MONETARY POLICY IN DEVELOPING COUNTRIES

MONETARY POLICY IN DEVELOPING COUNTRIES

Edited by
Sheila Page

London and New York

First published 1993
by Routledge
11 New Fetter Lane, London EC4P 4EE

Simultaneously published in the USA and Canada
by Routledge
29 West 35th Street, New York, NY 10001

© 1993 Overseas Development Institute

Typeset in Baskerville by Leaper & Gard Ltd, Bristol
Printed and bound in Great Britain by
Biddles Ltd, Guildford and King's Lynn

British Library Cataloguing in Publication Data
A catalogue record for this book is available from the British Library

ISBN 0-415-08822-4

Library of Congress Cataloging-in-Publication Data
Monetary policy in developing countries / edited by Sheila Page.
p.   cm.
Includes bibliographical references and index.
ISBN 0-415-08822-4
1. Monetary policy—Developing countries.   I. Page, Sheila.
HG1496.M633 1993
332.4′91724—dc20   92-24740
                                         CIP

CONTENTS

v

CONTENTS

Part II Country studies

CONTENTS

FIGURES AND TABLES

FIGURES

FIGURES AND TABLES

Kenya

Ghana

Côte d'Ivoire

Indonesia

Bangladesh

China

Informal sector

Exchange rates

Financial sector

ACKNOWLEDGEMENTS

This study of the role and the effectiveness of monetary policy in low income countries was initiated and designed at the Overseas Development Institute by Tony Addison and Lionel Demery. After they left the Institute, I directed the project. Christopher Lane wrote his three studies while at ODI. He also participated actively in the direction and editing of the other country studies, and thus had a major role in the analysis and focus of the research. John Healey assisted in the final editing of the special studies, as well as being the joint author of the conclusions. All of these therefore made a much greater contribution to the final study than the attribution of individual chapters can indicate, but they should not be held responsible for the final conclusions, or for any remaining errors and omissions.

The results of the study, together with those of parallel studies of monetary policy in Asia and Africa by the Harvard Institute for International Development, under David Cole, Betty Slade, Malcolm McPherson, and James Duesenberry, were presented at a joint conference in September 1991 at ODI. We are grateful to them and to all who attended that conference for their comments.

All of the country study authors are grateful for the information and cooperation which they received from government officials, bankers, and other researchers. I should also like to thank colleagues at ODI for their support and advice during this lengthy study, and particularly Margaret Cornell who edited the book with her customary skill and understanding.

We are grateful for financial support for the initial design of the research from the Economic and Social Research Committee of the Overseas Development Administration, for the principal part of the research from the Rockefeller Foundation, and for the African country studies from the International Development Research Centre of Canada. None of these has any responsibility for any of the views expressed here.

Sheila Page

Part I

THE NATURE OF MONETARY POLICY AND THE FINANCIAL SECTOR

1

THE NEW DEMAND FOR MONETARY DEVELOPMENT

Sheila Page

Practical need, new empirical evidence, and intellectual fashion have all contributed to a new interest in the role of the formal monetary sector and of monetary policy in developing countries. This poses particular problems for those which are least developed. Their interests and their problems were furthest removed from traditional analysis, so that both the problem (short-term stabilisation) and the recommended monetary instruments (broadly based and market-oriented banking systems and bond markets) are remote from their experience and remain under-researched in the context of their economies.

After the initial attempts to use monetary approaches, a widespread failure of governments to adhere to monetary ceilings or other policies was observed. This led to a variety of questions and possible explanations. Clearly these failures in part reflected the difficult political choices any policy of restraint entails. In this, they are similar to failures in developed countries. There are familiar disputes over the relationship between monetary instruments and policy targets such as the inflation rate and the balance of payments, and whether these targets can be met without imposing large costs on the 'real' economy. But there are major technical problems involved in monetary control and some of these can be more serious in developing countries. Other problems arise from the process of development. Financial systems are changing and becoming more sophisticated at the same time as they are being used to implement monetary policy.

The focus of this set of studies of monetary policy and of the financial sector is on how they affect development. It is necessary to say this because the assumptions, methods, and even the terminology of the study of developing country monetary policy are in some ways very different from those found in other development studies. Although the empirical evidence of what governments have done and of how the economies have changed is not sensitive to the intentions of those who examine them, the criteria for success or failure and the choice of significant results are. This is true in any social science study, but it has been particularly important in the field of monetary economics in developing countries. Much recent work on money in developed and developing countries has been directed specifically at how to implement monetary policy, rather than treating policy in the context of a study of the economic relationships within the financial sector and between that sector and other aspects of an economy, as is done in other branches of economics.

In developing countries, one of the major actors, the International Monetary Fund, has had a particular point of view, namely that macroeconomic intervention is good, even necessary, with sectoral intervention regarded, at least implicitly, as undesirable. Another major set of actors, the most vocal developing country governments themselves, appear to have held the view (for example in international negotiations like the GATT) that the development of their own financial institutions is so important in itself that it cannot be restricted by international agreements, although, as will be seen in the country studies presented here, others individually, in their own countries, have shown less commitment to this. Even those which do not accept the development of the sector as an end in itself may nevertheless take a direct interest in how it behaves towards other sectors, for example in sectoral lending which can have an impact on development. The criteria for a study of the financial sector are therefore particularly sensitive to the student's point of view.

Much previous work has started from the assumption that countries (or their advisers) have decided that they want to be able to implement monetary policies, and that they know what these are, and the purpose of a study is to identify the means and then to remove the obstacles. Even within this limited context there are different, not necessarily consistent, objectives. The inconsistencies and potential conflicts (and even the distinction among instruments, intermediate targets, and policies) have not always been recognised because a variety of immediate needs have led governments to seize on monetary instruments and policy as solutions, and in many cases these have been adopted because of external pressure, not from countries' own choice. The terminology used may be confusing, with liberalisation often being used to mean imposing an overall ceiling on credit rather than a set of disaggregated ones, or using indirect controls rather than direct ones.

It is necessary to go beyond this limited view of the study of monetary policy, and to ask additional questions. What do countries and analysts expect from monetary policy, and is it the same as in more developed countries? Are there additional benefits from strengthening the formal financial structure in a developing country? A variety of developmental arguments are now advanced for giving more attention to the financial sector. Although these may be well-founded, they are not newly relevant. It seems probable, therefore, that it is the changes stemming from monetary policy that explain the increase in interest. Taking both types of benefit into account, is developing the financial sector to permit monetary intervention an appropriate use of scarce resources? Under what circumstances, or how early in the growth process? All these uncertainties make it essential to be cautious in analysing the present and potential ability of governments to achieve the targets of their monetary policy.

This book, and in particular the country studies which form the central part of it, therefore starts by asking when countries have followed monetary policies, and for what purposes. It then attempts to assess how effective these have been. This provides the background to examine the first questions identified above, those of why many countries have found monetary policies difficult to implement, or have used direct intervention rather than financial sector tools. It focuses on whether the explanations can be found in factors peculiar to developing countries, and, if so, whether these can be changed by policy. This leads us back to the question of whether removing obstacles to, or developing the instruments of, monetary intervention does serve other purposes. A well-functioning formal financial system may improve the efficiency of the economy through its transfer-of-funds role, as well as the allocative functions emphasised in policy studies. It may mobilise or redirect domestic saving. One element in this analysis must be how far informal financial institutions can and do replace formal ones in developing countries.

To ask these questions together, about the effectiveness of monetary policy and the advantages of developing a financial system, illustrates two of the contradictions implicit in much discussion of the role of an efficient financial sector in implementing monetary policy. It is normally assumed to be preferable to use the financial sector, rather than more direct intervention, because this process permits the allocation of credit and the distribution of the effects of restraint to be determined by the market. But having an overall credit limit at all amounts to rationing, not a market solution, while deliberately developing the financial sector for this purpose amounts to accepting and implementing a sectoral priority.

The first part of this book will look at possible objectives for a financial sector and for monetary policy, and then identify possible ways in which developing countries and the financial sectors characteristic of them may differ from the conditions assumed in traditional approaches to monetary policy.

The country chapters in Part II will illustrate not merely the variety of experiences and degree of success, but the importance which policy in the individual countries gives to the different possible reasons for developing the formal financial sector. The six Asian and African countries included are not intended to be a representative sample of the developing world. They are all in the 'low' or 'low-middle' income category by per capita income. Foreign trade (exports/GDP) is relatively small for Bangladesh (6 per cent) and China (11 per cent), but the other four – Côte d'Ivoire (40 per cent), Kenya (27 per cent), Indonesia (25 per cent) and Ghana (21 per cent) – are fairly 'open' economies. The studies focus mainly on their experience during the two decades of the 1970s and 1980s. Over that period major changes occurred in many of their own policies, as well in the international environment facing them, but the countries chosen have all actively followed monetary policies during at least part of the period.

The chapters in Part III examine how the existence of informal monetary institutions and transactions and different international monetary arrangements, in particular the role of the exchange rate, affect the feasibility of operating different policies. The concluding Part IV will consider how successful monetary policy has been, and whether it could have been more successful, in terms of its direct objectives and of its more general effects on economic development.

A constraint on the methodology and any interpretation of the conclusions to the country and the special studies derives from the character of the financial sector. Because it functions efficiently through anticipation of effects, and because its participants tend to be more aware of this than other economic practitioners, it is particularly difficult to accept normal, sequential, 'proofs' of causality. It is therefore essential not to depend only on statistical relationships, but to use plausible models of transmission of effects, and to understand the operations (and failings) of the institutions and actors involved. It is also necessary to be clear about what, in the absence of intervention, the financial sector is determining or influencing, through both its existence and its degree of effectiveness – whether levels of output or prices, or allocation of resources, or control of inflation.

THE NEW INTEREST IN MONETARY POLICY

Monetary policy and the financial sector in low-income developing countries have been so neglected in development research that it may be an exaggeration even to identify a 'traditional view'. Whether the choice of priority activities or sectors was assigned to the public sector or 'the market', it was assumed that it was the 'real' choice which mattered and that such a choice could be made: either the financial sector was irrelevant, because intervention was direct, or it was assumed to function adequately (perhaps because finance and banking activities were importable). In the face of the many serious 'real' problems facing developing countries, developing the banking and financial sector took second place in the concerns of analysts and policy-makers. At the same time, the low incomes and savings capacities of poor people and poor countries, and the unfamiliar problems raised by heavy dependence on single commodities, often with a strong seasonal pattern of need for finance, did not attract the interest of commercial banks as providers of financial services. In practice, in most of Africa and Asia, the profitable parts of the market, upper-income groups and trade finance, could be assumed to be taken care of by expatriate banks. Research on monetary policy in developing countries was largely confined to the upper-middle-income countries of Latin America and East Asia, where the level of development made them nearer to familiar ground, and also where restrictions on foreign ownership limited the activities of foreign banks. It is also these countries which have led developing country concerns in international trade policy negotiations on the role of financial services.

The recent interest in monetary policy and financial sectors in low-income countries does not arise out of this background. In them, monetary policy has been introduced for external, macroeconomic, reasons. The countries which have introduced it have been forced, by external shocks (sometimes reinforced by domestic events or natural disasters), to make short-term adjustments of expenditure to income. Short-term adjustments used to be considered unsuitable for poor countries, a distraction from development, but they are now unavoidable, in the face of much more limited and policy-constrained external finance. External real interest rates are higher than in the past. This not only reinforces the need to adjust, rather than borrow, but increases the differential between world rates and the low or negative ones found in many developing countries, and therefore the strains and costs from isolating their financial system through controls. Countries must therefore act to reduce the strains, whether through direct intervention or financial policy.

Lower capital flows overall may also require countries to make more medium- to long-term adjustments in their dependence on deficit financing (whether external or domestic). They may therefore be using fiscal instruments and reforms more actively than in the past and they may need to make and implement decisions on where to cut investment, and how to mobilise savings other than through taxation. Another possible influence is the increasing exchange of experiences among developing countries: awareness of the success of the more advanced in developing their financial sectors to the point at which they become attractive to foreign portfolio investment has encouraged the less advanced to see a sophisticated financial sector as normal.

There are also some structural changes which may have encouraged the development of the financial sector, and would certainly be helped by it, but these seem in practice to have been secondary. More diverse economies, higher incomes, and more trade increase the demand for financial services, but the slow growth of low-income countries in the 1980s, and even in the 1970s, makes these unlikely to have been new or increasing forces for change in recent years. The general switch towards increasing the share of the private sector requires a mechanism for mobilising and allocating funds among possible investments. The shortage of external savings has encouraged more attention to mobilising domestic savings, and extending the financial system is an obvious means for this. There is, however, a potential conflict. The studies presented here confirm previous findings that it is the extent of a financial system (which may require subsidisation, like other physical infrastructure introduced in advance of demand) rather than monetary instruments as conventionally interpreted, such as the rate of interest, which encourages increased saving in the formal financial sector.

The switch to more emphasis on exports and on encouraging incoming foreign investment increases the demand for international banking services, but this is perhaps more likely to discourage the development of the national financial sector than encourage it. It is in trade that the advantages of trading-centre banks are greatest. An emphasis on import substitution has often gone with supporting and improving a local financial sector, along with other infrastructural investment. The question of whether using foreign banks has different effects on the rest of the economy from using domestic banks is not part of this study. If governments or countries do consider that financial services, like previous industries identified as 'commanding heights' or essential to national identity or to economic structure, cannot be left in foreign hands, this imposes a policy constraint. The policy must be either to develop the sector or to avoid committing the country to monetary policies or instruments which require a sophisticated financial sector. Such attitudes appear at present to be less common in developing countries than in industrial countries, and in Africa than in Latin America or in some Asian countries.

WHAT MONETISATION CAN DO FOR DEVELOPING COUNTRIES

The way in which monetary policy has been introduced into developing countries in recent years has led to an instrumental view of the financial sector. When monetary policy has been introduced for external reasons, frequently in the form of credit ceilings imposed by the IMF, it appears that its supporters initially have assumed that the means of implementing it existed (as they might in a developed country, and in line with the second reason suggested above for its traditional neglect). This view is reinforced by the unusually policy-oriented approach even in developed countries to analysis of monetary 'instruments' and the tradition of 'assigning' 'instruments' to 'targets'. In the unusually financially sophisticated context in which monetary policy operates in developed countries this has at least a circular justification if all know the convention, and play by it.[1]

When governments or analysts then respond to a failure of monetary policy by attempting to develop the financial sector of a developing country, this generates special problems for monetary control which have not been adequately identified or analysed in the existing research. The effects of policy may differ or, worse, change unpredictably as the financial sector becomes more sophisticated and at the same time expands to cover more of the economy. These are problems, if the sector is merely regarded as an instrument of control. But they may be advantages if the increased efficiency of the sector or its expansion, i.e. the monetisation of the economy, are beneficial. Research in this area is hampered – because it is outside the parameters and assumptions of monetary research; because non-monetary development research has neglected this area and offers little evidence on how important the effects are; and because government policy-makers are committed to such changes as goals, and have not reconsidered their inter-actions with the new monetary approaches. In addition, in the context which has normally provoked the turn to monetary policies – that of severe restraint on government resources – there is an obvious temptation to emphasise the developmental benefits of an improved financial sector, if this is a form of new investment which has legitimacy in the eyes of aid donors.[2]

The traditional motives for encouraging the growth of the formal monetary sector can still influence policy-makers, constraining their en-thusiasm for monetary control policies where there are possible conflicts between the new and old objectives. If the sector has been used to allocate credit, and if, as the country chapters will suggest, this tends to be associated with low interest rates, this may be one source of conflict with an active monetary policy of constraining total credit, or mobilising savings by using high interest rates. Introducing new instruments, or new uses of instruments like interest rates, will require a shift in industrial policy instruments, if not policy: at least to not subsidising through low interest rates, and possibly to not using credit allocation to favour particular sectors. The former could also have sectoral effects, according to capital intensity. Renouncing a tool of industrial strategy is not a trivial decision, unless there is also a renunciation of the idea of industrial policy.

WHY DEVELOPING COUNTRIES ARE DIFFERENT

The most obvious difference is that they have less money: this affects the development of a financial sector because their low income reduces their attractiveness to banks, but it also reduces their needs for transmission and savings services, and the opportunities for lending. The lack of complexity, of large numbers of economic actors transferring orders, investment, and finance among themselves, poses the same dilemma for financial services that it does for all forms of infrastructure, of whether the services should precede, and encourage, demand for them, or follow and be driven by such demand. There are also structural differences in the dependence on agri-culture or on a single commodity.

Even in richer countries, agriculture imposes unusually large demands and changes in demand for working capital, relative to income or fixed capital, because of the annual cycle of investment and production. This has been advanced as a reason for expecting a relatively developed financial sector in primary-producing countries. The reasons that this has not occurred in the countries studied here need examination, but clearly they include the roles of foreign banks in trade finance and of the government in seasonal credit. It is only when or in areas where the banks cease to be willing or able to operate, that the need for a special kind of commercial bank becomes obvious.

All poor countries are vulnerable to external shocks, which a financial system must be unusually strong to withstand or to mitigate. Those with dependence on a limited number of exports are particularly exposed. As the economic size of most developing countries is small, they can offer scope for at most a small number of banks, and little opportunity for these to spread their risks. Compared to banks in larger, more diversified economies, their banks are likely always to require either much greater government support, in the form of guarantees or insurance, or much greater prudence in their operations. Either raises the cost and lowers the supply of their finance and other services. This limits both banks' flexibility in use for monetary policy and their usefulness for any other services to development. All these factors suggest that there are special demands on a financial sector in a developing country, and also higher costs in fulfilling its normal tasks.

2

THE INSTITUTIONAL FRAMEWORK

Tony Addison and Lionel Demery

Financial markets can be divided into those for money and those for securities. The market for money is decentralised, and in less developed countries the market for securities may be as well. In more advanced developing countries, as in developed countries, the securities market is usually a centralised market, such as a stock exchange.

The most important features for the operation of monetary policy in developing countries are their low degree of monetisation and the dualism between informal and formal money markets; their underdeveloped banking systems; and the limited size of their markets for securities. Each is considered here in turn.

MONETISATION

The degree of monetisation is conventionally measured as the ratio of the broad money stock to GDP. A high share of economic activity for own consumption or in purely local trade reduces contacts with the general market, and therefore the transactions demand for money, particularly for personal deposits. While the level of per capita incomes is a crucial determinant of the level of monetisation, special conditions and government policies can account for much of the remaining inter-country variation in monetisation. In agricultural societies there are the problems of seasonality and shocks discussed in Chapter 1. Marketed surpluses can alter substantially between years; for example, in Bangladesh net buyers of rice vary roughly between 53 per cent of farm households in average years and 15 per cent in very good years (Ahmed 1981: 9, citing evidence from the 1970s). Good harvests may yield surpluses for sale.

The determinants of money demand are discussed further in Chapter 3. The strategy adopted for rural development can lead to large differences. Policies to promote sales of surplus through high producer prices will lead to a rise in the use of money. More directly, the development of rural banking facilities is crucial. The number of banks in the rural areas of South Asia is one reason why the monetisation ratio is higher in these countries

11

than in sub-Saharan Africa. There, the credit needs of most villages are served mainly by informal lenders, while modern banks concentrate on the towns.

INFORMAL AND FORMAL MONEY INSTITUTIONS AND MARKETS

One of the most important features of the financial systems of developing countries is the relative importance of 'informal' and 'formal' financial institutions. The formal 'modern' or 'organised' financial institutions include commercial banks, savings institutions, mortgage banks, etc. The informal market operates through small-scale money-lenders as well as others – such as merchants or rich farmers – who lend money as a sideline. Groups, often based on kinship, make loans within the network (Eicher and Baker 1982: 200). In Africa, rotating savings and loan associations – called *ekub* in Ethiopia and *chilemba* in Malawi – are very common (Holst 1985: 122). Rotating credit funds are prevalent in Asia, and are referred to as 'chit' funds in India and Thailand, where they finance a considerable volume of trade. In India 'indigenous bankers' are a very important source of finance (Timberg and Aiyar 1984). The Asian and Latin American informal markets are generally much more sophisticated than those in Africa; in other words, while there are many small-scale money-lenders, a greater proportion of their business is directed to medium- and large-scale enterprises, and sizeable loans may be made. Informal lending to formal sector firms can increase substantially when credit rationing in the formal financial markets forces firms to seek other sources of finance.[1]

In many ways the division of a country's financial system into informal and formal segments suffers from the same analytical deficiencies as the more general division of enterprises into informal and formal sectors. The division is most useful in the less sophisticated economies of Africa, but for the more diversified economies of Asia a three-way split – into informal lenders, indigenous bankers, and formal banks – may be necessary to categorise financial intermediaries.

Evidence on the nature and the degree of interaction between informal and formal money markets is fragmentary. The existence of very large differences in interest rates between the two markets is generally taken as a sign that the flow of funds between them is very small, but risks or the costs of risk may also diverge. The substitutability between formal and informal credit on the demand side and the degree of linkage among informal operations could also influence how an economy with a large informal sector responds to policy. Large net flows can take place between the formal and informal money markets in response to interest-rate changes and other factors. In Thailand the amount of private sector savings held in chit funds varies substantially from year to year – for example, falling by nearly a third between 1983 and 1986 in response to higher bank interest rates.[2] It is plausible to assume that interactions increase over time (as found in Wai 1977), and therefore are greater in East Asia and Latin America than in South Asia or sub-Saharan Africa.

The interaction between the formal and informal institutions, between the markets for lending to the formal and informal productive sectors, and between formal and informal markets – the line, for example, between extended trading credit and a loan of working capital – is one of the complexities of the 'money markets' in developing countries which is most important in analysing the role and effectiveness of monetary policy and policies for the monetary sector. The informal sector is discussed in more detail in Chapter 11, which draws attention to the importance of distinguishing between the informal financial sector and the financing of the informal production sector, and its interaction with the formal sector is discussed in Chapter 15.

THE BANKING SYSTEM

The relative importance of the banking system's role and of market determination, in direction of credit and in savings mobilisation, varies greatly among developing countries, reflecting differences in per capita incomes and saving rates, and in government policies. These functions are also changing because a number of adjustment programmes – particularly those supported by World Bank Structural Adjustment Loans (SALs) – have included some measure of financial liberalisation. There are strong grounds for arguing that financial liberalisation will encourage faster financial development over the medium to long terms, for the reasons suggested in Chapter 1. It is, however, by no means clear that it assists the task of implementing monetary restraint in the short term. The means of control are discussed in Chapter 4.

There are also substantial differences in the roles allotted to private versus public banks. In some countries the commercial banking system is either entirely state-run or dominated by state banks (for example, in Guyana and Tanzania), while in others privately owned banks play a central role (for example, in Kenya and Nigeria). The degree to which foreign banks are able to offer domestic banking services also varies greatly across countries.

Finally, the tasks undertaken by central banks differ significantly from country to country depending on institutional differences and the policy objectives of governments. The main functions of central banks are: to issue currency; to control the money supply in order to influence the key macroeconomic variables in a desired manner; to act as a bank to the commercial banking system; to be the government's banker; to regulate and supervise the financial system in order to maintain stability; and to promote the country's financial development. Different degrees of emphasis will be put on each of these objectives at different times, and they can conflict.

THE MARKET FOR SECURITIES

The common view has been that the market for securities is 'narrow' or 'thin' in developing countries, and that therefore it plays only a minor role in financial intermediation. There are a number of reasons for this, in addition to the obvious shortage of potential buyers. Many countries, by intention or default, pursue a strategy of financing long-term private investment through banks, rather than encouraging companies to issue shares. The pattern is more similar to continental Europe or Japan than to the United Kingdom or United States. Enterprises are often closely controlled by families. The legal and institutional mechanisms necessary to support the issuing and trading of securities are frequently lacking, taxation discourages such trade in some countries, and restrictions on foreign ownership or other ownership policies make a market difficult to develop. Finally, a very large share of investment is undertaken by the public sector, financed either through the budget or from banks.

Because they are thin, when stock markets do exist, they are often subject to violent swings in prices, further discouraging the use of securities to finance investment.[3] In recent years a few countries, for example the newly industrialised countries (NICs) and the emerging NICs of Asia, have officially promoted the expansion of markets in both private and government securities; their example has been promoted in other countries by the World Bank's International Finance Corporation (IFC).

The thinness of securities markets in developing countries has a number of consequences for monetary control. First, it is difficult to sell government debt. Consequently, there is a greater propensity to resort to monetary expansion. Second, central banks must rely heavily on quantitative and selective instruments (such as credit ceilings) rather than on indirect action, for instance, the sale of short-term government paper to the non-bank public to reduce their liquidity, and to influence the cost and availability of credit. The corollary is that private sector activity is much more affected by monetary restraint operating through bank finance (although family and informal finance operate in the opposite direction).

MEASURING MONEY

The choice of definition of monetary variables, for analysis or policies, depends on the purpose of the study or policy, the institutional structure of an economy, and inevitably on the available data. Conventionally, financial assets are grouped in two categories: money, with the special characteristic that it is the only asset which serves as a 'generally accepted' means of payment, and, on the other side, all other financial assets such as bonds, equities or stocks. The borderline with real assets, which may be held for the same transactions or store-of-value purposes, is always uncertain, especially when an economy is becoming 'monetised' or developed. If cattle are a generally accepted means of payment, there are grounds for incorporating such real assets in money definitions, since changes in the quantity 'held' will cause changes in expenditures. But the measurement problems would be insuperable, and no working definition of the money supply could be produced.

Most central banks consider a range of monetary variables to guide policy, starting from 'narrow money' and including an increasing range of deposits and financial assets. Whether because financial systems are more subject to constant change than other sectors, or because their agents are more conscious of economics and models, it has been harder to agree working definitions.[4]

One difficult issue for devising money supply measures in developing countries is the size of the informal money market. This can be very large indeed. Rough estimates by the Bank of Thailand suggest that in the mid-1980s between 7 and 16 per cent of private sector savings was held outside the formal banking system, and circulated through the chit funds. Most measures of the money supply – whether broad or narrow – cover formal financial institutions only. While it is conceivable that some estimate of informal money market flows could be included in a broader money measure (some estimates are given in Chapters 11 and 15), the measurement difficulties involved would probably preclude the construction of regular statistics. But the problem remains.

In some countries the reported money-supply statistics are an inadequate guide to the true monetary situation because foreign currency is being used extensively for domestic transactions. This is prevalent where high inflation has undermined confidence in the domestic currency. A more relevant empirical definition of the money supply therefore requires some estimate of domestically held foreign-currency deposits. Given that such deposits are often held illegally, the practical measurement problems may be insurmountable. Major difficulties with monetary control are likely to arise when the preferences of the public for holding domestic money – as against foreign – shift. The interaction between money and exchange rates is discussed in Chapter 12.

3

AN ANALYTICAL FRAMEWORK

Tony Addison and Lionel Demery

Our analytical framework consists of two core elements. First, there is a series of accounting relationships. The proximate sources of money creation are identified in an accounting sense, without behavioural content. The second element is a model in which the important parameters are determined by the decision-makers in the economy.

THE SOURCES OF MONEY CREATION

Taking a broad money supply definition (i.e. quasi-money), equation 1 gives the sources of the money creation, such that:

(1) $$M = PSBR - PLG + BLP + BCF + PAF$$

where PSBR = Public sector borrowing requirement
      PLG = Non-bank private sector lending to government
      BLP = Bank lending to the non-bank private sector
      BCF = Banks' net claims on foreigners
      PAF = Public sector acquisition of foreign currency

The first three terms on the right-hand side are all concerned with domestic sources of money creation, and are equivalent to the IMF's concept of Domestic Credit Expansion (DCE). The last two are the foreign impact; calling this F, we could write equation 1 as:

(2) $$M = DCE + F$$

Many different types of money-multiplier model can be constructed, depending on the degree of disaggregation needed. The following model is one of the most basic, but its transparency highlights the important relationships. We can write the balance sheets of the central bank and the commercial banking sector as follows:

(i) Central bank

Assets	Liabilities
Net foreign assets (NFA)	Currency held by the public (Cp)
Net government debt (NGD)	Currency held by the banks and net
Credit to banks (BCB)	deposits of banks held in the central
	bank (CDb)

(ii) Commercial banks

Assets	Liabilities
Currency held by banks and	Demand deposits (Dd)
deposits of banks held in the central	Time deposits (Dt)
bank (CDb)	Public sector deposits (PD)
Other financial and real assets	
(OFRA)	

Each balance sheet statement gives an accounting identity for the institution(s) concerned. For the central bank we therefore have:

$$(3) \qquad NFA + NGD + BCB = Cp + CDb \qquad \textit{Central bank}$$

The two items on the RHS of equation 3 comprise the 'monetary base' (MB).[1] The accounting identity for the banking sector therefore is:

$$(4) \qquad CDb + OFRA = Dd + Dt + PD \qquad \textit{Commercial banks}$$

Balance sheets and accounting identities for other sectors of the economy – such as the non-bank private sector – can be drawn up, or the banking system can be subdivided, but these are sufficient to construct a simple model of the banking system to show the relationship between the monetary base and the money supply.

A MONEY-MULTIPLIER MODEL

First, we need to define some preferences of the non-bank private sector (the 'public'). For the purpose of making transactions the public will have preferences regarding the ratio of cash relative to demand deposits that they want to hold. Let k be the public's decision about the preferred ratio:

$$(5) \qquad k = Cp/Dd$$

Similarly the public will allocate its total deposit holdings between time and demand deposits, where (t) is the preferred ratio:

$$(6) \qquad t = Dt/Dd$$

We can also define a ratio (p) between the deposits of the public sector (i.e. the government) and the commercial banks (PD) and demand deposits (Dd):

(7) $$p = PD/Dd$$

Unlike equations 5 and 6 this is not fixed by the preference of the public sector, but by the level of transactions being undertaken by the public sector.

The commercial banks maintain a given amount of cash and near-liquid deposits (CDb) at the central bank in order to meet daily transactions. We define the ratio (r) of bank reserves relative to their liabilities (known as the reserve ratio) as:

(8) $r = (CDb)/(Dd + Dt + PD)$

When a public sector organisation creates a deposit with a commercial bank it pays in a cheque drawn on the central bank. The result is that the net position of the commercial bank *vis-à-vis* the central bank changes, i.e. the deposits of the banking system with the central bank increase, which is from (3) equivalent to an increase in the monetary base.

To recap, our model consists of six relationships:

$$NFA + NGD + BCB = Cp + CDb$$
$$CDb + OFRA = Dd + Dt + PD$$
$$k = Cp/Dd$$
$$t = Dt/Dd$$
$$p = PD/Dd$$
$$r = (CDb)/(Dd + Dt + PD)$$

There are three exogenous variables: NFA, NGD, BCB; six endogenous variables: Cp, CDb, OFRA, Dd, PD; and four parameters: k, t, p and r. r can be a policy variable if the central bank fixes it. We can now use this system to specify the relationship between the monetary base and the money supply.

Equations 5 and 8 can be rearranged to give expressions for Cp and Cdb, to give:

(9) $$MB = [k + r(1 + t + p)]Dd$$

Therefore:

(10) $$Dd = \frac{1}{k + r(1 + t + p)} MB$$

Equation 6 can be rearranged, and substituted in equation 10, which upon rearrangement yields:

(11) $$Dt = \frac{1}{k + r(1 + t + p)} MB$$

We can also use equation 10 to derive an expanded expression for Cp, using the informaing that $Cp = kDd$:

(12) $$Cp = \frac{k}{k + r(1 + t + p)} MB$$

We are now in a position to derive the relationship between the monetary base and both the narrow and broad monetary measures. A narrow money measure (M1) consists of currency held by the public and demand deposits, while the broad definition includes time deposits as well, i.e.:

(13) $$M1 = Cp + Dd$$

(14) $$M2 = Cp + Dd + Dt$$

Substituting equation 10 and 12 into equation 13 yields:

(15) $$M1 = \alpha\, MB$$

where $$\alpha = \frac{1 + k}{k + r(1 + t + p)} > 1$$

and substituting equations 10, 11 and 12 into equation 14 yields:

(16) $$M2 = \beta\, MB$$

where $$\beta = \frac{1 + k + t}{k + r(1 + t + p)} > 1$$

The terms α and β are known as 'money-multipliers'. We see that the relationship between the monetary base and both the narrow and broad money supplies is dependent on the parameters: k, t, and p.

The accounting relationship highlights the role played by important sources of monetary growth, such as the unfunded portion of the government's deficit, bank lending and flows across the foreign exchanges. The money-multiplier model brings to the fore the parameters which embody the behavioural relations which underpin the working of the monetary system. The multiplier will change if the preferences of the public change or if the banks alter their reserve ratios.

For monetary policy to operate through variations in the money supply, policy-makers must be able to control the money supply, by operating on the public sector variables discussed in this section. They must be confident that the institutional difficulties of definition and the changes resulting from development which were discussed in the preceding chapter will be either small enough or predictable enough to make this effective. And they must also have confidence that the demand for money is stable enough or predictable enough for them to be able to estimate the behavioural response to a change in the supply.

THE DEMAND FOR MONEY

Econometric estimation of the demand for money has become increasingly sophisticated, using a wide range of independent variables and specifications.[2] Economic theory maintains that desired real money balances $(M/P)^d$ are positively related to a scale variable (Y) which may be current income, permanent income or real wealth, and negatively related to the opportunity cost of holding money, given by the yields on alternative real and financial assets. The forgone return on real assets is usually measured by the expected rate of inflation (P^e), while the forgone yield on financial assets is measured by a relevant rate of interest (R). At the most general level the demand for money function can therefore be written as:

$$(17) \qquad (M/P)^d_t = f(Y_t, P^e, R_t)$$

Equation 17 can be estimated for either broad or narrow money measures. Since desired money balances are unobservable, various assumptions about the speed at which actual money balances adjust to desired money balances are employed to substitute empirical money measures for $(M/P)^d_t$. Most empirical estimates settle for using either current or permanent income for Y_t, given the difficulties of measuring wealth, especially in developing countries.

It is generally thought that the income elasticity of the demand for money is significantly higher in developing, as compared with developed, countries (Thirlwall 1974: 107). While most studies of developed countries find an income elasticity close to one, most developing country studies find an income elasticity significantly greater than unity. This could reflect misspecification, for example arising from monetisation.

Demand-for-money estimations in developed countries usually use the rate of interest on private securities as a proxy for R_t. In developing countries rates of interest on government bonds are often used instead, because of the limited availability of private securities. Where domestic residents have access to foreign financial assets there may be a case for using returns on these assets to represent R_t. Even in countries with capital controls, capital flight indicates that returns in foreign financial markets still play a role. The relevant foreign rate of interest could be the interest rate prevailing in a regional financial system. In Asia, for example, this might be Hong Kong or Singapore. In developed countries with very open financial systems, foreign interest rates do not have statistically well-determined effects on the demand for money (Cuthbertson 1985: 117). Care must therefore be taken in ascribing too large a role to foreign interest rates in determining money demand in developing countries which have far less sophisticated financial systems.

Where there is an important informal production or financial sector, it is arguable that money-demand equations should be specified for different sectors. Estimations of the demand for money by firms have been under-taken in developed countries (see, for example, Miller and Orr 1966), and such studies could pick up some of the differences in money demand across dualistic economies. But in very low-income countries much finer disaggre-gations would be needed, since the demand for money by small farmers is probably very different from that of large farmers and agricultural enter-prises, and data are unlikely to be available. Alternatively, the population could be split into income groups, and separate equations run to pick up differences in portfolio choices. Such disaggregated money-demand esti-mations could be of considerable use to policy-makers in determining the effect of monetary policy on expenditure decisions. In the case of agriculture, time series data on agricultural incomes would be required. For each sector, the alternative assets would have to be identified in order to specify the opportunity cost of holding money for groups as diverse as peasant farmers and urban workers. This is a potentially fruitful road for applied work to take.

Once a money-demand function is estimated it is important to know whether it remains stable over time. This means testing the temporal constancy of the coefficients, for example by estimating the demand for money over two sub-periods and then using F-tests to determine the statis-tical significance of any shift in the function. Evidence on the temporal stability of money demand in developing countries is thin. In developed countries estimates of the demand for money in the 1960s and early 1970s showed temporal stability, but in later periods money demand became much less stable (Cuthbertson 1985: 118), perhaps because of higher in-flation. Such explanations could also be offered for the instability of money demand found in some Latin American studies (e.g. Darrat 1986: 68). For developing countries, greater instability may have been induced by the shocks of the 1980s. This would affect the ability of the authorities to achieve their objectives through manipulating monetary aggregates.

ISSUES CONCERNING CAUSALITY

One major problem for policy-makers is the degree to which changes in the money supply are independent of changes in the price level or nominal income. If significant feedbacks exist, they will have to assess the impact of money on incomes and prices in order to judge the final effect on the money supply. The dependence of government spending on prices and incomes is one source of endogeneity; the banking system itself may generate new sources of liquidity in response to demand.

Several tests of causality have been developed and applied to this problem, the most notable being those of Granger (1969) and Sims (1972). These depend on temporal sequence as an indication of independence (or lack of it) – an event occurring before another is said to be independent of it;

in econometric terms, this means an independent variable operates with a lag. As with any econometric relationship, such measures can only 'prove' absence of causality, not its presence. In the case of money markets, where information and anticipation are normal, it is questionable if they can even show that.

4

A FRAMEWORK FOR POLICY ANALYSIS

Tony Addison, Lionel Demery and Sheila Page

TARGETS FOR MONETARY CONTROL

Monetary targets may take several forms, depending on the objectives of the adjustment programme and the constraints imposed by a country's financial system. A target may be set for the overall rate of monetary expansion, or for one or more sub-components. If governments or their advisers believe that excess demand can be controlled by restricting monetary demand, and that they can determine the level of demand by influencing the supply, the intermediate target to set is the rate of growth of credit.

Which of the methods in Table 4.1 can be used in practice depends not only on the analytic factors identified, but also on international institutions (such as membership in a currency area, like the Franc Zone), domestic institutions and laws (which may affect use of any of the direct methods), domestic non-bank institutions (the size of the public sector, and its financial position), and political strength, commitment, and consistency (influencing the impact of direct measures and the coordination of monetary and fiscal policy). Which will be used, and with what degree of commitment, depends on domestic and external financial pressures. Failure, therefore, cannot be unambiguously attributed to any single one of these.

Table 4.1 Techniques of monetary control

		Price method	Direct controls	Indirect controls
1	Currency (Cp)		x	
2	Deposits (D)	x	x	x
3	Public sector deficit (PSD)		x	
4	Private (non-bank) lending to the public sector (PLG)	x	x	x
5	Bank lending to the non-bank private sector (BLP)	x	x	x
6	Foreign monetary impact (F)	x	x	x

25

In developing countries, one component – domestic credit expansion to the public sector – is commonly used, especially under IMF-supported programmes (for a justification of this in the context of balance-of-payments policy, see Lal 1984, and below). The target may be a ceiling or a range. IMF Stand-By and Extended Fund Facility (EFF) programmes almost invariably contain performance criteria ceilings on either total domestic credit expansion or domestic credit expansion to the public sector. Comprehensive surveys undertaken by Killick concluded that 'in most cases observance of these ceilings is the most serious hurdle the government must surmount in order to retain access to the [IMF] credit in question', and that for most governments 'credit ceilings (ccs) were far and away the most common objects of requests for waivers and modifications' (Killick 1984: 213). Systematic evidence showed the degree of failure in meeting targets: a 55 per cent success rate in meeting ceilings for a sample of 105 programmes in 1969–78 (ibid.: 253). This failure rate may have increased in the 1980s, as governments have had to implement monetary ceilings in a much more turbulent economic environment (IMF 1986). It is this type of evidence which led to concern about the feasibility of monetary control in developing countries.

METHODS OF MONETARY CONTROL

Reducing the public sector deficit

Where the public sector deficit (PSD) is large, and a significant contributor to monetary expansion, its reduction could have an important role in monetary restraint. Aside from cutting public expenditures and raising taxes, the deficit can be reduced by cutting public lending to the private sector. Privatisation gives a 'one-off' reduction of the PSD, although perhaps spread over several years, and could give time to implement one of the other means gradually. An advantage of this method is that its effects do not require an accurate prediction of bank behaviour, and there is no problem of evasion by banks.

There are problems, however, and at least one is likely to be more serious in developing than in developed countries. First, it is often difficult to vary expenditure and taxation decisions rapidly, either because of practical constraints or because of budget customs. Consequently, the role of deficit reduction tends to be confined largely to the medium term. Second, certain methods of reducing the PSD may be partly offset by unpredictable private sector responses. For example, the private sector may buy the public assets released through a privatisation programme by cutting their purchases of government paper. A reduction in public sector loans to the private sector may be offset by the public obtaining loans from the banks. Finally, the government may not be able to control expenditures and revenues. Not only are there problems in the day-to-day monitoring of expenditures and in the administration of taxes, but actual expenditures and revenues are affected by movements in the real economy. In low-income countries the dominance of agriculture can impart large fluctuations in the revenue base (whether taxes are based on profits or trade flows), as can exposure to external shocks. An unexpected drought can induce automatic public expenditures and sharply reduce tax revenues. These problems with controlling the PSD are separate from the usual political difficulties that governments have with fiscal restraint.

Increasing private (non-bank) lending to the public sector

In developed countries central banks employ a battery of techniques to maximise the sale of long-term debt to the private sector. Selling more debt reduces the public sector's reliance on bank borrowing. Short-term government paper, typically Treasury bills with a maturity of three months, can be bought from or sold to the public to influence private sector liquidity. Such 'open-market operations' can be used to deal flexibly with unexpected changes in liquidity.

One universal problem with open market operations is that they may be difficult to conduct at the chosen time, because market sentiment may not favour holding more government debt. There has been a long-running debate in both the United States and the United Kingdom on the optimal timing of bond sales. A second problem is that some short-dated government securities are very liquid and may be treated as money. Finally, the purchase of Treasury bills by banks can encourage them to lend more, since such bills count as assets in their balance sheets.

The thinness of the market for securities in many developing countries reduces the ability of the authorities to sell either long- or short-term government debt. The market's ability to absorb increases in government stock is limited. In most low-income and lower-middle-income countries the principal markets for long- and short-term government stocks are the commercial banks, insurance companies, provident funds, and housing finance institutions. Their demand for government securities arises out of the long-term management of their financial portfolios and not, generally, from any short-term speculative motive. In most of these countries the central bank reacts to the investment portfolio requirements of the institutions by making long-term government paper available when required. It is also common for the central bank to be the principal buyer of its own debt, when the cash needs of the savings institutions require it.

Nevertheless, although low income and savings limit the development of a country's financial system, government policy does play an important role in determining both the savings rate and the choice of assets. Low interest rates lead at least to a flight from domestic financial assets, even if they do not lower real savings rates.

The nominal interest rate on government paper is usually set at a low level to minimise exchequer interest payments, and bonds generally offer a poor return relative to other assets, and often a negative one. This will be observed in the country studies in this book. It is still unusual for governments to raise interest rates to compensate for higher inflation. The rate of return on government paper could be raised by offering a higher interest rate, discounting the price of the security, or giving tax concessions.

More direct quantity methods include requiring institutions to purchase government debt up to a specified limit or percentage of their assets. The authorities can apply different requirements to different types of institutions, to influence the structure of market liquidity.

Controlling deposits

If the central bank attempts to induce a rise in bond yields, interest rates on deposits will also rise, as banks compete with bonds for funds. Funds will be switched from demand deposits to time deposits, and thus, while the narrow money measure (which excludes time deposits) will be reduced, the broad money measure will be less affected than a simple model of switching would predict, and correspondingly there will be a smaller cut in bank loans and expenditure. (The effect will be further reduced to the extent that liquid, near-money assets are available.)

This may help explain why control of aggregate money supply through prices (interest rates) is limited in practice, and control of deposits through quantity methods is more popular among central banks. This may be especially true in developing countries where institutional changes, and unfamiliarity with instruments, make the choice of assets and their effective liquidity difficult to predict. A ceiling on the amount of deposits that banks can take will lead to a ceiling on the value of their loans. The main advantage of this technique is that it can be implemented quickly and monitored easily. But such quantitative restraints on bank deposits raise a number of well-known issues of equity and efficiency, almost identical to those raised by formal credit restrictions.

Restricting bank lending to the private sector

This is the most common technique in developing countries. In most of these, bank lending to the private sector is a major source of monetary expansion. It also poses serious problems of managing variations. The seasonality of bank lending is stronger because of the greater role of agriculture, and year-to-year variations may also be serious. In countries undertaking adjustment programmes with IMF support, variations for these reasons have on occasion been sufficient to breach monetary ceilings.

To control by price, the central bank induces an increase in the rate of interest charged on bank loans by increasing the 'bank rate', i.e. what it charges to banks. This should reduce the demand for credit by the private sector.

This method requires that the final effect on the money supply be predictable. Moreover, its usefulness also depends on the interest-rate elasticity of the demand for credit. If this elasticity is small, then a large interest-rate increase will be required to induce a significant reduction in credit demand. Central banks usually wish to avoid sharp increases in interest rates which create uncertainty in financial markets, and will therefore be loath to use this control technique. But where the demand for credit is relatively elastic with respect to its cost, the authorities can generate appreciable monetary effects with only small interest-rate changes.[1] In conditions of high inflation, the cash-flow costs of even low real interest rates may induce changes in behaviour, so that any relationship between interest and demand may be sensitive to both the real rate and the rate of inflation.

One drawback of this method is that other government policies, for example encouraging use of the formal banking sector, mobilising savings, or exchange-rate management, may also depend on the use of interest rates, and unless the markets can be segregated (which is itself a divergence from market methods), there may be conflicting government interests in setting the rate. It is also difficult to see any economic advantage in setting a rate indirectly, but with a known fixed chain to the actual target, over setting banks' interest rates or even their credit limits directly.

Furthermore, raising the cost of credit can have substantial effects on the real economy, because it raises the costs of old loans, which in turn will have ramifications for monetary control, as well as reducing the demand for new ones. This is particularly important in developing countries with a high share of private operations financed by bank credit. The problem can be reinforced if the credit squeeze induces a shortfall in demand, and the consequent depression of profits increases the need for external financing. Firms are left with the choice of borrowing or going bust, and their demand for credit increases. Large and adverse real-economy effects occur if companies eventually go bankrupt, but credit ceilings may be breached if they are not allowed to. Such 'distress' borrowing was observed during the stabilisation programmes in Argentina and Chile during the 1970s and early 1980s (Foxley 1983). In addition, this control technique has strong sectoral effects. Raising interest rates has more of a disincentive effect on long-term, compared to short-term, investments. The construction sector is often the first casualty of higher loan rates.[2] In the absence of any increase in the cost of credit, the introduction of credit ceilings will result in an excess demand, and will require rationing. Banks may be left to do this, or the authorities may specify ceilings on loans by type of borrower.

If the demand for credit for investment is more interest-elastic than credit used for consumption, using quantity methods will protect investment more than using price methods.

More generally, it is sometimes argued that the social benefit from directing credit to, say, exporters, exceeds that from directing it to speculators, but the latter may offer more collateral. (This is one reason why the effect of high interest rates on long-term investment is considered undesirable, as well as distorting.) It may also entail a bias away from agriculture. Many developing countries have regularly allocated credit to priority sectors and rationed others, so it may not be seen as unusual in the context of stabilisation.

Although theory would guide us away from using controls, since allocation by price is efficient (pareto optimal), this is on the assumption that externalities and other forms of market failure are absent and ignores the fact that intervention has already occurred in the setting of the target (or indeed in taking the view that the economy requires some form of stabilisation and government intervention). The arguments for and against controls to implement what is already an intervention must take a much more limited and non-absolute view of sectoral or sub-optimal efficiency. A stronger argument is that a straight subsidy to the sector concerned is more efficient than privileged access to credit. If the authorities try to favour certain sectors indirectly, the resulting response by the private sector can often produce an outcome different from the one intended. This is especially true if credit is offered to a particular activity, but the borrower may use his own resources to fund another activity.[3]

A problem with using credit controls instead of other sectoral measures is that banks may allocate the available credit to large, rather than small, firms since this reduces their transaction costs. The authorities can reduce this bias against small firms by allowing the cost of credit for them to be higher, to compensate.[4]

The main problem is that any credit controls can be easy to evade or misuse. The authorities need to define the credit ceiling by sector if the control is selective, and the final structure of controls may be complex. The financial institutions to be covered must be identified, and their lending activities monitored. Such systems generally start by covering commercial banks only. This immediately generates profitable lending opportunities for financial institutions which are not included within the control. Typically 'non-bank financial intermediaries' (NBFIs) expand during periods of credit controls. (Other types of monetary restraint can also encourage NBFIs.) Sometimes NBFIs are affiliates of the controlled banks. Kenya saw a very rapid growth of NBFIs in the 1980s; their share in the total liabilities of the banking system increased from about 36 per cent in 1980 to roughly 62 per cent in 1984; they are subject to less stringent controls on their operations than banks (Kenya, Republic of 1985: 65).

Usually some attempt will eventually be made to control the lending activities of the major NBFIs, but the smaller institutions and those operating on the periphery of the informal sector will typically pick up the lost business of their larger brothers. In Latin America, where the informal and formal credit markets have sophisticated links, when firms resort to informal credit they pay higher interest rates (Bruno 1979). As more of them switch from the rationed formal market to the unrationed informal market, the interest rate in the latter rises to clear the market. Thus, even if firms are able to circumvent controls on formal credit, the controls will have some impact. Containing the problem of evasion depends on the authorities' administrative capability and willingness to pay the costs of enforcement.

Credit controls can also lead to 'disintermediation'. It may be profitable for companies, which previously put their money on deposit, to lend directly to other companies at a suitable interest rate. The borrower will probably pay more for the loan (partly due to the higher risk incurred by the lender), so that his borrowings will be less than if he had access to formal credit. Alternatively, banks may charge a commission for introducing borrowers to lenders, and reduce the risk by guaranteeing the loan repayment.

Credit controls, if they persist for long periods, thus usually lead to structural changes in the financial system and the real economy. Some loss of efficiency in the banking system and resource misallocation occur. Nevertheless, not all structural effects are necessarily adverse. Through generating advantages for both formal and informal NBFIs, the range of financial institutions is widened, and the monopoly powers of the large banks are reduced. Weighing up the costs and benefits of credit controls for the development of the financial system is an important task for research.

Credit controls do distort official monetary measures. With disintermediation and increased reliance on informal credit, movements in the official money-supply measures can mislead policy-makers. In developed countries there has been a general movement away from the use of credit controls, partly because increasingly sophisticated financial systems make evasion easy, and partly because of a retreat from government intervention. Some developing countries are now moving towards greater reliance on price (interest-rate) methods. This is often part of a more general liberalisation programme, whereby prices, rather than administrative controls, are given a greater role in determining resource allocations.

Sterilising foreign monetary impacts

Given the 'openness' of most developing countries, fluctuations in the value of their exports, imports, and capital flows can have potentially large effects on their domestic money supplies through changes in their foreign-exchange reserves, depending on the institutional relationships between reserves and money supplies. Rapid changes can occur in the balances of payments of primary producers, following both seasonal fluctuations and major shifts in the prices and sales of their principal export commodities. Concentration of export sectors on a few primary commodities makes some countries especially vulnerable to this type of monetary disturbance. This greater exposure to external shocks is unfortunately accompanied by a reduced ability to avert or mitigate their impact on the domestic economy. This is sometimes by institutional choice and sometimes a consequence of their narrow financial markets.

In some developing countries the relation between the domestic money supply and changes in foreign-exchange reserves is a very direct one. First, there are those where a foreign currency is used as the domestic medium of exchange, for example the Australian and New Zealand dollars among some of the Pacific islands. Second, some countries operate a currency board system, under which the domestic currency is covered 100 per cent or more by foreign-exchange reserves. Singapore maintains the system, which has advantages for extremely open economies. In Lesotho and Swaziland, issues of domestic currency must be completely covered by their holdings of South African rand, South Africa being their main trading partner. A number of former British colonies operate a transitional system whereby issues of domestic currency must be backed partly by foreign-exchange reserves; the requirement is usually 50 per cent (Collyns 1983: 11). Finally, the Franc Zone countries use a common currency, backed by the French franc (see Chapter 7).

These systems institutionalise a government's unwillingness to 'sterilise' the impact of flows across the foreign exchanges on the domestic money supply, but, even without them, it can choose not to do so. The alternative, sterilisation, involves the sale or purchase of government securities, generally short-term Treasury bills, to lower or raise the public's money holdings in order to offset any externally induced change in them. Thus, in the case of an unusual outflow, the authorities would use domestic currency to buy Treasury bills from the public. An amount equal in value to the loss of reserves would need to be bought in order to offset the impact of the reserve loss on the money supply. If the authorities can do this successfully, then they are able to control the total money stock, and not just its domestic component. Of course in this case, the control will be bought at the cost of a persistent balance-of-payments deficit, and will be limited by the size of the reserves (the relationship between monetary control and exchange-rate policy is discussed in Chapter 12). In the reverse case, central banks will find it difficult to maintain sterilisation over the long run if it reaches a limit on the Treasury bills for which it can attract buyers.

These problems are greater in a narrow market, and therefore for developing countries. If the central bank buys Treasury bills, the scale of its purchases is limited by the stock of previously sold Treasury bills that the public holds. If the market is thin, sterilising monetary outflows could quickly exhaust the public's holdings of such paper. Alternatively, if the central bank sells bills to sterilise an inflow, the public may have a limited demand for this paper. Higher rates of interest will eventually be required to induce the public to hold more Treasury bills. In turn, these higher rates will, by altering the differential between domestic and foreign interest rates, attract inflows across the capital account of the balance of payments (assuming that there are no capital controls). In attempting to sterilise inflows across the current account, the authorities may find their efforts thwarted by capital account inflows. In summary, the authorities' ability to sterilise foreign monetary flows depends on the size of the market for government securities, the extent of controls on capital flows, the interest-rate responsiveness of foreign capital flows, the substitutability of domestic and foreign interest-bearing assets, and the costs of portfolio adjustment.

Among developed countries, capital flows are very responsive to changes in interest-rate differentials, and have become more so since the liberalisation of the world's main financial markets accelerated in the 1980s. But they also possess large markets for government paper. There is a wide range of sterilisation experiences among developing countries. Colombia offers a number of examples and studies, in which the importance of political factors in the choice of policy emerges clearly (Edwards 1984; Echavarria 1987).

Among the low-income group of countries, Sri Lanka has used open-market operations extensively. The Bank of Ceylon engaged in open-market operations as early as 1951 (Jayamaha 1986).[5] Since then, they have been used to offset the monetary inflows resulting from the early 1980s' boom in world tea prices. The common use of capital controls by many developing countries gives governments some degree of monetary autonomy, but the operation of parallel markets in foreign exchange may offset this.

Regulation of the banking system

Monetary growth can be restrained by altering reserve ratios. Banks are instructed to hold low-risk, but also low-return assets as a fixed percentage of their deposits. These include cash and deposits at the central bank (which earn low or zero rates of interest). In the absence of a specified reserve ratio, banks will minimise their cash holdings at a level which meets their daily transactions, subject to their own judgement on what is a 'safe' level of reserves with which to meet all claims. The authorities may set or change the reserve asset ratio as part of their responsibility for preserving solvency, or more deliberately to restrict credit. The effect is to reduce the average return to banks from new business by imposing an extra cost. In the terms used in Chapter 3, increasing r in equation 16 lowers the money multiplier.

Cash is the main reserve asset for banks in developing countries, so reserve-asset ratios are effectively 'liquidity ratios' in many cases. Changes in reserve requirements have tended to be infrequent. Greater use depends on the capacity of the authorities to monitor bank compliance, and on their control of the supply of eligible assets (normally done by including only currency and deposits at the central bank). Alterations in reserve ratios are ineffective if banks already hold reserve assets in excess of legal requirements. It is often suggested that banks in developing countries are characterised by a high degree of liquidity. Bhatia (1985: 20), for instance, provides evidence that the reserves of West African banks over the period 1965–74 were on average 15 per cent above their legal requirements. But if this occurs because profitable lending opportunities are limited, then this is obviously a time when credit restriction is either unnecessary or is being achieved by other means. It may be necessary to use it in combination with more direct sterilisation when there is a very large rise in external earnings. Raising reserve ratios is more effective when there is a balance-of-payments deficit, since bank liquidity will be falling. When different parts of the financial system have different degrees of liquidity, different reserve ratio requirements may be required.

If the authorities control the supply of eligible reserve assets then they can also achieve monetary restraint by reducing their supply. Such a system is conventionally termed a 'reserve base system' of monetary control.

The reserve base system is used in the United States, in some European countries (but not the United Kingdom), and in some more advanced developing countries, e.g. Venezuela. Instead of using a battery of open-market operations, credit ceilings, interest-rate increases and the like, the authorities can achieve their objectives through a simpler and more direct route, although in practice other instruments are used with it. Enforcing such a system has large administrative costs, so that central banks in many developing countries may not have the resources or the expertise to implement the system, but its costs may be less than the costs of a wider range of controls.

Proponents of reserve base control also claim that the system causes fewer distortions than applying more direct controls to each bank. Under the reserve base system, banks can still compete against each other. But, as with other controls, new institutions may appear and take business from the banks. Over time these problems grow. Financial institutions outside the system will be able to offer a higher interest rate to depositors; the share of deposits not controlled by the central bank will rise.

Finally, so-called 'moral suasion' is a common way for central banks in both developed and developing countries to impose monetary restraint. Banks are instructed to restrain lending, and although no legal penalty is specified for non-compliance, there is often an implicit threat from central bank disapproval. The degree of state involvement in the commercial banking system may influence its effectiveness.

POLICY QUESTIONS

This chapter has identified some major issues for the control of money:

The relative effectiveness of the different types of monetary control available The authorities in developing countries, are subject to constraints imposed by the characteristics of their financial markets. Constraints include the underdevelopment of markets for securities, the presence of large informal money markets, the lack of competition in the banking system, and a low level of monetisation. A careful case-by-case analysis of the characteristics of financial markets can illuminate how they affect both the choice of monetary instruments and their efficacy.

The effectiveness and the offsetting disadvantages of quantity instruments such as credit ceilings These are widely used, but they can have large costs in efficiency, and may distort the financial system. Moreover, they are difficult to maintain for long periods since they generate incentives for their evasion. Can price instruments, for example interest-rate policy, be effective in achieving monetary control under the constraints typically faced by policy-makers in developing countries?

The feasibility of increasing the use of instruments like selling government debt to absorb liquidity This depends on developing the market for government securities. Some constraints on this are inevitable in poor, small countries; some may stem from government policies on interest rates or capital taxation.

The size and impact on the formal sector of the informal sector There are potential links through demand (with informal credit being a close substitute for formal credit) or supply (with the informal sector on-lending funds drawn from the commercial banks). Flows between the formal and informal money markets may affect the ability of the authorities both to monitor and to control monetary aggregates.

The interaction between 'liberalisation' of interest rates and credit and effective monetary restraint Ceilings on interest rates encourage savers to deposit their funds in the informal money market; limits on credit encourage them to borrow from it. Liberalisation may make monetary restraint more difficult in the short run by drawing funds into the formal financial system, and will certainly make its effects less predictable by altering the parameters. It is also unclear, conceptually, whether policies to impose or strengthen monetary control can be called 'liberalisation'.

The interaction between money and prices   We need to identify the main determinants of movements in monetary aggregates in developing countries, especially the relative roles played by the public sector deficit, bank lending, and flows across the foreign exchanges. Whether each is controlled by policy depends partly on whether it can be; partly on whether the authorities want it to be. Do the uncontrollable linkages seriously weaken potential control of money and use of monetary policy?

Sectoral effects   These may vary because of differences in the 'gearing' of non-tradables relative to tradables, or the effect on capital-intensive sector, long-term returns. Of special importance is the potentially different impact of monetary policy on agriculture, industry and services. Informal credit markets may modify these sectoral effects.

Part II
COUNTRY STUDIES

5

KENYA, 1967–88

Tony Killick and F.M. Mwega

INTRODUCTION

In the economic history of post-independence Africa, Kenya has earned a reputation as one of the best performing and most stable economies. Much development has occurred, price rises have never spilled into hyperinflation, the substantial balance-of-payments difficulties that have occurred have never completely halted the economy. The worst excesses of macroeconomic mismanagement have generally been avoided. Of course, many factors have contributed to this relative success, but the absence of macroeconomic disasters suggests that the classical instruments of macromanagement – fiscal, monetary and exchange-rate policies – have made an important contribution. The purpose of this chapter is to focus on the monetary elements in this package and to enquire into the effectiveness and potentialities of monetary instruments in the Kenyan context.

As a prelude to addressing these questions, the next section provides brief summary information on the economic setting within which monetary policies have been determined, including an account of the development of the financial system. This is followed by the hard core of the chapter which presents the research findings. The final section briefly considers the implications of these for the future conduct of policies in Kenya.

THE ECONOMIC SETTING

Macroeconomic performance, 1967–88[1]

Our discussion of the performance of the economy is organised around the key economic indicators set out in Table 5.1, starting with the balance of payments. A general caution is in order concerning the reliability of Kenyan economic statistics: although the range of statistics is quite good, the quality is more suspect, with surprising discontinuities and unexplained changes in many series. Fortunately, Table 5.1 is used to reveal broad trends rather than

Table 5.1 Macroeconomic indicators for Kenya, 1969–88

	1969–73	*1974–8*	*1979–83*	*1984–8*[a]
Balance of Payments				
1 Purchasing power of exports (period av.)[b]	113	114	88	86
2 Change in import volumes (% p.a.)	0.6	4.0	−9.8	6.9
3 Current a/c as % GDP (period av.)	−4.2	−6.8	−7.8	−3.4
4 Basic balance as % GDP (period av.)	0.2	−0.5	−2.1	0.1
5 External reserves as months of imports (period average)	4.3	4.0	2.8	2.7
Inflation				
6 Rise in GDP deflator (% p.a)	4.1	14.0	9.6	9.2
7 Rise in consumer prices (% p.a.)[c]	5.1[d]	12.4[e]	11.8	8.9
Public Finances				
8 Govt. current a/c balance as % GDP (period av.)	1.5	2.3	0.7	−2.0
9 Overall budget deficit for financing as % GDP (period av.)	−4.9	−7.1	−9.4	−5.0
10 Govt. borrowing from banking system as % GDP (period av.)	0.7	1.6	1.5	1.7
Monetary Indicators				
11 Growth in money supply (M2) (% p.a.)	18.3	21.4	9.6	12.5
12 Growth in domestic credit (% p.a.)	21.0	22.0	11.5	13.7
13 Growth in credit to the public sector (% p.a.)	83.0	32.0	23.5	16.8
14 Share of private sector in total domestic credit (period av.) (%)	82	71	65	58
Investment, Saving and Income				
15 Gross domestic fixed capital formation as % GNP (period av.)	21.8	22.4	22.2	19.8
16 Gross national saving as % GNP (period av.)	17.9	17.5	18.3	18.4
17 Growth of constant-price GDP (% p.a.)	8.3	4.5	4.3	4.2
18 Change in per capita constant-price private consumption (% p.a.)	+4.4	+2.0	−2.6	+0.8

Sources: Derived from a wide range of statistical sources, chiefly publications of Government of Kenya and the Central Bank of Kenya.

Notes: a Many 1988 figures are provisional.

b Export earnings deflated by import price index. Index, 1980 = 100.

c Mean of lower-, middle- and upper-income indices.

d Mean for 1970–2, lower- and middle-income groups only.

e Mean for 1972–8.

small short-term movements, so the problem is, it is to be hoped, minimised.

The five-year sub-periods of Table 5.1 each record substantial current account deficits relative to GDP, particularly in the period 1974–83. The country has, however, been able to attract large amounts of foreign capital, especially official development aid, and comparison of lines 3 and 4 of the table shows that only in 1979–83 was there a significant current account deficit which could not be covered by inflows of long-term capital. From that point of view, the situation appears reasonably satisfactory. This needs to be qualified in three important respects, however.

First, concentration on the current account and its financing conceals a compression of imports – see line 1 of the table. In fact, between 1974 and 1983 an index of import volumes relative to constant-price GDP fell by a remarkable 60 per cent, and even though there was a subsequent increase in this ratio, there remained both an unsatisfied demand, held down by quota and credit restrictions, and a question about the ability of the system to sustain the volume of imports established in the late 1980s.

A second qualification is that it has only been possible to finance the current account deficits by running up a rapidly increasing external debt.[2] Even though much of this was secured on concessional terms and the government has not so far had to resort to debt reschedulings, debt ratios are rising rapidly. There is thus a prospect of the debt burden becoming un-manageable in the future.

Third, despite external borrowing, it has often not been possible to maintain desired levels of international reserves. By the end of 1988 they were only about half the target level and reserves net of liabilities to the IMF were substantially negative. Indeed, frequent recourse to stand-by and other high-conditionality credits from the Fund has been a further symptom of balance-of-payments distress.

The payments situation by the late 1980s was still far from satisfactory. While the long-standing stagnation of the export sector had apparently at last been broken[3] and import volumes also were beginning to recover, coffee prices and the terms of trade were worsening sharply. The years 1987–8 recorded exceptionally large current account deficits (equivalent in the two years to nearly 6 per cent of GDP), reserves were well down and reliance on external capital was particularly marked.

The most notable fact about Kenya's price history is that the inflation rate has never gone above 25 per cent and has usually been far below it. Within this overall record there have been distinct phases. The first decade of independence saw only very moderate price increases. There was then a steep increase during 1973, to average rates of around 12 per cent for 1974–83, followed by a fall to about 9 per cent in 1984–8. The decisive break in this latter period was a sharp fall in 1986, from about 13 per cent to under 6 per cent. Thereafter, inflation increased again, but it was unclear whether this marked the establishment of a new upward trend.

Public finances have become the Achilles' heel of the economy, despite an excellent record during the early independence years, when the government was able to expand its provision of education and other social services rapidly while actually improving the overall budget situation. Line 8 of Table 5.1 shows a substantial and growing surplus on the budget current account, and if the overall deficit was growing (line 9), this reflected development investments which could be largely financed by non-inflationary borrowing.

Things began to go wrong in the late 1970s, however, with large surpluses turning into large deficits. The government's current account has remained in deficit ever since. The overall deficit grew, relative to GDP, in the period 1974–83, and it became more difficult to avoid inflationary borrowings from the banking system. The figures for the final period are more difficult to interpret, showing a worsening on current account and a small increase in monetary deficit financing but a rather large improvement in the overall deficit. The overall fiscal situation remained weak, however, and this weakness will feature prominently later in this chapter.

Part of the problem has been a reluctance on the part of the government to use the tax weapon. Tax revenues rose as a proportion of GDP from 16 per cent in 1964–5 to 24 per cent in 1973–4 and have been around that proportion ever since. Inadequate expenditure control has been another part of the problem. Over the same period total government spending has risen relative to economic activity – from 23 per cent of GDP in 1964–5 to an average of around 35 per cent in the later 1980s, with serious budget financing difficulties emerging in the later 1970s. Not the least of the difficulties is that the two largest components of government spending are difficult to cut: the salaries of the civil service and the fast-growing local-currency costs of servicing the public debt. Annual budget presentations characteristically contain a mixture of statements of determination to bring expenditures under better control, marginal modifications of existing taxes, and systematically over-optimistic estimates of fiscal out-turns.

Confining ourselves to the data on monetary indicators in lines 11–14 of Table 5.1, we see first that the expansion of money supply has never been extremely rapid and, indeed, was rather moderate in the 1979–88 decade. Domestic credit grew rather faster in that decade, however, reflecting the decline in the foreign-reserve component of the money supply. The most significant statistics are in line 13, however, for it shows that the expansion of credit to the public sector has consistently been considerably more rapid than the growth of total credit.[4] This has led to the marked decline in the share of domestic credit going to the private sector, shown in line 14.

This brings us to the national accounting indicators in the final four lines of the table. These show that the investment and savings ratios have been fairly high and consistent throughout (although there have been year-to-year fluctuations masked by the averages in the table). Despite this, the growth of GDP since the mid-1970s has barely kept abreast of the (very rapid) population growth. The figures on per capita private consumption in line 18 show greater movement between the periods, but imply that by 1988 average private living standards were almost exactly the same as they had been in 1973. Health and mortality indicators show major improvements up to the earlier 1980s but a moderate tendency for worsening in the later years of the decade.

The perspective offered by the macroeconomic data is, then, of an economy performing moderately well: better than the average for all African countries but well below the record of non-African developing countries over the same period. Growth has never been totally halted but for the last fifteen years has rarely done much more than keep pace with the growing number of people.

A key feature of the economy which cannot be conveyed by the period figures in Table 5.1 is its vulnerability to large unforeseen changes in important economic variables which are beyond the direct control of Kenyan policy-makers. This vulnerability stems from the openness of the economy, including an only recently declining dependence on coffee and tea as the principal exports (which made up 47 per cent of total export earnings in 1988 and are subject to highly unstable world prices). The economy is wholly dependent on imported oil and remains essentially agro-based, leaving it open to the vagaries of the weather.

In consequence, over the period under analysis the economy has been buffeted by successive oil shocks, two periods of large but short-lived coffee and tea booms, and two major droughts. At the political level there was an attempted coup against President Moi in 1982, which undermined confidence, caused some capital flight and depressed investment.

In addition to these shocks, the economy has been exposed to a serious long-run deterioration in its commodity terms of trade. Although the terms of trade are subject to rather violent swings, the existence of an underlying deteriorating trend is clear, so that by 1988 the import purchasing power of a unit of exports was a mere half of the 1964 level.[5]

It is evident that the task of economic management in an economy so vulnerable to large swings in variables beyond the control of the policy-makers is particularly daunting, and this is part of the context in which our evaluation of monetary policies should be set. However, there are swings as well as roundabouts: booms as well as slumps. One of the key questions to ask is, how well has the government managed the booms? We address this question later.

The financial system

The financial system inherited at the time of independence in 1963 was typical of the colonial heritage of most British colonies in Africa: a Currency Board, in this case serving Tanzania and Uganda as well as Kenya; a commercial banking sector wholly dominated by two London-based banks; a Post Office Savings Bank (POSB); and a small number of more specialised institutions providing insurance, housing finance and other financial services. The government subsequently set up a government-owned bank, the Kenya Commercial Bank, which has grown to be the largest of the three major banks. Following the breakdown of the East African Currency Board arrangements, the Central Bank of Kenya (CBK) was created in 1966.[6] This had most of the powers usually associated with central banks at that time, except that a statutory limit (repealed in 1972) was placed on the amount of credit it could provide to the central government.

From the powers set out in its 1966 Act and from subsequent practice, four chief instruments of monetary policy can be identified:

1 The stipulation and variance of legal minimum reserve ratios that must be observed by the commercial banks. Minimum liquidity ratios (chiefly comprising cash, inter-bank balances and Treasury Bills) have been in operation throughout. Minimum cash ratios, on the other hand, have been laid down only rarely but were reintroduced in 1988 and show signs of becoming more permanently and actively used.

2 The laying-down by the CBK of quantitative ceilings for the expansion of domestic credit (or credit to the private sector) by the commercial banks.

3 The control and variance of interest rates. As at mid-1989, minimum rates were specified for banks' time and savings deposits, and for their loans and advances. Similar controls were in force for 'non-bank' financial institutions (NBFIs), for building societies, the POSB, etc.

4 The laying-down of guidelines by the CBK for the sectoral allocation of bank credit – a provision chiefly used to favour agricultural credit.

Various other devices have been used by the CBK from time to time, but chiefly in furtherance of non-monetary policy objectives.

Throughout much of the period with which we are concerned, Kenya's financial system exhibited most of the features associated with financial repression, but in a fairly mild form. Interest rates have been controlled throughout, at negative real rates during most of the 1970s and into the 1980s. This is shown by the following figures giving period averages of real deposit rates of interest.[7]

1966–70	+1.90	1981–5	−0.75
1971–5	−7.20	1986–8	+4.8
1976–80	−7.74		

A fixed exchange-rate policy was maintained during the 1960s and 1970s, with the currency gradually becoming overvalued, although not grossly so. Exchange controls have been in place throughout and the Kenyan shilling has never been a freely convertible currency. Another feature of repression, as we shall see later, has been a substantial volume of involuntary lending by the banking system to the central government and parastatal organisations. These features, plus occasional ceilings on bank lending and non-market CBK attempts to manipulate the sectoral composition of bank lending, have created disincentives to the development of the banking system, although the distortions have rarely been acute.

There has in recent years been a substantial easing of various aspects of financial repression. It has become stated government policy to move towards a liberalised system and the use of market-determined interest rates as the chief instrument of monetary policy. While they remain controlled and the subject of discontent within the banking community, interest rates have already been raised substantially and since the early 1980s have been positive in real terms (see above). There has also been a very important change to a policy of exchange-rate flexibility over the same period. As a result, there has in recent years been a major depreciation of the currency, with a real effective depreciation of 28 per cent in 1984–8.[8]

In the light of the above account, the indicators set out in Table 5.2 seem rather puzzling. What is shown there is substantial financial deepening in 1968–80, with various monetary magnitudes growing rapidly in real terms and rising relative to GDP, even though these were the years in which financial repression was most fully in evidence. Deepening seems, however, to

Table 5.2 Indicators of financial deepening, selected years (values in K£m)

		1968	1973	1980	1984	1986	1988	Growth rates 1973–80	1980–8
1	Assets/liabilities of banking system (a) in constant prices[a]	105	221	328	352	425	438	5.8	3.7
	(b) as % of GDP[b]	22	26	34	33	35	32	—	—
2	Money supply (M2) as % GDP[b]	24	32	31	31	31	28	—	—
3	Total deposits of commercial banks in constant prices[a]	11	187	257	277	318	333	5.4	3.3
4	Total deposits of NBFIs in constant prices[a]	7	28	89	152	169	174	18.0	8.8
5	(4) as % of (3)	64	15	35	55	53	52	12.9	5.1

Sources: Govt. of Kenya publications, including *National Development Plan, 1989–93*, Table 2.1.
Notes: a Deflated by GDP deflator (1968 = 100).
     b GDP at current market prices.

have been halted, perhaps even reversed, during the 1980s, despite liberal-isation in those years. Part of the explanation is that much of the development of the financial system in the 1980s occurred outside what is counted as the banking system, as is illustrated in lines 4 and 5 showing the rapid absolute and relative growth of the NBFI sector.

If we take all financial institutions together, from the small very basic system that existed at independence the sector by 1988 had grown into a substantial, relatively sophisticated one, comprising: the Central Bank of Kenya; twenty-four commercial banks with over 400 branches, agencies and other outlets throughout the country; fifty-four NBFIs with ninety-four branches, chiefly in Nairobi and other major cities; twenty-two building societies providing housing finance; thirty-nine insurance companies; 207 hire purchase companies; the Post Office Savings Bank, with a large network of offices around the country; about ten development finance institutions, providing longer-term capital; and over 900 savings and credit cooperative societies. Lest the statistics on the commercial banks mislead, however, it should be added that the commercial banking industry remains essentially oligopolistic, being dominated by four banks[9] with a long tradition of working together rather than of aggressive competition. This is a fact of considerable importance for the conduct of policy, because the direction in which the government has stated it wishes to go – towards more indirect instruments of monetary control – can only be expected to work well in the context of a competitive banking and financial system.

To some extent, the expansion outside the banking industry has been a response to the disincentives faced by the banks. This is particularly true of the NBFIs, many of which were created during the 1980s specifically to escape the tighter regulation than exercised by the CBK over the banks.[10] Their relative growth is shown in Table 5.2, and leaving aside the special case of the 1968 figures, which are from a time when the whole system was tiny, line 5 of the table shows that the deposit liabilities of the NBFIs grew very rapidly relative to those of the banks between 1973 and 1984, reaching over half of the banks' deposits by the latter year. They had become big business. Each of the major commercial banks created at least one NBFI subsidiary, precisely in order to take advantage of the less restrictive regu-latory framework within which these operated. On paper, the institutions in question appear to be constituted as merchant or investment banks, which would normally be undertaking much of the wholesale end of the banking business and providing longer-term finance than is normal for commercial banks. However, it appears that in practice they operate at least as much at the short end of the market as the banks, taking deposits and making short-term loans, with a particularly heavy exposure to parastatal bodies.

The NBFIs will feature prominently in the discussion of monetary policy in the next section. Their rapid expansion within loose regulatory rules predictably led to problems and a number of them (and a small commercial bank) got into serious liquidity difficulties during 1986. Some of them declared bankruptcy and the government set up a commission to assist those with prospects of viability. This crisis led to the withdrawal of deposits and abruptly halted the previous relative growth of this industry, as can be seen from Table 5.2. However, the impact of the reversal on total NBFI deposits was small, and already by end-1988 the real value of deposits with NBFIs was above the level of two years earlier. By 1989 the signs were that expansion had resumed, although some of them remained precariously dependent on the deposits of one or a few parastatal agencies, particularly the National Social Security Fund (NSSF).[11]

The growth of this sector is unlikely to be as dynamic in the future as it was in the 1980s, however, because CBK supervision of such institutions has been greatly strengthened. Already in 1985 major amendments were introduced to the 1968 Banking Act to strengthen the powers of the CBK over NBFIs. A study of the changes introduced then provides a graphic indirect account of the malpractices that had grown up in parts of this industry.[12] The 1985 amendments and further strengthening of the CBK's powers have since been consolidated into the Banking Act, 1989. The CBK has also moved to narrow the differential in the maximum lending rates which the banks and NBFIs are allowed to charge, and this too will tend to weaken their growth relative to the banks.

Despite the relative sophistication of Kenya's financial system, its capital markets are still in their infancy.[13] The market for short-term securities is dominated by Treasury bills, and the introduction in 1986 of longer-dated Treasury bonds has yet to change this situation. Despite government encouragement, there is still virtually no secondary market in government paper and almost none at all in commercial paper, although there is an active inter-bank market. There is also a Stock Exchange, but most dealings on this are in a limited number of stocks and it has scarcely been used as a source of new capital. The government wants to foster the growth of capital markets but the position for the period studied here was that there were severe limits on the extent to which it could finance budgetary deficits by non-monetary domestic borrowings, and that private agents had available to them only a narrow range of income-yielding financial securities which they could hold as alternatives to monetary assets.

RESEARCH FINDINGS

The presumption underlying this study is that money – and hence the conduct of monetary policy – matters for the performance of the Kenyan economy, so we start by testing this.

The effects of money on economic performance

Money and inflation   Controversy about the sources of inflation in Kenya has tended to centre around the relative strengths of inflationary shocks emanating externally in the form of rising import prices, which tend to be emphasised by the government, and of monetary expansion and its sources. A more recent point of interest is whether expectations, as conventionally represented by past inflation rates, have exerted a significant independent influence. We have therefore estimated a model which seeks to explain changes in the consumer price index using the growth of real income, changes in money supply (M2), changes in import prices and changes in the previous year's inflation rate as the explanatory variables, utilising data for 1971–88. The results obtained were as follows:

$$\Delta \log P = 0.055 - 0.574\Delta\log y + 0.253\Delta\log \ M2 + 0.208\Delta\log P_m$$
$$(2.981)^a \ (4.635)^b \quad\quad (3.166)^b \quad\quad\quad (3.402)^b$$

$$+ 0.076\Delta\log P_{-1}$$
$$(0.581)$$

where
$R^2 = 0.79$, DW $= 2.21$, and DF $= 13$.
Notes: a significant at the 5% level
b significant at the 1% level.

These results give us quite a good statistical explanation of the behaviour of prices with an R2 of 0.79 and a plausible set of results.[14] The strongest influence of all is a negative association between the growth of real GNP and inflation: when the economy expands rapidly the demand for money increases and inflation goes down. Both monetary expansion and import price inflation provide powerful – and statistically highly significant – offsetting factors, however. We find that a percentage point increase in M2 is associated (without time-lag) with a 0.25 per cent increase in the price level; and that a 1 per cent increase in import prices will raise the domestic price level by about 0.21 per cent. Expectations, as represented by $\Delta \log P_{-1}$, were not a significant influence. This latter result may perhaps be due to the absence of a strong trend in the inflation rate during the period in question, with temporary fluctuations around a rather flat trend line which Kenyans have learned to discount in making their decisions. It is also likely that the relative absence of a strong independent trade-union movement, and other organised interest groups that could provide a 'propagation mechanism' through which expectations could be translated into future inflation, contributes to this result.

Between 1985 and 1986 there was a sudden fall in the inflation rate. In the series used for our testing, it went down from 12.3 to 3.9 per cent and marked a sharp break from rates generally in the 10–12 per cent range for most of the earlier years of the decade. We therefore examined whether our model could retrospectively simulate such a fall, given the behaviour of the independent variables. The simulated values for the two years were 11.9 and 4.8 per cent, so it was indeed successful in tracking much of the decline. The same was true, although in varying degrees, with earlier turning points in the inflation rate. Specifically we explain the sudden fall in 1985–6 as chiefly the result of a fall in import prices in those years.

The finding that GNP growth, monetary expansion and import prices are significant explanatory variables is consistent with the results of other studies of inflation in Kenya. Thus, using a different model, Kiptui (1989) found both money and import prices to be significant, but (surprisingly) not real income growth. Nganda (1985) found money growth to be significant and also real income (negatively), but he unfortunately did not include a term for import prices. In common with our own results, both of these tests found past inflation to be non-significant. Despite variations in the models' tests, all studies of inflation in Kenya are unanimous in finding monetary expansion among the most important explanatory variables, which is the outcome most pertinent to our present purposes. On the presumption that causality principally runs from money to prices, the regulation of money supply appears to be a prerequisite for any adequate control and reduction of inflation in Kenya.

Causality does not run uniquely from money to inflation, however. If, for example, government expenditures are more elastic with respect to changes in the domestic price level than revenues, inflation will bring a tendency for budget deficits to widen and hence for a larger volume of inflationary money creation (Aghevli and Khan 1978). We therefore also tested for the influence of the feedback from inflation to monetary growth and this provided us with a still stronger statistical explanation of the process. In particular, the size of the coefficients for the income, money and import price variables was increased, with the impact of a percentage point of monetary growth on inflation going up from 0.25 to 0.44 per cent – a result which reinforces the importance, and difficulty, of monetary control as an anti-inflationary weapon.

Money and the balance of payments   There has been some controversy in the literature on the Kenyan economy about the influence of monetary variables on the balance of payments.[15] King (1979) and an unpublished paper by Grubel and Ryan (1979) reviewed the evidence for the 1960s and 1970s and, for different periods, both found monetary variables, particularly domestic credit to the government, to have a strong impact on the balance of payments, defined as the balance on monetary account. Others, notably Maitha et al. (1978) and Killick (1984 and 1985), while not denying the negative influence of domestic credit expansion, have placed more emphasis on the effects of external shocks and of structural weaknesses, particularly the poor past performance of the export sector. The monetary model of the balance of payments, of course, underpins the central role in the IMF's stand-by programmes of domestic credit restrictions, so it is of considerable policy importance to obtain the best understanding possible of the sources of Kenya's balance-of-payments difficulties.

A comprehensive examination of this subject is outside the scope of this study. We therefore examine the relationship between changes in international reserves (which we use as an imperfect proxy for the condition of the balance of payments) and domestic credit. This can shed light both on the determinants of changes in the balance of payments and on the feasibility of effective monetary policy.

The approach taken in our work has been to test (in statistical 'Granger' terms) for causal relationships between changes in net foreign assets (ΔNFA) and the supply of domestic credit by the banking system (ΔDC).[16] Taking quarterly data from 1972 to 1988, the results obtained are summarised in Table 5.3.

Looking first at line 3(a), we see a significant negative correlation between ΔDC and ΔNFA, with causality running from the former to the latter. That is, an increase in DC will lead to a reduction in NFA, as predicted by the monetarist model. A breakdown of DC into credit to the private sector (DCP) and credit to the government (DCG) provides a further insight, one which is also strongly consistent with the IMF's stress on the control of budget deficits. Line 2(a) shows a particularly strong negative correlation running from ΔDCG to ΔNFA, while line 1(a) shows a much weaker (and non-significant) negative correlation from ΔDCP to ΔNFA. Credit to government, then, is particularly likely to weaken the balance of payments, as was earlier found by King and Grubel and Ryan. Credit to the government is mostly

Table 5.3 Relationships between domestic credit and the balance of payments, 1973–88

Direction of causality		F Stat	Sign
1	(a) ΔDCP to ΔNFA	0.45	Negative
	(b) ΔNFA to ΔDCP	3.13[a]	Positive
2	(a) ΔDCG to ΔNFA	2.81[b]	Negative
	(b) ΔNFA to ΔDCG	0.70	Negative
3	(a) ΔDC to ΔNFA	2.16[b]	Negative
	(b) ΔNFA to ΔDC	0.90	Indeterminate
4	(a) ΔNBFIC to ΔNFA	0.93	Negative
	(b) ΔNFA to ΔNBFIC	1.80[c]	Positive

Notes: a Significant at the 1% level;
     b significant at the 5% level;
     c significant at the 10% level.

extended by the central bank in forms that increase the high-powered money base and which are thus more expansionary than credit to the private sector.

There are complications, however. In particular, there are feedback effects between ΔNFA and ΔDC. Line 2(b) shows that there is a (non-significant) tendency for changes in NFA to be correlated negatively and causally with changes in DCG. That is, economic conditions leading to a worsening in the balance of payments (reducing NFA) tend to cause a widening of the government's budgetary deficit and thus to an increase in DCG. If the balance of payments worsens because of a collapse in export earnings, this will reduce the domestic level of economic activity and the volume of imports. In turn, both developments will depress tax revenues and widen the budget deficit, although the relationship shows up as rather weak in our results.

Of much greater strength is the feedback mechanism from ΔNFA to ΔDCP, shown in line 1(b), but in this case the correlation is positive. What is shown there is a highly significant causal correlation between NFA and DCP: reductions in NFA are associated with reductions in DCP. In this case the mechanisms are easier to understand (although they would also merit further study). We suggest two. First, reductions in NFA reduce the quantity of high-powered money and thus diminish the reserve base upon which commercial banks undertake their lending. To some extent, therefore, the causal connection is automatic. However, we shall later suggest that bank lending is not highly sensitive to changes in their reserve ratios because they tend always to hold reserves in excess of the required minima. Of greater potency, we suggest, are the policy responses of the government. When the balance of payments is in difficulty and NFAs are declining, the government is likely to seek the assistance of the IMF and to impose (or tighten) credit ceilings. Since credit to the government itself (and possibly to parastatal bodies) is determined by the fiscal situation and is outside the direct control of the central bank, it is credit to the private sector which is cut, thus producing the positive relationship shown in the table.

The two feedback effects described above work in opposite directions, with a reduction in NFA leading to *increased* lending to government and *reduced* lending to the private sector. They thus tend to cancel each other out, leaving the net result indeterminate. This is confirmed in line 3(b) of Table 5.3, which shows a non-significant relationship between ΔNFA and changes in total DC, with an indeterminate sign.

The picture that emerges, then, is that increases in DCG are particularly prone to weaken the balance of payments, which is consistent with the monetarist position and with the thrust of IMF programmes which seek to strengthen the payments position by limiting bank credit to government. What we have also found, however, is that increases in DCG are, in turn, likely to result in reductions in DCP. We thus have prima-facie evidence of a tendency for the financial 'crowding-out' of the private sector – a subject to which we return later.

A further complication (not shown in Table 5.3) is, however, that the above explanation produces statistically much stronger results for the 1970s than it does for the 1980s. Application of the same methodology to 1981–8 produced only non-significant results, although the signs were as expected. It appears that there was a much weaker tendency for the mechanisms described above to operate in the 1980s, for reasons we have been unable to investigate. Some suggestions can, however, be offered. During that decade the government introduced a variety of 'structural adjustment' policy changes that are liable to have affected the ways in which the domestic economy interacts with the balance of payments. Probably the most important was the shift to a flexible exchange-rate policy, leading to a major real depreciation in recent years. It is likely that this change, in turn, contributed importantly to improved export performance (and tourism) and thus addressed a major structural weakness affecting the balance of payments. At the same time, increased amounts of external aid were received in support of these adjustment policies,and this too would have weakened the influence of domestic monetary variables on NFAs.

Our conclusion, then, is that non-monetary forces continue to exert major, perhaps increasing, influence on balance-of-payments out-turns – but that monetary variables matter too, especially the volume of central bank lending to the government. The process summarised in Table 5.3 has implications for the feasibility of an effective monetary policy in Kenya. If a given balance-of-payments target is taken as the policy objective, it would, in principle, be possible to promote this by manipulating DC to achieve the desired ΔNFA. However, the most potent element in DC for this purpose is ΔDCG – the government's deficit financing. We have suggested that DCP is already being manipulated in order to promote balance-of-payments objectives. ΔDCG is, however, determined by the behaviour of fiscal variables, including policy variables, and is thus outside the direct control of the central bank. What emerges as crucial, therefore, is the coordination of fiscal and monetary policy to achieve agreed objectives – another subject to which we return later.

Money, savings and investment   As was shown above, real interest rates became positive during the 1980s. Government policy is now to liberalise interest rates further and to move towards market-determined rates in the early 1990s. In the face of unsatisfied private sector demand for credit and a continuing large demand from the public sector, it is widely expected that the result of such liberalisation will be a sharp upward movement in the structure of nominal interest rates. It is also, of course, government policy to reduce inflation. There is thus a prospect of a major upward shift in real rates in the early 1990s and the question arises of the likely consequences of such a movement, particularly for savings and investment.

The effect of real interest rates (hereafter I^*) on savings in Kenya has been investigated by Mwega *et al.* (1989).[17] Their results were negative, despite the significant changes that had occurred in I* during the period covered. Neither total private savings nor that part of it channelled into the financial system was significantly influenced by I*; indeed, for the most part the signs were 'wrong'. The strongest influences on total private savings were the real growth of the economy and a dummy variable representing a variety of 'structural adjustment' measures (other than the changes in I*) adopted during the 1980s. There was also an apparently negative relationship between private saving and inflows of capital from the rest of the world, although that may have been a statistical artefact. Finally, a variable for the savings-income ratio lagged by one year was also found to have a strong influence, implying the existence of a strong desired level of saving on the part of private individuals and firms to which real saving rates adjust rapidly and strongly. One possible contributory factor to the relative unimportance of I* is that savers have few alternative reasonably liquid assets available to them.

These results were similar for that part of total savings channelled into time and savings deposits with the commercial banks and into the NBFIs (for which the data base is more reliable). Real income is by far the strongest determinant and I* is again insignificant. The expected negative correlation of I* with private sector demand for credit was found, although I* was only significant at the 10 per cent level. A 1 per cent increase in I* reduced the demand for credit by about 0.2 per cent. There is a presumption from the results of empirical studies of other developing countries that total investment would respond in the same direction.[18]

It follows from these results that a shift to higher real interest rates is not likely to make much difference to the saving rate but is likely to have a negative effect on the level of investment. The net effect will thus tend in some degree to be stagflationary, raising costs and retarding future economic growth by inducing reductions in investment.

Two important qualifications should be added, however. The first is that the tests could only be conducted on the relatively modest changes in I* that have actually occurred since independence. The results reported would not necessarily provide good predictions of the outcome of much larger increases in I*, which might occur as a result of liberalisation, although evidence from other countries provides at best mixed support for the proposition that aggregate saving is interest-elastic.[19] Secondly, while it is predictable from theory that investment will be a negative function of I*, theory also predicts higher productivity from that investment which is undertaken, as the interest price discriminates between high- and low-return investments.[20] In this event, productivity effects could offset the deflationary effects of reduced investment levels, leaving the net outcome indeterminate. We discuss below the impact of monetary movements on investment, in the discussion of the possible 'crowding-out' effects of government fiscal deficits.

To sum up, it is clear that monetary behaviour does indeed matter in Kenya. Its influence is perhaps strongest and most direct on domestic inflation, but it also contributes importantly to balance of payments outcomes. In turn, inflation and the availability of foreign exchange will have important effects on the performance of the 'real' economy. In addition, even though I^* may have little effect on the volume of savings, it probably does have an effect on investment, and we have also suggested that there is prima-facie evidence that monetary policy operates in ways that crowd out the private sector. It is evident, then, that effective monetary policies could make a significant contribution to the progress of the economy.

The demand for money

Monetarist policy models are based on the standard assumption that there is a stable demand-for-money function. We have therefore tested a model for the demand for money (m, the dependent variable) which takes as its explanatory variables:

1   Expected real income, taken to be determined by past real incomes (y_t),
2   Expected inflation, represented by past inflation (π_t),
3   The expected rate of interest on Treasury bills, taken as representative of the opportunity cost of holding money (r_t),
4   The demand for money in the previous period, to catch lagged adjustments to past discrepancies between the demand for and supply of money (m_{t-1}).

This was estimated in the log form for real M1, M2 and M3: $\log m_t = a_0 + a_1 \log \hat{y}_t + a_2\hat{\pi} + a_3 \log \hat{r}_t + a_4 \log m_{t-1}$, where a is a constant term. The results obtained for M1 and M2 were as set out in Table 5.4.

Past demand for money, the lagged adjustment term, is easily the largest influence (with the speed of adjustment working out at about 1.5 years). Expected inflation is also a significant variable, consistent with our earlier finding on the influence of money on the price level. More interestingly, the rate of interest is also significant at the 1 per cent level. The income variable has much weaker explanatory value – it is non-significant in the M1 test – and the income elasticities derived, of 0.25 for real M1 and 0.78 for real M2, are smaller than expected. The adjusted R^2s are large throughout.

What is most pertinent for present purposes is the influence of the policy variable, the rate of interest (r_t), to which the demand for money is sensitive. If our results are valid, the implication is that it would be possible for the government to influence the demand for money by shifting interest rates. It should be added, however, that other studies of the demand for money in Kenya have produced markedly differing results from those described above. Thus, Kanga (1985) found the income variable to be a statistically significant determinant, although his elasticity for M1 was almost identical to ours, and found the rate of interest an insignificant determinant. Ndele (1990) similarly

Table 5.4 Short-run money demand functions in Kenya, 1973:3–1988:4

Dependent variable	Log M1	Log M2	Log M3
Constant	0.945	0.196	0.173
	(1.524)	(0.535)	(0.583)
$\log \hat{y}^t$	0.040	0.074[b]	0.020
	(0.697)	(1.682)	(0.561)
$\hat{\pi}^t$	−1.280[a]	−1.319[a]	−1.206[a]
	(3.033)	(5.026)	(5.522)
$\log \hat{r}_t$	−0.037[a]	−0.017[a]	−0.009
	(3.091)	(2.687)	(1.574)
$\log m_{t-1}$	0.839[a]	0.905[a]	0.964[a]
	(12.752)	(19.686)	(30.909)
$\bar{R}^2$	0.82	0.92	0.97
DW	2.03	2.00	2.00
SSR	0.231	0.090	0.062
F(4,57)	72.06[a]	174.107[a]	534.02[a]

Notes: a significant at the 1% level;
b significant at the 5% level.

finds income to be a highly significant explanatory variable, but also finds the interest rate significant in some of his results. Both these studies differed from ours in the variables used, the period covered and the models employed, and we present our findings rather tentatively, despite the statistically robust results obtained. It is nonetheless possible that the authorities could influence money demand by using the interest-rate weapon. Less tentatively, the influence of the interest rate is likely to grow as the financial system develops and the range and liquidity of instruments available to the public increases.

This then brings us back to the stability of the demand for money. We tested this, using the Gujarati method,[21] with the result that the demand-for-money function of the type set out in Table 5.4 appears to be stable, although it is more so with narrow definitions of money (M1) than with broader definitions. This finding of stability was markedly different from the behaviour of the income velocity observed, but was consistent with the results of an earlier study by Darrat (1985). Stability does not mean constancy, however, for our tests also revealed a tendency for the income elasticity of demand for money to decline over time. This implies that it would not be appropriate to take a money demand function estimated for a long period such as ours as representative of the present-day situation. Estimates for a shorter, more recent period would be desirable (despite the resulting loss of degrees of freedom), with periodic re-estimations to catch changes in the income elasticities (and perhaps other coefficients).

Although these results indicate a stable demand function, as an effective monetary policy requires, the form of this function is actually rather unfavourable, for it includes a highly significant lagged variable, with the results implying a lag of about 1.5 years. Long-run demand stability is consistent with instability while adjustment is occurring and may mean that long-run stability may never actually be achieved – a conclusion unfavourable to the use of monetary instruments for the short-term 'fine-tuning' of the economy.

Controlling the supply of money

We tested a model which sought to explain changes in the real high-powered money base (ΔH^*). We found ΔH^* to be positively correlated with changes in real income, a result which is probably achieved via changes in NFA; and to be highly significantly negatively correlated with Δk, with a 1 per cent increase in k reducing the growth of H^* by about 0.8 or 0.9 per cent. The overall significance tests for the equations fitted were satisfactory and the results appeared robust. If k increases, meaning that a larger volume of credit can be created on a given H base, this will weaken the balance of payments, reducing the NFAs of the monetary authorities which, in turn, will reduce H and tend then to lead to some credit contraction. This result is similar to a finding for 1968–73 by Bolnick (1975). A form of sequenced automatic stabilisation process is at work, with shifts in k tending partially (but only partially) to offset ΔH and thus to moderate ΔM. We ran tests for the validity of the money multiplier model for Kenyan conditions and found that there was a significant negative correlation between the behaviour of H and k, but that H was far more volatile than k.

But while the behaviour of k does tend partially to counteract the effects of ΔH, this behaviour pattern suggests that discretionary interventions by the central bank to regulate M may be frustrated by countervailing movements in k, unless k is itself amenable to control by the CBK.

Whether H can be used as a policy tool for regulating M depends on the extent of the central bank's control over the components of H which, in the Kenyan case, are its net foreign assets (NFAs) and its lending to the government (CBG). The degree of CBK control over NFAs is slight. To a substantial extent, what happens to such balance-of-payments variables as the terms of trade, export volumes, long-term capital flows, etc., is beyond its control, except through the longer-term (but very important) use of the exchange rate, on which the CBK probably does have an important say. For any given period, however, the effect of any change in the real exchange rate on NFAs is problematic, so the most the CBK can do on this is to exert a general pressure (chiefly through the exchange rate) in the 'right' direction. Monetary variables do have an important influence on the payments situation, as we showed earlier, but the process was one in which the behaviour of NFA was chiefly driven by ΔDCG. We argue below that the CBK has only slight influence over the planned level of DCG and that, in any case, budgetary outcomes are not very predictable.

The CBK arguably has even less control over the domestic asset component of H than over the foreign assets. We conclude that it is unable to manipulate H in order to achieve a target level of M. It could seek to control M by using its powers over the commercial banks to manipulate domestic credit. We examine first M2, then M3.

Our starting point was pioneering research by Bolnick (1975). He also found k to be relatively unstable. He broke k into two components: α and β, where α = the ratio of public holdings of currency to bank deposits, and β = the ratio of the commercial banks' liquid assets to their deposit liabilities. Although there were movements in α, these were relatively small and had a limited impact on k. The behaviour of β, on the other hand, was both more unstable and had a more powerful effect on k. The reason for this, Bolnick found, was that the banks were slow to adjust their lending to changes in their liquidity ratios, thus damping the effect of changes in liquidity and tending to produce the type of automatic stabiliser described in the previous section, with Δk tending to offset ΔH.

Bolnick's work was confined to quarterly data 1967:4–1973:4, and we have therefore tested a similar model for 1971–88. The nature of our results was very close to his, with shifts in β inducing changes in k of the type already discussed.[22] We developed a model to try to explain $\Delta\beta$ and the strongest result we obtained (significant at the 5 per cent level) was changes in the banks' liquidity. Thus, if the banks experience an increase in their liquidity ratio, due to an increase in H, this does not induce them to raise their lending by the full amount that would be permitted by the increase in their reserve base. The relationship between bank liquidity and bank credit was not stable or predictable, thus making the outcome of any CBK attempts to regulate M by manipulating bank liquidity distinctly uncertain. This result is consistent with the findings of Kanga (1985), who tested for the elasticity of bank lending with respect to changes in their liquidity. He found that bank lending was not responsive to changes in their liquidity ratios *as defined by the CBK*. Specifically, he found that they did not regard their holdings of Treasury bills (the largest single component of the statutory ratio) as liquid assets in the sense of using them as a basis for credit creation; that this is still the case was confirmed to us during interviews in 1989. On the other hand, Kanga did find lending highly sensitive to other components of the banks' reserve base (cash, inter-bank deposits, etc.). This suggests, then, that much of the variability of k is due to an inappropriate specification of liquidity in Kenya and that modification of this could both stabilise k and increase CBK control of bank lending.

An alternative interpretation is that the observed unresponsiveness of bank lending to changes in their liquidity (conventionally defined) is due to the CBK's unwillingness to use its powers to vary minimum liquidity requirements in order to force the required ratio above the level that the banks would, in any case, choose to hold for prudential purposes.[23] Had they been willing to use this weapon more aggressively, raising enforced ratios above prudential minima, it seems likely that the banks would then have been more responsive to shifts in their liquidity.

Our tests identified other explanatory variables which help to explain banks' liquidity ratios, although these were significant at only the 10 or 20 per cent levels. We found a positive correlation with changes in lending rates, with liquidity rising when rates were raised, because of the effects on the demand for credit. Changes in the composition of deposit liabilities – as between current, time and savings deposits – also had an effect in some years, with shifts in favour of time and savings deposits associated with reduction in liquidity. For some periods we also found changes in the statutory minimum ratio to have an effect. It seems that the banks may actually have a policy of maintaining a prudential cushion of liquidity over and above their legal obligations, although the actual size varies from year to year.

It appears, then, that the behavioural pattern of the banks and its effects on k increase the CBK's difficulties in exerting reasonable control over M. Some degree of control is nonetheless evident, for, as noted at the beginning of this chapter, Kenya has never experienced a prolonged period of grossly excessive credit creation.

One explanation is the key role of the IMF, with which there have been programmes throughout the 1980s, with the exception of fiscal year 1986–7. The laying-down of maxima for the expansion of DCG and total DC is, of course, at the centre of Fund programmes, so agreement on a Fund programme implies acceptance of monetary ceilings. In the past the government and the CBK have not laid down credit ceilings when there has been no Fund programme. They have, of course, taken an active view of the ceilings proposed to them by the IMF, but have taken a very relaxed view in conditions when IMF programmes were either not needed or not feasible. This tells us that the government has not so far attempted very seriously to define and execute an independent monetary policy. It also means that monetary policy tends to be driven by the balance of payments in the sense that it is only in times of payments difficulties that a Fund programme will be requested.

Observance of Fund ceilings on credit to the government has to be attempted by means of fiscal measures, and the budgetary aspects of the monetary process are discussed in the next section. But since the Fund stipulates ceilings both for DCG and total DC, there is also an implied ceiling for DCP plus credit to the parastatals. The requisite control over DCP is then pursued by the stipulation of ceilings above which the commercial banks may not lend. For example, the government in December 1987 laid it down that bank credit to private and parastatal borrowers must not increase by more than 0.8 per cent per month.

How effective these ceilings are as a policy instrument is unclear. They are certainly not totally impotent; it has been possible to remain within Fund ceilings in all programmes since 1982. On the other hand, there is known to be a good deal of evasion of them, by a variety of routes. One, as we shall show later, has been to use credit from NBFIs as an alternative to bank credit – a possibility which seems to us seriously to undermine the economic rationale for having credit ceilings at all. Another device, we were informed, is that there is a good deal of inter-company lending, with some firms helping out others which are short of credit, the economic effects of which remain to be established. There is also a good deal of manipulation of the figures in order to bring them within the IMF performance criteria on the benchmark dates, although this is only possible so long as the underlying values are not too far out of line.[24] We suspect that the Fund has been willing to turn a blind eye to some of these practices in order to keep programmes on track and avoid the turmoil created by suspending them. A final thing that should be said is that Fund ceilings on total DC have not been very restrictive, permitting an average annual increase in the six programmes since 1982 of 12.4 per cent.[25]

The influence of the budget

It is evident that credit to government looms large in the overall behaviour of the monetary system. To examine this more closely, we consider the influence of different ways of financing the budget on total credit and the supply of money; and on the feasibility and extent of coordination between fiscal and monetary policies. We subsequently consider the implications for the private sector.

The period averages presented in Table 5.1 show sizeable budget deficits and significant government borrowing from the banking system, but they are too coarse to give more than a rough picture of developments over time. If we take the overall deficit, its development can be seen as falling into four distinct periods:

1   1965/6–1973/4: a period of modest overall deficits.
2   1974/5–1979/80: a period of substantially increased deficits but with no particular trend over time.
3   1980/1–1981/2: a period of large and rapidly increasing deficits.
4   1982/3–1987/8: the absolute value of the deficit was cut by two-thirds in 1982–3 over the previous year (following the attempted coup and a strong speech by President Moi stressing the need to restore fiscal discipline) but thereafter a strong upward trend was resumed until 1986–7, by which year it was equal to 8 per cent of GDP, but with a substantial fall in the following year.

We are interested, first, in the extent to which these deficits were correlated with changes in banking system credit to the government (ΔDCG) and then in the effects of this deficit financing on overall credit and money supply aggregates. Taking the period as a whole, we found that changes in the overall deficit were strongly and positively correlated:

1 with ΔDCG, with an $R^2 = 0.88$ (against a minimum R^2 value for 5 per cent significance of well under 0.4);
2 with changes in total domestic credit (ΔDC), with $R^2 = 0.96$; and
3 with broad and narrow definitions of money, with R^2s of 0.99 in both cases.

It is evident, therefore, the government financing needs exert a powerful influence on the overall monetary situation. We also obtained strong correlations in all periods starting in about 1972. Only in 1967–71 did the relationships fail to hold.

The government can, of course, seek to finance its budget deficits by borrowing either domestically or abroad. Taking 1967–87, we found that the use of external financing (F) was positively and highly significantly correlated with ΔDCG ($R^2 = 0.76$). Once again the early years were an exception; in 1967–71 these sources of finance were indeed substitutes. Thereafter, however, the correlation was consistently and strongly positive. Moreover, we found that almost throughout ΔF was strongly and positively correlated with ΔDC and ΔM1 and ΔM2. For 1967–87 the R^2s were 0.88, 0.95 and 0.94 respectively.

The position that apparently emerges here is a process in which, when the Treasury finds itself with an increasing budget deficit, it responds by borrowing more both from abroad and from the domestic banking system – with the process going into reverse when the deficit declines. The positive association between ΔF and the credit and money supply aggregates presumably comes about (i) because of discretionary policy decisions which cause ΔF to be positively correlated with ΔDCG, but also (ii) because ΔF automatically alters the size of the foreign asset component of the high-powered money base. This latter consideration explains why the correlations between ΔF and ΔM are stronger than between ΔF and ΔDCG. The nature of this transmission mechanism serves to underline yet further the central importance of control over the budget deficit for the behaviour of monetary magnitudes and for the feasibility of meaningful monetary policy.

It is unclear, from our understanding of the budgetary process, how much conscious and interactive coordination there is between the fiscal and monetary authorities. It seems fairly clear that the process is driven by the budget, but with the Ministry of Finance subjected to various constraints. One important constraint throughout most of the 1980s has been the ceilings on budget deficits and bank credit to government incorporated in agreements with the IMF (although we have suggested that these have not been particularly restrictive). Others were referred to earlier: the heavy presence in government expenditures of two large items which it is virtually impossible to cut (the wage bill of the civil service and the cost of servicing the public debt); and political reluctance to use the tax weapon. The combination of these constraints leaves the budget-makers with perilously few degrees of freedom and the domination of the Treasury over the central bank which exists in Kenya means that the management of the CBK is not normally in a position to exert any decisive influence on the overall arithmetic of the budget.

If this is correct – and it is consistent with our observations – it leaves the official Monetary Policy Committee with little option but to take the government's domestic financing requirements as given, leaving it the tasks of deciding the best ways of raising the necessary loans and of reconciling the government's financing needs with those of parastatal bodies and of private industry whilst remaining within the overall credit ceilings incorporated in IMF agreements.

A recent experiment in the marketing of Treasury bonds, with maturities of one to five years and bearing interest of 15 to 16.5 per cent, illustrates this aspect of the role of the CBK. These were introduced in 1986, with the principal objective of providing a non-inflationary form of financing for the government while at the same time mopping up some of the excess liquidity in the economy due to the coffee boom of that year. By using its control over bank interest rates and offering more attractive rates on the bonds, the CBK hoped to attract liquidity out of the banks and to tap the savings of the private sector. By mid-1988 a total of £458m.-worth of this paper had been sold, equivalent, for example, to the size of the exceptionally large budget deficit of 1986–7. However, this exercise was not the success that these figures might indicate, because we understand that by far the largest single purchaser was the National Social Security Fund (NSSF), whose purchases chiefly consisted of a switch in portfolio from shorter-dated Treasury bills, with probably only rather small effects on overall liquidity. The general public has remained reluctant to invest in the bonds, partly because they are illiquid, there being no established secondary market, and partly because the interest they pay attracts tax at 20 per cent.[26]

We have suggested that the CBK is largely in the position of having to accept government deficit-financing requirements as a given and then of having to make the best disposition of the remainder of its responsibilities given this (and other) constraints. This raises the issue of whether the Treasury is in a position to give the CBK reliable information about its financing requirements so that the CBK can at least plan the remainder of monetary policy realistically. The answer appears to be that it is not. In Table 10.5 we set out indicators of predictability and bias in the budgetary system for 1973/4–1980/1 and 1981/2–1987/8.[27] The first two columns provide measures of the predictability of key budgetary magnitudes, based on comparisons of original budget estimates and final outcomes.

We see there that in the earlier period the deficit (line 4) was subject to extremely large deviations from budget intentions, with a coefficient of variation of ± 259 per cent of the original budget estimate. By this standard, the result for the later period shows a considerable improvement, with a coefficient of 'only' ± 114 per cent. Nevertheless, this is a high degree of unpredictability and means that the CBK's Monetary Policy Committee does not have firm grounds upon which to base its decisions about credit to the rest of the economy.

The right-hand part of Table 5.5 indicates systematic biases in budget estimates. There is a bias towards optimism in all the budget magnitudes shown, except for external aid receipts in the later period. For the 1981/2–1987/8 period the mean size of the deviation on the deficit for domestic financing was equivalent to 9.0 per cent of average money supply (M2) – substantial but not huge.

Of course, the Kenyan Government is not alone in taking a consistently over-optimistic view of likely budgetary out-turns. It is likely that Treasury officials are aware that their forecasts tend to be over-optimistic, although to a degree the Treasury may nonetheless be systematically deceiving itself about likely budget outcomes. In principle, the consistent nature of the biases could be an aid to monetary policy-makers, allowing them to adjust for the over-optimism of the budget. However, the Monetary Policy Committee is manned exclusively by officials, including a strong representation from the Treasury, and we doubt whether they would feel free to disown their Minister's figures.

To sum up, the overall budget deficit has a powerful influence on trends

Table 5.5 Predictability and bias in Kenyan budgeting

| | | Coefficient of variation[a] | | Direction of bias[b] | | | |
| | | | | over-estimate | | under-estimate | |
		A	B	A	B	A	B
1	Current account balance[c]	119	302	6	7	2	0
2	Capital expenditure	40	26	5	6	3	1
3	External grants and loans	29	44	6	4	2	3
4	Deficit for domestic financing	259	114	2	1	6	6

Sources: A: Killick, 1984, Table 5.7;
B: G and K *Economic Surveys* (various issues).
Key: A = 1973/4 to 1980/1;
B = 1981/2 to 1987/8.
Notes: a In percentages of original budget estimates.
b Number of observations.
c In this case 'over-estimate' means *either* an actual surplus smaller than budgeted *or* an actual deficit larger than budgeted.

in domestic credit and money supply. The CBK has little influence over these, seriously weakening its ability to determine overall monetary outcomes. Finally, the Treasury cannot give the CBK even approximately reliable estimates of what its financing needs are likely to be. None of this bodes well for effective monetary policy.

Consequences for the private sector

One of the dangers inherent in the situation just described is that the government establishes a first claim on a substantial part of total domestic credit and, given a policy objective of avoiding excessive total credit creation, that this will pre-empt some of the credit needs of the rest of the economy to an extent which is inconsistent with the government's own stated objectives of encouraging the growth of the private sector. We referred earlier to the likelihood that much of this squeeze would fall upon the private sector, and Table 5.1, line 14, shows that the share of the private sector in total credit has consistently and substantially diminished over the years. Moreover, banking system credit to the government is causally correlated with a weakening of the payments situation (declining NFAs) and this weakening, in turn, has induced a reduction in credit to the private sector.

This process implies a 'financial crowding-out' of the private sector. To examine this, we first used Granger-causality tests to measure the possible influence of banking system credit to the public sector (ΔDCU) on its credit to the private sector (ΔDCP), and vice versa. The result was unambiguous. It supported the crowding-out hypothesis, with ΔDCU significant at the 5 per cent level in causing (in the Granger sense) ΔDCP in the opposite direction, whereas ΔDCP was found to have no significant effect on ΔDCU, implying that the public sector is given priority in the allocation of credit. The ΔDCU coefficients summed to -0.36, implying that a Ksh1m. increase in banking system credit to the public sector would result in a Ksh0.36m. reduction in credit to the private sector.

This result is strongly supported by earlier work by Koori (1984), who used a more structural model to test for crowding out. Among the differences between his approach and ours, are that he confined himself to credit from the 'competitive' part of the banking system, i.e. excluding the CBK, and that he focused on credit to the *non-household* part of the private sector. Despite these and other differences, his results were strikingly similar to ours. He too found the crowding-out hypothesis to be supported, with a coefficient very close to ours (-0.40) and with high levels of significance.

We then supplemented our Granger tests with an alternative approach which differentiated between alternative sources of credit to the public sector. The rationale for this is that when the public sector (in this case the central government) borrows from the CBK, this does not directly compete with credit to private enterprises, who do not have access to central bank loans. Competition between the two sectors is thus likely to be strongest when the public sector borrows from the banks. (We also incorporated NBFIs into the tests, with results reported later on.) The equations were tested for 1969–88 and the results obtained are summarised in Table 5.6

Where:

$\left[\dfrac{\Delta DCP}{P}\right]_t$ is real credit flow to the private sector;

$\left[\dfrac{Y}{P}\right]_t$ is real GDP;

$[L-\pi]_t$ is real lending rate as measured by nominal deposit rate minus the rate of inflation;

$\left[\dfrac{\Delta CBU}{\Delta DCU}\right]_t$ is central bank credit to the public sector (ΔCBU) relative to total domestic credit to the sector (ΔDCU) from the 'competitive' financial system;

$\left[\dfrac{\Delta DCU}{P}\right]_t$ is real credit to the public sector;

$\left[\dfrac{\Delta DCP}{P}\right]_{t-1}$ is lagged dependent variable; and

u_t is a random error term.

Equations 1 and 2 relate to credit by the banking system; equations 3 and 4 also include credit by NBFIs.

These results show that:

1   The real GNP coefficient is significant at the 1 per cent level, so that the real flow of credit to the private sector increases with output.
2   The real lending rate $(L-\pi)$ is significant at the 5 per cent level, confirming that private sector demand for credit is interest-elastic.
3   The higher the proportion of public sector needs that is satisfied by the central bank $(\Delta CBU/\Delta DCU)$, the less the competition faced by the private sector for funds. Although the sign is as expected, this variable is not significant in equations 1 and 2 (although it becomes so in equations 3 and 4 when NBFIs are incorporated).
4   The crowding-out coefficient $-(\Delta DCU/P)_t-$ is significant at the 5 per cent level, again confirming the results already reported. The coefficient value in equation 1 (-0.315) is very close to the -0.36 found in the previous test.
5   There are no significant adjustment lags in the real flow of credit to the private sector, with the lagged dependent variable insignificant throughout.

Econometric findings of a crowding-out process are supported by other evidence that such a process does operate in Kenya. King (1979) and Killick

Table 5.6 OLS estimates of private credit functions

Dependent variable	Constant	$\left[\dfrac{Y}{P}\right]_t$	$[L-\pi]_t$	$\left[\dfrac{\Delta CBU}{\Delta DCU}\right]_t$	$\left[\dfrac{\Delta DCU}{P}\right]_t$	Lagged dep. variable	R^2	DW	Period
1 $\left[\dfrac{\Delta DCP}{P}\right]_t$	−1937.93[c] (1.460)	0.080[a] (2.728)	−7243.06[b] (1.974)	48.901 (0.868)	−0.315[b] (1.817)	−0.146 (0.586)	0.46	2.12	1969−88
2 $\left[\dfrac{\Delta DCP}{P}\right]_t$	−1830.56 (1.506)	0.075[a] (2.867)	−6444.04[b] (1.994)	41.63 (0.749)	−0.337[b] (2.032)		0.44	2.19	1969−88
3 $\left[\dfrac{\Delta DCP}{P}\right]_t$	−7419.90[a] (4.870)	0.202[a] (5.943)	−7959.13[a] (4.419)	12.220[b] (2.308)	−0.371[a] (5.030)	0.085 (0.680)	0.75	3.16	1974−86
4 $\left[\dfrac{\Delta DCP}{P}\right]_t$	−7859.30[a] (5.867)	0.215[a] (7.698)	−8459.28[a] (5.288)	12.137[b] (2.367)	−0.363[a] (5.140)		0.73	3.09	1974−86

Notes: a Significant at the 1% level;
b significant at the 5% level;
c significant at the 10% level.

(1984) both record episodes in the 1970s; and Brough and Curtin (1981) have described a similar result as an aftermath of the 1976–7 coffee boom.

Instead of operating through interest rates (which were controlled throughout our period), crowding-out occurs in other ways. The CBK's control over the minimum levels and composition of the liquid reserves of the commercial banks and NBFIs is one of them. Liquid assets are defined rather narrowly, e.g. excluding commercial bills, so as to leave the institutions limited alternatives to holdings of Treasury bills and, in any case, the banks are required to hold not less than half of their liquid assets in Treasury bills. Since 1986 the CBK has used its powers over interest rates to attempt to transfer lending power from the banks into holdings of Treasury bonds, although with limited success. Yet another way of channelling involuntary finance to the government is through the use of its *de facto* powers over the NSSF and the POSB to require them both to invest extensively in government paper – sums that otherwise would potentially be available for on-lending to private borrowers.[28] Probably the most powerful mechanism of crowding-out, however, is through the use of ceilings on bank credit to the private sector, in order to accommodate the financing needs of the government. At the time of our research, in 1988–9, it seemed to be agreed that the ceilings then in force were adversely affecting private businesses.

The IMF apparently connived at this process during the 1980s. The mean permitted increase in total DC in its six programmes since 1982 was 12.4 per cent per annum. However, the equivalent value for DCG was 24.1 per cent (or 18.9 per cent, excluding one particularly high value). This implies that DCP was restricted to growth well below the overall ceiling and far below the permitted expansion in DCG (although the 1988 programme reversed this). This being the case, it is perhaps scarcely surprising that the government has been able to keep within the DCG ceilings.

As mentioned above, to some degree the rapid growth of the NBFIs has offered an escape route for private borrowers unable to satisfy their credit needs through bank borrowings, and has thus limited the degree of crowding out. To the extent that this has happened, it has imposed a cost on the private sector in terms of the substantially higher interest rates that have been charged by NBFIs. Perhaps more important is the fact that the extent of private sector access to this escape route may have been quite limited, for we suggest below that a large proportion of NBFI lending has been to parastatals. Including NBFIs in our econometric tests for crowding-out (3 and 4) actually strengthened our results, and it seems possible that their lending to the private sector goes down in periods of credit stringency. In principle, it is also possible that informal sector credit could have provided a safeguard against the effects of crowding-out, but this is unlikely in practice, except to the smallest businesses.

But while some crowding-out has undoubtedly occurred, its effects are uncertain. It does not appear that really draconian credit restrictions have been imposed; it has rather been a matter of slowing down the rate of expansion. It may well be that shortages of credit are for the private sector as a whole of secondary importance by comparison with the difficulties created, say, by price controls or foreign-exchange restrictions. Nevertheless, there is a strong presumption that crowding-out has had some discouraging effect on the output and expansion of private enterprises, particularly among small-scale, locally-owned businesses and those seeking to become established for the first time. And, quite apart from crowding-out *per se*, the fact that credit to the private sector tends to be treated as the residual must increase the uncertainties and riskiness of business, again discouraging investment. All such effects would be strongly contrary to stated government objectives.

Defining money and credit: the NBFIs

We tested the proposition suggested earlier that NBFI credit is a substitute for bank credit by examining whether changes in their credit are competitive with or complementary to movements in bank credit. Alternative equations were fitted (i) with credit to the private sector and (ii) with total domestic credit as the dependent variables and with NBFI credit as one of the explanatory variables. Both were run on two alternative bases, in one case relating to credit from the entire banking system and the other confined to credit by the commercial banks. Unfortunately, continuous data series were available only for 1973–86. The total 'explanations' of the various dependent variables were only moderately strong, with R^2s of between 0.34 and 0.60, but the results for the NBFI credit variable were consistent in all four tests.

The tests showed that bank and banking system credit to the whole economy and to the private sector were all negatively correlated with changes in NBFI credit, significant at the 20 per cent level and in one case at the 10 per cent level. Moreover, the coefficients in each case were close to unity,[29] implying an approximately exact offset between credit from the two alternative sources. In other words, if the CBK seeks to reduce total commercial bank lending, any reduction achieved is likely to be matched by an increase in NBFI credit. Although we would have wished for statistically more robust results, we regard this finding as important, for it implies that government credit control policies are likely to be undone if the NBFIs are left outside the control net. This policy conclusion is strongly supported in recent work by Ndele (1990), who obtained substantially stronger results when deposits with NBFIs were included in the definition of money, and who concludes (p. 29) that 'conduct of monetary policy without considering NBFIs will be in error and is likely to provide uncertain results.'

However, bringing the NBFIs within the coverage of monetary policy remains controversial within official circles. Those who defend leaving them outside argue that it is possible indirectly to control NBFI credit because, to a substantial extent, they are simply on-lending monies lent to them by the banks themselves and bank lending to NBFIs is counted within credit ceilings. However, this argument overlooks the fact that(as at end-1988) over three-quarters of total NBFI liabilities were to depositors, with only rather modest liabilities to the banks.

We also examined the results of incorporting a broader (M3) definition of money, which includes NBFI deposit liabilities, in various of the other tests reported above. For inflation, the differences in the results obtained were not large, but they were consistently in the direction of providing a stronger explanation. The R^2 was increased and so were the t-values of most of the explanatory variables. The influence of ΔM on inflation (significant at the 1 per cent level for M2 and M3) was somewhat increased, with the coefficient value rising from 0.324 to 0.361. We also examined whether adoption of an M3 definition would change the stability of the correlation between money and inflation, and found that it did so. Here again, then, we find support for the incorporation of NBFI deposits in the definitiion of M for the purposes of monetary policy.

Bringing NBFIs into the analysis of the influence of money on the *balance of payments* (in lines 4(a) and (b) of Table 5.3) reveals a non-significant tendency for changes in NBFI credit to weaken the balance of payments (reduce foreign assets) but a stronger (significant at the 10 per cent level) positive relationship from foreign assets to NBFI credit. The salient thing about this result is that it is qualitatively identical to the results obtained for the commercial banks (see lines 1(a) and (b) – credit to the private sector is dominated by the commercial banks so these entries are, in effect, results for the banks). This further strengthens the case for treating the NBFIs as analogous to the banks.

Incorporating M3 into the demand for money gave different results (see Table 5.4). The interest rate variable ceased to have significant explanatory power when the broader definition of money was used, with the presumption that depositors with the NBFIs do not perceive Treasury bills as an alternative to their NBFI deposits. Moreover, the tests undertaken for the stability of the money demand function showed that instability was greater the broader the definition of money (although even for M3 it was still relatively stable). The policy implication of these results, then, was that the use of a narrow (M1) definition of money might be more suitable for monetary policy in Kenya if it was to be chiefly directed to manipulating the demand for money than either of the broader alternatives, although the results were not strong.

Incorporating the liquid assets of the NBFIs into explaining the behaviour of the money multiplier made no difference to the variability of k, with virtually identical coefficients of variation with either definition of H. What the inclusion of NBFI liquidity did do was to eliminate (in econometric terms) any tendency for negative correlation between ΔH and Δk. This follows from the finding that NBFI credit tends to be negatively correlated with bank credit. In this case, if bank lending behaviour tends to produce a Δk which is inversely related to ΔH, the counter-cyclical activities of the NBFIs will tend to cancel this out. This suggests, in turn, that the task of predicting the consequences of a given change in H may be a little easier for the authorities if they use the broader definition, but only assuming that the NBFIs would still be allowed to operate counter-cyclically.

Using NBFIs in the tests of the crowding-out hypothesis (see Table 5.6, equations 3 and 4) results in a particularly strong tendency for credit to the private sector to be reduced when banking system credit to the public sector goes up. On the face of it, this seems at variance with the result reported earlier that NBFI credit is negatively correlated with bank credit. It is not clear why it does not dilute any crowding-out, with frustrated private borrowers turning instead to the NBFIs. Our understanding is that a great deal of NBFI lending is to parastatal agencies, and they are not an alternative for would-be private borrowers.[30] Moreover, a time of fiscal difficulty, when the government is making substantial claims for credit from the banking system, is also likely to be a time when the Treasury is particularly reluctant to provide subventions to meet the financial needs of ailing parastatals. If so, these agencies' credit needs and borrowings from the NBFIs would tend to increase in parallel with government requirements and counter-cyclically with the availability of credit to private borrowers. Depending on the relative magnitudes of the two influences, this might produce the complementarity effect reported earlier without alleviating the crowding-out effect. Indeed, it might strengthen it if the NBFIs reduce their lending to the private sector in order to meet the needs of the parastatals.

Special problems of commodity dependence

This book is addressed particularly to the special problems of monetary policy in countries dependent on exports of primary products. We have already shown that Kenya falls squarely into this category and that it is particularly reliant on revenues from two commodities with especially volatile world prices – coffee and tea. The chief interest in the Kenyan case is to examine how monetary policy responded to two temporary booms in world coffee and tea prices, which occurred in 1976–7 and 1986. Both were seriously mismanaged.

Taking the earlier one first,[31] when world prices for coffee, and subsequently tea, rose steeply, due principally to a frost in Brazil, export earnings and NFAs also rose, greatly increasing the lending power of the banking system (NFAs went up by nearly 50 per cent between end-1976 and end-1978). The political decision was made not to tax the windfall proceeds in order to neutralise their effects.[32] These were passed on to the farmers and there were large consequential increases in investment and imports. In the face of a boom, which was obviously only temporary, an appropriate, stabilising, response to large increases in NFAs would have been to use fiscal restraint to absorb purchasing power, and to raise bank liquidity ratios and take other measures to restrict the growth of DC (although whether it would have been feasible to do more than partially neutralise the expansionary impulses coming from the export sector must be doubted). No such attempt was made. The government embarked upon a huge increase in expenditures (mostly of a consumption nature) and took the view that DCP should actually be stimulated. Liquidity ratios were therefore lowered and DC rose by 76 per cent in 1977–8. It was not until 1978, when it was apparent that the boom was over, that an attempt was made to rein back on DC by raising liquidity ratios, but this had little effect.

Why the government should have acted in this way remains unclear. It is possible, however, that this episode illustrated a feature which is of long-term significance for the effectiveness of monetary policy, relating to the nature of Kenyan politics. It is generally believed that the decision to pass on virtually all the windfall gains to the farmers was taken personally by the then President Kenyatta. No doubt this was partly because the coffee and tea farmers are politically powerful, but it may also have been not unrelated to the fact that many key politicians and senior officials themselves own coffee and tea farms! More generally, it is a long-standing feature of public affairs in the country that those who are powerful in the state apparatus are positively encouraged to be active in private business, notwithstanding the large potential for conflicts of interest. It may be, therefore, that the subsequent decision to stimulate credit to the private sector was in some way related to the strength of representation of private business interests in government, although we have suggested earlier that this has not prevented a long-run crowding-out tendency.

Be that as it may, the consequences of this episode were major and long-lasting. Despite import controls, a very large import boom was triggered which led as early as 1978 to a major payments crisis and left controls even tighter than they had been at the beginning of the boom. The payments position was also more indirectly weakened by a relative rise in the price of non-tradables. There were also serious fiscal effects. The government expanded its own spending dramatically during the boom years, when revenues were also very buoyant, but was then unable to scale them back when world prices returned to more normal levels. A ratchet effect was at work. This was aggravated by the fact that the boom years had seriously weakened the control of the Treasury over the spending ministries, and it was not until 1982–3 that this control was properly restored.[33] Moreover, the increase in government current expenditures depressed private sector investment, both by absorbing resources and by its destabilising effects.

In a retrospective evaluation the CBK stated that the lesson to be learned from this episode was that

> next time a bonanza of the 1976 and 1977 magnitude occurs, the authorities would be well advised to pay out the resulting incomes to

70

society gradually in an orderly manner rather than in one season as was the case at that time.

(1981: 34)

However, Bevan *et al.* (1989) point out that in view of its low revealed marginal propensities to save and invest, it is not self-evident that the situation would have been improved by taxing off more of the windfall gains. This central bank assessment adds particular interest to the way the 1986 boom was handled. This was both smaller and shorter than the 1976–7 boom, with the world coffee price rising 'only' about 40 per cent, against 310 per cent in the 1970s, and with earnings from coffee going up by about two-thirds, against a nearly fivefold increase in 1976–7. It should, therefore, have been an easier boom to sterilise, had that been the objective.

It was not, however. Although the windfall was again passed on to the farmers, *pace* CBK, the government seized the payments relief brought by the boom as an opportunity for freeing itself from the restrictions of an IMF programme and greatly expanded its own spending, which went up by 29 per cent in FY 1986–7. In 1986 alone DCG rose by no less than 55 per cent, to be followed by a 30 per cent rise in the following year. Credit to the rest of the economy rose at far more moderate rates, although no credit ceilings were imposed and we are aware of no other attempt to engineer restraint on credit to non-government borrowers other than the (rather unsuccessful) sale of Treasury bonds reported earlier. Total M2 rose by 33 per cent in 1986. Relative to the (much smaller) size of the boom, the expansion of DC and of imports was even greater than in 1976–7. In consequence, and as in the earlier episode, enlarged balance of payments difficulties reappeared, illustrated by a huge decline in international reserves during 1987.

As in 1976–7, the CBK and others advised the government to adopt a prudent sterilisation approach, and once again that advice was largely rejected. It is, in short, difficult to see the 1986 boom except as again having been poorly managed in macroeconomic terms. There was one very important difference, however. It appears that most of the items on which the government so dramatically increased its spending in 1986–7 were of a one-off nature, with expenditure levels and budget deficits reverting to more normal levels thereafter. On this occasion there does not seem to have been a ratchet effect.

It is difficult to assess the extent to which the record of these episodes illustrates difficulties which are inherent in primary product dependence. If economic stabilisation is taken as the criterion, there clearly was serious mismanagement in both cases. It is less clear whether the government and the CBK would technically have been able to sterilise the booms had they been minded so to do, for we have pointed out the difficulties – and potential costs – of using DC to offset impulses emanating from abroad.

POLICY CONCLUSIONS

A recapitulation

The behaviour of monetary variables is important both for inflation and the balance of payments. Though it has a strong effect on these, and more directly through the influence of interest rates and credit policies on investment, money also has a strong effect on the real economy. The quality of monetary policy is therefore important to the performance of the Kenyan economy.

The demand for money is fairly stable, but with an adjustment lag of about one-and-a-half years. Such a substantial period would render the short-term effects of monetary policy instruments highly uncertain. More favourable for effective monetary policy is the finding that money demand is elastic with respect to the rate of interest, although we view this finding as only tentative.

We are deeply pessimistic about the ability of the central bank to manipulate the high-powered money base (H) for the purposes of controlling the overall supply of money, as it has scant control over the two most important determinants of H: the balance of payments and the credit requirements of government.

We also doubt the feasibility of regulating domestic credit through the mechanism of the money multiplier (k), for example, by varying bank reserve ratios. We confirmed earlier research results that k is unstable and that, in the short run at least, the credit creation decisions of the commercial banks are not very sensitive to variations in their reserve ratios, as conventionally defined. A degree of control has been necessary, nevertheless, in order to conform to IMF ceilings and, so far as the private sector is concerned, this has chiefly been achieved by the imposition of credit ceilings, which are liable to have adverse efficiency effects.

The overall budget deficit has a powerful impact on trends in domestic credit and money supply, whether financed by borrowing from the banking system or from external grants and loans. The CBK apparently has little influence over these determinants of the monetary situation, thus seriously weakening its ability to determine overall monetary outcomes, and the Treasury cannot give the CBK reliable forecasts of its financing needs.

Econometric and other evidence implies that credit to the public sector is crowding-out private borrowers. A variety of devices to secure involuntary lending by financial institutions to the state, reinforce the effects of the use of credit ceilings. The IMF has (at least) acquiesced in this process, with more generous provisions for credit to the government than for total domestic credit. How important this credit squeeze has been as a constraint on private enterprise development is, however, a matter for further investigation.

Although there is still much to learn about the behaviour and consequences of NBFIs, several of our tests indicated that they were similar in their effects to the banks. Overall their credit tends to act as a substitute for bank credit; including them in our tests for inflation gave us stronger and more stable results; the nature of their impact on the balance of payments is similar to that of the banks; their inclusion in tests on crowding-out strengthened our results. Only in one respect did our results point in a different direction: a narrow definition of money provides a better basis for predicting the demand for money.

The policy responses to the commodity booms of 1976–7 and 1986 were seriously mismanaged from a stabilisation standpoint. What now are the inferences to draw from these findings for the improvement of policy?

Strengthening policy

Since monetary variables have an important influence on the behaviour of the economy, monetary policy should be made effective. The changes necessary for policy to become more effective are: greater short-run stability in the demand for money; greater stability in balance-of-payments outcomes (possibly through a successful export diversification programme); a more predictable commercial bank response to changes in their liquidity, or the development of better ways of regulating bank lending; improved forecasting of budgetary out-turns and a generally lower public sector borrowing requirement; steadier government adherence to the precepts of macroeconomic management.

So far, attempts to use monetary instruments have been directed almost exclusively at directly manipulating the *supply* of money or credit; an alternative possibility is to operate on demand for it. The principal possibility here is for an active use of the interest rate. Even though we are not very confident about our results on the demand for money, they do indicate that this demand is interest-elastic. If so, when, say, there was an excess supply of money, it would be possible to reduce this by lowering interest rates – with the reverse possibility in the case of an excess demand.

Kenyan conditions would have to change in a number of respects for such a possibility to become a reality, however. Capital markets would need to be further developed so that the public would have available a wider range of financial instruments, which would have to be readily marketable, so as to increase the interest-elasticity of money demand.[34] Interest rates would probably have to be deregulated, or at least allowed to move over a wider range. And the government's own dependence on borrowings from banks and financial institutions would have to be restricted more than it is at present.

It is, in any case, unlikely that the tasks of monetary policy could be achieved simply by influencing money demand. The need would remain also to operate on supply. One possible improvement would be to try to exert greater leverage over k by operating more effectively on the banks' reserve base. One simple proposal is to raise it above prudential levels until it bites. An important obstacle here is that the banks are of unequal financial strength, so that to enforce minimum ratios well in excess of prudential levels could embarrass some of them. However, we cannot envisage this as being more than a temporary difficulty, especially if sensible transition arrangements were made. It is, in any case, a difficulty that would be reduced if interest rates were freed, for it is likely that the underlying lending rate would rise, and with it, bank profitability.

We should also like to recall Kanga's (1985) suggestion that liquidity be redefined by the CBK to include only those types of asset which the banks themselves regard as liquid, i.e. to exclude Treasury bills from the present definition. Treasury objections that this would cut off a badly needed source of deficit financing could be meet – if they had to be – by additionally requiring the banks to hold certain minimum levels of Treasury bills, which, however, would be treated as an 'above-the-line' bank asset rather than as part of their reserves.

A further policy change is to bring the NBFIs within the definitions of money and credit for the purposes of monetary regulation.[35] If this were done, and given the greatly strengthened powers of CBK supervision that now exist, the present prohibition on NBFIs offering chequing facilities should be lifted. This would widen the range of choice open to the public and strengthen competition in a banking system still dominated by an oligopolistic cartel of the four major banks. Alternatively, the Banking Act could be amended to define banks as any deposit-taking institutions, which would automatically bring in most NBFIs.

The development of the capital market would open another possibility: of manipulating bank liquidity (and interest rates) by means of open-market operations. Were it possible to move in these directions and in this way to increase CBK control over aggregate bank lending, it would simultaneously be possible gradually to move away from the present reliance on clumsy and inefficient quantitative credit ceilings.

In principle, moving away from them should reduce crowding-out (assuming that to be desirable). Without some downward shift in the government's demand for credit, however, this advantage could prove illusory. If the capital market developed and interest rates were freed without any such shift in the government's demand, its continuing large appetite for funds would drive interest rates to high levels and would crowd-out the private sector through that mechanism instead.

One of the strongest messages emerging from our research is: the budget dominates. Given some limit on the extent to which it is possible and desirable to accumulate further external debt, and in the absence of any major expansion of capital markets allowing the government to undertake more non-expansionary borrowing, continuation of the large overall budget deficits that marked most of the 1980s would effectively remove the possibility of a meaningful monetary policy. A strengthening of the fiscal situation (which would surely involve a rise in the tax ratio) is a prerequisite for a stronger monetary policy.[36] In addition to narrowing the budget gap, we have also pointed to the desirability of improving the predictability of budget outcomes and, especially, of removing the systematic over-optimism that mars the annual budget.

A reconsideration of the constitutional position of the CBK has also been suggested, with a view to reducing or removing its subordination to the Treasury and to increasing its independence, on the models of the Bundesbank in Germany and the Federal Reserve authorities in the United States. In principle, this would allow the CBK to limit banking system credit to the government, thus forcing the government to strengthen fiscal policies. However, such a suggestion is open to the charge of naivety in a highly centralised political structure. Genuine central bank independence can only grow out of a political culture which is supportive of the separation of powers that such an arrangement entails and we doubt whether the political realities in Kenya as they existed at the time of preparing this study would be tolerant of such a separation. However, fundamental political changes may be occurring and a possible redefinition of the constitutional position of the CBK should not be ruled out for the future.

We mentioned earlier government commitment to the development and liberalisation of the financial system. Perhaps surprisingly, when this occurs it is likely to widen the possibilities of monetary control. As the financial system becomes more diverse and sophisticated, the CBK has remarked:

> there are signs that direct controls such as ratio requirements, interest rate controls, exchange controls and lending guidelines are gradually becoming less effective as policy instruments

> (1989: 60)

The controls are easier to evade and attempts to close loopholes are only partly successful, as well as causing misunderstandings of government intentions. 'It seems inevitable', the CBK states, 'that they will be moved instead towards more market-based interventions.' The government's important *Sessional Paper No. 1, 1986* (p. 34) similarly states that 'monetary policy will continue to move towards greater reliance on market forces'.

This commitment notwithstanding, officials and politicians continue to see major obstacles in the way of movement in this direction. One is the continuing limited degree of progress within the financial sector. A shift towards more indirect, market-based approaches to monetary policy will not work well if commercial banking and financial markets remain oligopolistic. Even if competitive forces do assert themselves, there are fears that some of the more fragile existing banks and NBFIs might find it hard to survive in a more competitive domestic climate. Their bankruptcy could both cause political embarrassments and set back the development of the financial system itself. The most important obstacle, however, is the universal expectation that freer interest rates would mean higher rates. Among the unwanted consequences of this would be:

1   Its possible stagflationary effect, as described earlier, and the likelihood that this would have particularly adverse consequences for small, Kenyan-owned businesses.
2   Rises in costs to the Treasury of its own borrowing, adding to claims on government revenues.
3   Risks that the dominant major banks would collude to raise rates above free market rates.
4   Adverse effects on some politicians and other 'influentials' who are net borrowers and gain from the present artificially low interest rate structure.

This brings us straight back to the dominance of the budget. The reason why it is reasonable to expect that rates would rise if they were freed is that there is excess private sector demand for credit at present rates. This excess is a consequence of the crowding-out already described, resulting from the budget deficit. Were the government's own borrowing requirements to be reduced, the net result of liberalisation on the rate structure is indeterminate. In other words, the government's desire to liberalise and move towards market-based rates is inconsistent with its own present fiscal stance.

However, even with the present credit requirements of the public sector, we doubt whether liberalisation would send interest rates through the roof. The NBFIs have acted as a safety valve, as lenders of second resort, and their rates (in recent years) have not been enormously higher than those of the banks proper. Moreover, the scale of the excess demand mentioned to us by the banks was relatively modest, with a number of them saying they would increase their lending by about 12 per cent in the absence of restrictions.

Even if all our suggestions were adopted, however, there would remain severe limitations on what it is reasonable to expect of monetary policy in Kenya. The obstacles in its way, summarised in the previous section, are formidable and could give way only slowly. For the foreseeable future, the use of monetary instruments to 'fine-tune' the economy is out of the question, not least because of the lengthy adjustment lags. Probably the most that it is realistic to hope for is to mitigate the larger destabilising influences and to provide a useful supplement to the more powerful tools of fiscal policy.

Given existing circumstances, there is very little indeed that monetary policy alone can achieve in the management of the economy. In this connection, we are sceptical about the economic rationale in Kenya for the stress placed in IMF programmes on the control of DC in pursuit of balance-of-payments goals. Our results suggest that it is a considerable over-simplification to regard DC as a variable which is under the control of the authorities. We have suggested that instability in the velocity of circulation and adjustment lags makes the short-term macroeconomic outcome of changes in money supply somewhat unpredictable. Lastly, we have shown the relationships between DC and the balance of payments to be rather complex. On the other hand, our results are strongly supportive of programmes that see the limitation of the government's budget deficits as of key importance to the balance of payments, although in practice the IMF's ability to influence them seems rather confined.

Finally, we turn to the government's policy objectives. In concentrating here on the uses of monetary policy we have been implicitly assuming that macroeconomic management is important among the policy objectives of the Kenyan Government. Such an assumption may not be fully justified, however, for we have seen that monetary policy, in the sense of an official view of the desirable extent of the expansion of M and DC, exists only at times when there are IMF programmes (which admittedly covers almost all the 1980s) and has been effectively abandoned during the two major commodity booms of recent history. Moreover, we suspect that during the currency of a Fund programme the operative monetary ceilings were largely defined by the Fund rather than the government, even though it no doubt argued its own view during the negotiations. It is thus perhaps not stretching things too far to ask whether there has ever been a *national* monetary policy, in the sense of one principally defined by the government. To explain this it may be necessary to go well beyond our own professional expertise, to delve into the nature of Kenyan politics. As suggested earlier, it is possible that the interests represented within the ruling party stand in the way of action in this area, particularly the heavy engagement of key public figures in private business. At the same time, the party is able to adopt restrictive credit policies without any great drama when under pressure from the IMF to do so; it is not obvious, therefore, that political realities foreclose the possibility of an effective national policy.

6

GHANA, 1957–88

Nii Kwaku Sowa

INTRODUCTION

At independence in 1957, Ghana was a world leader in the production of cocoa, and its per capita income was at about the same level as that of Mexico or South Korea. The rate of inflation was a mere 1 per cent. However, positive real economic growth was not sustained for long; output fell between 1964 and 1966 and also from 1975 to the beginning of the Economic Recovery Programme in 1983.

From the 1970s, the country's money supply increased at a rate of over 40 per cent per annum and the monetary policies pursued up to 1983 were unable to check this trend. After 1983, when the Economic Recovery Programme (ERP) was instituted with IMF financing, fiscal discipline was restored; yet the country's money supply continued to increase at a high rate and inflation remained above 20 per cent. The increases in the money supply were no longer due to deficit financing, for budget surpluses have been registered since 1985, but rather to the inflow of funds from foreign multilateral and bilateral donor agencies and governments. This chapter contrasts the effects of these two monetary regimes on Ghana's economy.

From 1960, when the Bank of Ghana gained full central bank status, the Ghanaian authorities have had the chance to pursue an independent monetary policy. However, the effectiveness of central bank control of the money supply has been curtailed by government interference in the operations of the Bank of Ghana and a low degree of financial intermediation in the country. This study examines some of the constraints militating against the effective implementation of monetary policies in Ghana.

The next section examines the state of the economy in the post-colonial period; and the following one, the history and structure of the financial market, focusing upon the process of monetisation, the formal and informal sectors and the role of cocoa production and financing in the financial system. We then present a model of the determinants of money stock in Ghana, and the relationship between the money stock and macroeconomic aggregates, and finally, discuss the effectiveness of monetary policies in Ghana, and some of the obstacles to their effective implementation.

THE STATE OF THE ECONOMY

Economic decline, 1960–83

Table 6.1 presents a summary of the decline in the Ghanaian economy during the period 1960–83, and its partial recovery in 1983–8. The volume of output and investment declined, while population growth rose. Exports dropped both in volume and in value. Cocoa exports in the 1970s and 1980s were below the levels of the late 1950s. As the foreign-exchange constraint became more severe, imports contracted further. There was shortage of both intermediate imports and consumables.

During periods of economic decline (1970–83) agricultural production and services fared relatively better than industry in general and manufacturing in particular (Table 6.2). Severe foreign-exchange shortages meant that Ghana could not import the necessary spare parts and raw materials to maintain industrial plant and equipment, and industrial capacity utilisation dropped to below 25 per cent. The gains in the tertiary sector were mainly expansions in the share of government services, due to the political ideology and legacy of the Nkrumah Government. Nkrumah increased state participation in almost every sphere of the economy, through large state-owned holding companies.

In the early 1980s the situation worsened, with inflation running at over 100 per cent, the balance of payments in a very unfavourable situation, cocoa and other exports at their lowest production levels, and both unemployment and underemployment rife. By 1983, the country was a classic example of one faced with stagflation. There were shortages of almost all items: food, raw materials and even water. The country's economic plight was drawn to

Table 6.1 Basic indicators of real economic performance
(average annual growth rates)

	1960–70	1970–83	1983–8
GDP	2.2	−0.8	5.7
Population	2.3	2.4	3.6
Exports	0.1	−4.4	4.7
Imports	−1.5	−7.2	18.5
Gross domestic investment	−3.1	−5.9	13.6
Terms of trade	n.a.	−1.3	−2.8
Total agriculture (volume)	2.6	−0.5	3.4
Food production (per capita)	0.3	−4.5	5.6

Source: 1960–70, World Bank, *Towards Sustained Development in Sub-Saharan Africa* (Statistical Annex), Washington DC, 1984.
1970–83 and 1983–8. World Bank (1990b).

Table 6.2 Structure of production and consumption in Ghana

	% of GDP at factor cost		
	1970	*1983*	*1988*
Agriculture	55.6	57.2	51.3
Industry	14.3	8.4	10.8
of which: manufacturing	9.6	5.1	7.3
services	30.1	34.4	37.9
	% of domestic absorption		
Private consumption	82.2	82.4	82.7
General govt. consumption	8.4	13.0	10.8
Gross domestic investment	9.4	4.6	6.5

Source: World Bank (1990b).

the attention of the international community when in 1983, in the midst of drought and bushfires, nearly a million Ghanaians were repatriated from Nigeria.

Cocoa dominated exports, but had relatively low productivity. It employed 17 per cent of the labour force to produce only 8 per cent of GDP in 1968 (Steel, 1973). The neglect of the cocoa sector, combined with a poorly conceived programme of import-substituting industrialisation which relied on imported raw materials, contributed immensely to the deterioration in Ghana's economy. There were no clear policies to develop agriculture to feed the newly established industries. Subsequent governments after Nkrumah (1957–66) and the National Liberation Council, NLC (1966–9) did little to change the structure of the economy.

The causes of the decline can be attributed to both internal and external factors. The external factors include unfavourable long-run terms of trade and adverse weather conditions (especially the drought of the late 1970s and early 1980s). The instability of commodity prices on the international market exposed the economy to an unreliable and fragile source of earnings. Ghana, like other oil-importing developing countries, also suffered from the oil crises and the global economic slump of the 1970s.

In the face of a trend decline in the terms of trade (1.3 per cent per annum in the period 1970–83) and higher inflation than its trading partners, the country maintained a rigid fixed exchange-rate regime and refused to devalue. As the foreign-exchange constraint became more severe the government resorted to regulated pricing. Almost every commodity item in Ghana had a controlled price. This introduced distortions into the economy which threw everything out of gear and also brought in its wake corruption at unprecedented levels, which reached its height during the Acheampong era (1972–8). Perhaps the chief internal causes of the decline were gross economic mismanagement, corruption and political instability. Policies formulated were mere paperwork and were never properly implemented. In some cases, good policies drawn up and initiated could not be brought to fruition because of changes of government (mostly through the barrel of a gun). Since independence, Ghana has drawn up four development plans, none of which has ever been fully implemented.

The decline in the economy imposed a strong financial burden on successive governments, but efforts to reduce it by cutting expenditure led to opposition and often to overthrow. The NLC Government took over from Nkrumah in a military coup in 1966. Government spending in the NLC period was almost a fifth of GDP, as it had been during the Nkrumah era. The Busia Government (1969–72) tried to reverse the deficit financing it had inherited from the NLC and Nkrumah regimes. One such attempt involved the cutting of government expenditure on social services such as education and health. This move met with stiff opposition from both student groups and other opposition movements. A further attempt by Busia to adjust relative prices, by devaluing the currency, cost him his government.

When Colonel Acheampong took over from Busia in a military coup in 1972, he reversed most of the economic policies which Busia had initiated. He revalued the currency and repudiated most of Ghana's external debts. Acheampong increased government spending and between 1972 and 1978, when he was overthrown, registered the highest budget deficits Ghana has ever witnessed. Monetary and fiscal policies were either out of tune with the realities of the situation or were not properly implemented. As inflation and monetary growth accelerated in the mid-1970s, real government revenues fell sharply and the budget deficit widened from 4 per cent in 1974 to 8 per cent in 1975 and 11 per cent in 1976.

During the period 1979–83, with three different governments (the first reign of Jerry Rawlings, the civilian government of the Third Republic led by President Limann, and the second Rawlings Government), there was a slowdown in government spending and deficits dropped to an average of about 5 per cent of GDP. After the introduction of the Economic Reform Programme in 1983, the government of the Provisional National Defence Council (PNDC) restrained government spending, and for the first time in Ghana's post-independence history, budget surpluses began to be registered in 1987 (Table 6.3).

Persistent budget deficits over the years had forced successive governments to borrow from the central bank to finance the deficit. This increased during the Acheampong era. After the repudiation of Ghana's external debts in February 1972, the government could not borrow from external sources to finance the mounting deficits, and had to rely on the Bank of Ghana. High government borrowing 'crowded-out' the share of credit to the private sector and thus further depressed the chances for growth of that sector.

Until 1983, government borrowing from the banking system grew more

Table 6.3 Indicators of fiscal performance, 1965–88 (ratios)

Year	As ratios to GDP			Financing as ratio to deficit			Change in M2 %	Savings as ratio to GNP
	Revenue	Expenditure	Deficit	Internal loans	From Bank of Ghana	External loans		
1965	0.19	0.26	0.06	0.88	n.a.	0.03	1.7	0.08
1966	0.15	0.20	0.05	0.87	n.a.	0.34	5.0	0.08
1967	0.17	0.23	0.06	0.76	n.a.	0.19	1.3	0.08
1968	0.18	0.24	0.06	0.71	n.a.	0.27	10.3	0.13
1969	0.17	0.20	0.03	0.65	n.a.	0.41	10.5	0.13
1970	0.19	0.22	0.02	0.90	n.a.	0.96	9.8	0.14
1971	0.18	0.22	0.04	0.82	n.a.	0.27	11.2	0.08
1972	0.15	0.21	0.06	0.49	0.08	0.51	40.6	0.13
1973	0.11	0.17	0.05	0.90	0.83	0.10	18.9	0.14
1974	0.13	0.17	0.04	1.01	0.94	0.01	26.6	0.09
1975	0.15	0.23	0.08	1.00	1.51	0.00	38.0	0.14
1976	0.13	0.25	0.11	1.00	0.88	0.00	37.2	0.09
1977	0.10	0.20	0.09	0.99	1.36	0.01	60.0	0.10
1978	0.07	0.16	0.09	0.91	0.22	0.04	68.6	0.04
1979	0.10	0.17	0.07	1.00	0.21	—	15.8	0.06
1980	0.07	0.11	0.04	0.84	1.78	0.16	33.7	0.09
1981	0.05	0.11	0.06	0.92	0.38	0.08	51.5	0.04
1982	0.06	0.11	0.06	0.91	0.14	0.08	23.3	0.04
1983	0.06	0.08	0.03	0.78	0.09	0.20	40.3	0.00
1984	0.08	0.10	0.02	0.63	0.49	0.37	53.6	0.07
1985	0.12	0.14	0.02	0.53	0.27	0.46	46.2	0.08
1986	0.14	0.14	0.00	17.78	0.60	18.78	47.9	0.07
1987	0.15	0.14	0.01[a]	0.32	0.66	0.13	53.3	0.08
1988	0.15	0.14	0.01[a]	0.62	0.64	0.23	46.3	0.08

Source: Computed from IMF, International Financial Statistics, 1988 Yearbook, August 1989 issue, and from Ghana's Quarterly Digest of Statistics, March 1989.
Note: a Budget surplus.

rapidly than that of the private sector. By the beginning of the 1980s commercial banks' credit to the private sector was about a third of their total credit. In 1982, only 28 per cent of commercial bank credit went to the private sector. Credit to government was spent on the large and inefficient state sector which had developed. Thus, while private entrepreneurs were denied credit for investment, credit to government was not invested efficiently. The country's gross domestic investment declined from a level of about 24 per cent of GDP in 1960 to about 1 per cent in 1982.

In summary, both internal and external factors contributed to the decline. The internal factors included:

1   The maintenance of a fixed and highly overvalued exchange rate that discouraged exports and produced huge profits for traders of imported goods.
2   Large government deficits which resulted in inflationary pressures and distorted the real exchange rate.
3   The imposition of price controls on manufacturers, which discouraged production, while giving excessive profits to the unregulated small-scale trading sector.
4   Misallocation and misuse of import licences, which created further inefficiencies and denied critical inputs and equipment to high priority areas.

The external factors included:

1   Adverse weather in 1978–9 and 1982–3, which seriously reduced agricultural output.
2   The 1979–80 increases in petroleum prices, followed by world recession.
3   A trend deterioration in the terms of trade.
4   The expulsion of over one million Ghanaians from Nigeria in 1983.

The Economic Recovery Programme

In April 1983, the PNDC Government accepted an IMF economic adjustment package. Its major objectives were: to restore production incentives for food, industrial raw materials and export commodities; to increase the availability of essential consumer goods; to increase the overall availability of foreign exchange in the country; to lower the rate of inflation; to rehabilitate the physical infrastructure; and to undertake studies to restructure economic institutions.[1]

The major reforms relevant to the financial system were a comprehensive system of credit ceilings for commercial banks to restrain monetary growth, and radical changes in the operation of the foreign-exchange market. The share of the private sector in commercial bank credit rose to 74 per cent by

1987. Monetary policy was conducted in the framework of an annual monetary plan which set targets for credit expansion for every commercial bank. In September 1987 a liberalised system to determine borrowing and lending rates was introduced by the central bank for all commercial and secondary banks, which replaced the previous administrative fixing of rates by the Bank of Ghana.

There was a series of devaluations of the exchange rate until September 1986, when the government introduced a dual exchange-rate system. Transactions at Window I related to official transactions and were pegged at an exchange rate of 90 cedis to the dollar (compared to 2.75 in 1983). All other transactions passed through Window II, at rates which were determined by marginal bids at weekly auctions. In February 1987, the two windows were merged, with the rate determined in theory at the auction, but in practice by the Bank of Ghana which by deciding the allocation of foreign exchange to the auction can effectively determine the exchange rate. The first rate determined at the auction in September 1986 was ¢ 120 to the dollar; by December 1989 it had depreciated to ¢ 300. In 1988, the country moved towards a freely floating system of exchange-rate determination with the introduction of private forex bureaux which determine their own sale and purchase prices. This effectively eliminated the black market for foreign exchange.

Other major reforms in the ERP process were: removal of price controls on most commodities; selling off of most state-owned enterprises; and reductions in government expenditures and increases in revenue, leading to a reduction of budget deficits. For three consecutive years beginning in 1986, the budget was in surplus. A new Investment Code provided a package of incentives to attract foreign capital.

THE STRUCTURE AND OPERATIONS OF THE FINANCIAL SYSTEM

The process of monetisation

The foundations for the formal financial system in the Gold Coast were laid in the latter years of the nineteenth century as British silver coins started circulating in the region. A Government Savings Bank was set up in 1888, and in 1896 the first foreign commercial bank entered Accra. It still operates in Ghana, under the name of Standard Chartered Bank (Ghana) Limited.

A West African Currency Board was established in 1912 to issue and redeem the West African currency which was then circulating in The Gambia, Nigeria and Sierra Leone as well as the Gold Coast. However, it could not pursue independent monetary policies in the colonies as monetary expansions and contractions were tied to the balance of payments, and the exchange rate was pegged at par to sterling. The Board could only invest its funds in British Government or Dominion Government securities, and was barred from investing in the issues of the colonial governments. Thus funds which could have been invested in the colonies were diverted into British investments. On the other hand, the restrictions on monetary expansion did serve to contain inflation to the rate prevailing in the United Kingdom. When independent Ghana disengaged from the West African Currency Board in 1957, the issue and redemption of the currency became the duty of the Bank of Ghana, although the currency unit was not changed until 1965.

During the post-independence period, the economic declines in the mid-1960s and from 1975 to 1983 were associated with a falling real value of the cedi. This encouraged movement of financial holdings into physical goods and foreign currency, and correspondingly holdings of financial assets relative to GDP fell (see Figure 6.1). Furthermore, there was an evident financial shallowing, shown by relatively higher proportions of financial assets held as cash or demand deposits.

Some official policies also weakened confidence in the banking system. In 1978 the government decided to mop up excess liquidity by demonetising the cedi. Currency outside the banking system was changed at a 30 per cent discount for the new currency, i.e. holders of cash were given only 70 per cent of the face value of their currency holdings. In 1982, the PNDC government decided to vet all bank balances exceeding ¢ 50,000. Individuals without legal justification for the source of their balances forfeited their monies. This particularly affected small-scale businessmen who generally

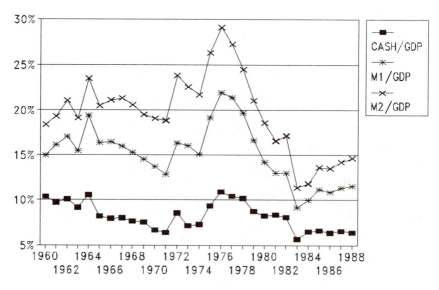

Figure 6.1 Ghana: Indicators of financial depth 1960–88
Source: World Bank (1990b)

did not keep records of their operations. The government also withdrew from circulation all 50-cedi notes issued by the Limann Administration the previous year. It was four years before the 50-cedi notes were refunded to their owners, in 1986, during which time inflation had substantially eroded their real value. The recovery during the ERP phase (post-1983) has so far brought only a relatively modest increase in the ratios of financial holdings to GDP, particularly in comparison to previous declines. This post-independence process of demonetisation and financial shallowing has limited the scope for the financial system to intermediate between savers and borrowers and to allocate financial assets efficiently.

The formal financial sector

The formal financial sector included by 1989 the central bank, six commercial banks, three development banks, a savings bank, a merchant bank, about 120 rural banks, a discount house, a building society, insurance companies and a trust holding company which also acts as a stock market. The Government of Ghana is the major shareholder in most of these financial institutions.

The Bank of Ghana was established on the eve of independence (in 1957). It became responsible for the external value of the currency in 1961; subsequently the Bank of Ghana Act (1963) gave it a development role:

> ... to propose to the Government measures which are likely to have a favourable effect on the balance of payments, movements of prices, the state of public finance and the general development of the national economy and monetary stability.

The Bank of Ghana operates, however, under the directions of the Minister responsible for Finance and Economic Planning. This subordination of the Bank to the government makes it difficult for it to follow independent policies which will counteract the government's fiscal policies. As regulator of the country's foreign exchange the Bank has, since September 1986, been supervising the weekly foreign-exchange auctions.

It is the supervisor of all banking operations in the country. Through the Bankers' Clearing House, it offers clearing facilities to the commercial banks. As part of a policy of decentralisation, it opened regional clearing houses in some of the regional capitals (six by 1985), although the use of cheques as a means of payment is still not widely accepted in Ghana.

Until 1953, Standard Chartered and Barclays Bank were the only commercial banks in the Gold Coast. They tended to direct credit to expatriate firms rather than to indigenous ones. This duopoly was broken by the establishment of the Bank of the Gold Coast (now Ghana Commercial Bank) as the first indigenous commercial bank. These three banks are generally referred to as the primary banks and hold about 60 per cent of the total deposits of the banking sector (Table 6.4). The government is a majority shareholder in the local banks and maintains minority shares in the three foreign-owned banks.

The commercial banks provide intermediary services such as keeping cash deposits and giving short-term advances for commerce and other businesses requiring short-term credit. They also deal in securities and other bills of exchange. About 50 per cent of the deposit liabilities of the primary banks are in the form of demand deposits and the greater part of them are private sector deposits.

The number of commercial bank branches, an imperfect indicator of changes in levels of intermediation, rose from 90 in 1958 to 244 by 1988. The spread of bank branches was concentrated in the regional capitals of Greater Accra, Ashanti, Western and Eastern Regions. Greater Accra alone accommodates about a quarter of bank branches. Despite the growth in the numbers of banks and branches, most rural areas have remained without any formal financial intermediary. Interbank activities centred upon cheque-clearing facilities in the Bankers' Clearing House, but were increased by the establishment in 1987 of a Consolidated Discount House which trades in securities.

There are four development banks. The National Investment Bank (NIB) started operations in 1964 with the objective of assisting Ghanaian entrepreneurs in the establishment and expansion of their enterprises. The Agricultural Development Bank (ADB), originally a division of the Bank of

Table 6.4 Distribution of bank deposits and branches, 1988

	Deposits (¢bn)	No. of branches
Commercial banks		
Ghana Commercial Bank	36	163
Barclays Bank	12	37
Standard Chartered Bank	12	24
National Savings and Credit	3	19
Bank of Credit & Commerce (BCCI)	2	1
Development banks		
Agricultural Development Bank	2	46
National Investment Bank	2	9
Social Security Bank	18	50
Bank for Housing and Construction	7	11
Other		
Ghana Co-operative Bank	3	49
Merchant Bank Ghana	3	2

Note: Deposits based on end-1988 deposit levels, excluding government and non-resident deposits.

Ghana, was established in 1965 to help small farmers. However, it followed the practices of the commercial banks in granting loans mostly to large-scale farmers. The Bank for Housing and Construction is, like ADB and NIB, owned by the government and parastatal organisations, and was established in 1972. By the nature of their objectives, these three banks advance long-term loans.

The Act establishing the NIB empowered it to advance credit without insisting on collateral, unlike the commercial banks. In common with the other development banks, and also some commercial banks, the NIB has accumulated a sizeable portfolio of non-performing assets. Without regular provision being made for bad debts, non-performing assets have become a major weakness in the banking system and encourage banks to keep assets in relatively low-risk government securities in order to balance the risk structure of their portfolios.

The depreciation of the cedi during the ERP has also led the banks and their customers into serious liquidity problems. This situation has become more acute in recent years with the continual depreciation of the cedi through the auction market. The development banks also received finance from foreign agencies to lend to their customers. Most of these loans were made when the cedi value was pegged at a high rate to the dollar. Recent devaluations have increased the cedi liabilities of the banks' customers and have caused many of them to default.

One major reason for setting up the Ghana Commercial Bank was for it to reach the countryside where the foreign-owned banks had been reluctant to go. Thus, the GCB opened up branches in several areas of the country, but their activities did not meet the needs of the rural people, since they insisted on stringent collateral before lending. This gap was partly filled by the Agricultural Development Bank and the Ghana Co-operative Bank. The latter is owned by two state financial institutions, some co-operative organisations and a few individual Ghanaians.

Despite these initiatives and specialised institutions, commercial banks devote on average only 9 per cent of their credit to agriculture, taken up mostly by large-scale farmers. This prompted the government to help establish rural banks; it was hoped that an expansion of unit-level banking facilities would reduce informal money-lending at usurious rates of interest. The rural banks were established as small unit-banking operations, owned and managed by local communities. The first rural bank was established in 1976 and 120 rural banks had been established throughout the country by 1989. The Bank of Ghana also owns shares in the rural banks and acts as their supervisor. The prime aim was to mobilise savings and to help cottage industries.

In addition to the banks, there are other financial institutions such as insurance companies, a building society, a Social Security Trust, a National Trust Holding Company and the discount house. Occasionally, a few corporate firms have floated shares, but generally indigenous Ghanaian businesses are funded with accumulated family wealth or by borrowing from the banks.

The informal sector

The informal sector includes money-lenders and several credit groups and thrift societies called *susu* collectors. Though these groups are made up only of smallholders, as a sector their operations have a significant impact on the functioning of the national economy.

The money-lenders are, generally, rich individuals who advance credit at rates well above commercial bank rates, primarily in rural areas. There are no official records on the rates charged by these lenders, but they are believed to be around 100 per cent per annum. These rates vary from one lender to another and are fixed rates unrelated to the term of the loan.

Farmers without access to bank credit approach the money-lenders during planting seasons. Businessmen also use the services of these lenders on occasion, normally to obtain credit to clear their goods from the ports and for other short-term operations. In 1951, the government passed the Money-Lenders Ordinance which tried to regulate the activities of the money-lender and to protect the borrower.

The *susu* is a rotational savings system usually operated by small-scale businesses formed into types of co-operatives. Each member of the group regularly contributes a given amount into a common pool and members then take turns in collecting the entire pool. In more sophisticated schemes, a special collector goes around with a notebook collecting various sums from different groups of traders and other small-scale business personnel each day. It becomes a type of compulsory saving, which the individual may take back at the end of a period. In the 1980s, some companies turned the activities of the small-scale *susu* collectors into larger ventures. These companies advertise in the public media as financial houses which receive and grant credit, and in effect they operate as unlicensed banks (with the corresponding risks). Although the success of the *susu* system depends largely on personal trust in the collectors' integrity and no interest is paid, the *susu* is very popular among small-scale businesses, especially traders and fishmongers.

Informal *susu* collectors have the advantage of being able to mobilise funds more easily than the formal sector by moving from door to door. They also help cultivate regular saving habits in small-scale businesses and provide easy access to credit for their clients, who are not bothered with bureaucratic procedures and the collateral requirements in the formal sector. Thus these informal financial groups fill an important gap left by the formal financial intermediaries. They intermediate between groups of small savers and rather larger individual borrowers.

Within the informal sector there is also a group of food sellers or 'chop-bar' owners, who offer credit facilities to workers for food and receive payment on pay-day. The special feature of this money-lending group is the fact that their customers need not save with them. Credit is advanced on a good introduction and a guarantee or a collateral. 'Chop-bar' owners normally make themselves known to the accounts clerks in the various work-places in order to improve the reliability of repayment. Another group of traders operate a hire-purchase system; these are mostly people having regular jobs, with trading as a secondary activity. They buy wares which they sell to their customers on credit with a premium which depends on the length of the payment period.

The informal financial market is composed almost entirely of small-scale borrowers and lenders who are unable or unwilling to utilise the formal banking sector, where procedures have followed those in higher-income European countries. The aggregate effect of the informal market in Ghana is difficult to ascertain. One effect may be to reduce the level of idle cash balances held by individuals and consequently to increase money velocity for a given money stock. This may have an impact on prices or output. It encourages additional financial saving and correspondingly increases investment and reduces consumption expenditure. For example, in the *susu* system the daily payments may represent small reductions in consumption and the lump-sum 'credit' may be directed towards investment activities. Clearly more research is required to investigate the economic impact of the informal sector.

Cocoa and the financial system

Cocoa was introduced into the Gold Coast from the middle of the nineteenth century; by 1911 its output of 41,000 tonnes made it the world's leading producer. Ghana's exports of cocoa peaked in 1964–5 with an output of 538,000 tonnes. The history of post-independence production mirrors the decline in the Ghanaian economy, with the most serious falls occurring in the mid-1960s (under the National Liberation Council) and in the Acheampong era (1972–8). Even though cocoa's share of GDP is only 8 per cent, it accounts for about 60 per cent of the nation's foreign-exchange earnings, with about another 11 per cent from processed cocoa exports. Cocoa also contributes about a quarter of the nation's tax revenue.

The Cocoa Marketing Board (CMB) was established in 1947 to co-ordinate the purchasing, marketing and export of cocoa. With the establishment of the Bank of Ghana, the CMB started investing in Government of Ghana Bills. The bill finance scheme for the marketing of the cocoa crop was introduced with a view to achieving two things:

1   to exchange CMB surplus liquid assets for the government's own

holding of longer-term sterling gilt-edged securities, or as a straight loan to government;

2   to transfer the Board's financial transactions from London to Accra (Bank of Ghana, *Report of the Board*, 1960; 1961).

Cocoa financing bills are still issued by the Bank of Ghana. The Bank is informed by the Cocoa Marketing Board of the amount required for cocoa purchases and issues cocoa bills to that value which are then purchased by the commercial banks. The Bank of Ghana takes up any unsold bills. Like other bills and bonds, the cocoa bills are discounted mostly by the Bank of Ghana.

The cocoa marketing system has tended to change with the various political changes over the years, reflecting the political and economic importance of cocoa in the Ghanaian economy. Between 1961 and 1966, the Nkrumah Government established the United Ghana Farmers' Co-operatives Council as the sole buying agent. In 1966, the NLC Government replaced the Council with indigenous private buying agents. Between 1972 and 1976, these private agents were, in turn, replaced by two semi-governmental agencies – the Produce Buying Agency (PBA) and the Ghana Co-operative Marketing Association (GCMA). In 1976, the Produce Buying Company Limited, which is wholly owned and financed by the Ghana Cocoa Board (COCOBOD), became the sole licensed buying agent.

Until August 1979, the payments for cocoa purchases from farmers were made mostly in cash, by purchasing clerks. The cash was obtained either from the buying agents' own finances or from bank loans. This system posed several problems for the industry. Some farmers took advances against future delivery of cocoa from one buying agent and sold the actual produce to another. Some farmers were forced to mortgage or sell their farms to pay off their debts. The cash system of payment was also beset with other problems, such as: long delays before payment; fraudulent practices, e.g. purchasing clerks investing the cash meant for produce purchases in other ventures and paying farmers after the maturity of their investments; and the security problems of moving cash over long distances (Atiemo 1989: 34).

Partly in a bid to eliminate these problems and partly to inculcate the banking habit into the cocoa farming communities, a new system of payment known as the '*akuafo* cheque' system was introduced in 1979 on a small scale. This involved the issue of payment vouchers to farmers, which they could then cash at commercial or rural banks. The *akuafo* cheque system was reorganised in 1983 and made the only system for the payment of cocoa farmers. The introduction of the *akuafo* cheques was certainly an improvement on the cash system, but it also faced some problems: inadequacy of banking outlets for administering the cheques; inadequate stocks of cash at some bank branches at certain periods of peak demand; fraudulent cheques.

Cocoa financing, because of the seasonality of the crop, influences the pattern of the banking sector's liquidity over the course of the year. But the fluctuations are predictable enough not to cause significant problems for monetary control, and move cyclically with income.

MODEL OF THE MONEY MARKET

This section discusses developments in the components of money supply and demand. It is followed by a multiplier model of the money stock determination, identification of the variables that are relevant for the control of the money stock, and a discussion of the directional signs of the effects of changes in these variables on the money supply. The model is completed by the inclusion of a demand-for-money function, the stability of which is necessary for the effective use of monetary policy.

The money supply

The Bank of Ghana defines money supply as demand deposits at the banks (both primary and secondary) plus currency in the hands of the general public. This definition, M1, treats money as a medium of exchange. However, the ease with which people can withdraw money from their savings accounts, without hindrance for transaction purposes, means that broad money, M2, defined as M1 plus time and savings deposits, may be more appropriate for policy purposes for Ghana. The importance of savings deposits for cash transactions in Ghana is a result of low confidence in personal cheques as a means of payment; it leads to little practical difference in the use of savings and current accounts. Data from the Bankers' Clearing House shows that cheques cleared in Ghana averaged 4,750 per day in 1978 and 5,851 per day in 1985. Even large commercial houses like the Ghana National Trading Company (GNTC), the Union Trading Company (UTC) and Kingsway Stores rarely accept personal cheques.

A broader measure of money as a means of payment would also include foreign-exchange holdings. When foreign exchange in formal markets became scarce and its rationing led to shortage of commodities on the local market, major foreign currencies became accepted, especially by traders and businessmen, as a means of exchange and a superior store of value. This was particularly so during the depressed conditions of the late 1970s and early 1980s. These currencies were accepted as means of payment by traders for most consumer durables. However, there are no accurate data on private foreign-exchange holdings.

The money stock in Ghana is made up predominantly of currency held by the public outside the banking system. The proportion decreased from a high of 54 per cent in 1960 to a low of 34 per cent in 1971, and then rose to a new high of 56 per cent in 1984. These trends reflect changes in the public's

93

confidence in the banking system. The ratio of M2 to GDP (Figure 6.1), which is a measure of the degree of monetisation in the country, increased until the late 1970s, when financial repression in the country, fuelled by negative interest rates, caused it to decline in the 1980s.

The decline may also be the result of a loss of confidence in the banking system as a whole. If the inverse of the M2:GDP ratio is interpreted as the velocity of money, then we observe a situation in which the velocity of money increased rapidly during the high inflationary period of the 1980s. Since 1978, even though the nominal money stock has been increasing rapidly, real money supply has been declining. The fact that real balances declined in that period was indicative of the high inflation rates then prevailing. These high rates of inflation caused all rates of interest in the country to be negative and thus depressed savings. Correspondingly, the gross domestic savings to GDP ratio dropped from a high of 13.8 per cent in 1970, averaging 10 per cent from 1967 to 1977, to around 6 per cent in the early 1980s, with a low of 0.4 per cent in 1983 (see Table 6.3).

Government finance and monetary policy

Large government deficits financed by borrowing from the banking system were the greatest source of changes in the supply of money, as shown in the lower half of Table 6.5. In some years, such as 1975, net credit to government accounted for almost the entire increase in domestic credit, whilst changes to the non-financial private sector were small in comparison. Discrepancies between banking sector figures and those of government accounts prevent any meaningful discussion of the post-1983 impact of government operations upon monetary control. However, Table 6.5 suggests that credit to central government continued to dominate credit expansion during the 1980s, although Table 6.3 showed clearly that net government borrowing from the banking system fell sharply between 1983 and 1986, and in 1987 and 1988 there were net repayments.

Money supply determination

The effectiveness of the monetary policy instruments of the Bank of Ghana can be analysed by the relation between the monetary base (liabilities of the central bank) and the money supply. This relation is demonstrated in the money multiplier formulation which relates the monetary base to broad money:

(1) $$M2 = \frac{1}{(rr + er) \cdot (1 - c) + c} MB$$

Table 6.5 Changes in money supply and sources of changes (cbn)

	1965	1970	1975	1980	1983	1984	1985	1986	1987	1988
Money supply										
Currency plus demand deposits	0.00	0.02	0.31	1.41	5.52	10.13	11.46	16.85	29.01	37.86
Quasi-money	0.01	0.02	0.07	0.60	0.46	1.02	3.30	5.55	7.84	11.18
Restricted deposits and other items	0.01	0.05	0.08	−0.05	1.85	−6.96	−0.99	−3.86	−25.40	−80.66
Total money supply	0.02	0.09	0.46	1.96	7.83	4.19	13.77	18.54	11.45	−31.62
Sources of changes	0.03	0.08	0.48	1.96	7.83	4.19	13.76	18.55	11.45	−31.62
Net foreign assets	−0.05	0.06	0.13	−0.12	−5.77	−12.1	−15.34	−22.77	−74.79	−21.79
Domestic credit:	0.08	0.02	0.35	2.08	13.60	16.29	29.10	41.32	86.24	−9.83
1 to central government (net)	0.06	−0.02	0.34	1.62	16.99	9.41	10.59	28.34	80.34	−8.69
2 to non-fin. public and other fin. institutions	−0.03	0.05	−0.04	0.33	−4.67	3.75	13.82	4.89	0.92	−10.61
3 to private sector	0.03	0.01	0.05	0.14	1.28	3.14	4.68	7.89	4.98	9.47

Note: Total changes in money supply may not be equal to total changes in sources, due to rounding.

Where:

MB = monetary base (banks' reserves at central bank plus currency with the public)

M2 = broad money (cash plus sight and time deposits)

c = cash ratio (cash/M2)

rr = required reserve to deposits ratio, and

er = excess reserve ratio.

To control the money supply (M2) effectively, the Bank of Ghana needs to control high-powered money (Mb); the rate of interest (Ir), which is assumed to influence excess reserve holding (er); the currency ratio (c); and the reserve ratio (rr). The interest rate here is the central bank's discount rate, which is the opportunity cost of holding excess reserves.

A restrictive monetary policy will involve a decrease in high-powered money, or an increase in the rate of interest, or in the currency ratio, or in the reserve ratio.

Equation 1 can be expressed in a general form as

$$M2 = f(Mb, Ir, c, rr), \text{ such that, } f_1 > 0, f_2 < > 0, f_3 < 0, f_4 < 0,$$

where f_i are the partial derivatives of M2 with respect to Mb, Ir, c, and rr respectively.

The sign of f_2 depends on whether the supply of credit or the demand for it is taken as given, or how changes in the discount rate affect the holding of excess reserves. From the point of view of savers, taking demand as given, an increase in the rate of interest might induce them to give more credit and increase the money supply. If interest rates increase, the opportunity cost of excess reserves in the banks' portfolio increases and the banks will have an incentive to reduce er. Thus, for a given level of the other variables (Mb, cr, and rr), a higher interest rate would increase the money supply. However, if the supply of credit is taken as given, an increase in the rate of interest will discourage borrowers from getting more credit and thus have a restrictive effect on money supply.

The currency ratio is based on a behavioural assumption about the public and is therefore outside the control of the central bank. Where the currency ratio is stable, the actions of the public become predictable and therefore the central bank can engage in 'defensive' actions to control the money supply. Figure 6.1 suggests that changes in Ghana may be difficult to predict with any certainty. A high currency ratio and greater use of cash means lower deposits, so less credit is created. Thus the high currency ratio in Ghana acts as an automatic damper in the money creation process.

The reserve ratio, based on the behaviour of the banks, is under the control of the monetary authorities, provided banks do not have excess reserves.

High-powered money = Securities + Advances − Government deposits + Foreign assets + Other assets

Advances are influenced by the central bank but are actually controlled by the commercial banks and other financial dealers. Other assets are generally influenced by technical and other external factors beyond the control of the central bank. In theory, the central bank can control the monetary base by engaging in defensive operations to neutralise the undesirable movement of a non-controllable item with counteraction on its controllable assets. The control of the monetary base is made difficult by changes in the level of foreign assets emanating from external shocks or changes in domestic demand.

Specified as a log-linear function, we have (abbreviations are explained in the Appendix):

$$(2) \quad \log(M2) = a_0 + a_1\log(Mb) + a_2\log(Ir) + a_3\log(Cr) + a_4\log(Rr) + u_1$$

The seemingly perfect fit for the money supply equation in Table 6.6a is due to high correlation (.99) between the monetary base and the money stock. An attempt was made to detrend the monetary base and re-estimate the equation. The result, shown in Table 6.6b, was not very good. With the exception of the rate of interest, no other variable was statistically significant.

The positive sign of the interest coefficient (in Tables 6.6a and 6.6b) indicates that an increase in the rate of interest would be expansionary.

Both the currency ratio and the reserve ratio exert significant influences on the supply of money in Table 6.6a, but not Table 6.6b. The currency ratio is always outside the control of the bank, while the reserve ratio could not serve effectively as a monetary tool for most of the time as the banks had excess reserves. The ability of the Bank of Ghana to control the money supply lies principally in its ability to influence the monetary base.

Table 6.6a Money supply equation (2SLS estimation)

Dependent variable is Y1 = Log(M2)
List of instruments: C, Log(Mb), IrEST, X13, X14
29 observations used for estimation from 1960 to 1988

Regressor	Coefficient	Standard error	T-Ratio
Intercept	−.4215	.1260	−3.3444
Log(Mb)	.9297	.0533	17.4285
Log(Ir)	.3069	.2092	1.4668
Log(Cr)	−.5328	.0957	−5.5675
Log(Rr)	−.2503	.0295	−8.4834
R-squared	.9995	F-statistic F (4, 24)	11847.2
R-bar-squared	.9994	SE of regression	.0526
Residual SS	.0664	Mean of dependent variable	7.6450
SD of dep. var	2.1642	DW-statistic	2.1112

Table 6.6b Money supply equation (2SLS estimation)

Dependent variable is Y1 = Log(M2)
List of instruments: C, TRX11, IrEST, X13, X14
29 observations used for estimation from 1960 to 1988

Regressor	Coefficient	Standard error	T-Ratio
Intercept	−.3175	1.1452	−.2773
TRX11	.3354	.3246	1.0332
Log(Ir)	2.7376	1.1763	2.3274
Log(Cr)	1.1385	.8058	1.4129
Log(Rr)	−.4800	.3576	−1.3423
R-squared	.9607	F-statistic F (4, 24)	146.6676
R-bar-squared	.9541	SE of regression	.4634
Residual SS	5.1541	Mean of dependent variable	7.6450
SD of dep. var.	2.1642	DW-statistic	1.9873

Estimating the demand for money

Our previous discussions have suggested that there have been sizeable shifts in the demand for money: money holdings relative to income have changed markedly over time as confidence in the cedi has changed and the proportions of money held as cash, demand and time deposits have also changed substantially. In this section we analyse the quantitative importance of income, interest rates, expected inflation and the exchange rate on the demand for money.

The strongest motive influencing the demand for money in Ghana is for transactions, which depend on income. Following Adekunle (1968) the demand for money in Ghana is treated as dependent on the level of current income. The speculative demand for money is not very pronounced in Ghana since the money market is not well developed and few alternative financial assets exist. Government bonds and Treasury bills are largely purchased by the financial institutions as investment for their idle funds. Consequently, we do not expect the rate of interest to have a significant effect on the demand for money.

As a store of wealth, money competes with such items as houses, land, cattle and so on. It is assumed that the rate of inflation is the opportunity cost of most of these 'durable' items. Hence the rate of inflation is also included as an argument in the money demand function.

From the mid-1970s, a new element of speculation emerged on the Ghanaian scene. Shortages of foreign exchange and the prolonged overvaluation of the exchange rate caused people to hold or release cedi balances, depending on the availability of foreign exchange and the exchange rate on the parallel market. If disaggregation of the demand-for-money function were possible, we would expect the exchange rate to affect the demand for money by businesses. The exchange rate is therefore included, although data constraints confined us to using the official exchange rate.

The demand for money in Ghana is therefore specified as:

$$(3) \quad (\frac{M2}{P})_t = g(Y_t, Ir_t, e_t, P_t, u_t^2)$$

Such that $g_1 > 0, g_2 < 0, g_3 < 0, g_4 < 0$; where g_i is the partial derivative of real balances with respect to Y, Ir, e, and P respectively.

We estimate equation 3 in a log-linear form with an adaptive expectations mechanism:

$$(4) \quad \log (\frac{M2}{P})_t = b_0 + b_1\log(Y_t) + b_2\log(Ir_t) + b_3\log(\frac{M2}{P})_{t-1} + b_4\log(P_t)$$

$$+ b_5\log(e_t) + u_t^2$$

The full model of the money market of the Ghanaian economy is as specified in equations 1 and 4. Since this is a complete simultaneous system with money stock and the rate of interest as endogenous variables, a method of two stage least squares (2SLS) was applied to data for the period 1960 to 1988.

Money demand results The regression results of the money demand equation did not present a good fit (Table 6.7a). Even though the adjusted R^2 is high, most of the estimates are individually not significant. It was found that using the price index in place of the rate of inflation presented a better fit.[2] Since the exchange-rate term was not statistically significant and carried the wrong sign, it was dropped from the equation. This improves the significance of the other explanatory variables and the R^2 increases from 0.81 to 0.86. The rate of interest does not exert a significant influence on the demand for money.

Using the improved regression in Table 6.7b, one observes a scale factor of .7259 in the short run; a long-run demand elasticity of 1.157 can be calculated. In a similar estimation of the demand for money in Ghana, Gockel (1983) found a scale factor of 1.553, apparently for the short run. For a developing country with an underdeveloped financial system, a scale factor of more than unity is usually expected. Our results, surprisingly, indicate apparent economies of scale in the use of money in the short run. The existence of long-run finite multipliers for the demand for money equation is an indication of its stability. Thus it should be easier for the Bank of Ghana to specify its monetary targets and set rates of growth in the money supply to achieve these targets.

Table 6.7a Money demand equation (2SLS estimation)

Dependent variable is Y2 = Log(M2/CPI))
List of instruments: C, X21, IREST, X23, X24, Y2(−1)
28 observations used for estimation from 1961 to 1988

Regressor	Coefficient	Standard error	T-Ratio
Intercept	−4.3956	2.1302	−2.0635
Log(GDP/CPI)	1.0531	.4081	2.5802
Log(Ir)	1.0215	.8015	1.2745
Log(CPI)	1.2474	.4161	−2.9982
Log(Er)	.1027	.1073	.9572
Y2(−1)	.1966	.2908	.6760

R-squared	.8475	F-statistic F (5, 22)	24.4493
R-bar-squared	.8128	SE of regression	.1949
Residual sum sq.	.8355	Mean of dependent variable	4.5793
SD of dep. var.	.4504	DW-statistic	1.8717

Table 6.7b Money demand equation (2SLS estimation)

Dependent variable is Y2 = Log(M2/CPI))
List of instruments: C, X21, IREST, X23, Y2(−1)
28 observations used for estimation from 1961 to 1988

Regressor	Coefficient	Standard error	T-Ratio
Intercept	−2.7934	1.1773	−2.3727
Log(GDP/CPI)	.7259	.2174	3.3399
Log(Ir)	.8381	.6420	1.3054
Log(CPI)	−.9478	.2160	−4.3876
Y2(−1)	.3728	.1740	2.1429

R-squared	.8794	F-statistic F (5, 22)	41.9376
R-bar-squared	.8585	SE of regression	.1695
Residual sum sq.	.6605	Mean of dependent variable	4.5793
SD of dep. var.	.4504	DW-statistic	2.1717

Joint test of zero restrictions on the coefficient of deleted variables:
Wald Statistic Chi−sq. (1) = .9162

MONETARY POLICY IMPLEMENTATION, 1957–88

The currency board system had the undoubted advantage, from the view-point of monetary control, of an automatic mechanism which contracted the money supply when the balance of payments was in deficit. As a result inflation was low. From our money demand estimations, we expect that low inflation would increase real money demand as a store of value. However, critics believed that such a system reduced the economic sovereignty of Ghana and it was abandoned (*de jure*) after independence although retained (*de facto*) for a number of years. Under the Bank of Ghana Act (1963), the increase in the money supply was restricted to 15 per cent per annum and the Bank of Ghana appears to have observed this (on a December-to-December basis at least) during its first fifteen years of operation, apart from 1964 (Table 6.3). A relaxation of monetary control (M2 up 40 per cent) followed the change of political control in 1972. The Bank of Ghana attributed this high monetary expansion 'mainly to net credit to the government and public institutions, particularly the Ghana Cocoa Marketing Board and the Ghana Supply Commission' (Bank of Ghana, 1972).

The subsequent sustained rate of increase in monetary growth and the simultaneous increases in the rate of inflation (despite widespread price control) (Table 6.8) led most people to believe that Ghanaian inflation was a monetary phenomenon, and therefore a substantial effort was made at the beginning of the Economic Recovery Programme to implement policies which would help curb expansions in the money supply. These included fiscal policies of curbing excessive government expenditure and monetary policies centred upon a credit squeeze. To a certain extent the axe was directed at the wrong tree. The 'squeeze' affected the private sector more than government and the public sector. This section considers in more detail the use of control mechanisms by the Bank of Ghana.

Credit control

Money and credit control are the main functions of the Bank of Ghana. Each year the Research Division of the Bank prepares a 'Monetary and Credit Plan' which describes the main trends in monetary and credit developments and includes the monetary and credit control measures guiding the operations of the financial institutions' operations. Credit control as a monetary tool was first instituted in 1964, ostensibly to direct credit to the industrial and agricultural sectors of the economy. The tools used by the Bank of Ghana to control money supply are interest rates, reserve requirements, sectoral credit ceilings and mandatory lending ratios.

The Bank of Ghana provides ceilings for all sectors of the economy in line with the country's stipulated development objectives. The 1964 regulation required that banking institutions should seek its approval before granting

Table 6.8 Key financial rates and ratios (1960–88)

Year end	Discount rate	Deposit rate	Lending rate	Inflation rate	Exchange rate ($/¢)	Liquidity minimum	Ratio actual
1960	4.0	3.0	7.5	0.9	1.400	45	77.5
1961	4.5	3.5	7.0	6.2	1.400	54	47.3
1962	4.5	3.5	7.0	5.9	1.400	50	55.0
1963	4.5	3.5	7.0	5.6	1.400	54	36.3
1964	4.5	3.5	7.0	15.8	1.400	54	70.0
1965	4.5	3.5	7.0	22.7	1.400	54	60.8
1966	7.0	3.5	9.0	14.8	1.400	54	78.7
1967	6.0	3.5	9.0	−9.7	0.980	54	66.5
1968	5.5	3.5	9.0	10.7	0.980	54	71.3
1969	5.5	3.5	9.0	6.5	0.980	35	60.9
1970	5.5	3.5	9.0	3.0	0.980	50	58.4
1971	8.0	7.5	9.0	8.0	0.550	40	50.9
1972	8.0	7.5	12.0	10.8	0.781	40	63.1
1973	6.0	5.0	10.0	17.1	0.870	40	60.5
1974	6.0	5.0	10.0	18.8	0.870	40	46.8
1975	8.0	7.5	12.5	29.8	0.870	40	57.0
1976	8.0	7.5	12.5	55.4	0.870	40	56.4
1977	8.0	7.5	12.5	116.5	0.870	67	62.4
1978	13.5	11.5	19.0	73.1	0.364	67	79.4
1979	13.5	11.5	19.0	54.5	0.364	67	89.1
1980	13.5	11.5	19.0	50.2	0.364	67	80.7
1981	19.5	11.5	19.0	116.5	0.364	60	80.0
1982	10.5	11.5	19.0	22.3	0.364	60	77.3
1983	14.5	11.5	19.0	122.8	0.033	45	79.1
1984	18.0	15.0	21.2	39.7	0.020	45	63.9
1985	18.5	15.8	21.2	10.3	0.017	40	65.4
1986	20.5	17.0	20.0	24.6	0.011	34	63.5
1987	23.5	17.6	25.5	39.8	0.006	29	40.8
1988	26.0	16.0	25.58	31.4	0.005	30	42.0

Source: Bank of Ghana, *Annual Reports*, various issues; *Quarterly Digest of Statistics*, June 1989, and IMF, *International Financial Statistics, 1988 Yearbook*.

loans exceeding £G5,000 to sectors other than agriculture and industry. These ceilings have been revised over the years. Currently, they are in the form of permissible percentage increases. This system is intended to have both a developmental and a rationing function.

Unfortunately, the credit ceilings did not channel funds to the intended sectors. Commercial banks continued to lend predominantly to the commerce and trade sectors of the economy. Most banks were averse to the high-risk agricultural sector. There was therefore no credit ceiling on lending to the agricultural sector. In 1982, the Bank of Ghana made it mandatory that at least 20 per cent of total bank credit should be to the agricultural sector. Industry also received only a small share of bank credit, although in 1982, for example, banks were allowed to expand credit to the manufacturing sector by 150 per cent. Even though it is not the wish of government to encourage credit to commerce, by 1982 there were shortages of so many essential items on the market that the Bank encouraged lending to the import trade sector, by allowing banks to expand their credits to that sector by 600 per cent. In 1985 credit ceilings for the priority sectors were increased by 300 per cent for export trade, 200 per cent for import trade, 80 per cent for manufacturing and 70 per cent for agriculture.

One reason for the ineffectiveness of credit ceilings in moving funds to the priority sectors is that they were set without any other incentives attached. Interest rates for the priority sectors were generally lower than for non-priority sectors.

Overall credit ceilings, however, seem to have been a more effective monetary control tool. In February 1989 six banks which had exceeded their credit limits were penalised by being barred from sponsoring clients to the foreign-exchange auction for two weeks.

The Bank of Ghana is empowered to set various reserve and liquid asset requirements. A higher ratio was specified for the end-year period because of the higher crop-financing demand for credit. In 1977, the Bank increased the reserves by introducing a system which made it mandatory for each commercial bank to maintain the average cash reserve ratio it had voluntarily maintained over the previous twelve months. When this failed to remove excess liquidity, the Bank demonetised the cedi in March 1978. The reserve requirements are not effective constraints on banks' lending, since their aggregate reserve holdings are always above the required ratios.

Interest rates have not been an effective monetary policy tool in Ghana. The high rates of inflation rendered most real interest rates negative. In 1989, when nominal interest rates ranged between 20 and 35 per cent, the rate of inflation was officially being quoted at 39 per cent. Rates of interest used to be specified by the Bank of Ghana. But, as part of the process of liberalisation under the Economic Recovery Programme, rates of interest snce 1988 have been determined on the free market by demand supply, taking a cue from the rates determined at the weekly auctions for government bonds and bill.

Growth in money supply

Evidence on the growth of the money supply shows that there were higher growth rates during the military regimes than during the civilian regimes. Under a parliamentary regime, the budget and its financing had to be reported to parliament. Under a military regime there was no control. Moreover, in a situation such as Ghana's where the central bank is more or less an appendage of government via the Ministry of Finance, it becomes very difficult to operate a restrictive monetary policy when the government is promoting an expansionary fiscal policy.

At the inception of the Economic Recovery Programme in 1983, the country's financial system was almost collapsing under strong inflationary pressure, an overvalued exchange rate and low savings rates. In order to curb the rate of inflation, which was then running at three-digit levels, a severe credit squeeze was applied and interest rates were increased to encourage saving. The increase in the rates of interest, however, discouraged investment (as suggested above, money demand did not respond to interest rates), without increasing deposits, owing to lack of confidence in the banking system. To encourage investment, liquidity reserve requirements were revised downwards, but this was a misdirected move as the banks were not under liquidity pressure. In anticipation of increased demand for credit, especially by the import trade and manufacturing sectors, selective and mandatory credit controls were used to direct credit to the priority sectors, as outlined above. Whereas the policies mentioned above could not by themselves lower the supply of money (since much of the increase in money came from the government and the above policies do not affect government very much), inflation in 1985, a year after the introduction of the ERP, dropped to 10 per cent from 123 per cent in 1983. This gave the erroneous impression that the policies had succeeded. However, 1984 had been a bumper harvest year and, in addition, Ghana had satisfied IMF conditionality under the ERP. External resources were flowing in and import pressures were eased. In other words, whereas the inflation in Ghana seems to have been demand-caused it was reduced by increasing supply.

CONCLUSIONS

The direction of monetary policy in Ghana has been almost completely overshadowed by the dominance of fiscal decisions in macroeconomic policy, although this was slightly modified under the Economic Recovery Programme from 1983. The government has been the chief cause of credit and monetary expansion in the country. Credit granted to the Cocoa Marketing Board and other parastatal organisations had to be financed mostly by creating new paper money. Most policies have tended to be *ad hoc* and directed only at solving particular problems. There was no evidence of monetary policies being directed at championing the developmental efforts of the country. In trying to solve some of the problems, such as inflation caused by unrestrained deficit financing, policies adopted by the Bank of Ghana have had little impact.

This inability of the Bank of Ghana to exercise effective control over the money stock may be exacerbated by the holding of a large amount of cash outside the control of the central bank. This is evidenced by the high currency to broad money ratio in the economy. However, this high currency ratio also provides an automatic damper to expansion in the money supply.

Education of the public in banking habits, and a programme to restore public confidence might help to restructure the banking system. Education about other financial instruments like government bonds and bills might ease inflationary pressures from deficit financing. The recent establishment of a stock exchange may help, but one doubts whether the full advantages of the market could be realised with an inexperienced public.

The Bank of Ghana is too much under the control of the central government. There are instances when one wonders who is in charge of monetary policy.[3] The Bank should be decoupled from the Ministry of Finance and Economic Planning. This would help the two bodies pursue independent monetary and fiscal policies. Once appointed, the Governor of the Bank should be assured of job security in order to enable him to pursue independent monetary policies without fear of recrimination from the government.

APPENDIX

List of variables and their descriptions

GDP	:	Gross domestic product
M1	:	Money supply
DT	:	Saving and time deposit
M2	:	Broad money supply
Cp	:	Currency with public
Dd	:	Demand deposits
CPI	:	Consumer price index
CDb	:	Reserves
Mb	:	Monetary base
Cr	:	Currency ratio
Rr	:	Reserve ratio
Ir	:	Interest rate (Bank of Ghana discount rate)
e	:	Exchange rate
Y1	:	log(M2)
X11	:	log(Mb)
X12	:	log(Ir)
X13	:	log(Cr)
X14	:	log(Rr)
Y2	:	log(M2/CPI)
X21	:	log(GDP)
X22	:	log(Ir)
X23	:	log(CPI)
X24	:	log(e)
IREST	:	OLS estimation of Ir
ER1	:	1/e
ER2	:	e1/cpi
X241	:	log(e2)
X231	:	log(cpi/cpi(−1))
C	:	Intercept term
X242	:	log(e/cpi)
P	:	rate of inflation

7

CÔTE D'IVOIRE, 1973–88

Christopher E. Lane

INTRODUCTION

Monetary policy in Côte d'Ivoire has a restricted range of policy options. As a member of a regional monetary union, Côte d'Ivoire cannot set interest rates independently of other union members, nor can it unilaterally change its exchange rate, which has remained pegged to the French franc since 1948.

Monetary policy instruments in Côte d'Ivoire have remained virtually unchanged since 1973. The economic environment, however, has altered from rapid export-based growth in the 1970s, to economic stagnation and prolonged adjustment to internal and external financial imbalances during the 1980s. Access to commercial foreign funds has been effectively cut since debt-servicing arrears emerged in 1983. Domestic monetary policy has therefore become more important than previously as a policy tool to increase the overall savings rate.

Following a brief summary of the economic environment, this chapter surveys the financial system and the monetary union. The following sections then analyse the scope and effectiveness of credit and interest-rate policies; the difficulties in managing money demand and supply; the real economy effects of monetary policy and the problems of inflexible exchange rates, and the role the monetary union plays in monetary policy.

THE STATE OF THE ECONOMY

The economy of Côte d'Ivoire is relatively open and is characterised by a high level of dependence upon primary product exports. About 35 per cent of GDP is exported (significantly higher than the other countries studied here: (Bangladesh 6 per cent, China 13 per cent, Ghana 20 per cent, Indonesia 26 per cent and Kenya 21 per cent). Of this 90 per cent is non-fuel commodities, cocoa and coffee being the most important. Exports are subject to considerable price instability, resulting in sizeable income changes from year to year.

Côte d'Ivoire had a rapidly growing government sector until 1980 (20–8 per cent of GDP) which contributed to a relatively rapid growth of services in GDP (see Table 7.1). Consequently, the real and financial positions of the economy were primarily determined by the effective terms of trade and the fiscal stance of the public sector.

From independence in 1960, the Ivoirian economy grew rapidly. Agriculture, the dominant sector in the economy employing nearly three-quarters of the labour force in 1973, grew more slowly but was the basis for strong export growth. Both political and economic factors were instrumental in stimulating rapid economic growth:

1   The political environment from the 1960s to the end of the 1980s has remained stable; the Partie Démocratique de la Côte d'Ivoire has been continuously in power since achieving independence.
2   A policy of encouraging immigration from neighbouring states provided a low-cost labour force in the construction, agriculture and service sectors, accounting for about 25 per cent of the workforce.
3   Buoyant prices for coffee and cocoa exports until the late 1970s, coupled with a successful marketing and development policy for cash crops, provided a large surplus for the expansion of the non-agricultural economy.

By 1980, however, severe disequilibria were present in the Ivoirian economy. Government borrowing had increased rapidly from 1976 with the consolidated government deficit reaching 12 per cent of GDP by 1980. Declining terms of trade from 1979 onwards contributed to a current account deficit equivalent to 17 per cent of GDP (1980) and debt service on nearly US$6 bn of foreign debt took almost 25 per cent of export proceeds. The 1980s were marked by a period of prolonged economic adjustment, notably characterised by World Bank Structural Adjustment Lending programmes and almost continual IMF financing of balance-of-payments imbalances. Drought and a contraction of government expenditure led to recession during 1982–4.

Temporarily buoyant commodity prices and a moratorium on foreign debt payments brought about a considerable recovery in 1985 and 1986, but

Table 7.1 Economic growth in Côte d'Ivoire (% p.a.)

	1965–73	1973–80	1980–7
Gross domestic product	8.5	7.0	2.2
Agriculture	4.9	3.3	1.6
Industry	12.5	11.7	−2.4
Services	11.2	6.5	4.2

Source: World Bank, 1988: xviii and 1989b for 1980–7 data

a reversal in the terms of trade in 1987 precipitated a new recession in 1987 and 1988. By 1989, the economy was in a critical situation: international coffee and cocoa prices in the local currency equivalent (CFAF) were at half the level prevalent in the 1985–6 season and the government deficit had increased to over 10 per cent of GDP.

THE STRUCTURE AND OPERATIONS OF THE FINANCIAL SYSTEM

The process of monetisation

The development of the monetary system in Côte d'Ivoire was based on the French franc as the legal currency. Soon after political independence the Union Monétaire Ouest Africaine (UMOA) was created in 1962 with Benin, Côte d'Ivoire, Upper Volta, Niger, Senegal and Mauritania as the founding member states. At this time, the Banque Centrale des Etats de l'Afrique Ouest (BCEAO) took on the usual responsibilities of a central bank such as reserve management, formulation of monetary policy, and credit facilities to banks, governments and other financial institutions, although the bank itself was located in Paris with agencies in each member state (Bhatia 1985). French policy-makers in the Trésorie and the Banque de France effectively had a power of veto in BCEAO decisions. In 1973, the UMOA was re-negotiated with a strengthened role for the BCEAO whose headquarters were moved to Dakar in Senegal. France's representation in the UMOA was restricted to two members of the central Board of Directors, the same as for all the UMOA member states.

In terms of monetisation of the economy, Côte d'Ivoire has been one of the most advanced countries in sub-Saharan Africa. The relatively early monetisation can be attributed to the importance of cash-crop agriculture in the economy, combined with the early incorporation of the indigenous rural population into production for exchange.

From independence until 1977 there was an increase in the 'banking habit', with two falls in the ratio of cash to narrow money (bringing it from .60 to .36) and rising ratios of both broad and narrow money to GDP (see Figure 7.1). This accompanied a sizeable expansion in the number of banking offices. The peak levels of financial intermediation in the mid-1970s were, however, a reflection of the export commodity boom rather than of a developing financial system. Windfall income receipts temporarily increased savings and lowered the income velocity of money.

There is little evidence that monetary policy has positively encouraged financial deepening. The continuity of monetary policy, in terms of instruments and approaches, over the 1970s and 1980s has implied a supportive rather than an innovative role. Although the economy has grown substantially,

109

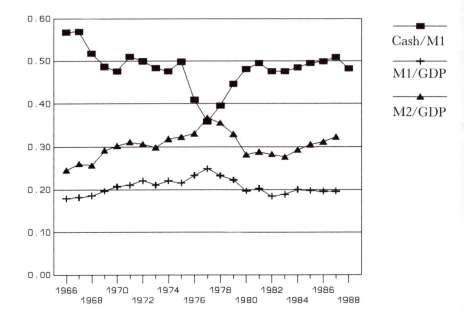

Figure 7.1 Indicators of financial development
Source: IMF, *International Financial Statistics*

financial instruments outside the commercial banking sector have not been developed significantly.

Union Monétaire Ouest Africaine (UMOA)

Membership of the UMOA is the most important feature of the Ivoirian financial system. The three main features of the UMOA are:

1   A common monetary area in which the CFA (Communauté Financière Africaine) franc circulates freely. The role of commercial banks or the government is confined to the issue of notes bearing the letter of identification of the relevant member country. Within the monetary union there is harmonisation of banking and monetary legislation and reserves are held centrally at the BCEAO.

2   Free convertibility of the CFA franc is assured by an operations account (compte d'opérations) at the French Treasury. The BCEAO is required to deposit not less than 65 per cent of its pooled foreign-exchange reserves in French francs on the operations account.

3   The CFA franc has a fixed rate of exchange with the French franc of CFAF 50 to 1 French franc.

The 1973 treaty envisaged that regional monetary union would contribute to rapid economic development and simultaneously 'harmonise' the economies of the member states. The linkage with the French franc was seen as increasing the availability of financial resources for development (presumably via the operations account and by encouraging foreign capital flows) and reflected a commitment to retain strong political and economic links within the Francophone community. The objectives of monetary and credit policy were to assure the value of the common currency and the ability to finance economic activity and development.

The Board of Directors of the BCEAO sets the amount of central bank credit accorded to member states each year and the discount rate, and decides on monetary policy changes to be made when appropriate. Monetary policy in each UMOA country is implemented by a local BCEAO agency and is administered by a National Credit Committee which allocates credit and implements sectoral credit policy. Côte d'Ivoire is by far the largest economy in the UMOA, with an output more than twice that of the second largest economy, Senegal. In terms of monetary aggregates it comprises nearly 50 per cent of UMOA broad money and more than half of total domestic credit.

The commercial banking system

Table 7.2 highlights the extent of the financial sector's dependence on the banking sector, with over 90 per cent of 1987 financial assets held in the banking system.[1] The number of banking institutions has increased substantially during the post-independence period, but four commercial banks dominate commercial banking, with nearly 95 per cent of total commercial bank assets and 69 per cent of total banking sector assets in 1987. Three of the 'big four' have a parent French bank as the principal shareholder, with

Table 7.2 Major financial system assets, 1987

	CFAF bn	%
Commercial and savings banks	1,546.2	60.3
Central Bank[a]	802.5	31.3
Bonds	95.1	3.7
Equity	122.0	4.7
Mutual funds, unit trusts	0.0	0.0
Total	2,565.8	100.0

Source: BCEAO, *Statistiques Economiques et Monétaires*; World Bank (1988).
Note: a Excludes some assets held by BCEAO not allocated by country.

remaining holdings distributed mainly amongst other foreign banks and the Ivoirian state. French parent banks typically supply credit lines to their counterpart Ivoirian banks which can significantly supplement domestic lending resources, particularly in situations of tight domestic liquidity.

Development banks were created, from independence onwards, with the dual goals of accelerating sectoral economic development and exerting government influence over investment patterns through direct intervention and credit policy. Capital funds are raised from government as well as from foreign donor and commercial agencies, but not from public deposits. These banks have experienced severe difficulties in the 1980s owing to a high proportion of non-performing loans and poor management. Four of the six banks existing in 1980 have since been put into liquidation; the total assets liquidated are equivalent to US$540m. at 1987 exchange rates, or 5.3 per cent of 1987 GDP. The proportion of bank loans recoverable is not known.

The agricultural development bank (BNDA) with 5 per cent of total banking sector assets continues to operate but is plagued by problems similar to those of the other now defunct development banks. BNDA has relied on 'temporary' BCEAO overdrafts at punitive rates of interest to keep afloat and its accounts are not publicly available, suggesting serious balance sheet problems.

The final development-type bank is the Compte de Gestion des Dépôts du Compte Autonome d'Amortissement (CAA), a public-sector agency which accepts deposits from the public sector, issues bonds and on-lends to state agencies, state-owned banks or the central bank. During periods of export boom the CAA can be a source of rapidly increasing liquidity in the banking system, as the surplus from the agricultural price stabilisation fund (Caisse de Stabilisation et de Soutien des Prix des Produits Agricoles – CSSPPA) enters as deposits into the banking system.

The detailed reasons for development-type banks' failures are not yet known, but the intertwining of politics and state banking at the highest levels is likely to have contributed to poorly performing loan portfolios. It is indicative that more than 25 per cent of total bank credits in the UMOA (which is dominated by Côte d'Ivoire) are reported to be non-performing (World Bank 1989b: 72), and it is likely that these credits have been concentrated in state-controlled banks. The liquidation of the four development-type banks was achieved without further bank runs for other troubled institutions but resulted in a substantial loss of banking liquidity and had a contributory impact on the banking sector liquidity shortage in 1987.

The direction of credit to less productive enterprises or towards consumption expenditure lowered the efficiency of the intermediation of the banking sector, and by implication restricted credit to more productive enterprises. This crowding-out argument is especially valid for credits from banks which are heavily exposed to a few near-bankrupt borrowers, where incentives are to lend more funds rather than demand repayment or servicing of existing debts which could threaten the borrowers' survival. Crowding-out in these circumstances favours the least creditworthy borrowers, whose interest payments are effectively capitalised by additional lending. The dominance of state ownership and support for development-type banks involved substantial losses of public funds, which, in turn, has retarded the process of fiscal adjustment during the 1980s.

Other financial institutions

The non-bank financial institutions (3.5 per cent of total financial sector assets in 1987) are, broadly, leasing and financing operations, and are frequently controlled by the commercial banks. Monetary policy will have indirect repercussions upon these institutions, as two-thirds of their deposits come directly from the commercial banks.

Insurance markets are a more important source of domestic savings mobilisation, with reserves of 6–7 per cent of the total assets of the banking system. Nearly half of premium turnover was accounted for by compulsory car insurance.

In 1976, the Abidjan Stock Exchange was opened to regulate and encourage an emerging market in bonds and equities. The government also wished to broaden shareholding amongst Ivoirians and hence to increase local ownership of foreign firms. Net issues of bonds from the CAA rarely exceed 0.5 per cent of GDP per year. This indicates that non-bank financing of the government deficit is limited in quantity. There is no significant short-term Treasury bill market, nor does there appear to have been a concerted effort to develop one.

In the long run the development of a securities market could lead to open-market operations to control liquidity in the economy, but at present several factors restrict the development of such a market. First, trading restrictions in the Bourse limit price movements and second, bond holders generally invest for tax reasons or because of statutory regulations requiring them to do so and therefore do not trade or arbitrage.

If these restrictions could be removed, which would increase the liquidity of government securities, an invigorated trading market in shorter-term securities could encourage additional domestic saving, particularly from funds currently flowing abroad. Furthermore, open-market operations could substitute for the present rediscounting system as a method of monetary control. Although a functioning stock market is not essential for an efficient process of financial intermediation, as a specialised agency providing long-term finance for the business sector it fills a particular role in the financial system which no other institution has taken up in Côte d'Ivoire.

Informal money markets

Unorganised money markets, including informal credit supplied by money-lenders and rural institutional credit (Wai 1977), are certainly prevalent in Côte d'Ivoire.

Rotating savings organisations, known as *tontines*, are operated by individuals making regular fixed savings and borrowing from the accumulated pool in turn. Allechi (1988) reports survey data from five Franc Zone countries including Côte d'Ivoire which show participation of 28.6 per cent of the (active) population in *tontines*, compared with 13.2 per cent holding a bank account and 13.4 per cent with a savings account. Touré (1985: 234–46) reports a similar type of system operating in urban areas where small daily savings, from traders in particular, are banked by an intermediary in the formal sector and returned less a commission charge at the month end. The intermediary also provides credit arrangements as a multiple of total monthly deposits.

Interviews[2] with cocoa and coffee farmers' representatives revealed that borrowing was predominantly undertaken in between harvesting seasons for consumption purposes (such as school fees, funeral and marriage obligations) and for the purchase of agricultural inputs. These *prêts à soudeur* (bridging loans) were made from the formal sector, including branches of the agricultural bank BNDA, and from *acheteurs*, the middlemen in the agricultural marketing system. More than half of farmers interviewed indicated that in the 1988–9 season loans were not available from either formal or informal sources; this coincided with acute liquidity shortages in the Ivoirian banking system. This anecdotal evidence suggests that the availability of rural informal credit is significantly related to formal credit availability, particularly in cases where informal loans are not the counterpart of informal savings.

Informal intermediaries may arise from restrictions in commercial banking. To obtain a demand deposit account a statement of regular income must be produced, which excludes the great majority of the Ivoirian population. A savings account in one of the big four banks requires a minimum deposit of CFAF 25,000, or 11 per cent of per capita GDP in 1988. Furthermore, banking remains a service for the urban community, with approximately 70 per cent of personal accounts being held in Abidjan. Thus the existence of informal credit markets should not be seen as a major impediment to the conduct of monetary policy but a consequence of the difficulties of providing banking services to low or intermittent income earners.

The existence of informal money markets as a substitute for saving and borrowing from commercial or development banks has the effect of maintaining the cash ratio at a higher level than it would otherwise be. For reserve base targeting of the money supply the existence of substantial informal money markets could reduce the effectiveness of monetary control by increasing the instability of the cash ratio, as cash is held for non-transactionary purposes and increases money multiplier instability. However, the observed stability of the cash ratio to total money supply (see below) suggests that informal markets do not strongly influence the conduct of monetary policy.

INSTRUMENTS OF MONETARY POLICY

The central bank has three direct instruments to influence the availability of credit: central bank credit ceilings, reserve requirements and prior authorisations. Indirect control of liquidity is effected through interest-rate adjustments, although interest-rate policy is more closely connected with sectoral allocation of credit. The BCEAO also has a sectoral credit policy which is based on preferential interest rates. Since this research was undertaken in 1989 the BCEAO has removed several aspects of the sectoral credit policy including sectoral credit coefficients and prior authorisations for credits.

Central bank credits

Table 7.3 shows the proportion of credit to the economy refinanced by the central bank, which has averaged close to 40 per cent since 1982. Refinancing has been the principal instrument used to influence the level and, to a lesser extent, the composition of credit in the economy.

Refinancing takes in three forms: short-term money market advances, rediscounts at either preferential or normal discount rate, and comparatively few fixed-rate loans of up to ten years' maturity. These credits are backed by discount bills deposited at the central bank.

Table 7.3 Credit and refinancing (%)

Year	Credit/GDP	Refinanced by BCEAO
1979	40.7	25.8
1980	40.0	30.6
1981	42.2	38.5
1982	41.1	40.4
1983	42.7	43.1
1984	37.7	40.8
1985	35.0	36.6
1986	34.4	38.0
1987	39.6	42.5
1988	n.a.	42.5

Source: BCEAO, *Statistiques Economiques et Monétaires.*

The annual ceiling for central bank credit usually defines the general monetary stance for the year. In theory the ceiling is set so that gross foreign assets cover 20 per cent of short-term liabilities of the central bank. This coverage rule would act as a strong constraint upon money creation if it were effectively applied, as sight liabilities comprise virtually all liabilities which the BCEAO agency has discretionary powers to adjust in the short term. When the 20 per cent ratio is breached, reductions of central bank refinancing should feed through to reductions in bank credit, thereby constraining the rate of money issue. The 20 per cent coverage requirement is, however, breached consistently at the country level and at the aggregate UMOA level. Côte d'Ivoire, for example, has operated at less than 2 per cent coverage for most of the 1980s.

Table 7.4 breaks down the BCEAO refinancing ceilings into three main categories: ordinary credit, rural credit and credit to the Treasury. The main component of ceiling overshooting is rural credit; credit to the government adhered closely to the targets, highlighting the important and effective restraint on direct credit to government. Credit to the rest of the economy (ordinary) was more likely to be significantly below target.

Refinancing of rural credit for purchase, stocks and export is regarded as priority credit in terms of both availability and the discount rate applicable. The ceiling is not binding, and was breached in every year but one to 1988. This soft constraint on borrowing allowed the Ivoirian Government to pursue a policy of agricultural stockpiling financed by the central bank between 1986 and 1988, whilst the world price of cocoa slumped. The demand for rural refinancing is derived from the public commodity stabilis-

Table 7.4 Central bank refinancing – ceilings and results (CFAF bn year end)

| | Credit to banks and financial institutions | | | | Credit to Treasury | |
| | Ordinary | | Rural | | | |
Year	Ceiling	Result	Ceiling[a]	Result	Ceiling	Result
1980	147.7	139.6	7.0	125.6	37.0	75.0
1981	188.9	177.4	163.0	193.9	87.7	65.0
1982	n.a.	239.9[b]	n.a.	172.5[b]	n.a.	90.0
1983	289.2	291.4	153.7	180.5	106.5	95.2
1984	311.0	295.3	150.0	147.5	115.0	107.4
1985	325.8	254.8	142.0	148.1	120.5	111.6
1986	255.0	243.5	145.0	180.4	124.3	119.5
1987	216.0	279.3	161.0	231.0	129.7	122.5
1988	n.a.	198.5	n.a.	302.8	n.a.	138.2

Source: BCEAO, *Notes et Statistiques.*
Notes: a Indicative.
  b Breakdown estimated from total.
  n.a. Not available.

ation scheme (CSSPPA). With weak cocoa and coffee prices, CSSPPA credit requirements have rapidly increased to meet the difference between world prices and Ivoirian producer prices and also to fund stockpiling.

An increase in rural refinancing either displaces refinancing of other activities or expands domestic credit overall. In practice, there appears to be a combination of monetary expansion and displacement of ordinary refinancing. During 1988, an expansion of rural refinancing by CFAF 71 bn accompanied an ordinary refinancing contraction of nearly CFAF 81 bn. The likelihood of crowding-out of non-rural borrowers during 1988 was also confirmed in discussions with commercial bank officials.

As CSSPPA had operated at a substantial deficit in 1988 and 1989, in July 1989 producer prices were reduced. Cocoa, for example, fell from CFAF 400/kg to CFAF 250/kg. Lower producer prices for the 1989–90 season should have reduced the amount of credit allocated as priority rural refinancing, but it is likely to have occurred because of the unsustainable credit requirements of stockpiling at the previous producer prices.

In summary, according a high priority to rural refinancing is the main cause of credit expansion in excess of target. As a result, foreign asset coverage remains far below the required minimum and monetary policy is rarely as contractionary as was intended. In extreme cases, such as in 1988, this system can crowd-out other types of borrowing. However, recent changes in agricultural pricing and sales policies would appear to reduce refinancing requirements below their 1989 peak.

Credit to government is strictly limited, to 20 per cent of the previous year's fiscal receipts. Between 1980 and 1987, the central bank was the source of about half of government's domestic borrowing, but only 15 per cent of total financing. Public sector borrowing from domestic banks is as important as central bank financing, and became more so in 1988 and 1989.

Table 7.4 shows that the ceiling is an effective means of curtailing direct central bank credit. Without specific coordination of fiscal and monetary policy, the limit on credit to government may be insufficient to fund borrowing requirements. However, there are several routes by which additional credit can be obtained, which make the ceiling less effective:

1 The ceiling does not include the financing of parastatal bodies. By reducing government net lending to parastatals the government direct borrowing requirement is reduced and the private sector must compete with parastatals for credit.
2 Delaying payment to the private sector, which creates increased private sector credit demand.
3 Foreign borrowing: with a convertible currency and booming exports Côte d'Ivoire borrowed heavily during the 1970s. Debt-servicing problems in the mid-1980s closed this route and increased the efficacy of monetary policy.

The final component of the global credit allocation from the central bank is the refinancing of ordinary credit from commercial banks and financial institutions. As it has low priority relative to government and rural credit, and the money issue is predetermined, other credit refinancing operates as a residual item, particularly in situations of liquidity shortage at the central bank.

Commercial banks know in advance that the amount of ordinary refinancing available is dependent on the liquidity of the local agency of the central bank. If the central bank has sufficient liquidity, the individual commercial bank can expect refinancing up to its portion of the ceiling. In positions of tight liquidity its allocation can only be known on a day-to-day basis.

From 1980, central bank control was extended by the stipulation of maximum monthly ordinary credit increases (i.e., credit eligible for rediscounting at the central bank) which operate counter-cyclically to the level of rural credit. Evaluation of monthly credit target compliance is hampered by BCEAO secrecy with respect to both targets and outcomes. Local banks reported general compliance with the targets, with the exception of the first quarter of the year due to delays in releasing credit targets.

Total credit ceilings   From 1976, the BCEAO set comprehensive annual indicative targets for monetary aggregates, although operational policy was confined to achieving the narrower central bank refinancing targets. Targets for overall net foreign assets, domestic credit components and total domestic liquidity are not published and appear to result from the framework used to determine the monetary stance in each UMOA country, which is basically an IMF-derived exercise of financial programming. Bhatia (1985) produced data for the years 1976–80 on targets and actuals, showing a substantial overshoot in UMOA domestic credit annually to 1979, principally because of rapid private credit growth in Côte d'Ivoire during 1976–9.

Reserve requirements

The central bank can require the deposit of funds from banks and financial institutions to restrict credit creation when deposits increase rapidly, or to ensure a certain minimum level of liquidity. In practice, reserve requirements have not been an important method of credit control as the refinancing system has been used for restricting credit growth.

The weaknesses in the development-type banks do suggest that a closer surveillance of banking liquidity would have been beneficial. The central bank has two instruments with which to supervise commercial bank lending operations, but these do not appear to be extensively employed. A minimum ratio between short-term liquid assets and sight liabilities can be imposed as well as a maximum ratio between non-guaranteed loans to a single enterprise and the banks' own capital and reserves. The thrust of central bank regulatory activity appears to be directed at ensuring that banks comply with complex regulations on the growth and distribution of credit, rather than at monitoring prudential regulation of banking liquidity and overseeing the quality of asset portfolios.

Prior authorisations (abandoned in 1990)

Loans in excess of CFAF 100 m. (US$0.3m.) required an *autorisation préalable* (AP) from the central bank which entitled a loan to be refinanced up to a certain percentage, according to sector of use. This instrument was intended both to control the amount of credit to the private sector and to augment the sectoral credit policy.

The effectiveness of the system was decreased by two factors:

1   Time delays in processing APs resulted in lending before notification. Authorisation typically took six months but applications could take one or two years, particularly in the case of new or foreign firms.
2   The limited amount of refinancing actually available at the central bank, especially in the late 1980s.

In practice, other sources of finance could be found for a loan which was refused an AP.

Sectoral coefficients (abandoned in 1990)

The BCEAO uniformly applied to each banking institution minimum proportions of total credit to the economy to be allocated to priority sectors and maxima for non-priority sectors. Table 7.5 shows that the sectoral distribution deteriorated substantially in terms of the priorities outlined by the BCEAO. For example, the primary sector credit target rose from 5 per cent of total credit to the economy in 1980 to 7.5 per cent in 1988, but actual credit fell from 5.9 per cent to 3.4 per cent; similarly the proportion of credit to industry fell from nearly 34 to 26.7 per cent.

In theory, breaching the sectoral coefficients resulted in the imposition of non-interest bearing deposits at the central bank. There is, however, no evidence that this sanction was ever applied.

The sectoral coefficient system was abandoned in 1990, as it clearly failed in its own stated objectives. The combination of credit allocation directives and a controlled interest-rate policy did not allow banks to adjust their lending terms to the perceived riskiness of the loan.

Table 7.5 Sectoral credit – objectives and outcomes (% total credit)

| Sector | | Objective = minimum | | Objective = maximum | | |
		Primary	Industry	Property	Tertiary	Other[a]
1980	Objective	5.0	37.3	11.5	22.0	24.2
	Outcome	5.9	33.9	12.1	20.7	27.4
1981	Objective	5.0	37.3	11.5	22.0	24.2
	Outcome	5.5	26.5	10.9	22.0	25.1
1982	Objective	–	–	–	–	–
	Outcome	5.6	36.4	10.2	20.3	27.4
1983	Objective	5.3	36.4	11.1		
	Outcome	5.6	34.3	9.6	22.4	28.0
1984	Objective	5.3	36.4	11.1		
	Outcome	5.3	34.4	10.7	20.7	28.9
1985	Objective	6.0	35.0	10.0	22.1	26.9
	Outcome	5.0	31.1	9.3	21.7	32.9
1986	Objective	7.5	37.0	9.0	21.1	25.4
	Outcome	4.3	28.1	8.2	26.7	32.7
1987	Objective	7.5	37.0	9.5	21.7	24.3
	Outcome	3.0	25.5	8.0	32.6	30.9
1988	Objective	7.5	37.0	9.5	21.7	24.3
	Outcome	3.4	26.7	6.3	35.6	28.0

Source: BCEAO, *Centrale des Risques.*
Note: a Energy, water, transport, communications, administration and households.

Interest-rate policy

Interest rates are set uniformly throughout the UMOA. Lending rates are defined in relation to the preferential discount rate (TEP) or to the normal discount rate (TEN), depending on the sectoral use of credit. The TEP and TEN are not usually adjusted more than once a year.

From late 1988 discount rates were raised and the spread between the normal and preferential rates was narrowed from 2.5 to 1 point. The increase in the preferential rate from 6 to 9 per cent represents a significant tightening of monetary policy and may signal an abandonment of the preferential refinancing role of the BCEAO.[3]

The money market rate for funds deposited at the BCEAO (overnight, one or three months) is adjusted several times annually at the discretion of the BCEAO Governor. In particular, it is set with reference to the French inter-bank interest rate to prevent the outflow of surplus funds from the UMOA, reflecting the ease with which funds can be transferred to and from France.

The UMOA interest-rate policy reflects the tension between maintaining rates at levels comparable to international rates in order to prevent the lodging of surplus funds in overseas accounts, and reducing the cost of borrowing to domestic borrowers as an incentive to investment. Lending rates are set in relation to the administratively determined discount rates, whilst marginal funds are priced at the more market-orientated money market rate. As capital is relatively scarce in developing countries, pegging interest rates to international levels is unlikely to equate supply and demand: excess credit demand must therefore be rationed in a non-price manner which is unlikely to reflect the borrower's ability to repay or the profitability of his investment. Furthermore, the fixed margins are not sufficient to induce banks to lend to more risky sectors such as small and medium businesses (for ordinary credit the maximum banking margin for lending was 5.50 per cent in April 1989).

Whilst there is some merit in arguing for more flexibility in deposit and lending rates, to increase competition for deposits and to increase lending incentives to higher-risk borrowers (or alternatively reduce collateral requirements), several other factors suggest that liberalisation is more likely to affect banks' lending than the level of savings mobilisation:

1   Since 1982 real deposit interest rates have been positive (see Figure 7.2), but low. Recent research indicates, although the debate is not yet settled, that the interest elasticity of savings in developing (and developed) countries is not particularly high; only severely negative real interest rates reduce financial intermediation (for example, Fry (1988) and Khatkhate (1988)).

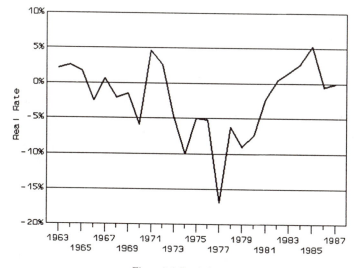

Figure 7.2 Real deposit rate 1963–88

121

2   Until recently the difference between the cost of funds from the central
    bank at the preferential discount rate and the rate paid on retail deposits
    was not significant: rates for large deposits were higher than the prefer-
    ential rate. Reliance upon the central bank as a source of low-cost funds
    is likely to have diminished incentives to attract private deposits. Wide-
    spread queuing at bank offices is indicative of low incentives for deposit
    mobilisation. The recent raising of the difference between the prefer-
    ential discount rate (TEP) and the deposit rate is likely to improve efforts
    at savings collection.

Whilst savings in aggregate do not respond to the real interest rate, allocations of savings among financial assets in Côte d'Ivoire do respond to
interest-rate differentials. For example, in 1985 the removal of interest
payments on sight deposits induced a significant shifting of deposits to
interest-bearing time deposits. Policy reforms should focus upon the interest-
rate differentials rather than levels, paying particular attention to French
interest rates, refinancing rates, and the effect of regulating rates and
lending-borrowing rate differentials on banks' lending policies.

PROBLEMS OF MONETARY CONTROL

In this section, we consider the interrelationship between the operations of
the central bank and the monetary system as a whole. As noted earlier, the
monetary authorities in Côte d'Ivoire cannot control the money supply. The
fixed nominal exchange rate against the French franc, absence of controls on
capital movements and limited scope for open-market operations severely
limit the central bank's ability to control counterparts of the money supply
(Khan and Knight 1981). In extreme cases an increase in domestic money
supply is completely offset by reductions in reserves, leaving the total money
supply unchanged. This conclusion assumes that monetary authorities are
unwilling or unable to sterilise the effects on the money supply of flows
across foreign exchanges.

The expansionary monetary effect of an export revenues boom could
theoretically be offset by a central bank open market sale of government
bonds. Côte d'Ivoire is, however, faced by a shortage of instruments to influence total money supply, with specifically limited scope for open market
operations by sale and purchase of government securities, and no independent interest-rate or exchange-rate policy.

Monetary control – refinancing and total credit

Coats and Khatkhate (1980) suggest that the limitations of the refinancing
instrument upon monetary control are: asymmetry, the maximum credit
restriction being a reduction of total refinancing to zero; reliance upon banks
to respond to the level of the discount rate when expansion is required; and

the unpredictable relation of the volume of refinancing to broader credit aggregates.

In Côte d'Ivoire, with over 40 per cent of total credit refinanced by the central bank, the refinancing instrument can be used in either an expansionary or a contractionary manner. However, we suggested above that commercial bank lending policy cannot be expected to respond very strongly to changes in the discount rate because of the importance of differentials with other deposit and lending rates. In practice, when the economy is buoyant and credit growth is rapid, refinancing is quantitatively an unimportant factor in funding credit growth, but the refinancing instrument is more effective when total credit growth is slow.

In the late 1970s, a unit increase in refinancing could be associated with a total credit increase which was larger by a factor of between three and nine. In the 1980s, some stability was restored to the credit/refinancing ratio, at about one. In the two consecutive years when refinancing was reduced (1984 and 1985) the associated change in total credit was low, giving some support to the weakness of refinancing operations in credit contraction and underlining the importance of other balance-sheet items which are not amenable to central bank control.

Whether the credit expansion corresponding to a given amount of refinancing is predictable is determined by the rate of growth of banks' liabilities and holdings of liquid assets. Apart from refinancing funds, this includes the availability of foreign finance from parent bank links and the willingness of the public and private sector to hold deposit liabilities in commercial banks and cash holdings. The variations of the credit to refinancing ratio are a result of limited official control over these other balance-sheet items. Only government deposits and cash holdings are directly controllable. Overall, the refinancing instrument appears to be least effective when it is most needed, i.e. when credit is growing rapidly and monetary restraint may be required to avoid inflation and to build up reserves.

Monetary base control

Table 7.6 shows how long-run changes in the monetary base are related to asset changes. The monetary base did not increase as fast as central bank credit to the private sector in either the 1976–80 (boom) phase or 1981–7 (adjustment) phase. This is primarily due to the financing requirements of balance of payments deficits, which resulted in a decline in the level of official foreign reserves.

Whilst balance-of-payments considerations reduce the effectiveness of control of the monetary base, it can still be concluded that a considerable degree of influence is potentially available in the central bank through control of lending to government and the private sector. The effectiveness of this depends upon the stability of the money multiplier.

Table 7.6 Changes in counterparts to monetary base (CFAF bn)

Year	Changes in:			
	MB	CBp	CBg	R
1976–80	+133.4	+176.2	+93.3	−136.1
1981–7	+180.5	+213.6	+168.0	−201.1

Source: IMF, *International Financial Statistics*.
Notes: MB = Cash issued plus banks' deposits at the central bank.
 CBp = Central bank credits to private sector.
 CBg = Central bank credit to government (net).
 R = Net foreign assets.

Money multiplier The money multiplier relationship, which relates the monetary base to the money supply, is determined by similar considerations to those defining the relationship between refinancing and total credit. The money multiplier is dependent upon private agents' and banks' willingness to hold cash, deposits and reserves in total and by category.

The broad money[4] multiplier has been declining annually since 1977, with an exception in 1982. The effect of changes in the monetary base and in the multiplier upon money supply is obtained from the approximation:

$$dM = dMB.m_{t-1} + dm.MB_{t-1}$$

where d = difference operator and m = multiplier

Increases in the monetary base explain monetary expansions over the longer term, but in particular years changes in the multiplier can be dominant. In most of the years considered, the multiplier and the monetary base have had opposite signs.

Although the central bank's role in controlling the monetary base level is important in the long run, other factors affect short-run money-supply behaviour. This helps to explain the unpredictability of the refinancing instrument in controlling liquidity. Detailed empirical studies could in principle determine private agents' short-run preferences over holding cash and different types of deposits, using monthly data where available.

Stability of asset and liability multipliers The stability of the money (liability) multiplier contrasts quite sharply with the previous discussion of the asset (credit) multiplier and the weakness of the relationship between refinancing and credit. The principal reason for this apparent anomaly is that the assets approach is rather partial in application; it does not consider the net foreign asset positions of the central or commercial banks. Both can fluctuate widely and this breaks the link between refinancing and credit.

At the central bank, refinancing levels are affected by the level of foreign reserves, to the extent that there is a constraint upon how far reserves can fall. So reserve shortages can reduce the level of refinancing independently of factors influencing commercial bank lending, whilst abundant reserves (or an export boom) may have the opposite effect.

In a similar way, reductions in commercial banks' net foreign asset positions may be unconnected to the central bank's refinancing policy at that time. In this case, domestic credit can move independently of the level of refinancing. There is considerable instability in the monetary system resulting from changes in the terms of trade, in particular the fluctuating price of exports.

The 'windfall gains' in export earnings from higher cocoa and coffee prices in 1976–9 did not translate into an accumulation of foreign reserves. Rather, they allowed a rapid increase in the volume and value of imports from 1977 to 1981. Bhatia (1985: 31) notes that a voluntary reserve deposit arrangement between the BCEAO and the CAA operated during 1977–9 partially to sterilise the rapidly rising liquidity of the banking system at this time. Despite this, domestic credit to both government and the private sector increased rapidly during this period.

Estimating demand for money

The quality of available macroeconomic data required for econometric estimation of money demand in Côte d'Ivoire is highly unsatisfactory in several respects, which bring into question the validity of almost any econometric results:

1　Quarterly macroeconomic data series are not readily obtainable.
2　Data are subject to wide margins of error. The retail price index, for example, is based upon a 1960 consumption basket.
3　There are time delays in producing recent years' data. Data for up to five or six years past are frequently estimates.

The general conclusions from ordinary least squares regressions are:

1　Real narrow and broad money aggregates were significantly and positively related to real income. Broad money demand also responded positively to the rate of income growth.
2　Generally, broad money demand was sensitive to interest rates. Increases in real and nominal rates resulted in reduced money demand. Inclusion of a time-trend variable, however, tended to lower the significance of the interest-rate variable substantially. As the discount rate is administratively set and rarely changed, its impact on money demand was likely to be low. In World Bank (1988) money demand is shown to be sensitive to differences between French and Ivoirian money market rates.

3   A partial adjustment mechanism did not greatly improve the equation performance, suggesting that money demand responds rapidly to changes in the economy.

The 'best-fit' equation shows that real money demand depends on lagged money, current real income and real income growth. The coefficient of the real rate of interest is insignificant. Both real income growth and lagged money were significant at the 99 per cent confidence level, and real income at the 95 per cent level. The Durbin-Watson statistic is in the indeterminate region. The short-run income elasticity of demand is 0.6, and the long-run elasticity 1.39, close to that of previous estimations. The real growth variable suggests that real income shocks have a substantial effect upon money demand, which is not adequately incorporated in the partial adjustment mechanism. When shocks are large, money holdings appear to adjust very rapidly. This feature may result from the fixed-rate regime whereby the effect of real shocks (if external in origin, or in the traded goods sector) will rapidly have a monetary effect via changes in reserve holdings.

Best-fit OLS money demand regression

$$M_t = -1.82 + .57M_{t-1} + .60Y_t - .28Rt_t + 0.86\,\dot{y}_t$$

$$(3.10) \qquad (2.30)\ (-1.19) \qquad (3.14)$$

SEE = .05, R-squared = .99, F-stat = 507.09, DW = 1.56

M = Broad money, i.e. M2, = cash + demand + time deposits,

Y = GDP, deflated, $\dot{Y}$ = rate of growth in GDP, and R = real rate of interest (discount rate, TEN).

Overall, there was no evidence to suggest that money demand was particularly unstable over time and that income was the most important determining variable. Money demand projections could therefore be made on the basis of income growth estimates.

REAL ECONOMY EFFECTS OF MONETARY POLICY

In Côte d'Ivoire there are limited substitutes for domestic bank credit, other than borrowing from an overseas parent company. There is no short-term company paper market, and access to finance from the stock market is restricted to well-capitalised large firms. This dependence upon bank credit suggested that changes in credit volumes might have real output effects.

Quarterly constant price production indices for eight industrial sub-sectors in the period 1982–7 were employed as indicators of output with corresponding real quarterly credit data. The production index was related to short-term credit lagged by one quarter, and to medium- and long-term credit lagged by one to three quarters.

Regressions carried out on both sector and pooled time-series bases for the industrial sub-sectors did not show a significant relationship between lagged credit, whether short-, medium- or long-term, or total credit, and the output indices. This indicates that bank credit may not be an important part of working capital. Company results for 1984 from the fifty largest companies in Côte d'Ivoire (*Bulletin de l'Afrique Noire*, 1988) show that total net losses of CFAF 97 bn were financed by a drawdown of cash reserves (deterioration of cashflow) rather than by increasing debt substantially.

Furthermore, the marked slowdown of credit growth in 1984–6 (including a contraction in 1984) was a result of both supply and demand factors, which are not adequately explained by supply-side credit constraints. Whilst the banking system's liquidity shortage was clear, as shown by a low cash ratio and a high loans-to-deposits ratio, extended recession and drought had reduced the number of creditworthy borrowers. In 1984, electricity shortages could also have contributed to credit demand reductions, but as production would also have been affected, the credit-to-output relationship is unlikely to have been affected.

At the sectoral level an interesting feature of credit allocation is that credit to the primary sector (80 per cent to agriculture) declined substantially (from CFAF 43 bn to CFAF 32 bn) between 1980 and 1988, yet the share of agriculture in GDP remained fairly constant. Between 1983 and 1988 credit to the primary sector halved in nominal terms, yet its GDP share increased from 30.6 to 34.0 per cent.

Although crop financing is excluded from primary sector credit, the low level and decline in the proportion of credit to the primary sector without a corresponding fall in output are evidence of a considerable degree of autonomy from the operations of formal credit markets. The apparent access to auto-finance (or perhaps informal finance) has permitted a reduction in formal credit, and indicates a healthy insulation from monetary policy actions.

Public and private sectors

The distribution of credit between the public and private sectors fluctuated widely between 1980 and 1988. In 1980, outstanding credit to public enterprises was 31.5 per cent of total credit. Over the next four years, outstanding credit fell sharply, reflecting the initiatives taken under adjustment programmes to address financial problems in the most important parastatals. By 1988, this credit had risen again to 22.5 per cent of total credit, at least in part a reflection of the renewed deterioration of the fiscal deficit which created pressures on the level of transfers to, or profits remitted from, public enterprises.

A weakly negative correlation is observed between the level of credit to government (net domestic bank financing) and net credit to public enterprises, suggesting a certain degree of substitutability between the two types of credit. The rapid shifts in the allocation of credit to public enterprises may therefore have been offset to some extent by a more direct financing role for the central government.

EVALUATING MEMBERSHIP OF THE UMOA

Until the early 1980s, the prevailing view was that Côte d'Ivoire was an economic success story. It was not therefore surprising that research concluded that the distinctive monetary arrangements of the UMOA had a part in this success, or, at least, that the monetary arrangements had not hindered development. However, the economic stagnation in Côte d'Ivoire since 1980, together with the more recent currency over-valuation resulting, in part, from commodity export price falls, has raised doubts about this received wisdom.

Growth performance

Table 7.7 shows how much Côte d'Ivoire's relative growth performance has changed during the 1967–87 period. Whilst a more sophisticated analysis is required to isolate the effects of monetary policy regime variables upon growth, certain noticeable changes have taken place (see Lane and Page 1991):

1   Growth in Côte d'Ivoire up to 1980 compared favourably with other developing-country groupings over substantial periods of time. Ivoirian growth in the 1967–73 and 1973–80 periods was clearly higher than the low-income Africa, sub-Saharan Africa and all developing countries weighted averages. Favourable comparisons can also be made against buoyant oil exporters such as Nigeria.

Table 7.7 GDP growth – Côte d'Ivoire and other African countries (annual rates[a])

Country/Group[b]	1967–73	1973–80	1980–6	1987
Côte d'Ivoire	8.5[c]	7.0	1.2	−3.9
Senegal (UMOA)	−0.3	2.1	3.2	6.2
Nigeria	6.9	9.6	−3.2	−3.6
Low-income Africa	3.2	1.2	1.4	2.9
Sub-Saharan Africa	5.6	3.3	0.4	−1.3
All developing economies	6.5	5.1	3.1	4.4

Sources: World Bank, *World Tables* (1989) and World Bank, *World Development Report* (various).
Notes: a   Period growth rates computed by least-squares method.
    b   Group figures are GDP weighted averages.
    c   1965–73.

2 Comparison of Côte d'Ivoire and Senegal, the two largest economies in the UMOA, shows that there is necessarily a process of convergent growth rates within the monetary union.
3 From 1980, Côte d'Ivoire's growth performance declined markedly, and more rapidly than in the low-income Africa, sub-Saharan Africa or developing country averages. Ivoirian performance is no longer markedly better than the groupings shown here, as had previously been the case.

Inflation

Inflation has been moderate in Côte d'Ivoire, only rising once above 20 per cent since independence, and remaining in single digits since 1981. Although membership of a monetary union is likely to be an important factor in maintaining low inflation rates, it is a separate issue whether this necessarily confers considerable benefits. We consider these issues in turn, arguing that inflation is likely to be lower than would otherwise be the case, but that nominal exchange-rate rigidity can reduce the benefits of low inflation.

Despite some shortcomings, the basic thrust of BCEAO monetary policy is counter-inflationary, and the monetary rules of the BCEAO are designed with this objective in mind, although it is clear that these rules have not always functioned ideally.

In the lexicon of the 'rules versus discretion' literature on the theory of economic policy (Kydland and Prescott 1977 and Barro and Gordon 1983), the anti-inflationary policy followed by the BCEAO has been both rule-based and a credible monetary policy. A credible monetary policy is defined as one in which the monetary authorities are perceived not to have an incentive to deviate from announced policy objectives. The rule followed is that money supply should be expanded with reference to the level of foreign-reserve coverage. There are two reasons why this is a broadly credible non-inflationary policy, despite the obvious difficulties experienced in the attainment of monetary objectives:

1 The BCEAO agency has no particular incentive or statutory authority during the course of the year to deviate intentionally from its policy.
2 Government cannot resort to rolling the printing presses to monetise fiscal deficits automatically.

Three facets of the UMOA have been important in sustaining this credibility. First, the supranational authority of the UMOA, where important decisions are made by simple majority or unanimity of opinion among member states. Secondly, the legal right of refusal of credit to government. Thirdly, the fixed exchange rate with the French franc.

Despite low inflation, particularly during the 1980s, Côte d'Ivoire has experienced substantial variation of its real exchange rate (Figure 7.3),

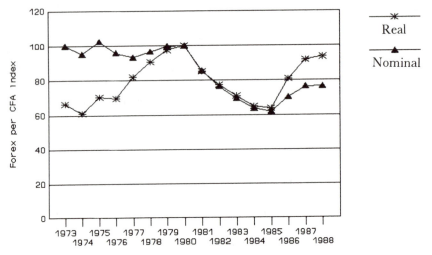

Figure 7.3 Côte d'Ivoire real and nominal effective exchange rates
Source: Derived from IMF *International Financial Statistics*

noticeably a sharp appreciation since 1985. A French Ministry of Co-operation report (Thill and Pelletier 1989) argues that overvaluation of the CFA franc relative to other neighbouring currencies, particularly those of Nigeria and Ghana, is undermining CFA country economies. This occurs through illegal cross-border trade into CFA countries, and price under-cutting on world markets. As an indication of how far the exchange rate had moved from purchasing power parity by 1988, farm labourers' wages paid in Côte d'Ivoire were more than three times greater than in Ghana.

Exchange-rate appreciation since 1985 resulted from appreciation of the peg currency, the French franc, against the US dollar, and domestic in-flation in excess of low foreign rates of inflation. Because currency appreci-ation has occurred despite fairly effective credit restraint, it is relatively straightforward to conclude that monetary policy is unlikely to be a complete substitute for exchange-rate flexibility.

Trade and investment

The valuation of the trade and investment benefits of monetary unions (see Mundell 1961 and Kenen 1961) need not be positive, nor constant, over time. During the stagnation of the 1980s in Côte d'Ivoire, the benefits were not evident. It is possible that monetary union has effects which reduce foreign investment and entrench inefficient trading patterns. Attracting foreign capital is fundamentally concerned with real factors such as productivity and growth prospects, labour relations and current business confidence. The monetary regime can facilitate such flows, but not deliver. In Côte d'Ivoire, private capital flows have been negative since 1985 without any marked change in Franc Zone arrangements.

The increase of intra-union trade has long been regarded as a probable development and benefit from the UMOA, despite the fact that monetary union is neither necessary nor sufficient for economic integration. Trade flows (Table 7.8) show that Côte d'Ivoire trade with other members of the Franc Zone expanded slowly between 1972 and 1986. Exports to other UMOA countries increased from 5.5 to 8.4 per cent of total exports but lagged behind the expansion of exports to other African countries. Conversely, the share of exports to the entire Franc Zone (France, the UMOA and the Central African Monetary Union) has fallen since 1972. Imports from UMOA have risen more substantially, from a 2.2 per cent share in 1972 to 7.3 per cent in 1986. Also the sourcing of imports from the Franc Zone has declined less rapidly than exports to the Zone.

Trade with France has declined substantially; the share of exports to France has halved, whilst only 31 per cent of imports as against 47 per cent in 1972 are sourced from France. However, trade with countries whose exchange rates are pegged to the franc or move within close margins to it (including European exchange rate mechanism (ERM) countries since 1979) has increased since 1981. Although there is a slowly rising trend within

Table 7.8 Côte d'Ivoire: trade shares (%)

Exports	1972	1976	1981	1986
EEC	63.4	61.3	54.7	59.3
of which France	29.1	25.4	18.6	14.2
Africa	11.2	11.9	17.2	15.6
of which UMOA	5.6	5.0	7.3	8.4
US	13.9	10.5	11.5	10.5
Other	11.4	16.3	16.6	14.6
Total	100.0	100.0	100.0	100.0

Imports	1972	1976	1981	1986
EEC	73.2	61.3	59.1	54.7
of which France	47.1	38.4	31.1	31.0
Africa	8.8	11.9	7.8	17.2
of which UMOA	2.2	5.0	1.6	7.3
US	6.1	10.5	7.4	11.5
Other	11.9	16.3	25.7	16.6
Total	100.0	100.0	100.0	100.0

Source: BCEAO, *Notes et Statistiques*.

UMOA, the rapidity of the decline of trade with France, which began well before the formation of the ERM mechanism, makes it difficult to come to firm conclusions on whether UMOA membership is sufficient to stimulate intra-Union trade.

Factor mobility

An important issue in defining whether a country is in an optimum currency area is that factors of production should be mobile within the area, but immobile internationally (Mundell 1961). This may allow more rapid non-inflationary growth by easing factor shortages.

Côte d'Ivoire is an important regional labour market and approximately 25 per cent of the population are immigrants, largely from Burkina Faso, Ghana and Mali. There are also French skilled workers and Lebanese traders. Significant amounts of cash flow as remittances to other UMOA and non-UMOA countries, as can be determined from inter-agency movements of banknotes within the UMOA. But the UMOA is not a unified geographic block, and labour movement takes place also with non-UMOA countries such as Ghana. The extent of monetary transfers between UMOA states for trade and workers' remittances (the factor mobility argument for union) suggests that there are considerable benefits from a regional currency, but not necessarily at the current pegged rate to the French franc, or for the historically defined UMOA.

Exchange-rate arrangements

If a political decision was made to increase the flexibility of the exchange rate, this would require renegotiation of the UMOA statutes and unanimous agreement from UMOA states and France. Several options are available:

1   A new devalued fixed rate against the French franc, either for the UMOA as a whole or for individual countries at different rates. Differing exchange rates would increase the incentives for monetary expansion in individual countries to maximise their use of pooled foreign currency. Increased inflation would probably hasten the demise of the entire monetary union.

2   A new type of peg. As the French franc is already a member of the ERM, the CFA franc is already almost *de facto* pegged to the ECU. A switch to an ECU peg could be carried out simultaneously with a devaluation. The problems with an ECU peg in the longer run will be similar to those of the present franc peg. Monetary restraint will be essential to avoid inflation and hence overvaluation of the exchange rate. A secondary problem would be the agreement of the other ERM members to supporting ECU–CFAF convertibility.

If European Monetary Union is achieved in the 1990s, European inflation could fall even lower, which would require greater CFA monetary discipline. Alternative pegs could take account of trade composition and prices, or currency composition of trade. Both measures would result in an increased weighting for the US dollar and regular exchange-rate changes.

3   Given the reluctance of many parties to move away from a French franc peg, the possibility of independent floating for the CFAF seems remote. There are also no developing country precedents of movement from a single fixed rate to sustained free floating. There are, however, examples of changes to a crawling peg.

CONCLUSIONS

For nearly twenty years following independence the monetary arrangements in Côte d'Ivoire functioned well, permitting low inflation and economic growth. Confidence in the value of the domestic currency was encouraged by the fixed exchange rate and guaranteed convertibility with the French franc. Importantly, credit to government from the domestic banking system was effectively limited by UMOA statutes, which eliminated a significant source of money creation. Foreign finance was readily available, which also reduced the pressure on domestic credit expansion.

By the late 1970s ineffective use of monetary control instruments coincident with rapid export-based economic growth permitted accelerated monetary growth, increased price instability, an overvalued real effective exchange rate and the emergence of large financial imbalances in the balance of payments and government operations.

Although the rapid monetary expansion in the 1970s had an external origin, it is clear that the monetary instruments of the central bank could not have been as effective in curtailing demand as they were to be in the 1980s. This was because the most important control instrument, the refinancing operation of the central bank, is ineffective at times of rapid liquidity growth. Individuals and firms moved from holding cash towards bank deposits, which permitted commercial banks to expand credit rapidly and reduced their reliance upon central bank financing. Commercial banks also have access to borrowing from foreign parent banks, beyond the control of the central bank in the absence of exchange controls. The poorly developed capital market precluded central bank intervention to mop up liquidity by the sale of securities.

The renewed application of restrictive monetary policy, during a prolonged period of adjustment in the 1980s, contributed to price stability and a reduction in the fiscal and trade deficits. Credit policy was more restrictive and closer to central bank objectives. However, the provision of subsidised credit to finance export crops, effectively without limit, has always meant that credit policy was not as restrictive as was intended.

There is little evidence to separate the effects of general economic stagnation from those of restrictive credit policies. The agricultural sector appears to be more insulated than other sectors from the general stance of money and credit policies, but there is evidence that informal rural finance performs essentially an intermediary role for formal institutions, unless rural credit is used for consumption purposes only. The implication is that much of the rural sector is self-financed, and not reliant upon formal or informal lenders to finance productive activities.

The emphasis of monetary policy in the 1990s is likely to be upon improving domestic savings mobilisation. The banking system has not been used for this purpose. In part, this is due to the lack of incentives to mobilise deposits which results from generous central bank provision of refinancing facilities. There is little evidence that commercial banks have made a significant effort to mobilise rural savings or provide savings instruments to small savers. Improving incentives to mobilise deposits, for example, by tying refinancing to deposit mobilisation, would improve service provision in this area.

There is little evidence to suggest that monetary and financial policy has stimulated financial development; the prime concern has been to maintain stability. Increases in financial deepening have been closely associated with income growth and not financial reform. If the private financial sector is to offer a wide range of financial services and instruments, some diversification from the present concentration of financial assets in the commercial and central bank sector would be beneficial. Whilst there are a number of emerging bank and non-bank institutions, their development could be accelerated by legislative changes. Financial innovation could occur at both ends of the spectrum of sophistication. There is considerable scope for mobilising informal savings in the traditional sector. The sizeable modern sector in the Ivoirian economy does not have access to sources of financing/saving such as short-term government and commercial paper, whilst equity financing could be developed with reforms of the currently restrictive stock market. In the longer term, the development of security markets could also supplement the refinancing instrument of monetary control.

Several aspects of central bank intervention in credit markets appear less than effective. Refinancing operations have limitations in controlling broad money aggregates, as mentioned above, and discourage saving. The liquidation of many development-type banks during the 1980s also suggests that refinancing operations may have allowed political lending considerations to override commercial concerns of loan repayment. Sectoral credit allocation policies, such as sectoral lending coefficients and prior authorisation, have not worked. Priority sectors have low and falling levels of credit. The most obvious reform of the current system would be to introduce more flexibility in interest-rate setting to replace administrative decision. This could be achieved by allowing commercial banks to trade directly with each other in the inter-bank money market. UMOA rules, however, prevent increased flexibility for interest-rate setting, unless the agreement of partner countries is obtained; the BCEAO could therefore play a coordinating function at an international level.

The net benefits of UMOA membership are now no longer as clear as they were in the 1960s or 1970s. Côte d'Ivoire is caught in a low growth, tight monetary policy environment, and the evidence points to an overvalued real exchange rate which strengthens the argument for a restrictive monetary policy. Abandoning the fixed exchange-rate peg will not be an easy decision to take, owing to the historical associations of stability connected to the arrangement and the uncertainty which change may create. Although monetary policy can be reasonably effective in achieving credit restriction to reduce inflation, externally determined exchange-rate changes or international price changes can have a far greater economic impact than domestic monetary policy responses can achieve. With increased exchange-rate flexibility, Côte d'Ivoire could respond to fundamental exchange-rate misalignment created by differential price movements, and, to a certain extent, offset these developments.

8

INDONESIA, 1974–90

Christopher E. Lane, David C. Cole and Betty F. Slade

INTRODUCTION

Recent Indonesian monetary policy experience can be classified under two distinct financial regimes characterised by contrasting monetary objectives and use of different policy instruments. The first regime (1974–82) of direct credit control and extensive central bank intervention in credit allocation was associated with rapid real economic growth led by oil, gas and timber export expansion, but slow growth of the financial system. The more recent period of financial decontrol (1983–90), in which development of market-based instruments of monetary policy occurred, was paralleled by a decline in oil and gas export prices and earnings and a reorientation of production toward other exports, including labour-intensive and resource-based manufactures. Real economic growth remained high on average (5.5 per cent p.a. 1984–9), while the financial system expanded dramatically.

Throughout the 1970s and 1980s Indonesia was unusual among developing countries in that it had minimal foreign-exchange controls and it avoided domestic budgetary deficits.[1] In the 1974–82 period, when oil export earnings and government revenues were both ample, the main concern of monetary policy was to curtail expansion of domestic credit and overall expenditure, while accumulating foreign-exchange reserves. After 1983, when both exports and budgetary revenues were weaker, the concern shifted to attracting capital from abroad, protecting foreign-exchange reserves and dealing with the tensions and shifts in expectations accompanying the structural transformation of the economy. As a consequence, monetary policy in this latter period has been characterised by frequent changes in instruments and approaches.

An important factor in maintaining a supportive counter-inflationary fiscal policy has been the political continuity since 1965. The Soeharto regime inherited a zero-growth, hyper-inflationary economy which remained a potent reminder of the costs of economic mismanagement to subsequent policy-makers (analysed in Woo and Nasution 1989).

The long-term objectives of monetary policy have been a satisfactory rate of economic growth with moderate rates of inflation, a sustainable balance of payments and adequate foreign-exchange reserves. Credit, interest-rate and exchange-rate policies have been utilised to achieve social or distributive objectives throughout the period studied. The intermediate objectives of monetary policy have varied considerably and have included targeting monetary aggregates, interest rates and foreign-exchange reserves.

The next section describes the main elements of the financial system. We then consider the experience of monetary control by direct instruments of credit and interest-rate controls, and in particular the response to oil price increases in 1973 and 1979. The focus of the section on post-1983 experience is the development of money-market instruments and the successes and setbacks experienced in indirect monetary control of an open economy. In the final sections we assess the effect of the open economy upon money demand and the role of Indonesia's fiscal policy stance and international financial flows in the transition from administrative control and intervention to a relatively effective market instrument-based monetary policy.

THE FINANCIAL SYSTEM

Commercial banking

The five state-owned banks in Indonesia have had two sometimes conflicting functions. First, they implemented the government's subsidised credit programme directing loans to priority sectors with cheap refinancing facilities from Bank Indonesia (BI), the central bank. Second, they were commercial banks in competition with private banks. During the 1980s, the government reduced the emphasis on their developmental role and encouraged them to respond more to market pressures: the extent of refinancing facilities available from BI was slimmed down and barriers to entry in the banking sector were removed.

At the beginning of the 1980s, the five state-owned banks remained in a dominant position in the Indonesian banking system, with 80 per cent of assets of the deposit money banks (Table 8.1). During the decade, largely as a result of deregulation, their share dropped to under 70 per cent. In October 1988, the so-called PAKTO reforms (see below) increased the freedom of entry for both new domestic private banks and joint-venture banks and initiated a new phase of competition between the state-owned banks and the rest of the commercial banking system.

Private Indonesian banks proliferated from the mid-1950s, although their functions were often quite limited. They have often been wholly owned by, and have existed to service, individual industrial conglomerates. They were at times able to provide cheap finance for conglomerates by borrowing excess funds from state-owned banks on the inter-bank market. The expansion of private banks accelerated during the financial deregulation undertaken in

Table 8.1 Banking system: number of banks and banking offices
(position at 31 March)

	Number of banks		Number of offices		Share of assets (%)	
	1982	*1989*	*1982*	*1989*	*1982*	*1989*
State-owned	5	5	712	818	80	69
Private	71	63	297	656	10	23
Foreign/joint venture	11	11	20	21	7	5
Regional development	28	194	29	292	4	3
Savings	3	3	14	82		
Rural	5,801	5,770				

Source: Bank Indonesia, *Report For Financial Year 1982/83* and *1988/89*.
Notes: Bank offices include head offices, branch offices and sub-branch offices.
Rural banks include village banks, paddy banks and petty traders' banks.

the 1980s. Table 8.1 shows that their share of total bank assets more than doubled (to 23 per cent) between 1982 and 1989.

Branches of foreign banks in Indonesia lost part of their small market share during the 1980s as restrictions upon their expansion (and employment practices) discriminated in favour of national banks. However, the PAKTO reforms in 1988 permitted entry to the Indonesian market in joint-venture deals with existing domestic banks with up to 85 per cent foreign ownership. During 1989 foreign banks expanded branch networks and initiated new joint ventures – particularly the Japanese banks.

Regional development banks act as localised government bankers. Lending activities have tended to be predominantly short-term, although the original intentions were to supply longer-term investment finance. Each bank is constrained in size because operations are confined to their individual regions.

Rural banking

The 5,800 rural banks consist of *lumbung desa* (paddy banks) and *bank pasar* (market banks). Prior to 1989, they were supervised by the state-owned Bank Rakyat Indonesia (BRI) which also provided loan and deposit facilities. They are now directly supervised by Bank Indonesia. The *unit desa* or village units of BRI are the most decentralised level of national banking and offer deposit and credit facilities. Until 1983, the *unit desa* acted principally as 'cashiers for special government programmes' (Patten and Snodgrass 1987:7), distributing subsidised credits for rice cultivation and small and medium credits for rural entrepreneurs. Patten and Snodgrass suggest three factors which led to the introduction of new credit facilities closer to the real market cost after 1983. First, the *unit desa* had no incentive to collect savings deposits which paid 15 per cent (i.e. higher than lending rates) so that lending was limited by the level of subsidy. Second, research had indicated that credit availability was more important to rural borrowers than the level of interest payments. Third, targeted credits, for example for rice cultivation, were becoming less appropriate as productive activities diversified in rural areas. With interest-rate decontrol in 1983, BRI introduced a new programme at the *unit desa* level to raise interest rates to between 1.5 and 2 per cent per month and expand rural credit without additional subsidies.

Other formal sector financial institutions

There were fourteen non-bank financial institutions in 1989 which operated in the money and capital markets. Their general function was to raise funds by the issue of promissory notes to other financial institutions and to carry out investment, predominantly in corporate loans or purchase of corporate securities. After 1983 there was growth in insurance and leasing companies as foreign firms took advantage of joint-venture opportunities. Pension funds were established as a result of income tax changes in 1984 exempting pension contributions from tax. Information on the size of pension funds is limited, but they are frequently cited in the local press as major investors in new companies and financial institutions.

Capital market

Until the end of 1988, the number of share issues and the level of trading on the Jakarta Stock Exchange (founded 1977) were relatively low. Capital market reforms in December 1987 and October and December 1988 simpli-fied listing requirements, allowed over-the-counter trading, provided access by overseas investors to domestic capital markets and permitted the esta-blishment of private stock exchanges. As a result stock market activity escalated rapidly and resulted in a shift of risk-bearing from commercial bank lending to a wider range of equity holders.

The informal sector

Rural informal credit is thought to be substantial, but is unrecorded. In order of importance,[2] intra-family transfers are probably the largest com-ponent, followed by traders' credit from wholesaler to retailer and retailer to customer. Next in importance are rotating savings and credit schemes, or *arisan*. Informal finance is also obtainable under the *gaduan* system where the produce of land is taken until a loan is repaid, or the Javanese *ijon* system where a share of the crop is taken in place of interest.

In the urban sector similar schemes exist for financing both consumption and small-scale investment, but the most substantial informal market is the offshore market. The removal of capital controls in 1971, together with the proximity of Singapore, encouraged substantial offshore holdings and borrowings in foreign currency. In many respects monetary policy is aimed at influencing the extent and direction of the flow of funds into and out of overseas accounts or Jakarta dollar deposits. We discuss below the influence of the open capital account upon monetary policy operations.

MONETARY POLICY IMPLEMENTATION 1974-82

Stabilisation by intervention 1974-8

In 1974, immediately following the first inflationary effects of booming oil prices on the Indonesian economy, the monetary authorities imposed direct credit controls on all banks as the principal means of controlling domestic monetary growth. This replaced reserve requirements as the primary instrument. From 1974 until 1983, the Indonesian financial scene was characterised by increasing government and central bank controls, negative real interest rates and widespread use of subsidised credit schemes. Although Indonesia during this period exhibited many features of a repressed financial system, buoyant oil exports, the balanced-budget policy, relatively low inflation and easy access to foreign financial markets minimised the long-term damage of domestic financial repression to the economy.

Credit ceilings on each bank were the dominant monetary policy instrument from 1974 until mid-1983. In addition, there were reserve requirements for all banks, and interest-rate controls on state-owned banks, whilst the private banks could set interest rates freely. The state-owned banks' deposit rates were rarely changed (twice in 1974, once in 1977 and 1978) and the real deposit rate was negative in each year apart from 1976 and 1977. Longer-term deposits were also subsidised by the government by between 6 and 9 percentage points in 1974, falling to 1.5-4.5 points after 1978. The main focus of interest-rate policy was to reduce the real cost of borrowing.

Reserve requirements were largely redundant for domestic credit purposes, as credit ceilings were the effective constraint on bank lending. With the open capital account, banks were able to place abroad any excess funds over their required reserves; reserve requirements therefore functioned as a limit to funds placed abroad. To limit such outflows Bank Indonesia paid interest on excess reserves after April 1974, but domestic financial savings still sought better returns abroad, as interest rates at home were negative. From around 1978, fears of, and then actual, devaluation of the rupiah also created incentives to hold excess liquidity in foreign currency.

The rationale for the introduction of extensive direct credit controls was different from the reasons for their retention for nearly a decade. The introduction of direct controls was a response to the ineffectiveness of reserve requirements in curtailing commercial bank lending (Asian Development

Bank 1987:955).[3] Reserve requirements were 30 per cent of commercial bank liabilities in 1977, but there was still excess liquidity in the banking system.

During the whole period up to 1983 domestic credit targets were set as a residual, with the influence of the government budget and balance of payments on money and credit assumed to be fixed exogenously. Overall monetary growth was targeted by taking into account target GDP growth and the inflation rate judged to be tolerable (Bank Indonesia 1989). The allocation of credit growth ceilings (and the targets for net domestic assets of commercial banks) was under the direction of Bank Indonesia. Table 8.2 demonstrates that the credit targets in the initial years were successful as a ceiling. Domestic asset growth targets were under-achieved in 1974–5 and 1975–6. Bank lending was cautious because credit ceiling allocation was linked to performance against ceilings in previous years and also because of close supervision of adherence to ceilings by Bank Indonesia.

Although the stance of monetary policy was relaxed in some respects as early as December 1974 when inflation had begun to recede (twelve-month deposit rates returned to 15 per cent and subsidies on longer-term deposits were reduced), the system of centralised control was maintained until new financial reforms were enacted in 1983.

The inadequate state of development of the financial and banking system was one of several factors which prevented the introduction of more indirect market-based methods of monetary control at this time. The balanced budget policy of the government meant that the central bank had no government paper with which to use open-market operations to influence the path of short-term interest rates. The banking sector was oligopolistic, dominated

Table 8.2 Monetary policy targets, 1974/5–1982/3 (% change)

Year ending March 31	Growth of domestic assets[a] All banks			Growth of domestic liquidity[b]	
	Target	Actual	Difference	Target	Actual
1975	31.1	25.9	−5.2	37	32
1976	33.5	24.9	−8.6	39	42
1977	24.0	26.4	2.4	31	26
1978	18.7	19.9	1.2	25	15
1979	21.3	25.7	4.4	20	27[c]
1980	22.1	25.3	3.2	23	40
1981	30.7	32.6	1.9	n.a.	36
1982	41.2	41.2	−0.0	n.a.	28
1983	40.4	38.8	−1.6	n.a.	21[c]

Source: Bank Indonesia, *Annual Report*, various issues.
Notes: a Domestic assets = bank loans + other assets.
     b Domestic liquidity = money + quasi money.
     c Domestic liquidity revalued for effects of devaluation.

by the state-owned banks, which provided little hope that interest rates would adjust to reflect the real scarcity of funds. Politically, there was a general interventionist bias to economic policy and a reluctance to rely upon market-based control mechanisms, reflected in the extensive level of government ownership and control in the economy. Finally, the abundance of financial resources generated by the oil boom led the government to focus primarily on allocation of those resources to desired uses, rather than on improving the efficiency of the financial system itself.

The emphasis on controlling the quantity of credit shifted to interest in its allocation as the system of direct control became more established. The ceilings on credit growth were used to affect the distribution of credit as well as its volume, by granting differing increases in credit ceilings to the banks. Foreign banks, for example, benefited little from the administrative system of credit-ceiling allocation. The rationale for selective credit intervention was to subsidise not only large government-owned or favoured enterprises but also small indigenous entrepreneurs (*pribumi*). This satisfied a political objective of maintaining a nationalist power base, which had been shaken by anti-Chinese riots in 1974. President Soeharto was himself of peasant origin. Directed credit programmes therefore were seen to be tackling genuine concerns of the ruling elite for the alleviation of rural poverty (Woo and Nasution 1989). By funnelling directed credit almost exclusively through the state-owned banks, the liquidity credit system maintained their dominance in commercial banking. The mechanism for directing domestic credit towards pre-defined priority sectors of the economy was via a complicated system of Bank Indonesia refinancing facilities called 'liquidity credits', giving varying rates of discount for many different categories of borrower and types of credit.[4]

The targets for commercial bank assets (credit and other items net) were fairly closely followed from fiscal years 1976 to 1978, with asset expansion less than 5 per cent over target (Table 8.2). Monetary growth was slower than had been expected because banks had few incentives to raise deposits when their lending was constrained by credit ceilings. In December 1977 reserve ratios were lowered and the availability of subsidised credits from Bank Indonesia was increased in order to stimulate domestic investment and monetary growth. During fiscal year 1978 monetary growth was higher than expected, largely owing to the 34 per cent devaluation of the rupiah which increased the rupiah value of local dollar deposits.

Credit ceilings were effective in the 1970s in controlling credit growth and damping down inflation. The combination of excess bank reserves and low deposit interest rates encouraged offshore financial intermediation which also served to reduce the potential expansionary effect of the balance of payments on the money stock.

Because of the government commitment to balanced budgets (introduced during the stabilisation programme of 1966–8), fiscal expenditures were closely correlated with revenues, even when changes in the oil price markedly changed oil tax revenues. The formulation of five-year plans (*Repelita*), with detailed programming of tax and non-tax revenue, foreign aid and borrowing, were intended to minimise domestic deficit-financing sources, and act as a safeguard against imprudent levels of foreign borrowing. Consequently Indonesia maintained substantial lines of undrawn credit with commercial foreign lenders throughout the 1970s and 1980s. Policies of fiscal balance acted as a constraint on inflationary financing if income fell, but were a constraint on curtailing expenditure if income rose.

Monetary impact of the two oil shocks

In 1973 and 1979, Indonesia experienced external shocks from sharp increases in oil prices. Although the impacts of the oil price shocks were in many respects similar, the policy responses were different. Table 8.3 compares macroeconomic variables for the periods 1972–4 and 1978–80.

The two shocks differed in magnitude. Fuel export prices for Indonesia rose by 42 and 315 per cent in 1973 and 1974 respectively, but by 44 and 64 per cent in 1979 and 1980. Nevertheless, both rises had profound macroeconomic consequences, as petroleum and associated products dominated exports, representing 51 per cent of total exports before the first shock and 64 per cent before the second.

Table 8.3 Comparing the oil price shocks: changes in economic indicators

	Fuel export price %	Broad money growth %	CPI %	GDP deflator %	Domestic credit %	Foreign assets Rp bn	Interest rate[a]
Pre Shock							
1972	11.3	48.7	6.7	13.3	33.7	221	18
1978	0.8	22.0	8.2	10.9	4.5	1,868	9
Shock							
1973	42.1	42.8	30.8	32.9	64.7	295	15
1979	44.2	35.0	18.2	34.8	8.5	3,509	9
Shock							
1974	314.9	46.3	40.6	47.3	41.3	661	18
1980	64.0	49.4	18.0	31.9	10.9	6,570	9
Post Shock							
1975	−2.7	39.1	19.0	12.4	47.6	72	15
1981	12.5	25.9	12.2	11.2	7.3	6,838	9

Sources: Central Bureau of Stastics, *Economic Indicators*, various issues; and World Bank (1990b).
Note: a State-owned bank twelve-month time deposit.

144

During each period the fiscal stance was broadly neutral with small overall deficit GDP ratios, and exchange-rate policy differed only slightly, moving from a fixed peg to the US dollar during the earlier shock to a very gently depreciating currency basket during the later one. In each case the shocks had inflationary effects. Inflation (the GDP deflator) rose by 20 percentage points in 1973 and 24 percentage points in 1979. Using the consumer price index, which is less influenced by the effects of the oil price rise than the GDP deflator, however, the increase in 1973 was far more substantial than in 1979. Although some of this differential can be attributed to the greater magnitude of the first shock and accompanying inflation from reduced food supply, the differing role of monetary policy was an important contributory factor.

The clearest difference was in the rate of credit growth, which rose from 33 per cent in 1972 to 65 per cent in 1973 and remained over 40 per cent in 1974 and 1975. During the second oil price shock domestic credit growth rose only moderately, from 5 per cent in 1978 to 9 per cent in 1979. The difference in credit growth is more surprising when the rates of monetary growth are compared: monetary growth was not appreciably faster during the 1973–4 period than in the 1979–80 period. Control of credit with similar rates of monetary growth meant that the banking system was accumulating stocks of foreign assets far more rapidly during the second shock than the first. After an increase in foreign assets up to 1974, the stock fell in 1975 to below the pre-shock level. During the second shock reserves increased steadily between 1978 and 1981 (excluding minor revisions for exchange-rate changes).

What may appear confusing is that the weak control and rapid expansion of commercial bank credit alone in 1978–81 (shown in Table 8.2) coincided with low rates of overall domestic credit growth (shown in Table 8.3). The key point is that the credit ceilings applied only to the commercial banks. Consideration must be given to Bank Indonesia net credit to government and the restrictive effect of accumulating government deposits. The slower growth of overall credit, and the associated lower rates of inflation, can, in large part, be attributed to the rapid increase in government deposits at the central bank which were recycled and financed the increase in subsidised credits without imparting an expansionary impetus to monetary growth.[5]

During the first oil shock, net credit to government decreased marginally between 1972 and 1974 (Table 8.4). In contrast, government deposits showed strong growth between 1978 and 1980 (and after) and in total their increase was greater than the increase in credit to the private sector. The rate of accumulation of government deposits, and correspondingly of foreign assets of both the central bank and the commercial banks, was such that the credit ceilings for commercial banks imposed between 1979 and 1982 were revised on several occasions in mid-year to allow a more vigorous expansion of credit to non-governmental borrowers in line with movements on the balance of payments, inflation and reserves.

Table 8.4 Comparing the oil price shocks: credit and government operations

	Govt. Rp bn	Other official entities Rp bn	Credit to: Private sector Rp bn	Other financial institutions Rp bn	Govt. savings/ GDP %	Govt. deficit/ GDP %
Pre Shock						
1972	9	2	592	0	5.1	−2.6
1978	−462	678	2,173	67	7.9	−3.3
Shock						
1973	−16	4	947	4	4.8	−2.4
1979	−1,163	893	2,855	19	9.7	−2.4
Shock						
1974	−137	1.1	1,377	42	5.1	−1.6
1980	−2,746	1,359	4,254	26	10.3	−2.4
Post Shock						
1975	51	201	1,115	45	6.2	−3.7
1981	−4,691	1,791	5,942	20	12.7	−2.2

Sources: As for Table 8.3

The remaining question is: how did the Indonesian Government manage to accumulate deposits and effectively sterilise the foreign-exchange inflow during the second shock but not the first, when the overall fiscal stance appeared to have been the same?

First, government savings (current revenue less current expenditure) during the second oil shock increased from 8 per cent of GDP in 1978 to 13 per cent in 1981, but remained at about 5 per cent of GDP during the first shock. Higher savings would have permitted a higher level of capital expenditure, other things being equal, during the second shock. If this expenditure had actually been implemented, no effective sterilisation would have occurred. However, the rate of increase of development expenditure commitments, which were largely assigned to state-owned construction companies, exceeded the implementation capacity. Foreign construction firms were barred from entry. In 1973 and 1974 development expenditure in constant prices increased by 7 and 5 per cent respectively. In contrast, at the height of the second boom, constant price expenditure as recorded in fiscal accounts increased by 27 per cent in both 1979 and 1980, but was actually unspent and accumulated in the government account at Bank Indonesia. The intention had been explicitly to sterilise the foreign-exchange inflows and these fortunate circumstances assisted in preventing a more substantial expansion of net domestic credit and expenditure.

The move to reforming instruments of monetary policy, 1981–3

The year 1981 was one of good growth (7.1 per cent), with inflation falling to 12.2 per cent. The decline in oil prices in 1982 resulted in the only fall in GDP since the mid-1960s, however, and an abrupt deterioration in the balance of payments. Monetary policy was unable to respond rapidly to the income change. The decline in real income and foreign-exchange earnings led to the reorientation of macroeconomic policies the following year. But already in 1982, a series of measures was implemented to increase non-oil exports and reduce the dependence of economic growth on oil. These included relaxed export credit terms, higher volumes of export credit refinancing facilities and a loosening of export regulations.

The government decided that the system of credit and interest-rate controls and extensive refinancing by Bank Indonesia impeded the growth and efficiency of the financial system. Thus a major focus of subsequent reforms was to increase competition in the banking sector and to reduce or eliminate the role of the central bank in credit allocation and control.

MONETARY POLICY IMPLEMENTATION 1983–90[6]

After 1983, in parallel with a series of market-oriented fiscal, financial, trade, foreign investment and exchange rate reforms, monetary policy shifted from direct controls to increasingly indirect instruments of intervention. Explicit monetary and credit targets were abandoned, interest-rate ceilings removed, and central bank-directed credits reduced. New money market securities were issued by the central bank after 1984, and it became a buyer of commercial bank (and non-bank financial institutions) endorsed paper and of foreign-exchange swap contracts (introduced in 1979). These three instruments were used to influence the supply of base money, interest rates and the demand for foreign exchange.

June 1983–August 1984

Removal of credit ceilings and emergence of the inter-bank market

On 1 June 1983, the Indonesian Government removed credit ceilings and eliminated most interest-rate controls on the state-owned banks. Bank Indonesia had yet to develop money-market instruments to influence the short-term interest rates and reserve holdings of commercial banks in place of credit ceilings. To reduce the possible expansionary effects of the removal of credit ceilings, 60 per cent of subsidised 'liquidity' credits (Bank Indonesia refinancing) outstanding in March 1983 were made ineligible for renewal. The substitution of other categories permitted the total amount of liquidity credits to grow, but at a slower rate.

The new government policies allowed the state-owned banks to raise their deposit and loan interest rates. Although the initial increase of state-owned bank rates was modest, all banks began to mobilise rupiah deposits to support new lending. This initiated the process of financial deepening which continued for the remainder of the decade. The demand for rupiah loans also increased as borrowers faced a higher cost of dollar loans resulting from the potential depreciation of the exchange rate.

Private banks soon discovered that they were better able to increase their loans than their deposits. The state-owned banks encountered the reverse of this. Private depositors apparently considered the state-owned banks safer than the private domestic banks, and therefore were willing to deposit funds with them at a somewhat lower interest rate than with the private banks. The state-owned banks also had a more extensive branch network. On the other hand, private bank lending procedures were quicker and less complicated than those of the state-owned banks, so that private borrowers were willing to borrow from them even at somewhat higher nominal interest rates than were charged by the state-owned banks. All state-owned enterprises were required to use only the state-owned banks, so this provided the state-owned banks with a captive clientele and a large interest-inelastic deposit base. This imbalance between the deposit mobilising and lending capabilities of the two groups of banks created a fertile environment for the development of the inter-bank money market.[7]

The inter-bank market grew very rapidly after July 1983 and then collapsed just as quickly after the change in policies in September 1984 (see below). The weighted average inter-bank interest rate was volatile, but was probably a good indicator of the liquidity conditions in the money market throughout this period.

While the domestic inter-bank money market was growing in response to normal market forces, the monetary authorities became more concerned with developing an indirect instrument to influence the total supply of reserve money of the banking system, as the repatriation of foreign-exchange holdings could lead to rapid growth of reserve money. Bank Indonesia introduced a new money-market instrument in January 1984, called a *Sertifikat Bank Indonesia*, or SBI, which was a short-term liability of Bank Indonesia (thirty- and ninety-day maturities).

September 1984–September 1986

Exchange-rate uncertainty and development of money-market instruments

The combination of unrestricted capital movements and erratic adjustments of the exchange-rate instrument made the domestic money market vulnerable to sharp contractions or expansions. In August 1984, the domestic inter-bank market became very unsettled, mainly because of an acceleration during July and August in the rate of depreciation of the rupiah. This led to speculation that there might be a further large devaluation. The response in the money markets was a heavy outflow of foreign-exchange reserves from Bank Indonesia, and a sharp rise in the overnight inter-bank interest rate to a peak of 90 per cent per annum in September from an average of 22 per cent in August.

The monetary authorities concluded that activity in the inter-bank market was contributing to the speculation against the rupiah, so they reduced the ceilings on the amount of inter-bank borrowing that banks could undertake (from 15 to 7.5 per cent of total deposit liabilities). Bank Indonesia also supplied emergency credits of up to six months to all banks that were short of liquidity. Most importantly, these reduced the rate of depreciation of the rupiah, which relieved the speculative concerns and caused a return flow of foreign exchange to Bank Indonesia. The volume of inter-bank lending dropped sharply and the inter-bank rate fell back quickly to below the pre-crisis level.

Having discovered that a short-term shortage of reserve money could be as troublesome as an excess, and with the SBI not developed sufficiently to meet this need, Bank Indonesia introduced a new money-market instrument in early 1985 called the *Surat Berharga Pasar Uang* (SBPU) that could be used to supply reserves. The SBPU was essentially a short-term security issued by a business or bank which Bank Indonesia was prepared to purchase at a discount from the banks via Ficorinvest, a Bank Indonesia-owned discount house. The rate of discount was set by Bank Indonesia through a quasi-auction process, and all banks had a ceiling on the volume eligible for re-discount. In effect, Bank Indonesia provided a committed credit line to commercial banks equal to the rediscount ceiling.

Initially the SBPU was used to replace part of the six-month emergency credits that had been given to many banks in September 1984. But there was continuing demand for reserve funds, especially from the private banks, whose borrowing in the inter-bank market was limited to 7.5 per cent of their total third-party liabilities. On the other hand, the state-owned banks had excess reserve funds which they could not lend directly to the private banks, because of the same limit. Instead they put their surplus reserves into Bank Indonesia's SBIs or into dollar deposits abroad. From June 1985 until June 1986 the level of outstanding SBIs rose from practically nothing to Rp 2,100 billion, while the level of inter-bank borrowing declined. The deposit money banks increased their net foreign-exchange holdings by about US$600 m., or Rp 650 bn.

Bank Indonesia itself served the former role of the inter-bank market by mopping up excess reserves from the state-owned banks through sales to them of SBIs and then lending reserves to the private banks (particularly foreign-exchange banks) by discounting their SBPUs. The interest rates set on these instruments by Bank Indonesia were adjusted only occasionally until June 1987.

A third money-market instrument utilised by Bank Indonesia during this period was the foreign-exchange swap facility.[8] Bank Indonesia set a fixed swap premium of 5.25 per cent per annum, which was less than the difference between foreign US dollar interest rates and the domestic rupiah deposit rates, and commercial banks could 'reswap' their swap contracts with Bank Indonesia, up to a preset ceiling, for a fixed commission. By subsidising the forward market in this manner, Bank Indonesia aimed to encourage the repatriation of working balances held abroad and at least temporarily increase its own foreign asset holdings. The swap facility encouraged repatriation of foreign assets by providing foreign-exchange cover for interest-rate arbitrage operations.

Thus, during this period the central bank set the SBI, SBPU and swap rates and rationed the quantity of SBPUs and swaps that it would buy from the individual banks. Since both of these instruments were sources of reserve money for the banks, Bank Indonesia essentially rationed the supply of reserve money for the individual banks. It also limited the amount of inter-bank borrowing that could be done by the private banks, and it bought up any excess reserves from the state-owned banks through the open-ended sale of SBIs. Not surprisingly, the volume of inter-bank borrowing diminished, and movements in the inter-bank interest rate were erratic and poorly correlated with the rates of either domestic or foreign money-market instruments.

The overall effect of these policies was that two of the new money-market instruments (SBPUs and swaps) were used primarily as quantitative instruments of monetary policy, to control the supply of reserve money, and they were not allowed to develop as flexible means of liquidity adjustment for the financial institutions. The SBI, on the other hand, was a fixed interest-rate instrument of liquidity adjustment primarily for the state-owned banks. Since the interest rates on all these instruments were effectively fixed by Bank Indonesia, they provided little information on the overall liquidity conditions or expectations in the money markets.

Problems were most clearly manifested by the persistent net outflow of foreign exchange from Bank Indonesia, whose holdings fell from Rp 6,600 bn at end-1984 to Rp 3,600 bn at end-1986 as the commercial banks continued to build up their foreign-exchange holdings. The rate of dollar outflow varied, depending on speculation about devaluation. The exchange rate was held fairly steady throughout this same period, especially after May 1985, which contributed to the pressures for, and the expectations of, a big devaluation.

The monetary authorities devalued by 31 per cent on 12 September 1986. The timing of this devaluation surprised many money-market participants, who expected it nearer the end of the year and had continued to hold rupiah assets earning 7 to 10 percentage points higher interest than comparable US dollar instruments.

October 1986–October 1988

Speculative pressures and stabilising monetary measures

There continued to be speculative surges against the rupiah following the devaluation. In December 1986 the central bank lost foreign reserves of US$1.7 bn; in May and June 1987, there was an outflow of US$1.1 bn (for comparison, 1986 imports were US$10.7 bn).

A major cause of these foreign-exchange pressures was the rather modest recovery of oil prices after June 1986, which many market participants interpreted as being likely to force a further large devaluation in order to maintain rupiah budget revenues. Management of the exchange rate relative to the US dollar during this period gave the impression of uncertainty, although it may have been more stable relative to a certain basket of foreign currencies.[9] This may have added to the speculation.

Following the devaluation, Bank Indonesia removed the ceilings on foreign-exchange reswaps for each bank, but also raised the swap premium from 5.25 per cent to 8 per cent. Despite the increase in price, the reswaps outstanding surged, and there was evidence of an apparent substitution of swaps for foreign-exchange asset holdings by the commercial banks. Inter-bank rates continued to rise throughout this period as many private and foreign banks had reached the rediscount ceiling for SBPUs and increasingly relied upon the inter-bank market for short-term funds. The Bank Indonesia reswap premium was raised again in May 1987 from 9 per cent. This was not sufficient to damp the speculative fever, and reswaps outstanding continued to rise in May and June. The central bank also raised the offer rate on SBIs and raised the basic discount rate to 19 per cent, but to no avail. The demand for SBIs practically disappeared.

The heavy loss of foreign-exchange reserves finally forced the government to take direct and drastic action in late June 1987. There were several reasons why the Indonesian authorities did not carry out another devaluation. First, a devaluation was not considered necessary for trade and general balance-of-payments purposes at the time. By the second quarter of 1987 the non-oil trade balance had started to improve and a firming of the oil price had raised net oil revenues to the highest level for over a year. Second, another de-valuation was seen as too destabilising and as working against the objectives of encouraging repatriation of private and banking foreign assets. Third, devaluation had not stemmed the tide of speculation in 1986.

The state-owned banks were the principal speculators against the rupiah, either by using their excess liquidity to buy foreign exchange directly, or by lending to the private banks and their own customers who could then lengthen their foreign-exchange positions. Therefore, the main attack by the monetary authorities was on the liquidity position of the banks, and es-pecially the state-owned banks. The contraction was accomplished by two specific measures. The first was an instruction to four large state-owned enterprises to transfer part of their time deposit balances at the state-owned banks into holdings of new SBIs issued by Bank Indonesia. The second was an immediate reduction in the ceilings on SBPU discounts at the central bank to zero, in effect forcing all the commercial banks to buy back their SBPUs from Bank Indonesia.

These two measures essentially wiped out, almost overnight, the equivalent of all the available legal reserves of the deposit money banks. The only way in which the banking system could meet its reserve requirements was by selling foreign exchange to Bank Indonesia, or by borrowing through the discount window. An increase in the discount rate for the use of the central bank discount facility from 20 to 30 per cent was intended to discourage the second alternative and to encourage sales of foreign exchange to the central bank.

The effects of the June–July restrictive measures were dramatic. There was a large return flow of foreign exchange to Bank Indonesia, amounting to US$1.3 bn from July to November 1987, and a US$1 bn decline in outstanding swap contracts with Bank Indonesia between April and December 1987. The improved domestic bank liquidity position was reflected in a drop in the inter-bank interest rate from an average of 23.5 per cent in June to 11.8 per cent in September, whilst SBI auction rates also fell during this period. All of these changes reflected changed expectations about the likelihood of a major devaluation in the near future.

The possibility for banks to use the SBPU rediscount with Bank Indonesia as a source of funds was eliminated in the short run as the rediscount ceilings had been used by commercial banks to borrow reserves from Bank Indonesia whilst simultaneously increasing foreign currency holdings. In the longer term the private commercial banks had lost a useful method of short-term reserve management and were more reliant on state banks supplying the inter-bank market, or external resources. The SBI was also tainted by the forced sale to the public enterprises, which may have set back the planned development of money markets. Bank Indonesia began a more discretionary period of money-market intervention. The rate set at the SBI auction served as the signal for the direction in which Bank Indonesia wished to see short-term interest rates move.

The focus of policy shifted to an attempt to extend the time horizon of stable expectations, especially for the exchange rate, from a few days or weeks to a few months. The major instrument that was used for this purpose was the rate of depreciation of the rupiah against the US dollar.

October 1988–December 1989

Activating domestic money markets

On 27 October 1988, the Government announced a broad package of financial reforms (PAKTO) that was designed to free entry into many types of financial activity and to give encouragement to the development of domestic financial markets. The major provisions that directly affected monetary policy included:

1   removal of specific limitations on inter-bank borrowing;
2   introduction of a flexible foreign-exchange swap premium based on the difference between the LIBOR rate and the time deposit rates of banks authorised to deal in foreign exchange;
3   reduction in the reserve requirements of banks (and NBFIs) to a uniform rate of 2 per cent of all third-party liabilities;
4   forced temporary purchase at fixed interest rates (16 and 16.5 per cent per annum) of three- and six-month SBIs by all banks to absorb 80 per cent of the reserves freed by the reduced reserve requirement;
5   allowing the entry of new banks wholly owned by Indonesian nationals or joint ventures with up to 85 per cent held by the foreign partner.

These policies increased the opportunities and facilities for the use of domestic money-market instruments and reduced the relative attractiveness of operating in the foreign-exchange markets for liquidity purposes. The flexible swap arrangement was intended to bring the premium under market forces. If the rate was simply fixed by Bank Indonesia, a change in the swap premium was likely to be interpreted by the commercial banks as a signal of a changed rate of depreciation and was likely to create instability in foreign-exchange markets. For example, increases in the swap premium in 1986 and 1987 actually raised the demand for swaps as a hedging option.

The forced sale of SBIs in November 1988 put a severe squeeze on the liquidity position of the commercial banks, because the reduction in legally required reserves was much greater than the reduction in reserves that the banks considered they needed to meet their own conception of reasonable liquidity requirements. Some banks, faced with this severe liquidity squeeze, had to turn to Bank Indonesia for what turned out to be long-term accommodation. Others managed to adjust by selling foreign-exchange holdings or by borrowing abroad and swapping foreign exchange with Bank Indonesia to acquire rupiah. The actual adjustment of the reserve holding turned out to be Rp 700 bn less than the forced purchase of SBIs.

This liquidity squeeze led to a one-off adjustment in the positions of many banks, and also to a sharp rise in the inter-bank interest rate. However, most banks managed to meet their legal reserve requirements in November by one means or another. After the adjustment, they began to explore their reserve-management practices and to work out new ways to meet the new reserve requirement rules.[10]

By late December 1988, a few banks began to sell some of their so-called 'PAKTO SBIs' either outright or under repurchase agreements, and thus a secondary market began to develop. In the first part of February 1989, 25 per cent of the PAKTO SBIs, which had a term of ninety days, matured and were redeemed by Bank Indonesia. This helped to ease further the liquidity position of the banks. In the meantime, the inter-bank market was becoming more active as a mechanism for redistributing available reserves among the banks.

The prospect of the remaining 75 per cent of PAKTO SBIs maturing in the first half of May 1989, and thereby supplying new reserve money of Rp 1,200 bn, which was about equal to the total reserves of the banking system (both required and excess), led to some concern about the money markets becoming excessively liquid and precipitating a significant loss of foreign exchange. To prevent this, Bank Indonesia gave further encouragement to the development of the secondary and primary markets for SBIs and also took several measures to discourage the holding of foreign exchange for liquidity management purposes.

These measures, which took effect from 1 May 1989, included:

1   setting net open foreign-exchange position limits for all foreign-exchange banks at 25 per cent of their total capital;
2   removal of foreign borrowing limits on domestic banks to permit them to acquire more longer-term foreign financing;
3   restrictions on the definition of capital for branches of foreign banks operating within Indonesia;
4   restrictions on the use of foreign-exchange swaps with Bank Indonesia by branches of foreign banks.

Steady depreciation of the exchange rate continued through the remainder of 1989 at about 4–5 per cent per annum. Bank Indonesia's foreign-exchange reserves held steady, while outstanding reswaps declined. Non-oil exports grew well and oil prices held steady. The inter-bank rate and SBI rates declined.

Thus, by the end of 1989 the cumulative effects of the various monetary and broader financial policies were basically favourable. Real economic growth was good (7.2 per cent), inflation moderate (7.0 per cent), the balance of payments was strong, bank assets and liabilities were growing rapidly, and the capital market was booming. The instruments of monetary policy were still in need of improvement to make them more indicative of and responsive to changing market conditions, but the array of instruments and the principles guiding their use seemed to be appropriate to the country's condition.

DEMAND FOR MONEY

There is a substantial body of work which analyses the demand for monetary assets in Indonesia (Ahmed and Kapur 1990; Boediono 1985; Odano and Soekarno 1988). In general, the behaviour of money demand conforms to theoretical reasoning. However, the work carried out has not focused on the stability of the money-demand function, because the sample size has not been sufficiently large. The general approach has been to disaggregate the components of money and to estimate several separate functions. This approach has shown that portfolio selection is strongly influenced by the relative rates of return on real and financial assets.

The speed of adjustment of money demand to changes in economic variables appears to have increased in the 1980s relative to that found in the 1970s (for estimations which use an adaptive expectations specification of a lagged dependent variable). For example, the coefficient on the lagged dependent variable in narrow money estimations fell from 0.749 during 1976.1–1984.4 (Boediono 1985) to 0.363 during 1984.2–1987.4 (Ahmed and Kapur 1990). This suggests that the increasing sophistication of money markets has improved the speed of financial transactions and that the degree of international financial integration has increased. The slow speed of adjustment (around 0.2 to 0.25) for major monetary aggregates in the pre-1983 period would lead to a more pessimistic view of the role for official intervention in the setting of interest rates than in the post-1983 phase. Even post-1983, with faster money-demand responses, the role of speculative money-market pressures in raising inter-bank and deposit rates appeared to override the authorities' attempts to control interest rates in the short term at specific times, as well as in the medium term.

Real narrow and broad money aggregates are predominantly influenced by a scalar variable (consumption or income) and reduced by domestic inflation. The income elasticity of demand has been high in all estimations undertaken and increases for less liquid forms of money indicating the process of financial deepening that has been undergone in Indonesia. Boediono (1985) finds a long-run elasticity of 1.09 for currency, 1.48 for demand deposits, 1.31 for narrow money and 2.03 for quasi-money for the period 1975–84. Higher domestic interest rates encourage real time and savings deposits, and in some cases lead to portfolio adjustments out of demand deposits.

The impact of the open economy upon demand for money has been tackled with a number of different methods: Boediono (1985) considers the role of the foreign–domestic interest rate differential (Rf–Rd), adjusted for exchange-rate expectations, upon quasi-money and by employing a measure of gross domestic income which incorporates terms-of-trade effects. Utilising quarterly data from 1975.1 to 1984.4 (straight-line interpolation for gross domestic income), the results showed that for quasi-money the interest-rate differential (with random walk exchange-rate expectations) had a significant negative effect upon the level of money demand. This result suggests that the fixed exchange-rate regime in the earlier half of the sample period had a strong influence on restraining expectations of devaluation. The gross domestic income variable also provided more significant parameter estimates than a GDP variable.

An alternative approach incorporates the open economy, with a devaluation expectations variable of trend decline that was found to have a significant effect upon demand for foreign currency deposits (at 95 per cent confidence level) for the period 1976.3 to 1986.4 (Odano and Soekarno 1988). For quasi-money, in the period 1984.2 to 1987.4, the influence of the open economy has been incorporated with the foreign interest rate plus the swap premium (lagged three periods) which has a significant negative effect upon money demand. Other external influences are the price of oil (positive) and the inflation-rate differential (negative) of Indonesia with foreign competitors and traders, but these are not significant at a 95 per cent confidence level (Ahmed and Kapur 1990).

Assessing money demand in the post-1983 period

Several problems remain with money-demand estimation for Indonesia. First, the incorporation of open economy variables remains partial at best. Second, estimations based on quarterly data cannot accurately capture the dynamics of changes in monetary demand.

Exchange-rate expectations have been extremely volatile. The oil price was at one time thought to be a good predictor of exchange-rate movements; for example, the September 1986 devaluation from Rp/US$ 1,134 to Rp/US$ 1,644 closely followed a decline in oil prices. However, even in this case, the financial markets were caught by surprise. In 1983, the devaluation actually preceded the oil price fall, whilst in years subsequent to 1986 the exchange rate did not respond to oil-price changes.

Because the swap premium was a managed tool of the Indonesian authorities, it did not give a clear indication of exchange-rate expectations. The premium was kept artificially low and market-determined swaps remained a small and imperfect market. The best indicator of exchange-rate expectations would appear to be the difference between foreign and domestic inter-bank rates. As discussed above, expectations of devaluation have led rupiah holders to convert into dollars and leave banks short of rupiah resources. Banks' short-term response has been to increase the use of inter-bank market funds and bid up the market rate. Ideally, the interest rate differential would be used as an indicator, but inter-bank rates are only available as a composite measure of differing maturities.

Thus, as an indicator of open economy effects, we use a series of measures:

1   the domestic inter-bank rate (a weighted average of maturities from one to ninety days) as an indicator of actual speculative pressure;

2   the foreign inter-bank rate (LIBOR three months US$) and the swap premium (three months) as the risk-adjusted return on foreign assets;

3   previous point rates of depreciation (one, three, six and twelve months previously) as an indicator of the risk premium associated with holding rupiah assets.

Monthly data are used to incorporate more complex dynamics into short-run money demand. For the scalar variable (GDP), a simple time trend was used in view of its reasonably stable annual growth path, and this proved markedly superior to interpolated series. Two functional forms were utilised: first an adaptive expectations model with a lagged dependent variable and, second, an autoregressive error process as a simplification of a dynamic specification. The demand for narrow money was specified as a function of the level of transactions (or a trend), the opportunity cost of holding money rather than goods (i.e., expected inflation) and the rate of return on alternative financial assets proxied by the time deposit rate. Open economy variables were not considered to be an important factor in determining this essentially transactions-determined variable. For quasi-money, open economy variables were added in addition to the variables considered in the narrow money estimations.

Estimations   The demand for narrow money and quasi-money was estimated for the period 1983.6–1989.9.

Functional forms:

$$
\begin{array}{c}
+ \quad - \quad - \\
(1) \qquad M1 = f1\,(Y,\ INF,\ Rd,\ Dummies) \\
+ \quad - \quad + \quad +/-- \quad +/- \quad + \\
(2) \qquad QM = f2\,(Y,\ INF,\ Rd,\ Rib,\ Rf,\ SWAP,\ EX,\ Dummies)
\end{array}
$$

Where:

M1	= Log rupiah currency plus demand deposits deflated by the consumer price index.
QM	= Log rupiah time plus savings deposits deflated by the consumer price index.
Y	= Log real GDP (interpolated) or time trend.
INF	= Consumer price inflation (over previous one, three, six and twelve months).
Rd	= Domestic interest rates (state-owned bank time deposits, one and three months).
Rib	= Weighted inter-bank rate.
Rf	= Foreign interest rate (LIBOR, one and three months).

SWAP = Bank Indonesia quoted swap premium (one and three months).

Dummies = Dummy variables to incorporate seasonality and the effects of policy regime changes in October 1988 (PAKTO) and May 1989 (limits imposed upon open foreign-exchange position of banks and NBFIs).
DJAN....DNOV monthly seasonal variation dummies, DJAN = January etc.

EX = US\$/Rp depreciation (one, three, six and twelve months).

Narrow money We report one result here for narrow money utilising an adaptive expectations model:

Regression 1
Independent variable – (real rupiah currency plus demand deposits)
Method – OLS

Variable	Coefficient	t stat
Constant	1.683	3.22
M1−1	0.645	5.80
Trend	0.0017	3.40
INF(3)	0.149	0.71
Rd(3 month)	−0.0068	−2.31
DJAN	−0.055	−4.84
DFEB	−0.015	−1.36
DAPR	−0.025	−2.26
DMAY	−0.016	−1.47
DJUL	−0.026	−2.38
DOCT	−0.020	−1.83
R^2	.953	F (10,65) 133.1
RBAR	.946	SEE 0.0246
DW	2.176	MLL 179.7
N	76	

Serial correlation rejected 1–12 lags.

The narrow money regressions generally show the expected sign of co-efficients, significant at a 95 per cent confidence level. Expected inflation, proxied by previous inflation of one, three, six or twelve months, had no significant effect upon real narrow money demand, demonstrating that the generally low and steady rates of inflation in Indonesia in the post-1983 period are likely to have created minimal disturbances to real money demand. The rate of interest on state-owned bank time deposits had a small but significant negative effect upon money demand, which indicates that lifting restrictions in 1983 on state-owned bank interest rates induced modest portfolio reallocation into longer maturity deposits from narrow money and developed financial deepening. Because a formulation with a time trend plus seasonal dummy variables was employed, the income elasticity of demand varies according to the rate of growth of income, being lower in years of high income growth. Finally, dummy variables for the PAKTO reforms in October 1988 and for reforms in May 1989 did not have a significant effect upon narrow money demand. Narrow money demand had a strong element of seasonality, in part because the trend variable exhibits no seasonality, with peak demand in December of each year.

Quasi-money   Regression 2 for quasi-money utilised the existence of serial correlation in residuals as a convenient simplification of a dynamic process.

Regression 2

Independent Variable – QM (real rupiah time and savings deposits)
Method   – Cochrane Orcutt Method AR (4)

Variable	Coefficient	t stat
Constant	4.065	85.09
Trend	.0019	51.16
Rd(3 month)	.00414	1.99
Rf+swap(3 mon)	−.0082	−2.68
INTBANK	−.0015	−4.73
Inf(12)	−.0062	−4.46
XR (6)	.0865	3.05
U(t-1)Rho	1.252	10.46
U(t-2)Rho	−.846	−4.68
U(t-3)Rho	.662	3.64
U(t-4)Rho	−.357	−3.29
R^2	.998	F (10,61) 3892.1
RBAR	.998	SEE 0.0168
DW	1.886	MLL 198.1
N	76	

Although regression 2 has a complicated lag structure and linear restrictions on the coefficient estimates, the effect of the independent variables upon money demand is very much as expected. The trend variable captures the scalar effects very strongly, domestic interest rates have a positive effect on money demand whilst inflation expectations (proxied by past annual inflation) reduce money demand. The open economy variables have a substantial effect upon quasi-money demand. Like Ahmed and Kapur (1990) we find that an increase in swap-adjusted foreign interest rates reduces domestic money demand, with no significant difference upon the coefficients of the swap rate and the foreign inter-bank rate if estimated separately. The domestic inter-bank rate also enters as an indicator of pressures upon money demand with a negative sign indicating that a high rate is largely a result of open economy pressures. Finally, the exchange risk premium, or risk of a depreciation not covered by the forward discount rate, is proxied by actual depreciation over the previous six months.

Prediction   The outcome of sample prediction performance turned out to be surprisingly good. Estimating the model upon the data for 1983.6–1988.12 permitted prediction of nine-months money demand. Apart from the final observation the model over-predicted money demand over the period 1989.1–1989.9 with a mean absolute prediction error of .38 per cent (of the log value). A comparison of the predictions of real quasi-money demand reveal an actual increase of 25.21 per cent and a predicted increase of 24.73 per cent. However, as a prediction model the accuracy of prediction will rest heavily upon the view taken of future movements in domestic and foreign interest rates.

CONCLUSIONS: IMPLEMENTING MONETARY POLICY – IS INDONESIA DIFFERENT?

There are two distinctive features of the Indonesian financial system that have a significant bearing on the implementation of monetary policy. One is the strict limitation on government budget deficits, which largely precludes domestic deficit financing and thereby prevents expansionary monetary pressures. The other is the open foreign capital account which permits sudden movements into and out of foreign exchange, creating problems for monetary policy. These foreign-exchange movements, however, also give clear signals of monetary imbalance and of the need for corrective action. The ability to maintain the open capital account for almost two decades has been dependent upon, and has supported, the conservative fiscal policy. These fundamental fiscal and foreign-exchange policies have set the conditions for the implementation of monetary policy.

Fiscal policy

Government deficits have been low, on average about 1.3 or 1.4 per cent of GDP, and almost entirely foreign-financed. There is essentially no provision for domestic financing of the budget deficit and no issuance of Treasury bills or bonds. Indonesian fiscal accounts must technically balance, i.e. the capital deficit equals the current surplus. Capital expenditures, however, are those committed; they may be unspent. Capital revenues include foreign financing and the surplus from the current budget.

   The practice of placing all revenues and accumulating budgeted expenditure commitments as deposits in Bank Indonesia has in many years had a significant depressing effect upon money supply.[11] In 1984, for example, broad money increased by Rp 3,300 bn (22 per cent), but only after allowing for a reduction in net credit to government (i.e. increased deposits) of Rp 3,400 bn. Thus government operations can have a considerable stabilising impact on monetary policy. Movements of state-enterprise deposits have also been used as a policy instrument. By shifting deposits from commercial banks into holdings of Bank Indonesia securities, commercial banks lose rupiah reserves and eventually require the repatriation of offshore foreign assets, an operation used to stabilise foreign-exchange outflows and to support the exchange rate in 1987.

Whilst many countries have variants of balanced budget rules, Indonesia is one of the few where the rhetoric is close to reality. The level of tax and non-tax receipts does appear to set a binding ceiling on the actual level of expenditure rather than the budgeted level. During the 1986 fiscal year, a fall in oil prices dramatically cut tax revenue from a predicted Rp 24,000 bn to Rp 16,000 bn. However, cuts in capital expenditures of Rp 2,500 and income in foreign grants and loans meant that the effect of the oil shock on net financing from Bank Indonesia was limited to Rp 2,000 bn. This fiscal austerity occurred despite nearly Rp 10,000 bn in government deposits at Bank Indonesia. From the monetary viewpoint, the conservatism of expenditure policy has been an important factor in maintaining or improving monetary control. There are social costs associated with such a policy, such as the delayed provision of urgently required social and physical infrastructure.

Two factors are central to explaining this fiscal conservatism. First, the experience of near economic collapse in the mid-1960s, and second, the strength of an economic technocratic group within the government (see Woo and Nasution 1990: ch. 3). It is likely that neither factor alone is a sufficient explanation.

In 1965, the year before Soeharto came to power, inflation was 595 per cent, government expenditure was 163 per cent greater than revenue, and Indonesia defaulted on its foreign debts. The root of the problem was simply monetisation of government deficits and government direction of credit to state enterprises and supporters in the private sector. In 1965, money growth (M1) was 283 per cent, and a sharp decline in the real money supply suggested that the use of money as a store of value had almost disappeared. The centrepiece of the reform programme instituted in 1966 was a firm commitment to avoid monetising government deficits. Foreign-financed government deficits were also limited to the supply of concessional loans as private capital adopted a 'wait and see' attitude. As Woo and Nasution aptly comment:

Soeharto obviously understood his first lesson in macroeconomic management because his balanced budget principle has never been compromised during his administration. To Soeharto, a prudent fiscal policy is understood to mean a 'balanced' budget.

(1989:59)

The second element of conservatism is the strong influence of a close-knit group of neo-classical economic policy-makers in the Ministries of Finance and Planning (BAPPENAS) and Bank Indonesia.[12] This group rose to prominence because of their competence in design and implementation of the 1966 adjustment programme and because of strong support for their policies from sources of external funding such as the IMF, the World Bank and the intergovernmental donor group, IGGI. Their influence was sustained, however, even when concessional funding was less crucial, as proven competence, for example in the resolution of the Pertamina crisis in 1975 (see below), led to continued patronage from President Soeharto.

In contrast to other developing economies, state-owned enterprises in Indonesia have not generally been used as a back door to uncontrolled credit expansion, despite comprising a large section of the formal economy. Ironically, a key factor in this control was the crisis of Pertamina, the state-owned oil conglomerate,[13] in 1975. Pertamina had rapidly expanded its non-oil investments by short- and medium-term foreign borrowing (the total outstanding amounting to perhaps US$10 bn at end-1974). IMF and World Bank concern at Pertamina's financial position with rising interest rates led to the imposition of restrictions on short-term borrowing. Pertamina defaulted on loan repayments in February 1975 and Bank Indonesia assumed responsibility for managing Pertamina's external debt portfolio. As a result, both foreign and domestic credits to other borrowers as well as government development expenditures were curtailed in succeeding years.

The political effect of the Pertamina crisis was to further strengthen the hand of the economic faction. They were given control of state-owned enterprise borrowing. Despite numerous examples of bail-outs and politically inspired lending to state-owned enterprises, the relatively early imposition of central authority upon state-enterprise borrowing limited the scale of foreign borrowing and also the share of total domestic credit to this sector. Effective legislative control of the government budget, combined with supervision of state-enterprise borrowing, has substantially reduced the scope for fiscal policy actions to destabilise monetary aggregates and monetary control.

Open capital account and financial flows

The open foreign capital account has created problems of control for monetary policy. The periodic emergence of speculative pressures has been the hallmark of the post-1983 reform period, as a result of exchange-rate uncertainty. Monetary policy instruments have had to be developed to offset the expansionary effect of inflows and to impose reserve-money contractions to stem outflows.

With the introduction of the Bank Indonesia Certificate (SBI) in 1984, Bank Indonesia moved to a position where it could, at least theoretically, intervene in the foreign-exchange market, without affecting the rupiah money supply (i.e. sterilised intervention, to buy [sell] foreign exchange and sell [buy] SBIs). In practice, this type of intervention was limited by the size of Bank Indonesia's reserves, and more importantly the size of the SBI market. Although the market for SBIs has developed, it remains small and there is still limited secondary trading, so the linkages between foreign flows and domestic money supply remain close.

Rather than intervening in the foreign-exchange market, Bank Indonesia sets rates at which it will buy and sell foreign exchange in the spot or swap market, and then stands to buy or sell whatever amounts are offered to and demanded from it in these two markets. Its principal short-run instruments are adjustments in the posted exchange rates and adjustments in reserve money to affect liquidity and short-term interest rates.

Exchange-rate adjustments, as we have noted, were quite erratic before 1988, often moving in perverse ways to try to influence, or 'fool', the market. Since early 1988, Bank Indonesia has followed a policy of fairly steady depreciation of the rupiah against the US dollar at 4–5 per cent per annum, and has looked to adjustments in reserve money and short-term interest rates as the principal instrument of policy.

In late 1988, a massive reduction in bank reserves through required purchases of SBIs by all banks raised interest rates and reversed a foreign-exchange outflow arising mainly from uncertainty over the expected package of financial regulatory changes. Throughout 1989, following the regulatory policy changes, monetary policy was more benign, permitting a steady expansion in reserve money and a decline in interest rates.

Nevertheless, given the open foreign-exchange system and the policy of steady depreciation of the exchange rate, domestic short-term interest rates must be kept within a narrow range of foreign interest rates plus the expected rate of depreciation. If domestic interest rates are pushed too low, foreign exchange will flow out, and if they are high enough, foreign exchange will flow in. This provides a fairly clear and simple rule for the management of monetary policy so long as there are no major shocks from the world economy or departures from the government's balanced budget policy.

9

BANGLADESH, 1973-85

Ashok Parikh

INTRODUCTION

Bangladesh is one of the least developed countries. It is a predominantly agricultural economy, with 60 per cent of GNP and 80 per cent of employment located in this sector (Taslim 1980: 28). Its monetised economy, which refers to the modern industrial sector, has two elements: the organised and the unorganised money markets. The organised money market includes the Bangladesh Bank, private and nationalised commercial banks (both foreign and domestic) and various other financial intermediaries, such as specialised banks and insurance companies. The Bangladesh Bank is the institution formally responsible for monetary policy, but the government plays a dominant role and most policy decisions are made by the Governor in close consultation with the Minister of Finance. The Bangladesh Bank assists the government in its borrowing operations. The structure of interest rates in the organised sector is highly diversified and subject to widespread government regulation. The unorganised money market dominates the provision of credit in the rural areas and is made up of local money-lenders, landlords and commission agents. Interest rates tend to be very much higher in the unorganised segment and there is little in the way of linkage with the organised money market (Wahid 1986). Over the period studied, Bangladesh has operated a very cautious policy at the behest of the IMF. Because of very low levels of monetary expansion it may be hard to detect the linkages which would be apparent in a more inflationary economy.

The period 1973-85 can be divided into three sub-periods: the Mujib regime (January 1972-August 1975), the Zia regime (November 1975-May 1981), and the Ershad regime (from March 1982). Monetary growth for the different regimes is analysed separately.

STATE OF THE ECONOMY

Bangladesh experienced relatively low GDP growth: 2.4 per cent per annum in the period 1965-80 and a somewhat higher rate in the 1980s, of 3.7 per

165

cent per annum (see Table 9.1). Inflation rates have averaged over 10 per cent for the entire period, although inflation measured by the GDP deflator was negative in 1975 and 1976 (fiscal years) and dipped below 10 per cent in 1982 and 1985 (Table 9.2). Table 9.3 summarises the growth of monetary and credit aggregates from 1972 onwards.

During the period 1973–75, the Mujib government resorted to large-scale deficit financing through money creation, mainly to finance increased expenditure for the rehabilitation of war-affected people and for the re-construction of the economy. The very high rates of inflation (38.5 to 81.0 per cent) during this period can also be associated with domestic crop losses and rapid rises in import prices. Large increases in bank credits to government and to public sector enterprises were the main reasons for an increase in money supply. The rapid increase in public sector credits was related to large losses suffered by nationalised industries (the jute industry in par-ticular). The increase in bank credits to the private sector was relatively small. Foreign-exchange reserves decreased substantially, and this produced a slightly contractionary effect on the money supply.

In the post-Mujib era good harvests and the decline in import prices

Table 9.1 Bangladesh economic indicators

Average annual rates of growth (%)	1965–80	1980–6
Inflation	14.9	11.2
GDP	2.4	3.7
Agricultural output	1.5	2.7
Industrial output	3.8	4.6
Services	3.4	4.7
Private consumption	2.7	3.5
Gross domestic investment	0.0	3.6

Share in total GDP	1965	1986
Agriculture	53	47
Industry	11	14
Manufacturing	5	8
Services	36	39

	1970	1986
Current account balance (US$m.)	−114	−538
Receipts of workers' remittances (US$m.)	–	586
Total external debt (US$m.)	–	7,868
1986: Population: 103.2 million.		
GNP per capita: US$160.		

Source: World Bank, *World Development Report* (1988).

Table 9.2 Percentage change in prices

Fiscal year beginning	CPI[a]	GDP deflator	Wholesale
1973	38.5	40.4	46.5
1974	61.9	71.2	56.0
1975	−6.9	−23.8	−12.6
1976	0.5	−3.4	−2.2
1977	15.5	30.5	10.2
1978	10.2	12.9	3.9
1979	15.4	13.1	21.2
1980	11.9	10.3	10.9
1981	12.9	12.8	10.6
1982	6.9	5.0	11.1
1983	9.9	16.4	6.3
1984	11.8	10.3	8.4
1985	8.9	5.6	−3.9
1986	11.5	12.3	10.1

Source: Bangladesh Bank; Bangladesh Bureau of Statistics; *Monthly Statistical Bulletin of Bangladesh*.
Note: a Dhaka, middle-class index.

Table 9.3 Percentage change in money and bank credit

Calendar year	Narrow money[a]	Broad money[a]	Bank credit[a]	Interest rates Advance	Interest rates Deposit	Exchange rate
1972	68.83	71.08	−	−	−	−
1973	23.72	23.37	33.95	−	−	7.742
1974	17.18	18.73	29.64	−	−	8.113
1975	−1.06	2.87	8.68	−	−	12.019
1976	7.56	18.11	17.97	11.29	4.31	15.397
1977	34.33	30.12	28.90	11.23	4.27	15.375
1978	20.86	21.05	21.25	10.57	4.23	15.106
1979	14.28	20.89	30.06	11.04	9.39	15.552
1980	19.77	18.84	24.42	11.53	4.97	15.454
1981	14.37	19.65	21.30	13.24	7.21	17.987
1982	12.59	18.66	36.77	13.66	7.54	22.118
1983	32.24	41.90	15.76	13.69	7.68	24.615
1984	28.29	30.40	34.84	13.82	8.33	25.354
1985	−	−	−	−	−	27.990
1986	−	−	−	−	−	30.270
1987	−	−	−	−	−	30.631

Source: Bangladesh Bank.
Note: a Percentage changes from de-seasonalised December monthly figures.

reduced the rate of inflation, improved the balance of payments, and also dramatically improved law and order.

During the Zia regime (1977–81), both bank credits and money supply increased more rapidly. The average annual increase in narrow money was about 21 per cent. Domestic bank credit also increased, at an average annual rate of 25 per cent, and on the fiscal front, the expenditure/GDP ratio increased from 8 to 17 points during the years 1976–81. However, as the economy experienced sustained economic growth, the increased money supply did not create inflationary pressures (Table 9.2).

The monetary and fiscal policies during the Ershad regime (from 1982 onwards) were similar to those of the Zia regime. Both the Zia and Ershad governments brought inflation and balance-of-payments deficits under control but they also benefited from higher levels of agricultural production, favourable world markets and a friendly world community (Hossain 1988). Domestic credit has been the main factor in higher rates of monetary growth. During the Zia and Ershad regimes, domestic credits to the private sector substantially increased, although credits to the public sector were reduced.

In 1979–80 and 1980–1, the deficit rose because government expenditure rose relative to revenue. Much of this deficit was financed by a sharp rise (29 per cent) in the availability of foreign assistance but there remained a large domestic resource deficit which was financed by heavy recourse to deficit financing. Net outlays on food rose as food grains were imported to minimise the impact of a severe drought.

Osmani et al. (1986) have found that, contrary to the assumption implicit in the IMF stabilisation programmes, unplanned deficit financing was not the predominant factor behind the breach of overall credit ceilings in Bangladesh. Moreover, in the two years when this did occur, the unplanned deficit financing was more a consequence of uncontrollable exogenous factors than an outcome of fiscal extravagance. It was found that deficit financing did not lead to an absolute reduction in private sector credit; it merely took a share of incremental resources. As a result, the private sector enjoyed an increasing access to real resources in both absolute and relative terms. The result seems to have been an example of 'reverse crowding-out', i.e. resources were pulled away from the government sector to the private sector through the process of inflation-induced transfer of resources.

During fiscal years 1982–4, the money supply increased by 28, 42 and 26 per cent respectively, as against the projected increases of 15, 15 and 16.5 per cent (Sohrabuddin 1986). The main reason for such large expansions of liquidity was the credit expansion to the private sector induced by the shift in policy towards increasing liberalisation and privatisation of the economy. Price increases were less than expected, mainly because of the increase in the asset demand for money. Smaller upward adjustments in administered prices and better management of the economy from the supply side were among the other factors which helped contain the increase in prices.

THE PROCESS OF MONETISATION

The process of monetisation since 1971 (see Table 9.4) has shown increased financial deposits (the share of time deposits in total deposits) and financial broadening (total deposits in GDP). However, high inflation in the mid-1970s is likely to have caused the sharp decline of deposits relative to GDP during the two years to 1974/5. The process of regaining confidence in taka-denominated financial assets can be seen over the next five or six years. From 1983, there was a more marked increase in the share of time deposits and a reduction in cash holdings, and the ratio of deposits to GDP rose to over 20 per cent. This is still comparatively low, however, even for low-income developing countries.

The improvement in intermediation during the 1980s can, at least in part, be associated with the liberalisation of the banking sector undertaken in 1983 which allowed the creation of private banks. The banking system now includes some 5,500 bank branches. The network is dominated by four state-owned retail banks (49 per cent of whose shares were offered to the public through the stock exchange in December 1986), the state-owned development banks, ten private national banks and seven foreign banks.

The state-owned banks' networks extend throughout the rural areas, but the 33 per cent of bank branches located in the urban areas distributed 73 per cent of credits outstanding in 1988 (*Far Eastern Economic Review*, 16 November 1989, 71–2).

Table 9.4 Indicators of monetisation (%)

Fiscal year beginning	Share of currency in total deposits	Share of time deposits in total	Share of total deposits in GDP
1972	40	58	16
1973	37	56	12
1974	29	58	8
1975	30	61	10
1976	29	61	13
1977	30	61	12
1978	29	62	12
1979	28	63	12
1980	29	64	14
1981	25	67	13
1982	25	70	16
1983	23	70	20
1984	22	71	20
1985	18	71	23
1986	17	74	23

Source: Bangladesh Bank; *Economic Trends*.

The reforms of the banking sector increased competition for deposits (in the form of improved services rather than interest-rate competition) and the development of new private Islamic banks would appear likely to further the process of monetisation of the economy.

MONETARY POLICY INSTRUMENTS AND CONTROL

Monetary targets and instruments

Monetary policy in Bangladesh has tried to achieve two conflicting objectives: controlling overall monetary expansion and ensuring an adequate flow of credit to the priority sectors. The principal instruments for achieving these objectives, namely, credit ceilings and reserve requirements, have not always been successful in reconciling the conflict between them.

The level and structure of interest rates have been regulated by the authorities since independence, to limit the cost of credit in general and to the priority sectors in particular. However, deposit rates are kept at relatively high levels in order to mobilise financial savings. In 1986–7, the interest rate on deposits was 8.59 per cent, while interest on loans was 14.7 per cent.

The basic framework of monetary policy is to fix a target level of money supply (broad money, M2), and to use various credit control and support measures to contain the monetary expansion within that level. At the same time credit is allocated to various sectors in such a way as to ensure the deployment of scarce bank credit in the best possible manner for increasing production, employment and real income.

In Bangladesh, the target growth rate of money supply is obtained on the basis of the expected rate of inflation and planned growth in real GDP, giving a target level of money supply. The rate of monetisation in the subsistence sector is taken into account and the rate of change of income velocity of money is assumed to be constant. The target level is discussed with the IMF and consultation sometimes leads to changes in targets. The actual change in money supply is likely to differ from the target, since the instruments for achieving the target are not precise. Following determination of the target level of money supply, the level of net foreign assets and other (net) liabilities of the banking system are projected to estimate what is called the safe limit to credit expansion.

Monetary policy in Bangladesh is restricted mainly to the use of direct or selective controls. The reasons for this are:

1   that the economy has a large non-monetised sector;
2   that commercial banks operate with excess reserves which vary seasonally;
3   that the money market is underdeveloped and unorganised, hence the market for securities is very narrow and confined to institutional investors;

4   that the rate of return on investment is very high, and investment demand for bank credit is interest-inelastic;

5   that the values of various monetary variables are supply-determined (Huda 1986).

Open-market operations   The share of government securities in total securities outstanding declined from 74 per cent in 1974 to 54 per cent in 1984. This is largely due to the broadening of the securities market through increased issues of private securities (Table 9.5).

It is interesting to note that despite their low yields, banks' investment in government securities has increased substantially. This investment by the commercial banks does not fall within credit ceiling regulations, and can be used as collateral for advances. Thus, both liquidity and credit policy have encouraged commercial banks to hold government securities (Huda 1986).

Discount-rate management   The Bangladesh Bank provides discounting facilities and makes loans to the commercial banks. The bank rate was raised from 5 to 8 per cent in 1974 and then remained unchanged for six years. It was raised to 10.5 per cent in October 1980, and to 11 per cent in 1985. It is clear that the discount rate is an inactive instrument of monetary policy.

In the initial years, when the discount rate was at a low level, use of the facility was also low. The upward movement did not discourage commercial banks from borrowing from the Bangladesh Bank, because the revisions were accompanied by simultaneous increases in commercial bank loan rates. For example, in 1980, when the bank rate increased by 2.5 points, it was accompanied by an increase of 4.5 points in the commercial bank lending

Table 9.5 Bangladesh securities: stocks outstanding (taka m.)

Year ending	Government securities	Foreign securities	Private securities	Total
June 1974	1,192.8	–	473.9	1,666.7
1975	1,547.8	0.30	751.4	2,285.5
1976	1,754.2	2.00	801.9	2,558.1
1977	2,454.0	–	845.5	3,302.2
1978	2,507.4	–	1,351.4	3,858.8
1979	2,609.7	–	2,101.3	4,711.0
1980	2,354.1	–	2,391.2	4,745.7
1981	3,328.0	–	2,185.6	6,513.6
1982	8,623.0	–	3,628.7	7,251.7
1983	6,193.7	2.1	4,112.8	10,308.6
1984	7,264.0	2.1	6,240.9	13,507.0

Source: *Bangladesh Bank Bulletin* (1985).

rate, resulting in a higher spread than previously in favour of the commercial banks.

Interest-rate policy The effect of negative real interest rates on savings seems to be small; in the absence of any statistics on other financial asset holdings, it is difficult to conclude that there is asset substitution. However, the increase in the price of real estate seems to indicate that people are bidding up its prices. Like deposit rates, lending rates were not changed in line with the rate of inflation.

Deposit interest rates were relatively low during the 1974–80 period, averaging 4 per cent. Real interest rates fell because of changes in inflation and were sharply negative during the inflationary bursts of 1974 and 1977. In the 1980s nominal deposit rates have risen to around 8 per cent and real interest rates became only moderately negative (Table 9.6).

Table 9.6 Interest rates

Fiscal year beginning	Interest on deposits	Rate of inflation[a]	Interest on loans	Interest differential
1974	3.51	70.21	11.28	7.77
1975	4.23	23.75	11.62	7.39
1976	4.32	3.28	11.03	6.71
1977	4.22	30.51	10.66	6.44
1978	4.27	12.99	11.12	6.85
1979	4.31	13.03	11.04	6.73
1980	6.98	10.81	13.07	6.09
1981	7.29	12.58	13.53	6.24
1982	7.36	4.90	13.55	6.19
1983	8.11	16.62	13.75	5.64
1984	8.13	10.02	14.50	6.37
1985	8.56	8.91	14.66	6.10
1986	8.59	11.51	14.70	6.11

Note: a Based on Dhaka cost-of-living index.

Selective credit control Credit control has been used as an instrument of monetary policy in Bangladesh on a wide scale. The case for selective credit control policies rests on the argument that financial intermediation does not by itself ensure optimal use of resources. Financial institutions tend to prefer projects which maximise private profitability, as compared to social welfare. Credit control policies have been instituted to divert funds to high priority areas, and particularly to help the self-employed on income-distribution grounds. There are various techniques to implement selective credit policies, including credit ceilings, interest rate subsidies, and differential margin requirements.

The Banking Control Department of the Bangladesh Bank is responsible for formulating various credit control measures which are passed on to the commercial banks for implementation. Selective credit control requires the diversion of supervision to non-priority, but more profitable, sectors.

PROBLEMS OF MONETARY POLICY IMPLEMENTATION

Monetary and real factors influencing inflation

From a structuralist point of view, bottlenecks in agricultural production and cost-push pressures via the balance of payments can cause inflation. Rising food prices can work through the cost of living index to increase wage demands. The demand for food in Bangladesh has increased dramatically, principally as a result of rapid population growth. While there have been efforts to increase agricultural production by introducing high-yielding varieties and improving irrigation and fertiliser technology, growth of output has nevertheless failed to keep pace with the growth of demand. This failure has been reflected in increased food prices, despite the widespread price controls exercised by the government.

The balance of payments has also tended to fuel inflation. Although the export sector has grown steadily since 1971, increases in imports – partly a result of ambitious government programmes – and rising import prices have resulted in persistent balance-of-payments deficits. Pressure from the IMF has at times led the government to devalue the currency, thus generating further inflationary pressures in the economy.

While the problems described above may raise the price level, the question remains of why inflation should persist. One explanation is that these price increases are either sustained or accelerated by the struggle between different classes (including the government) to maintain their respective real incomes and relative positions. Sunkel (1960: 111) and Parikh, Booth and Sundrum (1985) argue that budget deficits tend to rise because of continual attempts by the government to maintain real fiscal expenditures. In the absence of a well-developed financial market, the budget deficit is financed almost entirely from new money. Thus from a structuralist viewpoint, budget deficits and consequent expansions in the money supply are not autonomous. Rather, food shortages, rising imports and devaluation generate domestic inflation and subsequent efforts by government to maintain nominal fiscal expenditure in a period of rising prices produce budget deficits. Borrowing through the central bank increases the money supply, thus causing a further rise in the price level.

Monetarists argue that while an inflationary spell can be initiated by, for example, a shortage of food, its continuance is impossible without a supportive monetary expansion. Under a policy of tightly controlled money supply, an inadequate food supply can, except for a temporary disequilibrium, only alter the structure of relative prices without raising the general price level significantly (Kirkpatrick and Nixson 1976).

Structuralists generally claim that too tight a hold over the money supply may be damaging in the long run (by hindering growth, for example) but they do not deny that some degree of control is desirable. The key issue is the extent to which the monetary authorities are able to control the money supply. At the heart of the monetarist argument is the assumption of an exogenous money supply which can be tightly controlled by the monetary authorities in a developing economy. The following sections discuss the monetarist/structuralist controversy by examining whether the assumption of an exogenous money supply is valid.

Determination of the money supply

Data on the Dhaka cost-of-living index (P) and narrow money supply (M) are available on a month-by-month basis for the period November 1973 to November 1986, a total of 157 observations. There is a strong time-trend in both series. The monthly exponential rate of growth was 1.26 per cent for M and 0.84 per cent for P. The income velocity of money using annual data (July–June year) shows a strong downward trend declining from 9.76 in 1974–5 to 3.80 in 1984–5. This is obtained by using GDP at current market prices divided by broad money.

While we cannot establish exogeneity via causality tests, the observation that prices cause (in the Granger sense) money supply to rise can be used to refute the exogeneity of the money supply. The Geweke approach was employed to test for Granger causality (Geweke 1982). We concluded that for Bangladesh during the 1970s and 1980s there is evidence of causality running from prices to money supply, but no evidence of either contemporaneous causality or feedback in the opposite direction from money to prices. The estimation period was 1974(6) to 1986(10). Equations were also estimated using a broad money measure, M2. These results also found feedback from prices to money. Detailed results are available in Parikh and Starmer (1988).

The Bangladesh Bank administers credit policy by controlling the level of net domestic assets which it regards as an exogenous policy variable. The definition of exogeneity is not a lack of Granger causality but, operationally, that the Bank believes it can control the variable through the policy instruments at its command. We therefore decided to investigate whether the net domestic assets variable shows a lack of Granger causality. Hence, we related P and net domestic assets (NDA), using the Geweke framework. Data on net domestic assets were available in a consistent series from July 1982 to June 1987. The monthly exponential growth rates of NDA and P were 1.67 per cent and 0.82 per cent respectively. We found that net domestic assets 'Granger-cause' the price index with a fifteen-month lag. Similarly, the price index 'Granger-causes' net domestic assets with a lag of eighteen months. This is a case of two-way feedback causality, and neither net domestic assets nor prices can be treated as exogenous variables.

Our results indicate at least some pressure of excess demand; however, it seems unlikely that all monetary expansions will feed through directly to prices. Quite often, physical resources are under-utilised, owing to lack of finance and credit. Under these circumstances, credit expansion will tend to feed through to expansions in the supply of goods and services, rather than to inflation. In the case of Bangladesh, there is some evidence that this has happened. For example, for the years 1982–6, actual growth in money supply greatly exceeded planned growth while inflation rates were smaller than those predicted *ex post* by the quantity theory of money.

The explanation for the feedback from prices to net domestic assets may lie in Bangladesh Bank's procedure for fixing money supply targets. The Bank uses the quantity theory of money which gives the target growth of money supply as:

$$\dot{M} = \dot{P} + \dot{Y} - \dot{V}$$

where $\dot{M}$ is the growth in money supply which consists of a weighted average of growth in net domestic assets (excluding other liabilities) plus growth in net foreign assets, $\dot{P}$ is expected inflation, $\dot{Y}$ is the expected growth in real income, and $\dot{V}$ is the growth of income velocity of money.

Assuming that net foreign assets are exogenous, desired expansion of the money supply will be brought about by increases in net domestic assets. If the expected rate of inflation is proxied by previous rates of inflation, this yields a straightforward appearance of Granger causality running from prices to net domestic assets.

The Bangladesh Bank may have the ability at any point in time to adjust the net domestic assets to achieve its desired monetary targets. However, the extent to which the targets themselves are governed by expectations based on past information raises a question over the extent to which this can be regarded as 'control' over the economy as opposed to a fairly constrained response to existing economic conditions. Although the monetary authorities in Bangladesh take the view that they exercise control over the money supply, it may be more satisfactory to treat money as an endogenous variable.

The above arguments and statistical tests (see Appendix to this chapter) tend to suggest that both money supply and prices should be treated endogenously in an econometric model using annual data. On monthly data, lags shorter than twelve months can permit us to identify Granger causality running from prices to money, thus refuting the strict exogeneity of money which can justify the structural approach. Both money supply and prices could be Granger-caused by income, but this is not investigated because of lack of data on income.

The empirical results obtained from the model suggest some important policy implications.

1   Over the estimation period, Bangladesh has repeatedly suffered as a result of droughts, floods and famine. We believe that harvest failures may be identified as a prime cause of monetary expansions. Food shortages entail rising budget deficits (as government expenditure on development rises faster than revenues) and the accommodating policy to cope with the demand of the private sector for credit puts further upward pressure on the money supply.
2   There does not seem to be a significant impact of excess supply of real money balances on real expenditures.
3   Imports were significantly influenced by import and domestic prices, while exports were restricted on account of lack of capacity. Some capacity expansion may be possible if the necessary credit is forthcoming.

Development policy which is based on fiscal deficits cannot sustain economic growth in the long run, and inflation is likely to have an adverse effect on long-term investment. However, it does not follow that a tight monetary policy can control inflation when that inflation is caused by structural factors like harvest failures and resulting food crises. One possible response to this problem is to adopt measures which reduce the instability of food grain production. But as this is primarily the result of environmental factors, it is unlikely that the situation can be remedied in the short run. Nevertheless, the message of this study is that the Bangladesh Bank should be allowed to undertake a slightly greater level of monetary expansion than it has in the past after problems like harvest failures.

Money and the balance of payments

Table 9.7 shows the movements of current account and trade balance deficits in value terms and also as percentages of exports of goods and services. (The current account deficits are small as a percentage of GDP because the trade flows themselves are small relative to GDP.)

The Bangladesh taka was devalued against sterling by 53 per cent immediately after separation from West Pakistan in 1971. It remained overvalued, however, and the extent of overvaluation increased with the rapid increase in domestic prices during 1973–5. This overvaluation provided disincentives to jute traders and growers and induced smuggling of raw jute and food grains to India.

The external oil shocks, in 1973 and 1979, led to serious balance of payments problems. In 1974–5, the current account deficits were exceptionally high, at about 150 per cent of total exports. Lower exports, shortfalls in domestic production and higher import prices contributed to the serious

Table 9.7 Foreign trade

Fiscal year	Export price index	Import price index	Commodity terms of trade	Current account balance	Trade balance	Current account as % exports[a]	Trade balance as % of exports[a]
	(Indices 1973–4 = 100)			(US$ m.)		(%)	
1973–4	100	100	100	−240	−540	−57	−128
1974–5	160	168	63	−475	−625	−112	−147
1975–6	131	221	59	−606	−848	−153	−213
1976–7	115	201	57	−279	−420	−57	−87
1977–8	127	198	64	−283	−1,019	−50	−180
1978–9	146	203	72	−386	−1,340	−56	−196
1979–80	182	236	77	−84	−1,726	−10	−202
1980–1	221	300	70	−757	−2,353	−70	−218
1981–2	181	353	51	−1,014	−2,435	−97	−233
1982–3	156	368	42	−656	−2,221	−65	−213
1983–4	163	350	47	−60	−1,931	−6	−198
1984–5	193	339	57	−529	−2,340	−44	−194
1985–6	225	339	66	−578	−2,300	−45	−180

Source: IMF, *International Financial Statistics; Bangladesh Economic Survey, 1984–5.*
Note: a Exports of goods and services.

balance-of-payments problem. The debt-servicing ratio of Bangladesh has risen to about 10 per cent of total export earnings. This ratio is relatively low compared with ratios in other aid-dependent countries, mainly because of the large component of grants in Bangladesh's overall aid (IMF, *Bangladesh Economic Survey, 1984–5*).

During the Zia regime (November 1975–May 1981) Bangladesh did not face serious balance-of-payments difficulties until the oil shock of 1979. Good harvests in 1975–6 and 1976–7 substantially reduced food imports and, except for 1979–80, these imports remained relatively low. The government provided various types of incentives for export promotion and, as a result, exports of non-traditional items increased significantly. The Zia government also adopted a liberal import policy.

Although current account deficits were high, foreign reserves rose in 1978–9 because of a larger volume of foreign aid and remittances. In 1979–80 and 1980–1, the balance of payments came under severe pressure, resulting in a fall in foreign-exchange reserves. This was not only because of the rise in the oil price. In 1980–1, the inflow of aid declined significantly due, *inter alia*, to recession in donor countries. The delay in the availability of food aid led the government to borrow from foreign commercial banks for the first time. Private transfers from Bangladesh overseas workers did not increase as had happened following the first oil shock, owing to less buoyant economic activity in the OPEC countries.

During the Ershad regime (from March 1982) the balance of payments showed a significant improvement, with an overall surplus in 1982–3. The important contributory factors were a marked increase in overseas workers' remittances, an increase in export earnings, a reduction in the service-account deficit and an increased inflow of loans and grants. Non-food imports were 16 per cent lower in 1983–4 than in 1981–2, reflecting in large measure a depressed demand for finished goods and industrial raw materials. The country's commodity terms of trade improved by 11 per cent in 1983–4, reflecting an increase in export prices. The balance of payments, however, recorded overall deficits of US$29 m. in 1983–4 and US$122 m. in 1984–5. This deterioration was largely due to a significant decline in private and official transfers, an increase in debt payment, an increase in the service-account deficit and a stagnant level of aid and loan disbursement. But it coincided with a marked improvement in export receipts during the period 1983–5.

IMPACT OF AGRICULTURAL AND INDUSTRIAL POLICY ON DEMAND FOR CREDIT

In Bangladesh, agricultural production is very much governed by the weather, and the region is prone to cyclone, drought, floods and natural disasters. In August 1972, the country suffered a severe drought which affected the production of the major agricultural crops. Total loss of potential output was estimated at about 20 per cent of agricultural output in 1972–3. Floods in the last quarter of 1973 and during March–September 1974 were the most serious in the country's history. They created food shortages (Ahmed 1984) and these problems were compounded by large-scale smuggling of foodgrains and other essential goods to India. Foodgrain producers became major hoarders, withholding foodgrains from the market. The government's distribution system failed to deal with the inflationary situation and contributed towards the intensification of the problem.

The Mujib government faced substantial budget deficits owing to high subsidies on foodgrains, petroleum products and agricultural inputs, which were justified on the grounds that they would protect poor consumers and farmers. However, Islam (1977) and Islam (1980) considered that food subsidies were used for political patronage. The Mujib government also nationalised industries which incurred heavy financial losses.

The Zia government emphasised rural development. Adequate and smooth distribution of agricultural inputs as well as better weather conditions jointly contributed to an increase in agricultural production. Agricultural policies were designed to encourage foodgrain production, reduce the budgetary costs of agricultural subsidies and enable the private sector to play a more active role in agricultural development. A large amount of credit was made available to farmers to help meet the higher costs of fertilisers and irrigation equipment. The private sector was given more opportunity to compete with the public sector in importing, marketing and servicing minor irrigation equipment and in the wholesale and retail distribution of fertiliser.

In June 1982, barriers on domestic and foreign investments were relaxed and removed. Most of the nationalised industries were returned to their original owners. A number of steps were undertaken to improve the performances of the remaining public sector corporations and industrial enterprises, including the reorganisation of public enterprises, flexibility in pricing, capital restructuring, and programmes aimed at setting up an improved system for monitoring performance.

A large number of small-scale industrial units were set up with the help of cheap credits provided by the industrial and agricultural banks. In 1984, industrial policy widened the scope for domestic and foreign private investments. However, the volume of foreign and large-scale investment was much lower than expected.

The main objective of Bangladesh Shilpa Bank is to accelerate industrial sector growth by providing long-term loans, short-term bridging loans and working capital to projects financed by the Bank initially. Bangladesh Shilpa Rin Sangstha was established in 1972 for the purpose of providing credit facilities and other related assistance to industrial enterprises. Bangladesh Krishi Bank is one of the pioneering financial institutions in the field of rural finance. It extends credit facilities for the development of agriculture. Its range of activities varies from financing crops to agro-based industries, marketing and exports. Apart from its loan activities, the Bank also performs other ancillary activities, e.g. collecting deposits, providing advisory services to borrowers and extending foreign-exchange facilities. Table 9.8 suggests a very rapid rate of growth (22 per cent per annum) by Bangladesh Krishi and Shilpa banks. Disbursements of short-term agricultural credit increased by 77 per cent in fiscal year 1983 and by 66 per cent in fiscal year 1984. Medium-term credit increased less rapidly. Total disbursement of agricultural credit rose from 4.2 bn takas to 10 bn by 1984. Despite this very rapid growth in the 1980s, total disbursement of agricultural credit amounted to only 4 per cent of agricultural GDP in 1986 (World Bank 1987). Poor recovery of loans, however, has hampered the continued expansion of agricultural credit.

Bank credit in Bangladesh is of two types – advances and bills purchased and discounted by banks; bills are the single most important form of assets held by the banks. Yields on these assets are much higher than those on government securities. At the end of December 1974, trade and commerce accounted for 36 per cent of total bank credit, followed by the manufacturing sector, which absorbed about a third of bank finance (Taheruddin 1977).

Table 9.8 Total advances of Bangladesh Krishi and Shilpa banks (taka m.)

1974	June	1,485.5
	December	1,543.4
1975	June	1,793.4
	December	1,925.9
1976	June	1,894.3
	December	1,975.8
1977	June	2,131.0
	December	2,330.4
1978	June	2,599.4
	December	2,757.2
1979	June	3,433.7
	December	3,966.6
1980	June	4,540.6
	December	5,008.8
1981	June	5,792.9
	December	6,868.3
1982	June	8,498.4
	December	9,488.6
1983	June	12,527.1
	December	12,600.7
1984	June	17,127.4
	December	15,109.4
1985	June	22,220.9
	December	22,388.1
1986	June	25,929.0
	December	24,594.7

Source: IMF, *Economic Survey, 1986–7.*

APPENDIX: ECONOMETRIC MODELS OF BANGLADESH'S MONETARY SECTOR

This section summarises previous attempts to construct models for Bangladesh in order to assess the impact of monetary policy upon real income, the price level and the balance of payments. Two models were constructed: (i) monetarist and (ii) structuralist with some monetarist characteristics. The second model, developed by Parikh and Starmer (1988), establishes Granger causality running from prices to money. Strict exogeneity of money (in the Granger sense) cannot be maintained.

Model based on monetarist views

The model is similar to that of Aghevli and Khan (1980) except that it was estimated in a discrete framework. The Bangladesh Bank has been following a monetary policy designed to regulate the expansion of bank credit to the levels warranted by the economy's productive requirements and further to control the direction in keeping with overall economic projections. Monetary policy has been restricted to the use of direct or selective credit controls.

The model contains four stochastic equations which determine real expenditures, the rate of inflation, imports and exports respectively. Four identities defining the money supply, nominal income, the balance of payments and the monetary base complete the model. Capital flows are assumed to be exogenous in this model, and excess demand for money can be satisfied through the trade account by an inflow of money (reserves) from abroad, which corresponds to the surplus in the balance of payments under the fixed exchange-rate system. Under a floating exchange rate system, the balance of payments surplus would tend to induce currency appreciation which would reduce the price level and hence the demand for money, wiping out the surplus. The opposite chain of events would follow an excess supply of money.

To see how the model functions under the assumption of the monetary approach, let us assume that the monetary authorities expand the monetary base by increasing their stock of assets (credit creation). The increase in the money supply will induce increased expenditures, raising the levels of both imports and national income. Assuming that increases in imports (which may depress income) do not offset the increase in expenditure, there will be upward pressure on prices, stimulating a number of simultaneous effects: the expected rate of inflation will be adjusted upwards, real national income will rise, imports will expand and exports will decline. As a result, the balance of payments will deteriorate, resulting in a loss of international reserves and hence a contraction in the monetary base. Thus a once-for-all increase in the domestic assets of the central bank will increase real income and the rate of inflation in the short run. However, in the long run, contractions in the monetary base via outflows of foreign reserves will reverse the process. The long-run rate of inflation will tend towards the world rate, while real income is exogenously determined by full capacity output.

We used (non-linear) two-stage least squares estimates, with data for the period 1972-3 to 1985-6. The procedure allowed us to employ within-equation restrictions but not cross-equation restrictions. Since estimation takes place equation by equation, 2SLS has the advantage that the effects of any specification error will be restricted to the equation where it occurs.

The import equation was the only one of the four estimated equations which contained any significant explanatory variables (the expenditure variable and the lagged imports variable).

Using three-stage estimates, again most parameters were insignificant; a number of the signs were different from the 2SLS estimates but they conformed more closely to expected signs. The significant 3SLS estimates (each correctly signed) were again for imports.

These results suggest that it is difficult to sustain the monetarist model empirically in the case of Bangladesh. One of the reasons why the statistical results are insignificant could be the cautious monetary policy operated in Bangladesh over the period, which might have obscured the linkages between macroeconomic variables. A related factor is the relatively large non-monetised sector of the Bangladesh economy, which defies empirical representation.

Model with endogenous money

In equation 1 the (annual) desired demand for real cash balances $M1^d/PC_t$ (where M1 stands for narrow money and PC for the Dhaka cost-of-living index) is a function of real income (RGDP). We assume that the expected rate of inflation captures the opportunity cost of holding real money balances[1] and proxy the expected rate of inflation by food price inflation (FINF) of the current and past year. This seems a plausible assumption, given the prime importance of food in the average household budget and the tendency for food prices to grow at a much quicker rate than the overall cost of living index. Hence we derive:

$$(1) \qquad \log\left(\frac{M1^d}{PC_t}\right) = a_0 + a_1 \log RGDP_t + a_2 FINF_t + a_3 FINF_{t-1}$$

Substituting the partial adjustment mechanism for the log of real money balances, we obtain

$$(2) \qquad \log\left(\frac{M1}{PC}\right)_t = a_0\sigma + a_1\sigma \log RGDP_t + a_2\sigma \log FINF_t$$
$$+ a_3\sigma \log FINF_{t-1} + (1-\sigma)\log\left(\frac{M1}{PC}\right)_{t-1}$$

In this formulation,[2] the income elasticity of demand for real money balances is a_i in the long run (and likewise for elasticities with respect to other variables). Income elasticity is expected to be positive, while the elasticities with respect to the inflation variables are expected to be negative.

In using real money balances as the dependent variable, we are assuming that the demand for nominal money is homogeneous of degree one (i.e. the demand for nominal money balances increases in the same proportion as the price level measured by the Dhaka cost-of-living index.)

The target variable for the Bangladesh Bank is broad money (M2), which is given by the definitional relationship:

$$(3) \qquad M2 = M1 + TD$$

where TD represents time deposits held by the non-bank public. In developing countries, time deposits are the most important asset for middle-class income earners. The holding of time deposits depends upon the return on such deposits, the level of real income and the inflation rate. In poor economies, high expected rates of inflation encourage saving among the well-off. (In Bangladesh, real estate may be a substitute asset, but as we have no source of data on real estate prices and so on, proxying the opportunity cost of time deposits by the expected rate of inflation is our only viable strategy.) Hence our equation is:

$$(4) \qquad (\frac{TD}{PC})_t = b_0 + b_1 DINT_t + b_2 logRGDP_t + b_3 (logPC_t - logPC_{t-1})$$

with $b_1 < 0$. An increase in the interest rate reduces the speculative demand for money. An inflationary variable can encourage asset-building, since higher amounts of assets will be required to maintain the same standard of living in future with the higher rates of inflation. The annual growth in time deposits of 21.1 per cent in nominal terms during the period 1974–5 to 1984–5 far exceeded the growth in currency and demand deposits (15.26 per cent) and the average annual rate of inflation (9.4 per cent). However, it should be pointed out that while the rate of return on time deposits varied from 3.51 to 8.13 per cent during the period, the rate of inflation was generally higher and hence the real rate of return on deposits was, for most of the time, negative. Real estate is not a highly liquid asset while time deposits are a short-term highly liquid asset.

The money supply

The money supply is modelled using the balance-sheet approach. In this approach the changes in money supply result from changes in (i) bank lending to the private sector, (ii) lending to the public sector and (iii) changes in foreign assets (equivalent to the balance-of-payments surplus/deficit and reserves). *Economic Trends* (1988) is the source for data on total net foreign assets (NFA), domestic net government credit (NEWPUB), other public domestic credit (OTHPUB), credit to the private sector (PRIV), and other items of liabilities and assets (OL). The last four components together are defined as net domestic assets (NDA) and net domestic assets plus net foreign assets yield the money supply (M2), as in equation 2.5.

$$(5) \qquad\qquad\qquad M2_t = NDA_t + NFA_t$$

$$(6) \qquad M1_t + TD_t = PRIV_t + NEWPUB_t + OTHPUB_t - OL_t + NFA_t$$

Equations 5 and 6 indicate the relations between the main components of the money supply and we subsequently present an equation for each of these components.

To understand the functioning of the model, let us suppose there is a harvest failure which produces an increase in food prices. The increase in the cost of living tends to raise the demand for currency and demand deposits and, to a certain extent, time deposits. The supply of bank credit to the private sector rises and government expenditure rises faster than government revenue, which puts upward pressure on the central bank to increase credit to the government sector. This will result in an increase in total money supply (M2) which will raise PC, the Dhaka cost-of-living index, further. Thus the money supply is the proximate cause of inflation, although the ultimate cause is to be found in the initial supply-side shock.

Data on money, prices, government revenues, government expenditures, and gross domestic product have strong time-trends. The collinearity, among explanatory variables is serious. We resist the temptation to drop variables in the presence of collinearity, and instead of equation-by-equation evaluation, the model was evaluated according to its performance in static and dynamic simulation.

A model of twelve behavioural equations and two identities was estimated using two-stage least squares. The model decomposed the money supply into its components following the balance-sheet approach and each component was separately modelled. Food and non-food prices were introduced as determinants of monetary expansion acting via fiscal deficits and the demand for bank credit (we assumed throughout that credit is demand determined). The money demand (M2) was explained by decomposing it into its components, i.e. currency and demand deposits (M1) and time deposits (quasi-money).

The model was estimated using 2SLS, and a serial correlation correction was performed on three equations. The model was then simulated, and on the whole the results were satisfactory in terms of various criteria. However, net foreign assets was a difficult variable to endogenise and our predictions were rather poor, given the volatile nature of foreign aid received by Bangladesh during the period 1974–87.

The model suggests that food price increases play an important explanatory role in monetary expansions. Of course, increases in money supply may well produce further inflationary pressures, although this is not necessarily the case at all times: there may be short time periods during which monetary expansions increase output. Our simulations of real output indicate that, historically, inflationary pressures and real output growth are all consistent with a structuralist framework in which food prices are identified as the leading factor underlying monetary expansions.

10

CHINA, 1949–88

Anita Santorum

INTRODUCTION

From 1949 to 1978 China's economy was based on a strict system of central planning. In the late 1970s, an ambitious programme of economic reform was started, which involved both market liberalisation and a partial decentralisation of production decisions to the level of enterprises and agricultural units.

The role of monetary policy and of the financial system, which was limited to providing financial support for the economic plan during the central planning period, changed rapidly and dramatically as a consequence of the reform. A different banking system structure and a more dynamic monetary policy were required to support the economic reform and to control excess demand. The transition period from planning to market system was the most dramatic stage of the reform. The way the banking system and the central bank's monetary policy responded to the state's withdrawal from some activities and the reductions in subsidies strongly influenced the success of the reform.

From this perspective, China's experience is relevant to both centrally planned economies (CPEs) and other developing countries at a similar stage of economic development and liberalisation. The first among the CPEs to set up a two-level banking system (in 1984), China has also been particularly successful, compared with other developing countries, in developing an extended banking system despite the size of the country. The high degree of dispersion of small banking institutions in rural areas seems to have provided an adequate basis both for the successful collection of savings during the period 1978–84 and for the extension of credit to small agricultural units, during the transition from the commune system to the production responsibility system (PRS).

In comparison with other developing countries, China had been an almost closed economy until 1978. The volume of trade was modest relative to GDP. Furthermore, balanced trade was the main target of external trade policy, achieved almost every year until 1978. After that date a rapid increase

185

in imports, mainly of equipment and technology, produced a considerable increase in the volume of trade and a trade deficit. The Chinese authorities, however, have always been concerned about running a trade deficit for prolonged periods and keep strict control over the size of both foreign-exchange reserves and foreign debt, being ready to cut imports drastically whenever reserves drop or foreign debt increases. China's move to market liberalisation was determined by domestic political and economic pressures, rather than by any economic policy advisers from the IMF.

Still based on a fixed exchange-rate system, most foreign trade operations are carried out by the Ministry of Foreign Trade or by companies under the strict supervision of the Ministry. Any difference between foreign and domestic prices is subsidised by the government. There is an illegal market in foreign-exchange certificates (FECs – currency notes for foreign visitors) in most cities, since they need to be used for purchases in Friendship Stores, and in most hotels and expensive restaurants. The unofficial exchange rate in 1987 was between 170 and 200 RMB (Ren Min Bi = people's money) for 100 FEC. In some coastal cities and areas near Hong Kong and the special economic zones there is also an illegal market in US and HK dollars. The secondary market for foreign exchange appeared only around 1983, but it developed fast in the richest areas of the country. Its size is unknown; it is believed, however, still to be of only limited importance.

Before the economic reform, the role of the banking system and of monetary policy was limited to accommodating the economic plan finan-cially and to controlling excess demand in the consumer goods market. After the economic reform, the banking system gained rapidly in importance, with a role in mobilising funds and providing finance for enterprises and agri-cultural units. Monetary policy, however, was still less important than other economic instruments, and its main target remained the control of inflation. Despite the introduction of reserve requirements and interest on loans to specialised banks, the monetary policy of the People's Bank was still based on a vertical system of credit control.

This chapter aims to describe the role of the banking system and monetary policy in China, both before and during the economic reform, giving an evaluation of the effectiveness of monetary policy over the whole period 1949–88, with particular reference to the targets and effects of monetary policy after 1978. The next section looks at the structure and role of the banking system and how the banking system and the central bank's monetary policy have responded to changes in the economy and in economic policy from 1949 to the 1984 reform. We then analyse the determination of money supply and the issue of stability in the demand for money. The last two sections examine the impact of monetary policy on major macro-economic and sectoral indicators, and present conclusions.

FINANCIAL INSTITUTIONS[1]

Four economic periods can be distinguished in the evolution of the Chinese banking system: the reconstruction period, soon after the Revolution and before the establishment of the planning system, from 1949 to 1954; the centrally planned period, from the First Five Year Plan in 1954 to the beginning of the economic reform in 1978; the first wave of economic reform, from 1978 to 1984; and the second wave of economic reform, after 1984. The structure and function of the banking system evolved according to the changes in the economy and in economic policy.

Understanding the history of the Chinese banking system is important, since most features of its past structure and functions can still be found in the present. As in other CPEs, before September 1983 China had a monobank system: the People's Bank functioned both as central bank and as a commercial bank and firmly controlled all the other banks. In 1984, a series of economic reforms dramatically changed the banking system and its functions. The financial system has been entirely restructured, a two-level banking system has been established, and new financial intermediaries (banks, insurance companies, leasing and investment companies) have been created. This section examines the targets and instruments of monetary policy of the People's Bank, specialised banks and the inter-bank market, and Treasury and other bonds and shares.

Changing role of the banking system in a changing economy

The reconstruction period, 1949–54   After the Revolution in 1949 the banks' functions changed from the general mediation of funds to fulfilling the directives of the new Chinese Government. All other financial institutions and markets were closed. Cash, deposits and some irredeemable government bonds were the only financial assets.

The People's Bank of China, established in 1948, was designated as the central bank soon after the Revolution. Its role was fundamental in shifting the economy to socialism. Its immediate tasks were the unification of the banking system under state control (more than 900 private banks existed before 1949) and control of the hyperinflation which hit the economy at the end of the Kuomintang regime. The unification was completed in 1955 and inflation was halted by strict credit controls on enterprises and implementation of the centrally planned system of investment, pricing and production.

By the end of the period, the People's Bank was virtually the sole financial institution in China. It had resumed control of the Bank of China (in 1953) and of the other two specialised banks: the Bank of Communications and the Agriculture Co-operative Bank. Both banks were, however, later replaced by other similar institutions at the beginning of the First Five Year Plan.

The basic structure of the monobank system, however, as well as its main functions, remained virtually unchanged during the period of planning and the first stage of reform, until 1984. At times, when the economic Plan required special financial support for some priority sectors of the economy (agriculture and construction), the specialised banks reappeared as separate units.

The establishment of the planning system, 1954–77   In accordance with the Soviet economic model, all key resources were to be centrally allocated. The function of the banking system was confined to financing the economic plan, with the aim of preventing the creation of excess liquidity outside the enterprise sector (de Wulf and Goldsborough 1986).

The allocation of financial resources relied upon the tax system: all enterprise profits were delivered to the state, which, in its turn, assigned budgetary grants, free of both interest and repayment of principal, to enterprises, according to the economic plan. The intermediation function of the banking system was strictly limited by the principle of separation of responsibilities between bank lending and budgetary grants, as modelled on the Soviet experience of the 1930s and after. The budget supplied investment and construction funds as well as a minimum working capital (quota capital) to both state enterprises and agricultural collective units. Bank lending was to cover only transitory and unexpected financial requirements, above the assigned quota. Loans were generally short-term, mostly granted to finance the accumulation of stocks or the purchase of raw materials, acting as a substitute for buyers' credits and commercial bills. The banks charged interest on the funds provided, to encourage more accurate planning of funding, but the interest rates were low compared with rates on savings deposits and administrative costs, with preferential rates for priority sectors.

The aim of the whole system was to reduce enterprises' liquidity to a minimum and to control it through the banking system. In fact, the separation between budgetary grants and bank loans has never been completely effective. Since enterprises were not allowed to reinvest their own profits, in order to avoid fund shortages they tended to overestimate the amount of working capital they required from the state budget and often diverted the funds granted from short-term expenditures to long-term investment projects.

Since most of the funds allocated to enterprises were budgetary funds and performance was judged exclusively on the fulfilment of production plans, enterprises had no incentive to ensure an accurate and profitable use of financial resources (Zhang 1981). Budget constraints did not operate; if losses occurred, either budget support or liberal bank lending would be provided in order to avoid bankruptcies or reorganisation of the enterprise. A large part of bank lending served to keep unprofitable production units afloat and to finance the accumulation of stocks of unwanted goods in the commercial sector (de Wulf and Goldsborough 1986), the option of unprofitable use of financial resources being preferred to carrying out changes in the economic plan.

After Mao's death in September 1976 and the arrest of the Gang of Four the following month, the 'moderate' wing of the CCP led by Deng Xiao Ping grew strong enough to establish itself in power, with good prospects for imposing political stability. Under these conditions, a general long-term programme of economic reform could be launched.

The first economic reform, 1978–84   The macroeconomic situation in 1977 was characterised by a decrease in the rate of economic growth, declining growth in labour productivity, lower returns to capital and a clear dominance of investment in the capital goods sector over investment in the production of consumer goods. The main targets of the new leadership were rapid modernisation and economic growth. Agriculture, light industry, consumer goods and the welfare of the population became economic priorities.

The first wave of the reforms was aimed at decentralising production decisions both in agriculture and industry, and at gradually introducing some market forces. In 1979, wages and procurement prices of agricultural products were raised, and enterprises were allowed to use part of their profits for wages and bonus payments. The development of the private economy was actively supported, both by the provision of credit and by political and legal encouragement.

The Production Responsibility System, based on contracts between the brigade and single production units, decentralised production and investment decisions from the communal organisations to the farmers. The PRS was given official status in 1982; however, in selected geographical areas experiments had been in operation since 1978.[2] Decentralisation in the industrial sector, among other innovations, allowed state enterprises to retain and allocate themselves a fixed part of their profits.

The switch to a decentralised system of production, together with the expansion of the private economy, caused a sharp increase in monetary income, in demand for working capital and, consequently, in the money stock. Nominal currency in circulation grew much faster than either the net material product or retail sales. The demand for credit and currency in rural areas increased rapidly after the end of the commune system and the introduction of the PRS. Decentralisation in the production sectors and the growth of private small businesses in the marketing sector all required efficient financial intermediation, in order to mobilise capital funds and give economic units prompt access to financial resources for new investment. In order to sustain the economic reform, the financial system needed to be changed accordingly.

The structure and functions of the banking system were reformed in 1979. The State Council announced that the allocation of investment funds would no longer consist exclusively of budgetary grants and would be gradually substituted by bank loans, subject to interest rates and repayment of principal; this directive was to have a major impact on the whole financial system.

From 1979, both the People's Bank and the specialised banks were authorised to issue medium-term and even long-term (five to ten years) loans for the purchase and improvement of equipment and other approved investment projects. The composition of funds allocated to industrial enterprises changed rapidly from 70 per cent budgetary grants, in 1978, to 80 per cent from bank lending in 1982 (Bortolani and Santorum 1984).

Loans were granted on the basis of the following criteria:

1   that the project for which funding was requested had been previously included in the economic plan of the borrowing unit and/or the project conformed to the general guidelines of the economic plan of the area where the borrowing unit was operating;
2   that the goods to be purchased with the loan were available on the market. The profitability of projects and the borrower's repayment ability were not taken into consideration in the monitoring process.

In order to improve the allocation of financial resources to specific sectors of the economy the specialised banks were needed once more. Both the Agricultural Bank and the Construction Bank were re-established as separate units. The Bank of China benefited from the effects of the 'open door' policy in foreign relations and a programme of partial decentralisation of import-export decisions to selected economic units. Two more financial institutions for foreign investment dealings were established: the China International Trust and Investment Corporation (CITIC), under the control of the State Council, in 1979, and the Investment Bank, under the control of the Construction Bank, in 1982. Under the new system, the People's Bank controlled directly or through the specialised banks all financial institutions, with the exception of the CITIC, and continued to perform the functions of both a central bank and a commercial bank.

The second economic reform, 1984   In October 1984 the State Council decided to push further the programme of economic decentralisation and market liberalisation (*Beijing Review* 1984). Budgetary funds for state enterprises were cut further and bank lending became the major financial source for short- and medium-term investment. Reform of the tax system allowed enterprises to retain and use a significant part of their profits, and the decision-making power of state-owned firms was expanded. The role of the individual economic unit was enhanced further; free markets grew rapidly in both rural and urban areas. The price system underwent further changes: a new range of prices was introduced and the range of products with flexible and free market prices was enlarged. The role of the market mechanism involved not only agricultural products but also the distribution of industrial goods. A two-tier system emerged: part of the total production of each good was to be allocated by the economic plan, and part by the market.

The second wave of economic reforms further changed the requirements of the banking system. The tax reform which gave state enterprises the full responsibility for the use of their after-tax profits changed the destination and size of enterprise deposits: enterprises could use their funds to settle approved goods transactions, for wage and bonus payments, and to finance working capital and short-term investment. Bank loans had replaced budgetary grants for working capital by 1983, and for investment and even capital construction by 1985, with the exclusion of sectors of national interest such as infrastructure, welfare, education and health (Zhou and Zhu 1987).

The whole economic reform process after 1978 produced dramatic changes in the distribution of income. Between 1978 and 1986, households' income increased from 53 to 65 per cent of disposable national income, while government revenue declined from 34 to 23 per cent. Thus, the control of about one-eighth of national income shifted from government to households (Naughton 1988).

Between 1978 (the earliest year available) and 1986, government savings, measured as the surplus on the state budget, fell from 20 per cent of disposable national income to 9.5 per cent (Table 10.1), while household savings increased dramatically from 1.6 per cent of national income to 12 per cent. During the same period, total savings declined from 33 per cent of national income in 1978 to 28 per cent in 1982, climbing again after 1983 to 32 per cent in 1986. The 1978–82 drop in the savings rate reflects the central authorities' decision to reduce the investment rate (36.5 per cent of net material product in 1978) in favour of total consumption. The savings rate increased later when the economic reform had already produced a major shift in the

Table 10.1 Net saving as percentage of national income

	Total net saving	Government	State enterprises	Non-state enterprises	Households
1978	33.2	20.0	6.7	4.9	1.6
1979	31.2	13.8	8.7	5.0	3.6
1980	30.2	12.2	7.7	3.9	6.4
1981	28.7	10.7	8.8	3.1	6.1
1982	28.0	9.1	8.5	3.4	7.0
1983	29.5	9.6	7.2	3.5	9.3
1984	31.5	10.4	4.9	3.6	12.5
1985	30.1	11.8	4.8	3.7	9.7
1986	32.2	9.5	5.2	5.5	12.0

Source: Macroeconomic Research Office, 1987.

source of savings. The increase in domestic savings after 1983 was derived from households' and non-state enterprises' savings, while saving by the state economy (government and state enterprises) declined from 17.6 per cent in 1982 to 14.7 per cent in 1986. The shift in the composition of savings, together with the decreasing role of the economic plan in allocating funds, increased the importance of providing adequate financial intermediation.

In 1982, the central authorities recognised that the existing structure of the banking system could not adequately support the economic reform. A State Council directive reforming the banking system was issued in September 1983, a year before the second wave of economic reforms was launched.

The People's Bank was restructured as a central bank only and its commercial banking functions were given to the newly established Industrial and Commercial Bank. Urban credit cooperatives were opened in 1986, following the example and successful experience of the rural credit co-operatives. All government financial institutions, including insurance companies and the CITIC, are now under the direct control of the People's Bank. China was the first socialist country to set up a two-level banking system. Hungary followed only in 1986, at a similar stage of its economic reforms. The present structure of China's banking system is illustrated in Figure 10.1 and described in de Wulf and Goldsborough (1986) and Zhou and Zhu (1987).

The People's Bank has the functions of a central bank with the rank of a ministry, and also has Treasury functions. Its control over the banking system, however, appears to be rather weak, for a number of reasons.

1 There is no banking law which regulates banks' lending and deposits, the fixing of interest rates, monitoring, etc., but only a series of directives, which are at times contradictory.
2 The size of the banking system is such as to prevent effective direct control from the centre over all branches of the specialised banks: the pyramidal system of competences and responsibilities translates into bureaucratic complexity,
3 Local government at various levels, as well as departments under the State Council, can still hand out mandatory loans, with different priorities which the banks then have to follow (Zhou and Zhu 1987).

During the transition from the old, centrally controlled financial system, to the new system, in which banks will ultimately be responsible for both sources and uses of their own funds, the central bank will have to strengthen its supervision over the specialised banks and issue adequate regulations.

The main obstacle to a more efficient banking system, however, is government intervention, which determines priority sectors as well as 'prime-rate' borrowers and puts direct pressure on bank branches at the local level.

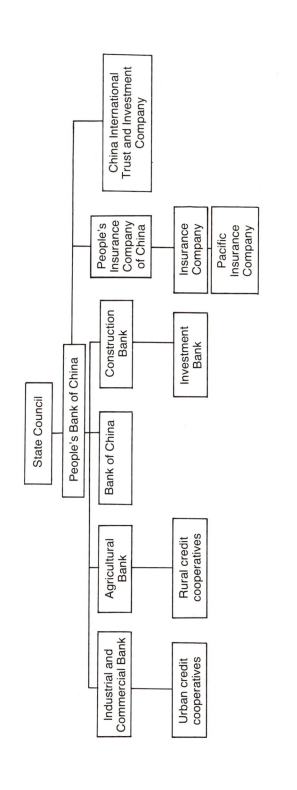

Figure 10.1 China's banking system after 1984
Source: Zhou and Zhu (1987).

Targets and instruments of monetary policy

The principal targets of monetary policy have been control of total credit within the limits imposed by the economic plan and control of currency in circulation in order to achieve macroeconomic equilibrium in the consumer market, without inflation. Both targets strictly derive from the accommodating function of the banking system during the planning period, when the banks were supposed to provide the financial resources necessary for the achievement of the plan goals without generating excess demand.

The use of monetary policy instruments is still quite limited. Although a few experiments have been attempted and widely publicised, the monetary base is still determined by a vertical system of control, with the central bank directly controlling the specialised banks and their local branches, based on the implementation of the credit plan and the cash plan. Other instruments of monetary policy are interest rates on loans and savings deposits, reserve requirements, interest rates on loans to specialised banks and Treasury bonds. Better monitoring, based on both project profitability and borrowers' trustworthiness, would dramatically improve the efficiency of the banking system.

The choice of M0 as the target of monetary policy followed directly from the 'surplus purchasing power' theory, according to which households' purchasing power, strictly determined by cash holdings, is to be matched by an adequate supply of consumer goods, in order to avoid inflation and excess demand (Shi 1982; Huang *et al.* 1981). Currency in circulation is therefore the intermediate target, whereas equilibrium in the consumer goods market is the final macroeconomic goal. The M0 target was determined on the basis of a balance of income and expenditures, so that the volume of currency in circulation to provide household purchasing power would match the total value of retail sale goods available. This system of determining the desired stock of currency in circulation is conventional in planned economies.

Before 1984, if surplus purchasing power was predicted, the planning authorities generally followed three options: an increase in imports of consumer goods; control over the purchasing power of departments and institutional units (through credit restrictions); and an increase in production of consumer goods. Sometimes the prices of certain goods in excess demand, or of luxury items such as cigarettes and alcohol, were raised, with the aim of withdrawing part of the excess currency in circulation through retail sales. There were no taxes on personal incomes (except on very high incomes). The tax system was not used with the direct purpose of controlling aggregate excess demand, but rather income allocation.

Whenever the enforcement of the cash plan was likely to miss its targets, the central bank's power over the money supply appears to have been limited to the use of the interest rate on saving deposits as an instrument for affecting households' liquidity preference.

The reform of the banking system in September 1983 aimed to give more power and instruments of monetary control to the People's Bank. At present, however, the stock of currency in circulation remains the main target of monetary policy.

The credit plan and cash plan   In accordance with its accommodating function, each year the People's Bank prepares the financial plan, which includes the credit plan, the cash plan and the government budget. The credit plan and the cash plan are based on information available from each branch of the People's Bank and of the specialised banks and are formed according to a pyramidal system of responsibilities, from local offices to the central bank. The 'desired' amount of currency in circulation is determined by the central bank through the compilation of both the cash plan and the credit plan, see Cheng (1981), de Wulf and Goldsborough (1986), and Bortolani and Santorum (1984).

Even after the reform of the system in 1984, the central bank still used the credit plan in order to implement its direct control over the other banks' credit operations. The effectiveness of the credit plan and the cash plan, however, is limited by the inability of the central bank to enforce the plans themselves. It had been hampered before 1978 by economic plan errors, lack of monitoring, illegal practices and corruption, and local government intervention. Liberalisation brought the major problem of accurately predicting both currency and credit supply. The rapid monetary growth which occurred after 1978 showed the central bank's inability to enforce the credit plan and the cash plan; the reform of the banking system in 1984 also aimed at providing the People's Bank with other instruments of monetary policy.

Interest rates on loans have never been used as a means to control total bank lending. Until 1984 they probably only had the purpose of encouraging enterprises to use the funds borrowed from the banks more carefully than the funds provided free of charge from the government budget. Designated priority sectors have always benefited from preferential interest rates.

Real interest rates were at times negative, as was the spread between interest rates on savings deposits and on loans (Table 10.2). The banking system could make profits by setting a low rate on enterprises' sight deposits and higher rates on loans. Time deposits, of up to one year, for enterprises were only introduced in 1982. Until 1982, therefore, all enterprise deposits (about one-third of total deposits at the People's Bank) were sight deposits and, since they were compulsory, they could bear otherwise unattractive rates.

The annual interest rate on enterprises' sight deposits was set at 1.80 per cent, while that on loans for working capital (the great majority of loans to enterprises) was set at 5.40 per cent and raised to 7.20 per cent in 1982. Interest rates on time deposits under one year ranged from 3.60 to 5.04 per cent. Interest rates on medium-term loans (one to five years) ranged from 5.04 to

Table 10.2 Real rates of interest, nominal spread between interest rate on loans and savings deposits, and inflation (%).

	Working capital loans from People's Bank	One-year saving deposits	Nominal spread working capital loans—sav. dep.	Change in cost of living in urban areas
1978	3.50	2.54	0.96	0.7
1979	2.30	1.79	0.51	1.9
1980	−2.74	−2.46	−0.28	7.5
1981	2.54	2.90	−0.36	2.5
1982	4.48	3.67	0.81	2.0
1983	5.20	3.76	0.81	2.0
1984	4.50	3.06	1.44	2.7
1985	−4.22	−5.06	0.84	11.9
1986	0.92	0.20	0.72	7.0
1987				11.7

Sources: Bortolani and Santorum (1984) for data from 1978 to 1983 on interest rates on loans; Byrd (1983) for 1978–81 interest rates on saving deposits and *Zhongguo Jinrong* for 1982–6; State Statistical Bureau: *Statistical Yearbook* 1987, and *China Statistics Monthly* 1988.

6.48 per cent. Preferential rates varied from 3.60 to 4.32 per cent.

Banking operations with enterprises were thus profitable, while losses on household savings collection were probably covered by profits from other sectors. The whole banking system seems to have been profitable until 1984. Since the reform, a wider range of loans and deposits has been introduced and deposit rates have been revised upwards because of inflation, while most loans rates have been kept low for economic and political reasons. This reduced the profitability of the banking sector.

When price liberalisation rapidly raised the cost of living (Table 10.2), the banks had to raise their interest rates to take account of inflation. The People's Bank revised upward the rates of interest on both loans and saving deposits three times over the period 1978–83.

Flexible rates of interest on loans were introduced in 1984: they can fluctuate, according to local market conditions, within a spread fixed by the central bank. However, those enterprises which suffer from the increased cost of capital can ask for a subsequent tax reduction.

The structure of interest rates, both term and across-sector, will eventually need to be changed. The present price structure (with free, flexible and fixed prices) causes considerable distortions in the evaluation of opportunity costs both to borrowers and to the banks.

Credit rationing and misallocation of resources have occurred repeatedly. Preference has traditionally been given to investments which guaranteed quick and high nominal returns, because they appeared the safest and simplest to finance. Low prices have been maintained in the primary sectors and in the construction sector, while those in other sectors have been raised and, at least partially, liberalised. Certain low-priority sectors (such as processing industries) have, therefore, benefited from the financial reform and the credit expansion more than higher-priority sectors (such as transport and energy). Since banks base their evaluation on nominal prices rather than the true opportunity costs, resources have repeatedly been allocated to comparatively low-yielding investment.

Monitoring loans   Until 1984, credit operations were guided by the principle of what was called the 'commodity inventory system', introduced in 1955. According to this principle, loans were granted to projects in relation to the specific economic plan of the borrowing unit, and backed by material stocks held by the unit. The loans had to be repaid promptly soon after the stocks used to back the loan were sold (de Wulf and Goldsborough, 1986).

A widely used indicator for monitoring loans was the ratio of the enterprise's total production to the working capital financed by bank borrowing. This ratio was compared with the ratio of the whole production sector and the ratios of the enterprise in the past. When it fell below one, or was lower than either of the other two indicators, the enterprise's performance was checked. The power of the banking authorities, however, was limited to reporting their findings to the planning authorities, who would take the final decision on the future of the enterprise. In effect, very few defaulting borrowers were ever restructured or closed down, while it is known that 'a large number of bad debts emerge and are cancelled from the bank's asset column periodically by the State's orders' (Zhou and Zhu 1987).

Since the banking reform of 1984, monitoring has become more effective and is based on the profitability of the project as well as on the repayment ability of the borrowers. The shortage of trained personnel and the difficulties in establishing an efficient information system are the main obstacles to proper monitoring of loans.

Interest rate on savings deposits   The interest rate on savings deposits was used in the period 1978–86 as an instrument for influencing households' liquidity preference, in an attempt to reduce the excess currency in circulation by increasing saving deposits. An empirical model of households' portfolio and expenditure behaviour in China, estimated by Santorum (1987) over the period 1955–83, confirms a positive relationship between this interest rate and savings deposits and a negative relationship between the interest rate and currency in circulation.[3]

Santorum (1987) shows that in China consumers' expenditure and decisions on portfolio allocation are interdependent: the composition of wealth in the previous period affects flow decisions, and expenditures affect the next-period portfolio allocation. The interest rate on savings deposits can therefore be used as an instrument of monetary policy in order to influence consumers' decisions. An increase in the rate, by reducing currency in circulation and increasing savings deposits, causes a change in portfolio liquidity, with a final negative effect on next-period expenditures. The predictive ability of the model, however, is dramatically affected by the structural changes which occurred during and after the economic reform, so that the model can say very little about a similar policy carried out in later years. The estimated model also suggests that saving deposits represent an accumulated purchasing power which could be subsequently released, causing an unpredictable increase in expenditure in later years.

Interest rates on saving deposits were changed only eight times during the period 1953–78, remaining unmodified sometimes for years, while they have been raised every year (with the exception of 1983) since 1979. In 1985, in response to the rapid increase of inflation (to 11.9 per cent), which was due to the uncontrolled expansion of the money supply, the monetary authorities raised the rates twice in the same year. Their levels remained below the rate of inflation, however.

The rate was not linked to changes in prices of consumer goods. A State Council directive of August 1988, however, suggested the introduction of price-index-linked interest rates on savings deposits of three or more years duration. At the end of 1988, the rate on one-year savings deposits was raised to 16 per cent, as a consequence of the accelerating inflation in the major cities and the widespread withdrawals of savings deposits which followed.

Table 10.2 shows that over the period 1978–86, the real rate of interest on one-year savings deposits was negative in 1980 and 1985. This rate is *ex post* and based on the official index of inflation. In view of the fact that the 'true' rate of inflation (without considering repressed inflation) was reported to be higher than the official figures, and that expectations of inflation were rising dramatically, the 'true' real rate of interest, as perceived by economic agents, was probably deeply negative by 1987–8.

In 1988, inflation was around 24 per cent in cities and towns, according to official data, while the true figure was probably twice as high, according to the local press. The decision of the Politburo to speed up the price reform (*Renmin Ribao*, 21 August, 1988) had a dramatic impact on households' expectations. Chinese sources reported massive withdrawals of savings deposits, a widespread rush to buy any consumer goods available in the shops and a sharp increase in household stocks of non-perishable consumer goods. Speculation by commercial enterprises, ready to exploit the sudden increase in excess demand, worsened the situation. Ten days later, the State Council announced that no radical price reform would be undertaken in the next two years and issued directives to the People's Bank to link the interest rate on savings deposits of three years' duration or more to inflation (ibid., 31 August, 1988).

Reserve requirements   Since 1978, the Agricultural Bank and the other specialised banks have kept some reserves at the central bank, in proportion to their deposits: before 1984, however, the proportion was not fixed, and the authorities did not permit them to be used as reserve requirements. After 1984, a more traditional system of reserve requirements was established. Reserve requirements are entirely composed of deposits with the People's Bank. Their ratio was originally fixed, in 1984, at 40 per cent of urban households' deposits, 20 per cent of enterprises' deposits and 25 per cent of rural deposits, including the redeposits of the rural credit cooperatives with the Agricultural Bank (*Zhongguo Jinrong* 1984). In 1985, the requirements were reduced to 10 per cent of deposits for all specialised banks, except the Construction Bank, for which 30 per cent was imposed (Zhou and Zhu 1987).

The formal reserve requirement was pegged at 10 per cent of deposits until late 1987; the specialised banks, however, had been maintaining larger deposits with the central bank, with such excess reserves amounting to 11.56 per cent of deposits at the end of 1985. Excess reserves have been falling steadily with the development of the inter-bank lending market (see below on the specialised banks), which provided the opportunity for more profitable investment, and amounted to only 6.4 per cent of deposits in October 1987 (Naughton 1988). This is likely to have contributed to the growth of money supply over the period 1985-7.

The reserve requirement quotas were too low to be effectively used as instruments of monetary policy. The indecision shown by the monetary authorities about using the reserve requirement ratio as an effective instrument to control monetary expansion reflects the difficulties, the lack of preparation and sometimes the political pressures that have affected the process of transition to a new kind of monetary policy. In a period of rapid inflation, the opportunity to switch decisively to new instruments of monetary policy was discussed in a leisurely way, while the traditional vertical control of bank lending was strengthened. In October 1987, the reserve requirement quota was raised to 12 per cent and the rural credit cooperatives were required to maintain an additional 5 billion yuan in deposits at the central bank over and above their reserve requirement.

Interest rate on loans to specialised banks   Loans from the People's Bank to other banks were introduced in 1984. However, they seem to have been used for purposes other than the control of the monetary base. In 1984, the interest rate on loans to the specialised banks was exactly the same as the rate on their redeposits at the central bank (0.36 per month), so that there was no financial disincentive to borrow from the People's Bank (de Wulf and Goldsborough 1986).

Specialised banks can borrow from the PB at a 0.39 per cent monthly interest rate on borrowing previously included in the credit plan and at a 0.42 per cent monthly interest rate on temporary (unplanned) borrowing

(Zhou and Zhu 1987). The interest rates, however, have been mainly changed for specific purposes, such as to facilitate borrowing by the Agricultural Bank during the harvest period.

Savings collection   Households have three choices of financial asset: cash, savings deposits and Treasury bonds. The last have been sold to households only since 1982; they are not negotiable and in 1988 represented about 1 per cent of total savings. Some enterprises have been allowed to issue 'shares' to be purchased by their workers. These 'shares' have the characteristics of bonds rather than shares: they bear a fixed minimum dividend, are not negotiable and are issued with the specific purpose of raising the worker's salary above the ceiling imposed by the government on bonuses to workers. They cannot, therefore, be considered as savings deposits substitutes. Their volume is also extremely modest.

There are two kinds of savings deposits: sight and time. Time deposits offer a range of various durations at different interest rates. Withdrawing the deposit before the end of the prescribed term is possible but is penalised by the application of a lower interest rate. The effective liquidity of all kinds of deposits depends on the cash reserve of the bank branch and on the general monetary policy directives of the People's Bank. Before the economic reform, some political pressures were used by bank managers on depositors who wanted to withdraw their savings. Since the reform, this sort of action is less common; in a period of widespread withdrawals, however, as in the second half of 1988, the authorities have delayed payment considerably and, in some cases, have issued IOUs because of cash shortages.

Savings deposits increased very rapidly during the period 1978–86 (see Table 10.3). Three main factors behind the rapid increase of households' savings can be identified (Naughton 1986):

1 the unprecedentedly rapid growth of households' money income, due to the economic reform;
2 the changes in the nature of household income in rural areas, as a consequence of the Production Responsibility System, and the corresponding transfer of responsibility over agricultural production and investment from the collective organisations to individual households;
3 the changes in the nature of expenditures, introduced by the increasing availability of large-scale consumer goods, such as radios, bicycles, televisions, fans, tape recorders.

The increase in savings resulted in an increase in cash and savings deposits – the two basic assets in households' portfolios. Before the economic reform, currency was 50 per cent of the money stock (M2, currency plus saving deposits). After 1979, savings deposits increased more rapidly than currency in circulation, reaching 60 per cent of the money stock by 1982.

Table 10.3 Households' savings deposits (yuan bn)

	Rural areas Rural credit cooperatives	Urban areas	Total
1977	4.65	13.51	18.16
1978	5.57	15.49	21.06
1979	7.84	20.26	28.10
1980	11.70	28.25	39.15
1981	16.95	35.41	52.36
1982	22.81	44.73	67.54
1983	31.99	57.26	89.25
1984	43.81	77.66	121.47
1985	56.84	105.78	162.62
1986	76.61	147.15	223.76

Source: *Statistical Yearbook*, 1987.

The 'switch' in the components of household portfolios can also be attributed to the successful savings collection policy of the People's Bank. After 1978, the PB stressed the importance of savings collection in withdrawing the excess currency in circulation (not, it is interesting to note, in order to mobilise funds). Interest rates were raised, more types of term deposits were offered, and, most important, the number of savings offices was rapidly increased (Table 10.4). The population/savings offices ratio has dropped continuously in the rural areas and, until 1984, in the urban areas. The number of savings offices in proportion to population is much higher in the rural areas; this is due to the high number and flexible structure of the rural credit cooperatives. This has been one of the key factors behind the rapid increase in savings deposits. Table 10.3 shows how successful the collection of savings has been: by the end of 1982, the total savings deposits figure was nearly four times higher than in 1977. Both the number of depositors and the average size of deposits increased (Bortolani and Santorum 1984).

While not underestimating the effects of the increase in the interest rate on savings deposits and the expansion of bank savings offices, it should be noted that the same 'switch' occurred in other CPEs at similar stages in their economic growth: currency in circulation ceased to be the major component of M2 from the early 1950s in Czechoslovakia and the GDR, and from the early 1960s in Hungary and Poland (Rudcenko 1979). Given the limited range of existing financial instruments, savings deposits seem likely to have responded mainly to the increased accessibility of deposit institutions and, more generally, to the improvement as well as innovation in banking services.

Table 10.4 Number of savings offices in urban and rural areas

| | Urban areas | | Rural areas | Population/savings office ratio | |
	People's Bank	Agricultural Bank	Rural credit cooperatives	Urban areas	Rural areas
1979	6,750	0	n.a.	27,400	n.a.
1980	8,600	0	n.a.	22,256	n.a.
1981	9,948	199	389,726	19,879	2,050
1982	11,100	280	393,164	18,589	2,045
1983	11,612	549	418,805	19,839	1,871
1984	11,783	2,158	421,582	17,550	1,672
1985	n.a.	2,158	406,581	n.a.	1,630
1986	n.a.	6,342	393,534		1,574

Sources: Bortolani and Santorum, 1984, for 1979–80 data; *Statistical Yearbook*, 1986 and 1987, for other years.
Note: The PB ceased to operate as a commercial bank in 1984. Data on savings offices of the Industrial Commercial Bank are not available.

Services   Post-1984 directives from the People's Bank stress the importance of banks becoming self-sufficient and of their performance being evaluated on the basis of their profitability. Though this statement appears meaningless in view of the fact that the spread between interest rates on loans and rates on savings deposits is still far from covering administrative costs, it has started to produce some effects at the branch level. More services were gradually offered to depositors: cheques, cashier's cheques, bill payments, and even credit cards. As usually happens with any kind of innovation, these services are being introduced on an experimental basis in selected areas and to priority customers.

Specialised banks   Any assessment of the degree of independence of these banks from the central bank since the reform is difficult, as China still lacks a proper banking law. This also makes the control of the People's Bank over the specialised banks hard to define and to enforce. The shift in enterprises' sources of financing which occurred after 1978 enhanced the role of the specialised banks, which also seem to have been given more responsibilities since the reform of the banking system in 1984.

The Agricultural Bank and the Construction Bank, when in operation, were responsible for the allocation of funds to agricultural collective units and construction units respectively. There was no competition among banks, since they were allocated funds directly from the People's Bank according to the economic plan, were given their own sphere of responsibility, and their customers (enterprises, collective units, households) were assigned one bank with which to do their business (de Wulf and Goldsborough 1986). No direct liquidity transfer from one economic sector to another, or from one province to another, was possible: all mobilisation of resources had either to go through the central bank or through the central government, or to remain within the same sector and the same area from which the resources originated.

At present, there is still a high degree of specialisation and each bank is assigned its specific sphere of responsibility. The first sign that this rule might be overcome in the near future came in 1986 when individuals were allowed to use the bank of their choice for deposits (Sherer 1988).

Willingness to increase competition within the financial system has been made evident by the opening of the Bank of Communications and of the first non-governmental bank, the Shanghai Aijian Banking, Trust and Investment Company, in 1986. Their operations, like those of the few operating branches of foreign banks, are strictly limited and virtually do not conflict with other banks' areas of responsibility. They represent, however, initial exploratory experiments, and the Chinese experience suggests that experiments of this sort might, at times, evolve quite rapidly. In the long term, competition among specialised banks could be allowed and promoted, with benefits resulting from reduction in administrative costs, increased efficiency of the service and a new range of services offered to the public.

The two other financial institutions, the Bank of China and the rural credit cooperatives, had seemingly passed through the whole political succession cycle without undergoing dramatic changes: the Bank of China, because its functions were confined to the foreign sector, and the rural credit cooperatives, in existence since 1933, because of their importance in mobilising savings in rural areas.

The rural credit cooperatives   These are collectively owned units under the direct control of the Agricultural Bank, which they use as a clearing bank. Their structure is simple: a main office at the commune level, branch offices at the brigade level and the credit stations at the 'grass-roots' level. The ability of the rural credit cooperatives physically to reach a high number of depositors derives from the extremely flexible structure of the credit stations: consisting of one or three workers, they employ both full-time and part-time workers, up to a total of 706,000 employees in 1986. Part-time staff have decreased as a proportion of total staff since 1982, when they were 52 per cent of the total personnel; they still represent 43 per cent, however, equivalent to 28 per cent of total staff employed in the banking sector in rural areas.

Inter-bank lending market   The dramatic increase in the demand for credit which followed the economic reform put the banks under heavy strain and is now pushing them to become competitive. Since 1985, recommendations from the People's Bank have stated that loans can be granted only in proportion to deposits. At fixed interest rates, the excess demand for bank loans has produced a shortage of funds within the banking system.

The specialised banks, which used to borrow directly from the central bank, had to look for alternative sources when the People's Bank imposed a 'credit squeeze' on the whole financial system by granting loans to them strictly in accordance with the credit plan and charging higher interest rates on above-quota funds. The two sources to which they turned were inter-bank loans and bond issues. In 1985, both the Agricultural Bank and the Industrial and Commercial Bank issued bonds. The inter-bank loan market appeared officially in 1985 and slowly became an important source of short-term funds.

Since 1985, regional offices of the People's Bank in ten major cities have started to act as clearing houses for short-term (ten-day) inter-bank funds, 'by temporarily releasing a specialised bank's excess deposits and permitted but unutilised credit to other specialised banks' (de Wulf and Goldsborough 1986). The interest rate is negotiable within a fixed spread, which is linked to the People's Bank's lending rates (Sherer 1988).

The introduction of the inter-bank lending market has had the immediate effect of reducing the excess reserves of the specialised banks at the central bank. In the short term, its development seems problematic. At present, contractionary monetary policies are intended to affect economic sectors differentially, while the development of the inter-bank lending market would give the more penalised banks a chance to overcome their credit plan quotas. In September 1988, there was even an attempt by the central bank to limit drastically the operations of the inter-bank market, in order to cut credit; this attempt, however, met with strong resistance from enterprises and other units which complained that they could not find the necessary capital to finance wages and working capital.

A well-functioning inter-bank lending market would avoid situations in which banks, and therefore economic sectors, were affected differentially by the same monetary policy measures (Fry 1988). Agriculture, for example, has always been penalised in favour of other sectors. The allocation of resources as well as the effectiveness of monetary policy could both be improved dramatically.

Treasury and other institutions' bonds and shares In 1979, total government expenditure overtook total revenue for the first time after a long period of budget surpluses. A budget deficit was recorded each year from 1979 to 1984, and then again from 1986 to 1987. In the first two years, the People's Bank intervened directly, financing most of the deficit by net lending (53 per cent of total deficit financing, in 1980, according to IMF estimates).

Though the deficit/GDP ratio was rather low compared with other countries (5.3 per cent in 1979, 3.5 per cent in 1980 and 1.3 per cent in 1982, according to IMF estimates), the financial authorities regarded the government deficit as a possible source of inflationary pressures and looked for alternative sources of financing.

In 1981, Treasury bonds were issued for the first time since the 1950s (Table 10.5). The 1981 issue covered 84 per cent of the deficit, as measured according to standard Western criteria by the IMF (Bortolani and Santorum 1984). Treasury bonds were allocated through the central bank. The first issue was compulsorily allocated among designated institutions. After 1982, however, Treasury bonds could also be purchased on a voluntary basis by individuals as well as enterprises. They are not negotiable; after 1985, however, they were discountable at the central bank and used by enterprises as collateral for borrowing (Grub and Sudweeks 1988).

Treasury bonds pay interest, and their duration is between five and ten years. Their nominal interest rate was 5 per cent in 1981. The following year it was raised to 8 per cent on bonds purchased by individuals, but reduced to 4 per cent on bonds purchased by enterprises and other institutions. In 1985 the rate was raised to 9 per cent for individuals and 5 per cent for enterprises.

Although the Treasury bond yield for individuals has been maintained 1–2 percentage points above the interest rate on one-year saving deposits, Treasury bonds still cannot compete fully with savings deposits, because of their limited degree of liquidity. Furthermore, the low yield for enterprises and institutions means that compulsory purchases of Treasury bonds, which still often occur (e.g., by banks), are equivalent to a tax imposition.

Since 1984, state enterprises, banks and local government units have also been allowed to issue bonds. Bond issues increased dramatically in 1986, particularly from rural enterprises, as the credit squeeze started. By the end of 1986, 7,000 enterprises had issued shares, and stock exchanges had opened in the major cities. The size of the market, however, is still negligible in terms both of participants and of the amount of funds deriving from bond and share issues as compared with bank borrowing. Bond regulations include the designation of potential investors: for example, banks can only issue bonds to their depositors; enterprises can only issue bonds to their

Table 10.5 Treasury bonds and government deficit (yuan bn)

	TB	Government deficit	Deficit/GDP (%)
1981	4.87	−2.55	−0.6
1982	4.38	−2.93	−0.6
1983	4.16	−4.35	−0.8
1984	4.25	−4.45	−0.7
1985	6.06	2.16	0.3
1986	6.25	−7.05	−0.8

Sources: *Statistical Yearbook*, 1987 for TB and government deficit; *Jingji Yanjiu*, for GDP.
Note: GDP = disposable national income.

workers. Experimental stock exchanges have opened in Shenyang, Shanghai and Beijing; the People's Bank and the Industrial and Commercial Bank may act as dealers.

MONEY SUPPLY AND DEMAND

Definition of money

The definition of money in a centrally planned economy is different from standard classifications. Government production units can settle transactions among themselves only by bank transfer and can keep only a fixed amount of cash for unpredictable transactions. Cash is used for retail sales, wages and state purchases of agricultural products. Two monetary circuits can thus be identified: one in which cash plays the role of the means of exchange and the other, restricted to government and production units, in which most payments are made by bank transfer.

Monetary aggregates in CPEs are generally defined as:

M0 = currency in circulation
M2 = M0 + saving deposits
M3 = M2 + enterprises' deposits + budgetary deposits + capital construction deposits + deposits of government agencies and organisations.

Determination of the money supply: a flow of funds analysis

We have seen that one important target of monetary policy has been the control of currency in circulation. Two kinds of analysis can be used in order to examine the process of money creation: the deposit multiplier approach, and flow of funds analysis. The former requires (i) that bank reserves are exogenously determined and (ii) that there is a rigid link between bank reserves and the money supply (Chick 1973). In view of the fact that loans have been granted in proportion to bank deposits only in recent years and that reserve requirements have never been used efficiently, neither condition is likely to hold for the Chinese case. Flow of funds analysis gives useful insights into why the control of currency in circulation by means of the credit plan and the cash plan has become less and less adequate during the process of liberalisation.

Before 1984, currency was put in circulation by the central bank through other banks, state enterprises and government units, and was withdrawn through the same institutions. Forty-two per cent of the currency outflow was due to wage payments and 38 per cent to state procurement of agricultural products. Eighty-two per cent of currency in circulation was held by households and the remainder by enterprises, agricultural units and government units. Retail sales accounted for 70 per cent of cash inflow (People's Bank of China, 1983).

The balance sheet of the People's Bank up to 1984 was something like the following:

Assets	Liabilities
Loans to enterprises	Enterprises' deposits
Loans to government	Government deposits
Loans to non-state sector (private	Savings deposits
and agric. units)	Currency
Reserves (gold and foreign	Other banks' reserves
exchange)	Agricultural bank reserves

The People's Bank cannot control total credit directly, since it is primarily determined by the economic plan and the government budget.

Under a flow of funds analysis, and assuming fixed bank reserves, changes in the money stock result as follows:

$$\Delta CU = (\Delta L_c + \Delta L_g + \Delta L_{ns}) - (\Delta D_c + \Delta D_g + \Delta SD)$$
$$\Delta CU = (\Delta L_e - \Delta D_E) + (\Delta L_G - \Delta D_G) + (\Delta L_{ns} - \Delta SD)$$
$$\Delta CU = SEBR + PSBR + NSBR$$

This implies that if:

$$SEBR + PSBR > - NSBR$$

then:

$$\Delta CU > 0.$$

where:

CU = currency; L = loans and D = deposits; subscripts e and g are respectively for enterprises and government units; subscript ns is for the non-state sector; SD = saving deposits; $SEBR$ = state enterprises' net borrowing requirement; $PSBR$ = public sector net borrowing requirement; $NSBR$ = non-state sector borrowing requirement. SD includes the Agricultural Bank deposits at the People's Bank.

In principle both SEBR and PSBR are determined by the economic plan. The central bank has no power over them; it can only ensure that the borrowing requirement does not exceed the plan targets.

Only cash loans will produce changes in the money stock, since any other kind of loan is counterbalanced by corresponding change in enterprise or government deposits. Cash loans are mainly for wage payments and purchases of agricultural products. They depend on the plan, enterprises' economic performance (since bonuses have been introduced) and the (unpredictable) agricultural production. Interest rates on these loans had no incentive effects on enterprises or government units until perhaps 1985, when production units' performance became important and interest on loans finally became greater than the corresponding interest rate on deposits.

This leaves the People's Bank with the task of controlling NSBR. With fixed interest rates on loans, ineffective loan monitoring, and non-binding reserve requirements, the central bank had virtually no means of controlling NSBR, except by increasing the interest rate on savings deposits.

Money creation in rural areas is very important. We can reasonably assume that nearly half the currency in circulation is in the rural areas, where production units used to keep cash for payments to members of the brigade and purchases of various inputs, and peasants were paid only once or twice a year (although only part of their income was in cash). The Production Responsibility System introduced in agriculture between 1979 and 1983 contributed considerably to the increase in the volume of currency in circulation in the rural areas: most of the payments are made in cash, while peasants are given land for their own personal needs rather than goods, in a new form of income in kind which is quite difficult to value. The rural credit cooperatives contributed in recent years to a very large savings deposit increase relative to the rural areas, while on the other hand they lent less than one-third of the money they collected.

Another main concern for the next few years will be the process of accumulation and investment in the rural areas, which, after the dismantling of the communes, depends largely on peasants' own decisions (see Reynolds 1987). In the two years 1985–6 the growth of savings deposits in real terms declined, while peasants showed more interest in spending on consumer goods than in investing in agricultural inputs; as a result, investment in agriculture declined so sharply that the planning authorities feared for the long-term growth of agricultural production. The role of banks in this particular problem area could be vital: credit facilities could be extended and better monitoring implemented; a structure of interest rates on both loans and savings deposits which takes into account the real opportunity cost of alternative investment could guide households' portfolio and investment decisions towards the desired mix of investment and consumption expenditure.

Is the money stock exogenous?

The question of the exogeneity of the money stock is important in order to assess whether the money stock can be used as an instrument of monetary policy. Two studies have addressed the issue in relation to China: Portes and Santorum (1987) and Chen (1988). Both reached the conclusion that the money stock is not exogenous. Although both studies used a causality approach (Portes and Santorum used the Granger test while Chen used a vector autoregression model), and exogeneity, in its more technical sense, should be determined in the context of a particular model (and might not hold in other models), their results provide evidence that the money stock in China is largely demand-determined.

It remains to be established how the private sector can command the money supply it wants. One reasonable explanation for China (where securities do not play a relevant role in monetary policy) could be the following: an original increase in the demand for bank loans (due to exogenous changes in aggregate demand) induces banks (in aggregate) to over-expand; this would produce a 'cash drain' which would oblige the specialised banks to borrow from the central bank, thus increasing the money supply, to support the increase in deposits, initiated by the increased desire to spend (see Chick 1973), in a typical 'accommodating' monetary policy fashion.

In contrast to an 'accommodating' policy, following the economic reform, the People's Bank is interested in acquiring further instruments (e.g. open-market operations) and in implementing a better use of the existing instruments (e.g. reserve requirements, discounting operations) necessary to a 'dynamic' monetary policy. This would allow the central bank to initiate changes in the monetary sector, in order to promote broad macroeconomic targets of stabilisation and growth. In this 'dynamic' policy, changes in cash supply would be exogenously determined, at least in the sense that they would be initiated 'outside' the private sector.

Demand for money

Several studies have estimated demand-for-money equations for China. The most interesting findings are in Portes and Santorum (1987) and in Feltenstein and Farhidian (1987).

Portes and Santorum estimated a standard general demand-for-money equation. Their best estimated equation for M0 was the following (equation 3 in Table 3 of their paper):

$$m = 0.32^* + 0.35^* m_{-1} + 0.73^* y + 0.74^{**} p + 1.64^* \Delta p - 0.12^{**} R$$

where all variables are in logs, except R, and m = M0, y = households' disposable income, p = retail sales price index, R = interest rate on one-year saving deposits. * and ** mean significant at the 5 and 10 per cent confidence levels respectively.

According to the estimated equation, the income elasticity is 1.123 and the adjustment coefficient 0.65, that is, money balances adjust within six months. The interesting result is the negative correlation between interest rates on savings deposits and money balances. The odd result is the positive correlation between prices and money balances: this is probably due to the use of official prices, which do not include hidden and repressed inflation. The effects of excess demand on the consumption goods markets should enter the demand for money equation.

Feltenstein and Farhidian (1987) estimated a demand-for-money equation which takes into account repressed inflation. Although their theoretical model might be questionable (see Portes and Santorum 1987), their results are rather interesting. Their estimates are the following:

$$m = -1.60 + 1.373y - 4.023\pi^E_{\Gamma}$$
$$\Delta m = 0.255 \, (m^d - m_{-1})$$

where all variables are in logs and m = $M2/\pi_{\Gamma}$, y = real disposable income deflated by π_{Γ}, π_{Γ} is the virtual price index defined as π_{Γ} = pα (p = official price index), and m^d is the long-run demand for money. The use of virtual prices, instead of official prices, gives less weight to income and more weight to inflation. Most important of all, the coefficient of the expected true rate of inflation is negative.

These results suggest that demand-for-money equations for China need to include the effects of excess demand on the consumer goods market and the interest rate on savings deposits.

A crucial factor for setting realistic targets in monetary policy is the stability of the demand for money. The dramatic and continuous changes in the structure of the Chinese economy, however, have deeply affected agents' behaviour. Estimates of long-term behavioural equations display parameter variance over time; the changes generally occur either in 1978–9, when the economic reform started, or in 1984, when the first programme of reform reached its full effect and the second wave of economic reform was on its way.

One possible explanation is the change in liquidity due to the financial reform and to the partial liberalisation of the economy. The former increased the range of cash loans and financial sources available to private units as well as the number of financial intermediaries (insurance companies, local governments, etc.), while the latter raised the number of private units entitled to borrow money and increased the volume of cash kept as working capital by those units.

The pattern shown by the velocity of money (defined as the ratio of currency held by households over households' expenditures) gives some further insights into this particular matter. The velocity of M0 continued to fall from 1979 to 1984; in 1984, however, M0 increased by 4.4 per cent over the previous year. In 1985, velocity increased suddenly by 7.5 per cent over 1984, while currency held by households showed a further increase of 24 per cent. The 1985 changes in currency and velocity are rather peculiar: in previous years (e.g., 1970, 1976, 1977) when velocity increased considerably over the previous period, the change in velocity had always been matched by a moderate increase, or even by a reduction, in currency in circulation. In this perspective, the 1984 and 1985 data suggest that important changes in the liquidity of assets and in the financial intermediaries sector must have taken place. These changes continued to have a strong effect on the demand for money after 1985.

Until 1983, the People's Bank used to fix its M0 target on the basis of the balance of purchasing power and expenditures, which corresponds to using the quantity equation MV=PQ for predicting M (money), given P (general price level) and Q (quantity of traded goods), and assuming a stable velocity of money (V). Velocity was measured as the ratio of retail sales to currency in circulation. The base period was 1953–7, which was considered to be financially stable (de Wulf and Goldsborough 1986). The instability of the velocity of money, not taken into account by the economic authorities, hampered their ability to set and reach their targets (ibid.).

Monetary policy cycle

A macroeconomic model, at the Research Centre for Technological, Social and Economic Development of the State Council, includes the banking system and considers the effects of disequilibria both in the consumer goods market and in the labour market. Zhou and Zhu (1987) used this model in order to evaluate the performance of the banking system since the economic reform. The model indicates that, under the 1988 regulations and price system, the banking system would generate a monetary policy cycle from periods of credit squeeze and tight monetary control to periods of rapid monetary expansion.

AGGREGATE AND SECTORAL EFFECTS OF THE CENTRAL BANK'S MONETARY POLICY

Effects on consumer goods market

Excess demand   There have been a number of studies on excess demand for consumer goods in China: Feltenstein and Farhidian (1987), Feltenstein, Lebow and van Wijnbergen (1986), Naughton (1986) and Portes and Santorum (1987). All these studies attempt, using different methods and approaches, to give some estimate of the size and pattern of excess demand for consumer goods. Their findings are similar and consistent with each other. All indices show a similar pattern of excess demand over the period 1955–83 and indicate that general excess demand has been the dominant regime during the past thirty years.

According to Portes and Santorum's estimates, the pattern of excess demand has been strictly linked to the political cycle and changes in economic priorities. Plotting the Portes-Santorum index of excess demand and the percentage changes in currency in circulation over the period 1955–83 (Figure 10.2), we can note a strong correlation between monetary growth and excess demand for consumer goods.

Figure 10.2 suggests similarities between the period of the First Five Year Plan and the Great Leap Forward, and the economic reform of the 1980s, both characterised by large excess demand. The main characteristics

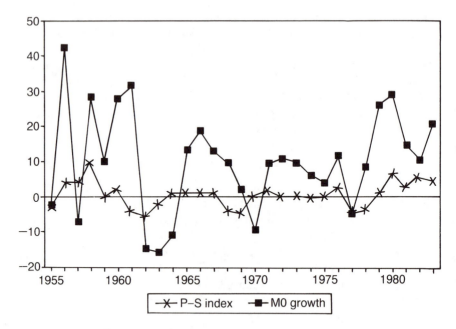

Figure 10.2 P–S index and monetary growth, 1955–83

common to both periods are: rapid economic growth and transition to different systems of production in agriculture (from private production to communes in the 1950s and from communes to household production in the 1980s), sustained by a large increase in bank credit and uncontrolled expansion of currency in circulation.

General excess demand seems to characterise those periods in which the economic authorities try to regulate a mixed-economy system while still using a direct-from-the-centre control, without having at their disposal suitable and powerful instruments of macroeconomic policy.

Katharine Hsiao (1971) identified 1953 and 1956 as years of high repressed inflation by use of a simple index based on the velocity of money; her findings for 1956 are confirmed by the Portes and Santorum estimates. In 1953, the process of introducing socialism was not yet completed: the state was in control of 41 per cent of retail sales of consumer goods and about 69 per cent of total transactions; the first economic plan was only just on its way. The main reasons for the unexpected increase in the money supply were the government deficit and the introduction of state procurements for the main agricultural products, which were paid for in cash. In 1956, the Agriculture Bank and the Rural Credit Cooperatives increased the amount of loans to peasants, helping them to join the new collective units. At the same time, industrial wages were raised and a large share of investment was financed by bank credit.

Similarly, in 1979 and in the early 1980s, the money supply rose sharply because of the growth of agricultural loans together with the increase in agricultural prices and the privatisation of rural markets, while the procurement practice was maintained (see Sicular 1988, for a theoretical model which analyses the economic disadvantages of such a mixed market system). Furthermore, at the same time a large share of investment and the whole working capital of enterprises were to be financed by bank loans, and salaries in industry were raised to counterbalance the increase in prices for agricultural products.

Referring to the monetary expansion of the early 1980s, Byrd (1983) and Balassa (1982) suggest an additional explanation: that the reform of the banking system itself, decentralising the collection of deposits and the issues of loans to local branches, has been a main factor in the rapid monetary growth, through the deposit multiplier.

Open inflation   Considering that China was a planned economy from 1954 to 1978 and a 'mixed' economy from 1978, we can search for direct links between monetary expansion and open inflation.

Chow (1987) investigates the effects of the money supply on the price level, testing the hypothesis that inflation in China has been mainly a monetary phenomenon. His analysis is entirely based on an econometric model derived from the quantity equation $MV = PQ$. His results are interesting: he finds a long-run positive relationship between price level and M/y (where M = currency in circulation and y = NMP, net material product, in real terms) and a less than unit price elasticity with respect to M/y, indicating that the velocity of money is not constant. However, the model used by Chow depends strictly on the assumption that the money stock is exogenous and that changes in output are independent of changes in the money supply.

Following Chow's approach, but removing the assumptions of money stock exogeneity and non-correlation between money and output, I have examined the relation between price and money supply in a rather different framework. The econometric structure of the model is borrowed from the rational expectations approach, but the assumptions are quite different.

It is intended to be strictly a model of planners' behaviour. Planners are assumed to follow rational behaviour; they plan/forecast current-period changes in the money supply on the basis of information available at the end of the previous period. The money stock is not completely under their control and is affected by unpredictable demand shocks, since the banking system is willing to supply any cash that is demanded.

Planners respond to *unanticipated* changes in the money stock by changing either output or prices, or both, in order to reduce households' surplus purchasing power. They respond to *anticipated* changes in the money supply by changes in the supply of consumer goods. Imports are not considered in the model because of the lack of separate data on imports of consumer goods. The planners' final target is assumed to be equilibrium, defined as balance on the consumer market without inflation, to be achieved through the combined adjustment of the supply of consumer goods, prices and interest rates. Variables in period t−1 are assumed to be already available to planners at the beginning of period t.

The empirical model is composed of a money growth equation, on the basis of which planners are assumed to formulate their expectations, and a price equation. The empirical variables have been chosen to take account of the planners' monetary policy target, M0. Therefore, the money variable is currency in circulation, the corresponding output variable is personal consumption, and the price variable is the retail price index.

The empirical model has been estimated first by OLS on single equations. The first step was to obtain the best possible regression of actual monetary growth on a set of exogenous variables which contains only information available to the planners at the beginning of period t (only lagged variables are included in the equation). The underlying assumption is that rational planners would use all the available information and the 'best' statistical description of the process determining money growth for formulating their expectations. The following equation seemed to be the best obtainable description of the process governing monetary growth over the period 1956–83 (all variables are in logs):

(1) $\Delta M_t = 0.37 - 0.78\Delta M_{t-1} - 0.53 M_{t-2} + 0.42\Delta SD_{t-1} + 0.70\Delta SD_{t-2}$
$\quad\quad (.17) \quad (.20) \quad\quad\quad (.19) \quad\quad\quad (.12) \quad\quad\quad\quad (.15)$

$\quad\quad - 0.36 SD_{t-3} + 1.24\Delta(c_{t-1} + p_{t-1})$
$\quad\quad\quad (.12) \quad\quad\quad (.49)$

$R^2 = 0.70$ $\bar{R}^2 = 0.72$ $s = 0.0827$ $\xi^2(2,25) = 1.91$ $\xi^3(2,25) = 0.77$
$BJ(2) = 0.43$, $LM1(1,20) = 0.003$ CHOW(6,15) = 1.86 (break in 1977)
CHOW(4,17) = 3.07 (break in 1979) N=28
See note to Table 10.6 for explanation of the tests.
M = currency in circulation; SD = households' saving deposits;
c = real consumption; p = retail price index; Δ indicates changes in the logarithm of variables.

The supply equation is assumed to be simply:

(2) $\quad\quad\quad C_t^s = \beta_0 + \beta_1 C_{t-1} + \beta_2 T + \sum_{i=1}^{n} \beta_{3i}\epsilon_{t-i} + v_t$

where T is time trend and ϵ_{t-i} are the residuals from (1), i.e. unanticipated disturbances in the money supply. The price equation, corresponding to (2), which has been finally estimated is:

(3) $\quad\quad P_t = \gamma_0 + \gamma_1 M_t + \gamma_2\epsilon_{t-1} + \gamma_3 T + \gamma_4 C_{t-1} + \gamma_5 P_{t-1} + \gamma_6 R_{t-1}$
$\quad\quad\quad\quad + \gamma_7(M_{t-1} - P_{t-1}) + v_t$

214

The mathematical explanation of (3) is in the Appendix.

Because of disequilibrium on the consumer market, and since the planning authorities can respond to expected changes in excess demand by increasing either output or prices, the supply equation is not directly observable. In equation 3, we expect $\gamma 2 > 0$, since unanticipated money should induce the authorities to increase prices, because the production plan is inflexible in the short term: this is exactly opposite to what is expected in a free economy, where, according to the RE theory, unanticipated money should increase output and reduce prices.

Results from the estimation of equation 3 over the period 1958–83 are given in Table 10.6 column (a). The equation is well defined and appears to

Table 10.6 Price equation, dependent variable p_t, period 1958–83

	(a)	(b)
constant	1.05	0.66*
	(.35)	(.08)
M_t	0.18*	0.20*
	(.04)	(.02)
ε_{t-1}	0.11*	0.13
	(.05)	(.05)
Time	0.006	–
	(.005)	
c_{t-1}	−0.35	0.24*
	(.10)	(.03)
p_{t-1}	0.39*	0.52*
	(.12)	(.06)
R_{t-1}	0.80	–
	(.57)	
$M_{t-1} - p_{t-1}$	0.03	
	(.04)	
R^2	0.94	0.94
s	0.0163	0.0160
BJ(2)	0.60	0.15
ξ^2 (2,22)	0.01	0.08
ξ^3 (2,22)	0.50	0.72
LM 1	1.11 (1,17)	0.87 (1,20)
CHOW $T_1 = 20$	0.74 (6,12)	0.50 (6,15)
SSR	0.0048	0.0054
N=26		F(3,18)=0.75

Note: Standard errors in brackets. * indicates values significant at the 5% confidence level. s is the standard error of the regression, BJ is the Bera-Jarque normality test, x^2-distributed with 2 degrees of freedom, ξ^2 is an F-distributed linearity test, ξ^3 is an F-distributed homoskedasticity test, LM 1 is the Lagrange Multiplier test for first order autocorrelation, CHOW is the standard Chow test, SSR is the sum of squared residuals. Column (b) reports also the F-test for the restrictions against equation (a).

be reasonably stable. The ϵ_{t-1} coefficient is positive and significant, suggesting that the authorities respond to previous-period unanticipated money by increasing the price level.

Testing the RE hypothesis gave a likelihood ratio of 13.014, χ^2 distributed with six degrees of freedom; χ_2 values are 12.95 at 95 per cent confidence level and 14.45 at 97.5 per cent level. In view of the fact that we are dealing with small samples and asymptotic tests tend to over-reject, I do not consider the result from the likelihood ratio test as providing enough evidence for rejecting the RE hypothesis.

Tests of the hypothesis that only unexpected monetary growth has an impact on the price level gave a likelihood ratio of 4.088 χ^2 distributed with one degree of freedom; at the 95 per cent confidence level $\chi^2_{(1)} = 3.841$ and at the 97.5 per cent, $\chi^2_{(1)} = 5.024$. Again, since we are dealing with a small sample, I do not consider the test gives enough ground to reject the hypothesis that only unanticipated money growth causes changes in prices.

Finally equation (a) and equation (b) in Table 10.6 have been used separately in order to forecast 1984 and 1985 values of monetary growth and price level. The predicted growth in money was +11 per cent in 1984 (compared with an actual increase of +49 per cent) and +2 per cent in 1985 (actual increase +25 per cent). The price equation performed only slightly better, predicting a price index of 1.69 in 1984 (actual value 1.60) and of 1.80 in 1985 (actual value 1.74). Both equations become unstable when 1984 and 1985 observations are included: no matter where we break the series, the Chow test always rejects the hypothesis of parameter time invariance.

Estimating the restricted price equation (b) in Table 10.6 over the period 1958–76 only, I could still get a well-defined model. I then used that model for forecasting over the period 1977–85. The results were as follows:

General retail price index (1950=1.00)

	$\hat{p}$	p
1977	1.31	1.35
1978	1.33	1.36
1979	1.39	1.39
1980	1.48	1.47
1981	1.54	1.50
1982	1.51	1.53
1983	1.55	1.57
1984	1.70	1.60
1985	1.84	1.74

Theil's inequality coefficient (Spanos 1986: 402–5) was only 0.00356, which indicates that the prediction power of the model was indeed rather good.

The only contradiction is in 1982, when the model predicts a decrease in prices, while in that year the price level actually increased. It is interesting that again the model tends to overestimate the price level in 1984 and 1985, while equation 1 greatly underestimated the monetary growth in those years.

On the basis of the results obtained, unexpected monetary growth seems to have been a major cause of inflation in the 1980s.

Causal relationships between money and other macroeconomic variables

We have seen that money supply changes in China affect both prices and the demand for consumer goods. Chen (1988) addresses the more general issue of the existence of a causal relationship between money and four macroeconomic variables: national income, the budget deficit, the trade deficit and an index of total inflation, inclusive of both official inflation and a measure of repressed inflation, derived from the *ex-post* identity MV=PQ. Chen also attempts to determine which definition of monetary aggregate is more appropriate for defining targets of monetary policy. He estimates three VAR models using, alternatively, M0, M2 and M3.

According to Chen's results, M0 seems to be the best indicator of changes in the other macroeconomic variables; changes in M0, in their turn, have effects on all four macrovariables under consideration. M2 and M3 can also be used as indicators (their response to changes in the other macrovariables is significant, even if to a lesser degree than M0); their own causality effects on the other variables, however, are restricted to national income for M2, and to the government deficit for M3. There is a high correlation among the three variables.

Caution should be used, however, in considering the causality effects suggested by the results, in particular by the relationship between the money stock (defined either as M0 or M2) and national income. The estimates indicate that both M0 and M2 are extremely significant in predicting national income, which would suggest the possibility of a Keynesian effect running from money to national income: the result is surprising, in view of the fact that for twenty-seven years of the estimation period (1952–83) China was strictly a CPE.

Bidirectional causality has been found, however, for all three monetary aggregates. Although this is not a proper exogeneity test, the results do suggest that the money stock could be used as an indicator/target of monetary policy, but not as an instrument.

Sectoral effects of monetary policy

Empirical studies of periods of general economic reform, when changes in macroeconomic variables are due to several reasons, most of which are structural and, therefore, non-quantifiable, are extremely difficult. Table 10.7 reports the percentage changes in M0 and compares them with the rates of

Table 10.7 Monetary growth and economic performance (% changes)

	M0	NVIO	NVAO	NMP	Job-waiting rate
1978	4.0	17.7	3.9	12.3	5.3
1979	11.5	8.1	6.4	7.0	n.a.
1980	−4.4	10.9	−1.8	6.4	4.9
1981	8.7	1.7	7.1	4.9	3.8
1982	26.4	6.0	11.7	8.3	3.2
1983	29.1	9.8	8.5	9.8	2.3
1984	14.5	14.9	13.0	13.5	1.9
1985	10.9	19.1	1.7	12.7	1.8
1986	20.7	9.1	3.7	7.4	2.0

NVIO = Net value industrial output
NVAO = Net value agricultural output
NMP = Net material product

Sources: Chen, 1988, for monetary data, and *Statistical Yearbook 1987*, for other data.

growth of net value of industrial output (NVIO), net value of agricultural output (NVAO), net material product and the job-waiting rate in cities and towns (ratio of people waiting for jobs over total workers), in an attempt to identify some correlation between monetary growth and changes in other macroeconomic variables.

There have been two reductions in the rate of growth of M0: in 1980, where there was an actual contraction, and in 1984–5, when the rate of growth decreased. The first monetary contraction seems to have had an effect on NVIO in the following year (rate of growth reduced to 1.7 from 10.9) and on NVAO the same year (negative rate of growth). Net material product increased by only 4.9 per cent in 1981, compared with 6.4 per cent in 1980. No effect can be found on the job-waiting rate.

A clear correlation is shown between the reduction in monetary growth in 1985 and the reduction in the rates of growth of GVIO, GVAO and NMP, as well as the increase in unemployment. Furthermore, both in 1980 and in 1985, contractionary monetary policies were accompanied by a reduction in the growth rate of NVAO, in the same period, and a reduction in the growth rate of NVIO, in the following period.

The effects of the 1984–5 contractionary monetary policy can be seen in a reduction in the rate of growth of NVIO in 1986 (two years later). More significant is the reduction in the rate of growth of NVAO in 1985 (one-year lag) and the still slow rate of growth, compared with the previous period, in 1986. The NMP growth rate also declined in 1986, while the job-waiting rate suddenly increased.

The effects of monetary policy largely depend on the response from production units. Therefore, while the monetary authorities set their macroeconomic targets, they must also pay attention to the way the chosen monetary policy is likely to affect different sectors of the economy.

Table 10.8 reports data on agricultural credit and the volume of sales of chemical fertiliser and tractors, which are quite sensitive to credit availability. In spite of the fact that variations in the sales of fertiliser and of tractors have also been affected by changes in prices (for which we do not have data) and by the availability of products on the market, we can still attempt to draw a

Table 10.8 Agricultural credit and sales of agricultural inputs (% changes)

	Total bank lending to agriculture	Sales of chemical fertiliser	Sales of tractors, walking tractors, motor-driven agricultural machinery
1979	n.a.	21.1	−0.9
1980	56.5	11.8	−30.5
1981	−0.3	10.5	−23.2
1982	16.4	11.7	−8.6
1983	18.3	1.7	20.0
1984	−6.8	−1.9	−28.7
1985	−12.8	−8.0	1.7
1986	32.7	21.1	1.9

Source: *Statistical Yearbook*, 1987.

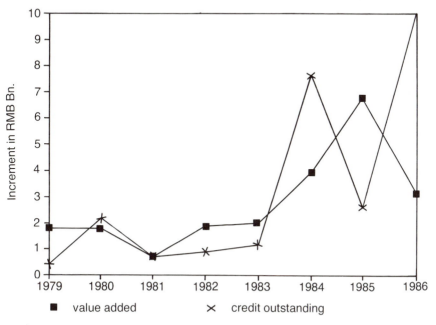

■ value added   × credit outstanding

Figure 10.3 Rural value added and credit, 1977–86
Source: Naughton (1988)

few conclusions. Although we cannot find a clear correlation between credit and sales of agricultural inputs over the period 1979–86, in 1984 the imposition of a tight credit policy appears to have caused a dramatic decline in the sales of both fertiliser and tractors; the decline in the sales of chemical fertiliser continued in 1985, probably as a consequence of the imposition of a tight credit policy in the second quarter of that year.

Rural enterprises are also dependent on credit from the banking system for their start-up costs (Naughton 1988). A comparison of the increase in value added in township and village enterprises and the net increase in credit extended to those enterprises each year (Figure 10.3) shows that in most years, these are quite close; the rapid growth in this sector in 1983–4 was closely related to credit resources. The credit squeeze in 1985, however, seems to have had an effect on the value added of the sector a year later, in 1986.

CONCLUSION

Despite the radical changes in the structure of the banking system since 1978, and more especially since 1984, the central bank maintained control of inflation as its main monetary target and continued to rely on direct credit control as the main instrument of monetary policy. Other instruments, such as reserve requirements and interest rates on loans to specialised banks, were gradually introduced but as 'experiments', not used for specifically monetary policy purposes.

Since 1978, the monetary policy of the People's Bank has been characterised by a stop-go pattern, under which periods of restrictive policy, of an average duration of one year, were followed by periods of expansionary policy during which the banking system supplied virtually all the funds demanded. The policy cycle deeply affected the behaviour of enterprises and resulted in a loss of credibility for all restrictive monetary measures.

In periods of monetary contraction enterprises use their own funds and working capital loans in order to pay wages and bonuses to workers and to finance the accumulation of precautionary stocks, simply preparing themselves to wait for the next expansionary period (Naughton 1988). Investment drops, while the demand for intermediate goods as well as the demand for consumption goods increase. This process obviously affects the efficiency of credit control. In order to break the cycle, realistic rates of interest should be adopted, lending criteria should be revised and enforced, and 'hard' budget constraints should be imposed on enterprises. The last implies the revision of fiscal benefits to enterprises as well as the reduction of government intervention in establishing priority sectors and priority borrowers.

After 1978, as a consequence of the economic reform, the money supply increased rapidly despite attempts by the monetary authorities to control it. A restrictive monetary policy was implemented in 1981 and in 1985–6. In both cases the monetary restrictions had effects on economic growth and on both agricultural and industrial production. The effects on inflation, however, were limited in 1981 and virtually unidentifiable after 1986. Furthermore, agriculture seems to have been the sector most penalised during both periods of monetary restriction.

Monetary policy has become less and less effective as a means of controlling inflation, as widespread and accelerating inflation (with rates ranging from 20 to 40 per cent) in urban areas in the second part of 1988 indicates.

Before reform, the central bank was able to enforce the use of properly set reserve requirement ratios and interest rates on loans to the specialised banks in order to tie money creation to a controllable monetary base. It was also able to use the inter-bank lending market to protect vulnerable sectors, such as agriculture, during periods of restrictive monetary policy. In the late 1980s, however, it seemed to prefer to return to the old system of credit plans in order to control monetary expansion and to increases in the savings deposit interest rate (up to 16 per cent, more than double that of the previous year, at the end of 1988) in order to withdraw excess currency from circulation.

In the short term, the central bank urgently needs to recover the credibility of its monetary policy. This could be achieved by implementing an efficient loan-monitoring system as well as by giving banks the power to enforce it effectively. This requires both less central and local government intervention in selecting priority borrowers and a fiscal system which does not allow enterprises to deduct the cost of higher interest rates from their tax charges.

Interest rates on loans do not provide realistic indications of the real opportunity costs of alternative investments. In order to avoid misallocation of resources to low-yielding sectors, as has repeatedly happened in the past, the structure of interest rates across sectors should be revised.

There has been a widespread debate about opportunities to allow most enterprises to issue shares, to introduce more financial instruments and to expand the capital market. Shi Lei and Ao Huicheng, two experts at the Planning Department of the People's Bank, have identified four major obstacles to a rapid growth of the capital market: lack of development of the credit system; scarcity of funds; the public's lack of confidence in the new financial instruments; and the issues of specific regulation and the development of well-trained personnel (Yue 1988).

Another limit to development comes from the structure of the interest rates on bonds. Yields on bonds purchased by enterprises are too low compared with alternative investment. Competition between savings deposits and bonds issued to individuals is also limited and the interest rates on bonds have already been pegged to bank rates (with a ceiling of 20 per cent above banking rates on savings deposits) in Guangzhou province (Grub and Sudweeks 1988).

APPENDIX

The conventional RE model is composed of a long-run demand-for-money equation 1 and an output equation 2:

$$(1) \qquad M_t - p_t = a_0 + a_1 y_t^d + a_2 R_t + u_t$$

$$(2) \qquad y_t^s = \beta_0 + \beta_1 X_{2t} + \sum_{i=1}^{n} \beta_{3i} \epsilon_{t-i} + v_t$$

where: M = nominal money stock
  p = price level
  y^d = quantity demanded
  y^s = quantity supplied
  R = nominal interest rate.

X_{2t} is a set of explanatory variables, u_t and v_t are independent serially uncorrelated error terms. All variables are in logs, except the interest rate. ϵ_{t-i} are unanticipated disturbances in the money supply, given by

$$\epsilon_{t-i} = M_{t-i} - E(M_{t-i} | I_{t-i-1})$$

Expectations are assumed to be formed on the basis of information available at the end of the previous period. Equation 1 describes equilibrium in the monetary sector. Assuming $y^d = y^s$ the model can be solved with respect to p_t by substituting (2) for (1), giving:

$$(3) \qquad p_t = -(a_0 + a_1 \beta_0) + M_t - a_1 \beta_1 X_{2t} - a_1 \Sigma \beta_{3i} \epsilon_{t-i} - a_2 R_t \\ - (a_1 v_t + u_t)$$

This is the conventional equation tested by Barro (1981) and others. The key hypothesis is that anticipated movements in the money stock (with the expected rate of inflation-type effects held fixed) would be reflected in one-to-one, contemporaneous movements in the price level (Barro 1978). Alogoskoufis and Pissarides (1983) build a more general model which includes the hypotheses of real partial adjustment in the monetary sector and price sluggishness.

Monetary adjustment assumes that the demand for money does not adjust instantaneously to its long-run values. Current period demand for real money balances is assumed to adjust with respect to previous period deviation from its long-run value according to:

$$(M_t - p_t) - (M_{t-1} - p_{t-1}) = \mu[(M_t^* - p_t^*) - (M_{t-1} - p_{t-1})]$$

which yields:

$$(4) \qquad M_t - p_t = \mu(M_t^* - p_t^*) + (1 - \mu)(M_{t-1} - p_{t-1})$$

where $(M_t^* - p_t^*)$ is the long-run demand for real money balances and μ is the parameter which indicates the speed of adjustment: when $\mu = 1$, we have full adjustment and the current period demand for money is equal to the long-run demand. When $\mu = 0$, there is no adjustment and current demand is equal to previous period demand.

Similarly, prices can be assumed to change according to the following adjustment process:

$$p_t - p_{t-1} = \lambda(p_t^* - p_{t-1})$$

which yields:

(5) $$p_t = \lambda p_t^* - (1 - \lambda)p_{t-1}$$

where p_t^* is the equilibrium price. When $\lambda = 1$, $p_t = p_t^*$ (full adjustment), while when $\lambda = 0$, no adjustment occurs and $p_t = p_{t-1}$.

In a conventional market model where prices are expected to move towards equilibrium, the parameter λ describes the movement of the aggregate price level and not the behaviour of any particular agent in the economy (Alogoskoufis and Pissarides 1983). In our specific context, λ is probably far from describing the movement of the price level and might explain planners' behaviour only as long as they follow the adjustment rule in (5): neither hypothesis may hold; however, they can be tested.

Substituting (3) for (4) and equating y^s and y^d yields:

(6) $$p_t = -\mu(a_0 + a_1\beta_0) + M_t - \mu a_1\beta_1 X_{2t} - \mu a_1 \Sigma \beta_{3i}\epsilon_{t-i} - \mu a_2 R_t$$
$$-(1 - \mu)(M_{t-1} - p_{t-1}) - \mu(a_1 v_t - u_t)$$

The price equation including both monetary adjustment and price sluggishness is obtained by substituting market clearing prices, as derived from (6) for (5):

(7) $$p_t = -\lambda\mu(a_0 - a_1\beta_0) + \lambda M_t - \lambda\mu a_1\beta_1 X_{2t} - \lambda\mu a_1 \Sigma \beta_{3i}\epsilon_{t-i} - \lambda\mu a_2 R_t$$
$$-\lambda(1 - \mu)(M_{t-1} - p_{t-1}) - (1 - \lambda)p_{t-1} - \lambda\mu(a_1 v_t + u_t)$$

If the price-adjustment rule of equation 5 holds, (7) can be rewritten as:

(8) $$p_t = -\lambda\mu(a_0 - a_1\beta_0) + M_t - \lambda\mu a_1\beta_1 X_{2t} - \lambda\mu\Sigma\beta_{3i}\epsilon_{t-1} - \lambda\mu a_2 R_t$$
$$-\lambda(1 - \mu)(M_{t-1} - p_{t-1}) - (1 - \lambda)(M_t - p_{t-1}) - \lambda\mu(a_1 v_t + u_t)$$

When $\lambda = 1$, there will no longer be equilibrium in the goods market; in this case, we cannot observe the output equation unless we specify the rule determining excess demand. Empirical tests gave $F(1,19) = 0.39$ for H_1: $\mu = 1$ and $F(1,19) = 11.48$, for H_2: $\lambda = 1$ (critical value $_{95}F(1,19) = 4.38$). Therefore, we reject the full price adjustment hypothesis, but we cannot reject the full monetary adjustment hypothesis.

The demand for money adjusts completely within a one-year period to its long-run value. This could mean that the monetary authorities are actually willing to supply any amount of cash they are asked for and households can return any unwanted quantity of money simply by depositing it in the bank. The price index, on the other hand, does not adjust within the period to its equilibrium level, which inevitably implies disequilibrium in the consumer goods market. Moreover, the sum of the current money coefficient (λ, in equation 8) and the lagged prices coefficient, $(1 - \lambda)$, is different from 1.

This implies that the planning authorities do not follow the adjustment rule assumed in equation 5.

Part III
SPECIAL STUDIES

11

THE INFORMAL FINANCIAL SECTOR: HOW DOES IT OPERATE AND WHO ARE THE CUSTOMERS?

J.J. Thomas

INTRODUCTION

The discussion of monetary policy elsewhere in this book has concentrated on the formal financial sector (FFS), that is, the commercial banks and various specialised financial institutions created and licensed by the governments in many developing countries to target long-term investment to particular regions or groups. The picture would, however, be incomplete without some consideration of the informal financial sector (IFS) that exists in developing countries.[1] 'Financial dualism' involves more than simply the dichotomy between FFS and IFS. The customers of the institutions in the FFS and IFS are also both 'formal' and 'informal' (see for example Germidis *et al.* 1991: 13, and for a fuller discussion of the IFS, Thomas 1992).

This 'double dualism' may be criticised from a number of points of view (see Thomas 1991), but of relevance here is the omission of sectors that are important in developing countries. First, while in general the customers of the FFS tend to be in the modern (or formal) sector of large-scale industrial and manufacturing production, there are also rural customers in the modern agricultural sector. Second, while in general there is little contact between the FFS and potential customers in the rural traditional sector, this is also true for potential customers in the urban informal sector. As a result, the concentration on the FFS tends to ignore the financial needs of two important groups; those working in the urban informal sector and the rural poor – groups that represent a high proportion of the population and the labour force in most developing countries. The fact that the needs of these groups are not generally catered for by the FFS has meant that informal financial institutions (IFIs) have played an important role in supplying these needs.

The FFS in most developing countries offers the basic services of money transfers, chequing services, credit cards, facilities for saving and the provision of credit. Why are these services not available to potential rural or urban informal customers? There are six main reasons:

1　The commercial banks do not have branches in the city slums and squatter settlements or in the countryside, so access to banking facilities by potential customers is limited.
2　Commercial banks are inflexible and tend to grant credit only for investment purposes, not for consumption.
3　 Transaction costs are high as a proportion of the size of potential transactions, and may become very high if they include adequate project appraisal.
4　The commercial banks lack information about potential customers from these groups, thus raising risks and costs.
5　Potential customers do not possess acceptable collateral to substitute for creditworthiness.
6　Given the lack of information about these customers, it is believed that they are too poor to be able to pay a commercial rate of interest on a loan.

The main purpose of this chapter will be to examine in more detail the response of formal financial institutions, often in reaction to government or international persuasion, to the problems listed in the previous paragraph and the extent to which institutions in the IFS are able to overcome these problems and provide financial services to other customers. The next section will present evidence on and discuss the problems. The following sections will look at a variety of informal financial institutions and examine how successful they have been, and consider the implications of the IFS for monetary policy, before the final section of conclusions.

FORMAL FINANCIAL INSTITUTIONS AND THE RURAL TRADITIONAL AND URBAN INFORMAL SECTORS

It is necessary first to compare the services offered by the commercial banks with the needs of these sectors. These sectors, particularly the urban informal, are heterogeneous. The concentration here on the urban sector reflects its relative neglect in discussions of financial institutions and monetary policy. Many of the same issues arise in connection with problems of rural savings and credit, but these have already been widely discussed (see, for example, Von Pischke, Adams and Donald (eds) 1983), and relevant evidence on rural credit problems and programmes will be presented below. The normal banking services provided by the FFS are not well matched with these needs. Some small enterprises and some farmers may be sufficiently well-established to make regular use of commercial banking facilities, but the majority of those working in these urban and rural sectors are not. The majority in the urban sector tend to operate with cash, since their incomes are low and they are dealing with or selling to people who do not have bank accounts, so the advantages of a bank account for trade are not obvious, except to put the individual in touch with other bank services. At the subsistence level at which many peasants operate, many have little regular contact with markets and do not need to use cash as much as those in the cities.

There is also a problem of distance, since most commercial banks are physically distant from many potential rural customers, who are too poor to travel to the local towns or cities to make use of bank services. For the urban worker, the distance is 'social' rather than 'physical', since many of the slums or squatter settlements they inhabit are close to the downtown offices of the commercial banks.

This absence of contact with commercial banks for transfer services tends to mean that, where saving is possible, it will be undertaken through other channels, and this is one important service that is provided by some institutions in the IFS. In addition to the absence of links with banks, the small size of increments of savings and the relatively short saving periods involved tend to make saving through the FFS both difficult and unattractive. Some saving is the precautionary (rainy day) variety, which may need to be liquidated frequently, while some is intended to build up capital.

The needs for credit are very diverse, particularly in agriculture, to cover seasonal fluctuations in income flows; the provision of short-term liquidity or emergency credit; the supply of working capital; and finding funds for investment.

It is clear that those working in the urban informal sector do not receive much credit from the FFS. For example, in a large-scale study of Lima, Carbonetto et al. (1987) found that 91 per cent had not obtained any formal credits and an additional 2.6 per cent had obtained credit of less than US$10. Of those who had obtained credit, only 5.6 per cent received loans from commercial banks and 6.3 per cent from state banks, whereas 41.7 per cent obtained loans from parents or friends. Less than 1 per cent had taken loans from money-lenders for very short periods (from one day to a week) at real interest rates of 40–70 per cent per annum. Chandavarkar (1989) cites data for a number of African countries showing that the initial investment for the start-up of small enterprises came overwhelmingly from the entrepreneur's own savings or those of relatives and at most 2 per cent came from banks (see also Harper 1984: ch. 5).

There are two main reasons for this. The first is that the quantities of credit required by a majority of potential borrowers from these sectors may be too small to cover the fixed costs involved in making individual loans. For example, Levitsky (1986b) quotes studies of the Philippines in the 1970s showing that the transactions costs in lending to small businesses were between 2.5 and 3.0 per cent of the value of the loan, as compared to 0.5 per cent of loans to large businesses. Bundling savings or loans into larger units is one method of reducing the effect of high fixed costs, but it is not a costless process. Some ways of dealing with this problem will be discussed in the following section.

The second is the problem of assessing risk; this presents particular difficulties. Here again the lack of customer contact with the commercial banks works against potential borrowers as they cannot build up a credit record with a lending institution. The possibility of supplying collateral as a substitute for reputation is also denied to most of them, since they do not possess the necessary assets. Many live in slums or as squatters on land that has been acquired illegally or to which they have no title. This removes housing and land, a source of collateral that is used extensively by those operating in the formal sector. This can also be a problem for would-be borrowers in rural areas. As Johnny (1985) notes for Sierra Leone, 'Farmers cannot use their most tangible property – land – as credit collateral because of the customary communal system of land tenure which prevails in the provinces' (p. 21). Even where land may be owned individually, women may face a problem, since many cultures exclude them from the ownership of land (see Mayoux 1988; Mayoux et al. 1989, for examples from Africa). Even where small enterprises own capital in the form of machinery, it is often obsolescent and of little market value and so is of little use as collateral.

Commercial banks and other financial institutions may well feel that they do not need this business. However, policy-makers in many developing countries have long been concerned with the problem of providing rural credit and some have wished to encourage the urban informal sector. As a result there have been efforts to involve the FFS, through funding from state banks, credit guarantee programmes and the creation of special banks.

Credit guarantee schemes   One method of making loans on the basis of little or no collateral more attractive to formal financial institutions is to provide credit guarantees against default. This has been tried in a large number of countries, both developed and developing, with somewhat mixed success.

> The purpose of such schemes is to encourage financial institutions, and in particular commercial banks, to lend to small businesses with viable projects and good prospects of success.
>
> (Levitsky and Prasad 1987: 1)

Success depends on ensuring a number of conditions are satisfied. First, while the objective is to reduce the risk of certain kinds of loan, the guarantees should not remove risk altogether. If the lending banks bear none of the risk, they will have little or no incentive to assess the viability of the loans made under the scheme, which is then likely to run into financial problems by having to pay out its initial capital quickly in default payments. The percentage of the loan (the principal and possibly interest payments) covered

230

by the guarantee should be large enough to make the scheme attractive to commercial banks, while not so large as to discourage proper profit appraisal. With the exception of Japan, where 100 per cent credit guarantees are offered and seem to work, in many countries the maximum cover is around 60 per cent.

Second, the scheme must ensure that proper evaluations of viability are carried out, and this raises the question of who is to do it. One argument is that the commercial banks should do it, since they are making the loan. However, in some cases, the participating commercial banks will be dealing with new kinds of customers and may not have the expertise to assess projects. There may be a case for the agency providing the credit guarantee to charge a fee and provide the necessary evaluation. It is important that one assessment should be made, but in a well-designed scheme it should not be necessary for both to carry out a study of viability. It is important that charges should be high enough to cover these evaluation costs, as a number of credit guarantee schemes have run into problems on this matter. Borrowers in these sectors have been able to repay loans at interest rates above those charged in the FFS, so a fee sufficient to ensure proper assessment of viability should be feasible.

Third, the scheme should lay out explicitly and clearly the evaluation criteria to be followed by the commercial banks if they are responsible for the viability assessment. This is to prevent problems arising later when defaults occur if claims are rejected because the commercial banks failed to meet unclear or implicit requirements for project evaluation.

Fourth, the conditions to be met before a claim is accepted need to balance sufficient generosity to encourage the commercial banks to participate with the need to ensure that this generosity does not discourage them from pursuing bad debts with all possible vigour before making a claim. Again, the requirements need to be spelled out explicitly at the outset.

Fifth, once claims are submitted and are found to be valid, it is necessary to ensure prompt settlement. There is evidence from a number of countries that scepticism about the probability of guarantees being met, or bad experiences with delays over settlement of claims, have been the main causes of commercial banks either refusing to participate in credit guarantee schemes or leaving them.[2]

Sixth, it is necessary to set the ratio of guarantees to the credit guarantee agency's capital, taking proper account of risk. Levitsky and Prasad suggest that a ratio of guarantees to capital of about 10:1 is appropriate for most developing countries.[3]

Seventh, the scheme should induce the banks to make loans they would not otherwise have made (that is, provide additionality), rather than allowing the participating banks to obtain credit guarantees for risky loans they would have made anyway. Additionality is often difficult to achieve. Furthermore, Levitsky and Prasad report that in many of the countries they studied, the participating banks continued to demand collateral even where credit guarantees should have provided adequate protection.

Finally, there is the problem of making the schemes attractive to the participating banks. Reporting on a scheme in Barbados, Levitsky and Prasad noted:

> the commercial banks regard the scheme as a way of making them approve loans to very risky small businesses. In addition, the commercial banks are not very enthusiastic about granting small loans on which the risks are high and the profitability is low. They prefer to make larger loans where the risks are high but the profitability is higher.
>
> (1987: 79)

This problem may be particularly severe when the credit guarantee scheme tries to provide credit at subsidised low interest rates, since this may not provide sufficient spread for the banks to make a profit.

The survey by Levitsky and Prasad found evidence of major problems facing credit guarantee schemes in many of the countries they studied, and few schemes met most of the criteria listed above. The most frequent problems were failure to lay out the risk assessment criteria clearly, with considerable disputes between the participating banks and the agency running the scheme, and slow settlement rates. In some instances, the number of guarantees being issued dropped sharply after the initial period as the participating banks either withdrew or cut back. In others, the schemes became unviable when faced with high default rates, and were unable to continue.[4] The authors conclude:

> Credit guarantee schemes appear to be an attractive form of support for small enterprise development in developing countries, where non-availability of finance has been a serious constraint in developing the small business sector. However, guarantee schemes only have meaning to the extent that the commercial banking system is ready to participate in the scheme. Schemes in which the only participants are publicly-funded development finance institutions have little meaning, since ultimately the losses of these institutions must be made good from the public treasury. The evidence from developed countries is that the government, the business community, and the banking system must all assume some part of the risk. Credit guarantee schemes cannot and should not completely absolve banks from taking a normal level of risk as such risk-taking is acceptable banking practice.
>
> (1987: 13)

The credit guarantee scheme has the advantage of persuading the FFS to participate and may therefore be more flexible and responsive than more direct approaches that ignore this sector.

Alternative approaches might involve acting as a broker between the informal and formal financial sectors. While such approaches have not been widely tried to date, Seibel (1989) and Seibel and Parhusip (1990) report on interesting experiments in the Philippines and a number of other countries with financial self-help groups acting as intermediaries between micro entrepreneurs and commercial banks. These schemes deserve further study.

The reluctance of the FFS to become involved in schemes aimed at small-scale enterprises (SSEs) is illustrated by the experience of the World Bank. During the late 1970s, the World Bank accepted the case for supporting SSEs because of their potential for job creation. Between July 1977 and June 1985, it lent more than US$2.2 bn through seventy different projects in thirty-seven countries. Even though loans to the SSEs involved in the Bank programmes were in the range of US$20,000 to US$50,000 and were thus much larger financially than most small enterprises, the Bank had difficulty in finding appropriate financial intermediaries for its programmes. In its early projects, the funds were channelled through Development Finance Companies (DFCs), but these were found to be too centralised, with few branches outside the metropolitan centres, and, conditioned by their role in appraising complex projects, they demanded extensive documented information, which could not be provided by small enterprises.

Given these problems, the World Bank switched its policy towards channelling its credit through the commercial banks. The advantages of these institutions over DFCs are:

(1) they have the necessary domestic resources and as such are better able to meet the need for working capital and term loans for fixed assets;

(2) they offer a greater variety of banking services;

(3) they usually have a large branch network permitting contact with small enterprises on a local basis;

(4) they are better able to respond quickly to the needs of small businesses; and

(5) they are more experienced in debt collection than the DFCs.

(Levitsky 1986a: 20)

However, Levitsky reports the same lack of enthusiasm on the part of commercial banks towards the World Bank credit programmes as was found above.

It is clear that much of the Bank's lending was made through conventional channels and the programmes were not intended to tackle the creditworthiness/collateral problem. Levitsky (1986a) shows that the programmes did create employment, even if the costs per job created were somewhat higher than those envisaged in the Bank's plans.[5] This resistance on the part of formal financial institutions to becoming involved in credit programmes for enterprises that are small by World Bank standards, but large in comparison with the size of most enterprises in the urban informal sectors, confirms the problems faced by small-scale borrowers when trying to obtain credit from the FFS.[6]

In summary, the FFS has not been much involved in providing financial services to the rural and urban informal sectors, and programmes to increase its involvement have often failed. It is time now to see how institutions in the IFS have dealt with the problems listed above.

INFORMAL FINANCIAL INSTITUTIONS

In discussing informal financial institutions, we may identify two groups with different degrees of linkage with the formal financial sector. The first, which might be called 'self-help saving and lending schemes', involve no direct linkage with financial institutions and rely on the mobilisation of savings within the rural and urban informal sectors to provide the capital for loans. Important here are the so-called Rotating Savings and Credit Associations (ROSCAs). The second group involves institutions that operate independently of the commercial banks, but which may be linked to the FFS, depending on whether they are licensed or not. For example, money-lenders are generally outside the FFS, but pawnbrokers may or may not be licensed. Also in this category would be included special programmes, often organised and funded by non-governmental organisations (NGOs), to provide financial services (especially credit) to those in these sectors.

Informal financial institutions across a large number of developing countries in different continents show a considerable variety, as well as common approaches to basic problems. One interesting phenomenon that has resulted from the movement of Chinese and Indians, especially during colonial times, is the popularity of certain informal financial institutions in particular countries. Thus Ng (1985) comments on 'the conspicuous presence of professional moneylenders of Indian origin in those SEACEN countries which had been under British rule' as compared with 'the relative predominance of rotating savings and credit associations (ROSCAs) and pawnshops ... in those countries where overseas Chinese represent a significant percentage of their population' (pp. 2–3).[7] Religious and cultural differences (such as the caste structure, see Bhattacharya 1984) also play an important role in determining what kinds of financial institutions are acceptable and tolerated, in particular for women.

In examining alternative financial institutions, one will need to consider the way in which they deal with a number of problems:

1 how to keep down transaction costs;
2 how to offer competitive interest rates to lenders and/or borrowers;
3 how to keep default rates low; and, in some cases,
4 how to target particular groups of potential savers or borrowers who may have special needs, such as women.

Self-help savings and lending schemes

Since the increments in savings tend to be small and the periods of deposit may be relatively short, low transactions costs are very important and may outweigh the rate of interest being offered. In addition, Vogel and Burkett (1986a, b) suggest that reciprocity (that is, enhanced access to loans) may be important in attracting small savers to particular institutions. As evidence of its importance, they cite the dramatic decline of postal savings deposits in many African and Asian countries in recent years (with the exception of Singapore and Taiwan, where interest payments were tax-free). Whereas postal savings accounts offered accessibility (there were post offices in many areas where there were no branches of commercial banks) and were prepared to handle very small transactions, they generally did not offer credit to depositors (again with the exception of Singapore, where postal savings offices made housing loans to individuals).

This need is met by the formation of groups of individuals in associations to pool their savings in order to provide loans.[8] Rotating savings and credit associations (ROSCAs) are of considerable antiquity and are found widely in Africa and Asia, but somewhat less in Latin America.[9] They are normally small groups (from ten to forty members) that agree that for a specified period the members will pay a given amount into a kitty at regular intervals. The kitty is then allocated to the members of the ROSCA in rotation until all members have received it, at which point the ROSCA either disbands or starts on a new cycle. It may be formed by a group of friends or acquaintances and carried out informally, with at most a member chosen to provide some minimum organisation. Alternatively, the initiative to form the ROSCA may come from an outside organiser or manager, who may provide the group with services in return for privileges, such as being the first borrower.

The method of ordering the rotation is determined in various ways. In some cases where hierarchies are important, the order may depend on seniority or social standing. In other cases it is determined by lot, but this method, while appearing fair, may fail to provide sufficient incentives for the members to take part. Since no rates of interest are involved, the first borrower gains most in terms of obtaining an interest-free loan and subsequent borrowers gain decreasingly as the implicit repayment period shortens, until the last borrower, who gains nothing as he will have contributed exactly the amount he receives in the final kitty. For this reason, while ROSCAs formed from groups of friends may accept the random draw method of rotation, most have developed methods of auctioning the kitty that provide incentives to members. For example, Ng (1985) reports that 86 per cent of ROSCAs surveyed in a study in Thailand in 1970 allocated the kitty by some form of tendering.

One method of auctioning that is practised in Pakistan (Asian Development

Bank 1990: 199) is by an open auction at each meeting with only members who have not yet received the kitty being eligible to bid, the kitty going to the member offering the biggest discount. Suppose a ROSCA of thirty members agree to contribute $1,000 each to a kitty every two weeks for fifteen months: if, at the second meeting, the highest discount offered by one of the twenty-nine bidding members is $5,000, each member of the ROSCA then pays in a contribution of $862 (i.e. ($30,000–$5,000)/29). This system provides considerable flexibility, since those who are keen to borrow early and offer large discounts are paying a relatively high rate of interest, while those who put in bids with small discounts and are content to wait until late in the cycle receive relatively high rates of interest on their contributions.

How does the ROSCA deal with the four problems listed above? First, the simple nature of the organisation and its small size tend to keep transaction costs low. Little organisation or book-keeping is necessary and the collection of contributions and the distribution of the kitty may be carried out simultaneously if members bring their contributions to a meeting and the winner departs with the kitty. Providing the member contributes regularly to the kitty and fulfils his obligations, the ROSCA is not concerned with the purpose of the loan, so project appraisal is unnecessary.[10]

Second, the question of interest rates depends on the method of rotation. If the order is culturally determined or if friends agree to rely on the fortunes of a random draw, interest rates are of little relevance. However, the majority of ROSCAs that use an auction system to determine the order of rotation provide a considerable degree of choice over the interest rate, within the constraints of the fixed time-cycle of the system. One point to note is that the need to pay a rate of interest through an auction system does not keep the poor from taking part in ROSCAs.

The third problem is potential default, in this case by members who received the kitty early refusing or being unable to continue contributing to the ROSCA for the rest of the cycle. Collateral is not provided, so safeguards vary. If the rotation is determined by social or cultural constraints, these may well be sufficiently strong to ensure compliance. If friends or homogeneous groups, such as neighbours or fellow workers, are involved, the risk of default may be very low, since would-be members who are judged to be potential problems may be refused entry. If the groups are not homogeneous, the rules of entry may be strict enough to ensure that members about whom there are doubts are only eligible to borrow late in the cycle. In any event, all accounts of the operations of ROSCAs suggest that the default rate is not a problem.

Finally, the basic simplicity of the system and the considerable flexibility in terms of the size of the group, the size of contributions, the length of the cycle and the method of rotation suggest that ROSCAs should be capable of allowing particular groups to target themselves. Those likely to be excluded from the possibility of forming or being invited to join ROSCAs are those who do not have access to the funds to make the required regular contributions and/or those who are isolated from contact with potential ROSCA members. In many societies, women are likely to be disqualified on both counts, and descriptions of ROSCAs suggest that they are predominantly male organisations.

Informal lending institutions

Cooperative thrift and credit societies   A number of examples are quoted in Mayoux (1988) of institutions that arrange for the collection of savings and the granting of loans at low rates of interest. These may involve larger groups than are found in ROSCAs (Moepi 1988 reports that thirty-one such groups in Botswana had a membership of 3,650) and the membership rules may be much more formal (Jallow 1988 describes some in The Gambia in which members have to pay an entrance fee of D2.50, about US$1.00 in the early 1980s, purchase a share of D10.00 and save for six months, earning interest at 8 per cent per annum before becoming eligible to borrow at an interest rate of 12 per cent per annum). The success of these institutions is difficult to evaluate, since the reports do not discuss transaction costs and there is little discussion of recovery rates.[11]

Money-lending   Among sources of credit that do not involve a savings commitment, money-lenders have been the traditional source in many poor communities, particularly in rural areas. Judgements concerning their operations vary, and while some have seen them as usurers whose monopolistic position allows them to exploit their poor victims, a number of studies that have examined the evidence for such stereotyping have concluded that this picture may be misleading. For example, the Asian Development Bank (1990) reports on a study of fourteen villages in Thailand which showed that eleven of the villages had at least four money-lenders and that outside money-lenders were also active. This suggests that the view of the monopolistic position of the money-lender may be exaggerated in some cases. This is a result one would expect if there is an opportunity to compete for monopoly profits and freedom of entry is not blocked.

However, the freedom of entry is conditioned by the need to obtain the information necessary to assess the creditworthiness of the borrowers, which is essential in the absence of collateral. In many cases this is obtained by the proximity of the lenders to the borrowers, which may give the local money-lender sufficient advantage to earn a rent on his specialised knowledge. This tends to keep transaction costs low.[12] However, the fact that money-lenders from outside the villages can compete suggests that this advantage is not decisive. In examining the interest rates charged by money-lenders, Ng (1985) presents data for Malaysia which suggest that when the risk premium and alternative returns are taken into account, any monopoly element is a relatively small proportion of the interest rate. Many rural borrowers need loans to smooth consumption over the year, and surveys suggest they do not see the food provided on credit from the money-lender during the non-harvest period as exploitation. As Johnny (1985) points out regarding Sierra Leone, the need to obtain credit annually provides a strong incentive for borrowers to repay their debts, in order to ensure the provision of loans in future years.[13]

In summary, close proximity of money-lenders to the borrowers can reduce transaction costs, and use of the resulting knowledge obtained by this proximity can provide an assessment of risk that enables them to charge a risk premium, which replaces the demand for collateral by other lenders. This makes the quoted interest rates charged by money-lenders higher than those charged by institutions in the FFS. The borrower also has advantages – of informal procedures and locational convenience (Holst 1985: 141).[14] There is some evidence of competition.

Pawnshops While the pawnbroker has become less important as a source of credit in most developed countries, the pawnshop still has a role to play in many developing countries. Since money is only advanced against collateral, there is no need for the lender to devote resources to assessing the credit-worthiness of borrowers, though some expertise is required to assess the value of the item pledged, which may typically be jewels, ornaments, gold, silver and other items of value such as various consumer durables.[15] The expertise necessary to assess the pledges may have been acquired independently of the activity of pawnbroking, since jewellers or gold dealers often operate as pawnbrokers, so that this cost does not have to be covered by profits from pawnbroking. Given such expertise, the time involved in arranging the loan is minimal and this tends to reduce transaction costs. This means that a potential pawner can expect short waits and can transact business directly with the pawnbroker.

Pawnbrokers have a bad reputation because they are said to charge exorbitant interest rates and to make considerable profits by selling the goods that are not redeemed (see Bhaduri 1989: 245), but empirical evidence does not support this. Bouman and Houtman (1988) present data for Sri Lanka, where pawnbrokers are officially licensed, though there are unlicensed pawnshops operating illegally. They found that a legal pawnbroker made a return on capital of about 10 per cent, which was not particularly usurious, but that an unregistered pawnshop was making a return of 70 per cent on capital. They concluded that this high return reflected the extra risk incurred in part through the illegality of the unregistered operation and also through racial problems; many of the unlicensed pawnshops in Colombo belonged to Tamils and some were destroyed in riots in 1984. They question the validity of the argument that pawnbrokers make their profit from unreclaimed pledges and suggest that it is more profitable for the lender to provide credit repeatedly to the same customer using the same pledge.

Sri Lanka is an interesting case, because rural banks saw the possibilities and offered pawning facilities. While this business expanded rapidly at first, it was unable to dominate the private pawnbrokers for a number of reasons. First, the price offered by the banks for gold did not adjust as rapidly in response to inflation as did the pawnshops. Secondly, the rural banks put conditions on the purposes of loans, that they should be for essential or productive purposes, whereas pawnshops did not interfere with their customers' affairs. Thirdly, the rural banks operated at hours that were less flexible than the pawnshops, and took time to process applications (see Chandavarkar 1989).

There are a number of reasons for the popularity of pawnshops as a source of credit. While the borrower loses the pledge if the loan is not repaid in full, that is the end of the matter and the borrower incurs no liability to pay further interest on the loan. This avoids an ever-increasing debt load. Transaction costs are low and access to funds is very rapid. As in the case of other forms of informal financial credit, it seems that rates of interest higher than those operating in the FFS, from which the borrower may anyway be excluded, are not the major consideration.

If it is the case that most customers who use pawnshops redeem the pledge, then in principle this form of collateral should be acceptable to the FFS, though the small value of many transactions and the need for the expertise to assess the pledges might make the costs too high for this to be economical. Given the generally negative view of pawnbroking in many developed countries, it is unlikely that commercial banks in developing countries would be enthusiastic to detract from their 'Westernised' images by undertaking this kind of business.

Credit unions   These are larger and more formal versions of the basic idea of the ROSCA, with a more elaborate organisation, and they illustrate some of the effects of extending the scale of the operations. Credit unions became popular in Latin America as a result of encouragement from the US Peace Corps and church groups. The basic idea 'was to provide an outlet for savings that would be available as credit to the same group and to rely on voluntary contributions of labour and a "co-operative" spirit rather than on the profit motive' (Vogel and Burkett 1986a: 432). In many instances, they received funds from aid organisations. They link savings closely to the provision of credit. Vogel and Burkett (1986b) report studies from Latin America that suggest that transaction costs in credit unions were lower than in commercial banks, and costs did not rise too rapidly with increased scale. There were problems of members' control over those running the unions (for example, members of the board were often found to receive a disproportionate share of credit union funds). Default rates, while generally not a problem, were sometimes considerably higher than for the ROSCAs.

A major difficulty faced by credit unions in Latin America, as well as in parts of Africa (Vogel and Burkett 1986b) is that the link between savings and credit was often undermined by governments or NGOs, which have seen credit unions as instruments for achieving other objectives, such as increasing agricultural output or improving the incomes of the rural poor. These additional objectives have meant that credits have been tied to schemes that were not the choice of the borrowers, which has tended to undermine the incentives for mobilising savings.

In addition to the traditional sources of credit available through the IFS, innovations have come from both indigenous and external NGOs, as well as international organisations such as USAID and the World Bank aimed at providing financial help to some of those working in the informal economy.

Credit programmes run by international organisations and NGOs

Other programmes have been more directly created and run by donors. Harper and de Jong (1986) report the work of a number of NGOs in financing small enterprises, while IFAD (1985) details the effort of the International Fund for Agricultural Development (IFAD) to provide credit to the rural poor. Both studies report many problems with defaults and highlight the difficulties and costs of the supervision of loans when the amounts are relatively small and there is little or no collateral. Given that NGOs lack the local knowledge of those involved, the costs of assessing creditworthiness add considerably to transaction costs.

Further problems may be caused by programmes that attempt to provide cheap credit by offering loans at low rates of interest. The philosophy underlying some of these programmes seems to be based on the assumption that because the poor live close to the margin of subsistence, they can neither save nor afford to borrow at 'high' (i.e. commercial) rates of interest. While well-intentioned as methods of undercutting what are seen as the exploitatively high rates of interest charged by money-lenders, the effects of subsidised credit programmes have not always been successful. The high rates of interest charged by money-lenders contain a risk premium, and the absence of this and of the information possessed by these lenders has led to serious problems of default, without the resources to bear the cost. In addition, the low rates of interest discourage local savings, and deprive the borrowers of potential channels of saving that could increase the amount of funds available for loans. On balance, in the case of rural credit programmes, the evidence seems strongly against the provision of cheap credit as opposed to encouraging savings through price incentives (see Adams *et al.* 1984 and Remenyi 1991).

The work of the World Bank in lending to small-scale enterprises was discussed in the previous section in the context of its attempts to encourage the commercial banks to participate. In contrast to the approach of the

World Bank, the Grameen Bank in Bangladesh set out to develop a system that would deliver credit to the rural poor, especially women, independently of the FFS.

The Grameen Bank stems from work by Muhammad Yunus in a small-scale project in the village of Jobra (Chittagong) in August 1976. The first few years saw some experimentation with the way in which loans were made, but by 1979 the basic structure had evolved. It received sponsorship from the Bangladesh Bank and some commercial banks in 1979 and the experiment was extended to include the whole province of Tangail (see Siddiqui 1984; Yunus 1989). In September 1983 it was transformed into an independent bank. The government of Bangladesh provided 60 per cent of the initial paid-up share capital of the bank, while 40 per cent was held by borrowers. In July 1986 the share capital was increased, but with the government's proportion reduced to 25 per cent and 75 per cent being subscribed by borrowers.

The Grameen Bank demonstrated not only that it was possible to provide savings opportunities for, and operate credit programmes with, very poor women in rural areas, but also that it was possible to obtain extremely high rates of punctual repayment of the loans. This success attracted the attention of international agencies, and the bank received loans from IFAD of US$3.4m. in 1981, and US$37m. in 1985. IFAD lent to the Bangladesh government for fifty years at 1 per cent, the government lent to the Grameen Bank for twenty years at 2 per cent, while the bank charged 16 per cent on the loans it made (Yunus 1988: 9–10). At the end of 1988, the bank obtained a new loan of US$125m. from IFAD and aid agencies, including the Norwegian agency NORAD, the Swedish SIDA and the Canadian CIDA.

From twenty-five branches with under 15,000 members in 1980, the bank had grown to over 630 branches with about 630,000 members in 1989, and planned to have 1,700 branches operating by 1995 (Yunus 1988). The total disbursement of Tk 21m. in 1980 (US$1 = Tk 15.48) grew to nearly Tk 550m. in 1986 (US$1 = Tk 29.89) and with a target of Tk 1,500m. in 1989.

Yunus has been an impassioned and articulate proselytiser for the institution, and the Grameen Bank has published a stream of books and papers outlining in detail the poverty of its clients and the improvements in their lives that have resulted from taking its loans (see, for example, Ray 1987 and Yunus 1987). These publications contrast strongly with the more sober reports and advertising from the commercial banks in developing countries, with their emphasis on middle-class customers and services. From the outset the Grameen Bank had a wider aim than merely providing a credit programme. For example, it set out to help women, who were particularly constrained in rural Muslim communities, to teach discipline and to inculcate habits of saving and financial planning, if only on a small scale.

The Grameen Bank seems to be extremely successful in making loans without collateral, achieving repayment rates of 98–9 per cent, but many economists are puzzled as to why it works. Its operating procedures indicate how it deals with the problem of assessing creditworthiness in the absence of collateral.

It works with a basic unit of five people, with six such groups being formed into a centre of thirty members. In addition to weekly loan repayments, members are required to pay a small group tax and to make small weekly personal savings into a group fund. Members are able to borrow from the group fund for consumption and investment purposes, with the agreement of the other members (Ghai 1984). Fugelsang and Chandler describe the system:

> The units are made up of five like-minded people who are in a similar economic condition and enjoy mutual trust and confidence. Whereas group members must be inhabitants of the same village, only one member of a household may be in a group. If several people from a household want to join the Bank, they must take membership in different groups .... Women comprise their own groups, ... given the Islamic milieu of Bangladesh ....
>
> When a 'new' group is formed, it is kept under close observation for a month by bank workers and other staff to see if the members are conforming to the discipline of Grameen Bank. If satisfactory, two members will receive their loans and be observed for a month or two to ascertain if they pay their instalments regularly. Only then will the next two members be eligible for loans. The fifth member of a group will receive his or her loan when the second set of loanees have established their reliability ....
>
> The individual is kept in line by a considerable amount of peer pressure. Equally, an individual is sustained by a considerable amount of peer support .... In practice what often happens in the case of financial difficulties is that the group arrives at a private arrangement to pay a member's instalment. This is one of the reasons the Bank has a repayment rate as high as 98 per cent.
>
> A member may leave the group at any time as long as any loan is fully repaid. If a member leaves without repaying the entire loan, the responsibility for paying the balance falls on the remaining group members ....
>
> One of the most significant features of the centre meetings is that all bank business is conducted openly in front of the members.
>
> (1988: 55–60)

When the Grameen Bank system has been exported to other developing countries, most of the basic characteristics outlined above have been transplanted. Thus Hulme (1990), in summarising schemes in Malaysia, Malawi and Sri Lanka, reports that all of them operated (i) with groups of five members, (ii) of the same sex, (iii) formed into centres of thirty, (iv) that membership was restricted to the poor, (v) that loans to women were favoured, (vi) that repayments were made at the weekly group meetings, (vii) that groups were penalised for individual non-repayment, (viii) that all trans-actions were conducted openly at centre meetings, (xi) that members had to contribute savings and to the group tax, and (x) that the offices of group and centre leaders rotated annually.

While all of these characteristics may be desirable and important from some points of view, it is possible to argue that some are more important than others, considering the basic problem the Grameen Bank set out to overcome. Focusing on the economic rationale underlying the Grameen Bank system would suggest classifying the ten basic characteristics into the following groupings:

1   Aims of bank: (iv) and (v), with the position of women in many rural communities requiring (ii).
2   Essential: (i), (iii), (vi), (vii) and (viii), since these characteristics provide the basis for peer-group pressure.[16]
3   Non-essential but probably useful: (ix) and (x).

When looked at from the lender's viewpoint, a poor borrower represents a high risk, since he or she has neither a known credit rating nor collateral. The crucial factor in the success of the Grameen Bank is that it provides a system for shifting most of the risk of default from the Bank to the borrowers. The borrowers use local knowledge and group pressure to ensure that risk is minimised. Potential borrowers know that they will be penalised if members of their group default. They have access to local knowledge denied to the Bank and can use it to weed out potential bad debtors at the outset. The fact that the group is penalised for individual defaults acts both negatively to provide group pressure on the potential sinner, and positively to provide group support for individuals who get into genuine difficulties.[17]

The fact that within many Grameen Bank schemes the loans get larger at each stage tends to reduce the risk of a group decision to default on a loan. The members' credit cycles do not coincide, reducing the risk of group default at the end of a cycle.

If the interpretation of the Grameen Bank system proposed here as a way of tapping local knowledge and transferring risk from the bank to the borrowers is correct, it would suggest that the system should not be specific to Bangladesh, or even to the particular characteristics of rural communities (Hulme 1990); Thomas (1990b) discusses the transfer of the Grameen Bank approach to urban workers in Lima.[18]

Having provided an ingenious method of solving the collateral problem and keeping default rates low, and shown its ability to target specific groups, how does the Grameen Bank perform with respect to the two other problems of providing credit to the poor? The evidence on transaction costs is difficult to interpret as lending is often combined with the provision of other non-credit services, such as the distribution of seeds and hire of tools in rural areas, or very basic training in book-keeping and stock control in the urban applications of the system. Without access to detailed financial accounts, it is difficult to allocate costs between the different activities, but the general picture is that overall costs are low, since the Grameen Bank system does not need expensive office facilities and the staff tend to be 'dedicated' workers, so that the salary bill is also relatively low. As far as rates of interest are concerned, borrowers are charged the going commercial rate, so that this is not a subsidised credit programme. The fact that poor borrowers can pay this rate of interest and still achieve such high repayment rates confirms the fact that access to credit is more of a problem for the poor than the particular level of interest rates.

Risk aversion, however, is a double-edged weapon: it may work well when potential group members are being assessed by barring those who are likely to be bad risks when it comes to repayments, but when combined with low income levels, it is also likely to reduce the range of investment opportunities considered by borrowers.[19]

One question concerning the success of the Grameen Bank programme is whether it can be adapted to provide loans to the less poor, or to encourage more adventurous use of loans without losing the advantages of the system. The policy of small loans to the poor and small, homogeneous groups is more amenable to the use of peer-group pressure than is the provision of loans to those who are better off and who tend to be able to approach sources of credit individually.

Devereux and Pares (1987) quote Avandhani's analysis of repayment data for India, from which he concluded:

> A larger proportion of farmers repaid loans among marginal, small and medium farmers than among large farmers, both in 1961–62 and 1971–72 .... This would imply that repayment performance of the large cultivators was generally bad in both periods ... richer farmers had defaulted more than smaller cultivators in their repayment performance.
>
> (p. 31)

They also quote one of Oxfam's Assistant Country Representatives who ascribed many of the difficulties met in two Oxfam planting schemes in Orissa to the fact that the schemes were directed at large, non-homogeneous groups, so that:

> Since the programmes' structure was community based rather than based on a particular social or economic class (where there are more likely to be feelings of common identity and solidarity), this mixed membership neutralised any social pressure that a group as a whole could otherwise place on defaulters.
>
> (p. 44)

In summary, with the exception of the pawnshop, which solves the problem of assessing creditworthiness by obtaining physical collateral, other sources of credit, such as money-lenders and indigenous banks, make use of their detailed local knowledge to assess risk. The Grameen Bank has found a way to tap into local knowledge without needing to transfer this information to the Bank and has generally produced impressive repayment rates. Most informal sources of credit charge interest rates that are higher than those that would apply in the hypothetical situation in which their borrowers could obtain loans from formal financial institutions. The message that emerges from many studies is that the level of interest is often of less importance than high transaction costs, complex application procedures or long delays in processing applications. These are problems to be addressed if credit is to be forthcoming from the formal sector. It is also clear that the poor can save and that providing channels for savings is important, both to enable the poor to obtain a reasonable rate of return on their savings and to mobilise savings as a source of credit.

THE INFORMAL FINANCIAL SECTOR AND MONETARY POLICY

To evaluate the relevance of 'financial dualism' and 'financial repression' for monetary policy in developing countries, it is necessary to estimate the size of the IFS. This is difficult since the unregulated nature of the IFS means that statistical data are not routinely recorded by governmental or private agencies.[20] Two recent surveys (Asian Development Bank 1990; and Germidis et al. 1991) contain estimates of the size of the IFS for various developing countries and Table 11.1 presents a consolidation of the results from these sources (which should be consulted for bibliographical details of the individual studies).

Quantitative data may relate to different dimensions of the IFS, such as (i) the proportion of the population which participates in the IFS, (ii) the volume and (iii) the value of transactions in the IFS. Much of the information that is available has been collected through sample surveys, and this method of data collection has produced mainly estimates of (i) and (ii) rather than (iii), since it is generally easier to obtain accurate data on the number of households participating and the proportion of loans involving the IFS than it is to collect data on the value of the loans in question. Many of the estimates presented in Table 11.1 relate to (i) and (ii). The relatively high percentages of households involved and the high proportion of total credit obtained from informal sources confirm the extent to which the informal sectors are reliant on the IFS for credit. However, they do not provide much information about the size of the IFS in relation to the FFS.

Little or no information exists on the value of IFS transactions for most developing countries, making it difficult to evaluate the impact of the IFS on monetary policy. Despite the large percentage of the population participating

Table 11.1 Some indications of the size of the informal financial sector

Country	Rural credit	Credit for urban informal sector
Bangladesh	33–67% of rural borrowing from informal sources. 63% of credit from informal sources.	— —
China	33–67% of all borrowings from informal sources, mid-80s	—
India	38% of rural household debt owed to IFS, 1982. 1961: 83%, 1971: 71%, 1981: 39% of rural household debt from IFS.	40% of urban household debt owed to IFS, 1982. 30% of urban credit from IFS.
Indonesia	83% of agricultural households received no formal credit.	93% of capital of households with informal business activities came from own funds and 'other sources'.
Korea	51% of average liabilities of farm households from IFS. 50% of average outstanding loans of farm households from IFS.	— Urban informal credit was 15% of deposit money bank loans, 1978.
Malaysia	70% of rural borrowing from IFS. 62% of all farm loans from IFS.	— —
Mexico	50–5% of farm credit from IFS.	—
Nepal	76% of farm family credit from IFS.	—
Nigeria	95% of farm loans from IFS.	—
Pakistan	69% of rural credit from IFS.	—
Philippines	70% of rural credit from IFS in 1987. 1950s and 1960s: 60%; late 1970s: 78% of rural credit from IFS.	45% of urban credit from IFS in 1987. Less than 10% of small and medium businesses received formal credit.
Sri Lanka	45% of credit to paddy farmers in 1975–6 from IFS.	—
Thailand	45% of outstanding credit from IFS in 1987. 52% of rural credit from IFS.	— 17% of total deposits and 20% of total loans with IFS.
Zambia	43% of farm credit from IFS.	—
Zimbabwe	87% of farm credit from IFS.	—

Sources: Asian Development Bank (1990: 189, Table 3.1). Germidis *et al.* (1991: 44–5, Table 1.3).

in the IFS, the generally small scale of credit transactions involved suggests that, in aggregate terms, the total value of IFS transactions is small in comparison to the FFS. This conclusion can only be speculative.

The other problem in evaluating the importance of the IFS to monetary policy is the absence of data on the IFS for most countries over time, so that it is difficult to judge whether the IFS has been increasing or decreasing in importance in recent years. It would clearly be desirable to obtain such data, which would also provide insight into the cyclical behaviour of the IFS.

However, it is possible to shed some statistical light on a related question: what effect does monetary policy have on the IFS and its customers? Studies examining the welfare effects of monetary policy are rare in the financial analysis of developing countries. Given the high percentage of poor people in the populations of these countries, these effects should not be ignored. The previous section showed that some institutions in the IFS, such as ROSCAs, are widely used by clients in the modern sector as well as those in the informal and traditional sectors. The evidence suggests, however, that for such clients, these IFS transactions are small relative to their involvement in the FFS, so that the main impact of monetary policy on them is likely to come through its effects on the FFS rather than the IFS.[21]

The impact of monetary policy is likely to be very different on those clients of the IFS who are effectively excluded from the FFS. The importance of this difference may be illustrated by considering a change in monetary policy that leads to an increase in prices and examining the relative impact of the resulting 'inflation tax'. Evidence from various developing countries suggests that because the poor hold relatively large proportions of their assets in the form of cash, they are subject to high rates of 'inflation tax'. Gil Dìaz (1987) presents data for Mexico, dividing government debt into non-interest-earning debt (bank notes and coins plus any non-interest deposits) and interest-earning debt. For the former group of assets, the inflation tax is the rate of inflation, which was 29.8 per cent in 1980. For the latter group of assets, the inflation tax is less than this by the rate of interest the government pays on these assets, which in 1980 reduced the inflation tax to 12.7 per cent. He also presents data which show that families were more likely than firms to be affected by the inflation tax because they held 91 per cent of non-demand deposits and 60 per cent of currency. Among families, those in the lowest income decile held the highest percentage of currency (relative to income by decile), so that the poor would be particularly susceptible to the effects of an inflation tax.[22]

CONCLUSIONS

This chapter has concentrated on the problems faced by workers in the rural traditional and urban informal sectors in obtaining access to credit. While rural credit has been widely discussed in the past, this has been less true of the needs of those in the cities. In turning to the implications of credit provision for monetary policy, it is noticeable that, in contrast to the prominence of the urban informal sector in studies of employment and poverty in developing countries, it is hardly, if ever, mentioned when monetary policy is discussed, even if there is reference to the problems of the rural sector. While a number of the country studies in this book (Bangladesh, Côte d'Ivoire, Ghana and Indonesia) discuss banks and credit programmes in rural areas, there is no discussion of the urban sector, and the same is true of such a widely used textbook on monetary policy in developing countries as Fry (1988).

Why is this? One may suggest a number of reasons. First, the concept of the urban informal sector had a relatively late and limited impact on the well-established dichotomy between the rural sector and the urban (i.e. formal) sector that characterised the early dualist models of development economists. Even when the informal sector was recognised as an element in the adjustment of the urban labour market, it was seen as one of the job-search options open to the rural migrant in search of a formal sector job (see Fields 1975); as a staging post on this route, it was generally ignored in macroeconomic modelling and policy discussions.

The second reason is the attitude of politicians and policy-makers to this sector, which has varied from being strongly negative to one of ambivalence and, at best, neglect. In the 1960s, during the industrialisation and export-orientated phase of development, the informal sector, with its supposed reliance on traditional techniques, was seen as an anachronism. The activities of street-sellers in the modern business and tourist areas, together with the growth of slums and squatter settlements on the fringes of affluent areas, were seen as blots on the modernity of the country, and the middle-class assumption, based on observation from a safe distance, that they were full of petty criminals produced a generally hostile attitude. With the growing realisation that, even under the most favourable economic conditions, the modern sector could not expand fast enough to absorb the rapidly increasing urban labour force and that neither public nor private housing programmes could provide enough places for them to live, governments tended to become more tolerant of informal labour and informal (or spontaneous) housing. The result was a policy of benign neglect, in which there was less overt hostility. Finally, with the world recession and the effect of the debt crisis, many developing countries have seen employment in the formal sector falling and some governments have begun to see a more positive role for the informal sector, with its ability to create jobs for the poor and the unskilled.[23] This final phase has led to some policy changes and increasing interest in supporting it.

The third factor may be that, although the urban informal sector is important for employment, productivity is low and it generates so little income that it has a small effect on monetary policy. For example, Carbonetto and Carazo (1986) estimate that in Peru in 1981 it only generated the equivalent of 7 per cent of GDP, while the formal sector generated 79 per cent. This supports the suggestion above that even relatively large changes are unlikely to affect monetary policy. It is possible, however, that the sector's ability to absorb labour and the evidence for counter-cyclical movements demonstrated above for some countries could reduce the effectiveness of policies intended to operate on the labour market by increasing unemployment (cf. Charmes 1990; ILO 1988).

Finally, monetary policy is mainly concerned with the formal financial sector and the role of the commercial banks. The commercial banks are linked to the formal sector through their dealings with private sector customers, the public sector, government and, to some extent, the rural sector, though generally only with large-scale agricultural production. The one sector with which they have little or no contact is the urban informal sector.

This neglect is potentially risky, especially now, because the urban informal sector represents an important component of non-agricultural employment in most of the developing countries in Africa, Asia and Latin America. If anything, the effect of the world recession and the international debt crisis has been to increase its importance, and evidence from a number of countries suggests that it may have moved counter-cyclically and helped to soften the effects of recession.

The evidence presented here shows that some small borrowers have obtained loans through a variety of informal financial institutions. These institutions have dealt with the basic problems that such borrowers usually lack creditworthiness and do not possess collateral in a number of ways, usually through the mobilisation of local knowledge or local group pressure and support. Dealing with these problems has its costs and this is reflected in interest rates and other charges that are higher to borrowers using informal financial institutions than they would be in the FFS.

The view that people in the informal sectors cannot save tends not to be accurate, and schemes to mobilise savings from such people are often successful (see Padmanabhan 1988; Seibel 1989). While risk evaluation is as important in the informal as the formal financial sector, often commercial banks impose inappropriate standards (for example, in granting loans only for investment and not for consumption) on applications from the informal or rural sectors. All of these factors reduce the access of small borrowers to the FFS.

Attempts to involve the commercial banks in providing small loans, for example through credit guarantee schemes, have not been very successful. One approach that is worth further exploration is the possibility of linking the IFS to its formal counterpart. Some encouraging small beginnings have been made in a number of countries, but a great deal of further work will need to be done to persuade commercial banks to participate.

As this chapter has shown, there has been a considerable amount of research on the characteristics of small borrowers and the different credit institutions in the IFS that provide the bulk of what credit they get and the limited channels for mobilising their savings. It may now be time for the emphasis in future studies to focus on the examination of potential linkages between small borrowers and the FFS (cf. Seibel 1989; Seibel and Parhusip 1990; and Germidis *et al.* 1991). These could involve the FFS acting through existing institutions or the creation of new intermediaries. It is important that, in analysing the possibilities, arguments for market efficiency are not overemphasised at the expense of welfare considerations relating to the current customers of the IFS.

12

EXCHANGE RATES AND THE EFFECTIVENESS OF MONETARY POLICY

Christopher E. Lane

NOMINAL ANCHORS AND REAL TARGETS

Exchange regime type

Table 12.1 summarises the possible combinations of monetary policy targets and the type of foreign-exchange regime.

With a fixed exchange rate, monetary aggregates are difficult to control over an extended period. The main operational problem is a lack of control of reserve money, as injections (withdrawals) are made by central bank purchases (sales) of foreign exchange. By attempting to place limitations upon changes in reserve money (for example, on convertibility of the exchange rate) the market exchange rate is likely to diverge from the officially quoted central bank rate. This is also the case for a managed peg type of exchange regime.

Problems of monetary control are likely to be particularly severe if there is substantial dependence upon primary commodity exports, since the outcome, and therefore the net monetary effect, of the balance of payments is likely to be less predictable. For many of the country studies in this book the history of monetary policy with fixed or pegged exchange rates has been one of accommodating the large monetary impacts of substantial changes in the price and/or volume of commodity exports.

In Côte d'Ivoire and Kenya, commodity price rises in the mid-1970s rapidly expanded money supply (and inflation), whilst the oil price booms in 1973 and the late 1970s had a highly expansionary effect upon Indonesian monetary aggregates. In the 1980s, Côte d'Ivoire had the opposite problem of declining real money supply, as commodity prices plunged. Only in China have the problems of money-supply endogeneity been addressed effectively by a complete insulation of domestic from foreign money.

With flexible rates the central bank has greater potential to affect the level of foreign reserves and reserve money and hence to control money supply. This assumes that foreign-exchange flows and market-determined changes

Table 12.1 Monetary instruments and exchange-rate regimes

	Fixed or pegged exchange rate	*Flexible exchange rate*
Credit target or ceiling	Feasible – effectiveness dependent upon real and financial economy	Feasible – ditto
Monetary target or ceiling	Money endogenous – loss of reserve money control and hence aggregates. Exacerbated by commodity export dependence	Potentially effective – dependent upon extent of instruments to affect reserve money

in the price of foreign exchange adjust simultaneously, so that the effect of imbalance in the supply and demand for foreign exchange is reflected primarily in exchange-rate changes and not changes in reserves and domestic money holdings. Given that exchange rates are rarely fully flexible in developing countries, although the recent introduction of auction systems does provide some examples of increased flexibility, the scope for control of monetary aggregates in developing countries is likely to be limited. Developed countries have also found that trade flows can adjust very slowly to substantial changes in exchange rates.

The efficacy of direct credit controls, which is the predominant operational monetary control in developing countries, in many respects does not depend upon whether exchange rates are fixed or flexible. Credit ceilings are imposed to influence the level of domestic spending, economic activity and the balance of trade.

A constructive division of types of exchange-rate policies is into those following 'real targets', those reliant upon a 'nominal anchor' (Corden 1990) and finally those with market-determined exchange rates. The predominant exchange-rate policy in developing countries has been a fixed exchange rate acting as a 'nominal anchor' upon monetary policy. The commitment can be to keep exchange rates fixed for long periods or to a pre-announced rate of depreciation such as a crawling peg (perhaps in line with planned or expected inflation). For the nominal anchor to be effective, domestic monetary policy in the long term must be constrained to avoid the emergence of higher than anticipated inflation and to maintain a sustainable current account balance. For policy purposes, this means that the money supply is endogenously determined and generally cannot be used as an independent policy instrument.

However, there are two routes which relax the grip of the exchange-rate anchor upon monetary policy. First, import tariffs and restrictions can be imposed, and second, reserves can be run down and foreign borrowing increased to sustain current account deficits. A successful nominal anchor policy is one which maintains real exchange rates at levels of international competitiveness and a sustainable balance of payments. It requires that people behave as if they believe that monetary policy is adjusted to contain inflation and that they correspondingly adjust their price and wage demands.

To follow a real target also involves a policy-determined exchange rate, with intervention in response to macroeconomic developments to achieve a non-accelerating rate of inflation (not necessarily low inflation), in order to maintain international competitiveness and a target balance-of-payments position. The essence of the real targets approach is that it is inefficient to defend a nominal anchor (for example, from reserve depletion by imposing import controls) as exchange-rate overvaluation has substantial long-term costs. The essential difference from the nominal anchor policy is that the nominal exchange rate responds to economic developments rather than leads them. Without a nominal anchor, monetary policy must have developed a reputation for being used in a sensible and consistent manner to contain inflation. The nominal exchange rate can thus be a separate but complementary instrument to monetary policy, and adjustment of the exchange rate in response to variables like inflation and the reserve position is assumed to have a real effect upon economic activity. Examples of real target exchange-rate policies in our country studies are Indonesia (from 1978) and Kenya (from 1980).

The degree to which exchange-rate policy is actually separable from monetary policy depends upon the extent of capital mobility and the potential for sterilised intervention. Countries which have developed capital markets but maintain effective capital controls of some kind can operate the most independent exchange-rate policy through sterilised intervention. However, this combination is rare, especially in developing countries where capital flight is difficult to prevent and most capital markets are under-developed or are captive markets for government securities.[1] Nonetheless the experience and success of some recent experiments (see, for example, Chapter 8 on Indonesia) indicate that regular adjustment of the exchange rate as a responsive variable can complement a disciplined monetary policy.

A combination of factors, including the breakdown of the Bretton Woods system of exchange rates, the subsequent volatility of the dollar and increasing capital mobility, have slowly shifted exchange-rate policy in developing countries to a more flexible policy based upon real targets. However, neither nominal anchors nor real targets can be sustained without increasing import and/or capital restrictions if monetary policy leads to real appreciation (and expectations of depreciation).

Fixed exchange rates have not been effective nominal anchors over the long term in many developing countries. Monetary policy is rarely effectively constrained to be compatible with a predetermined nominal exchange rate.

Either the nominal rate does not in practice provide sufficient discipline or it is not feasible to operate the necessary monetary control. Pressures to expand money and credit, particularly to finance government, override the other objectives of monetary control (as is clearly the case in Ghana, and partially so in Kenya and China). Inflation with a fixed exchange rate encourages the demand for foreign currency holding in preference to local, as a hedge against devaluation. As the exchange rate is overvalued, production for export is discouraged, foreign-exchange receipts are likely to decline and imports must be restricted, possibly constraining growth.

In the next section, we survey how fixed nominal rates in developing countries were weakened by the changes in developed countries' exchange-rate arrangements since the early 1970s to more freely floating exchange rates; this is followed by an examination of the contrasting experience of the Franc Zone economies which have a formal fixed rate of exchange with the French franc (as in Côte d'Ivoire). In these countries the fixed nominal exchange-rate regime has clearly disciplined monetary policy, but international competitiveness and balance-of-payments stability have not been sustained.

We then consider the experience of countries forced to abandon a nominal 'anchor' because of a lack of monetary control. In general, the lack of credibility attached to economic policy has dictated a movement to a free market-determined exchange rate. In Ghana, for example, a fiscally driven expansion of money supply created a strong demand for foreign currency far in excess of the supply of foreign exchange at the official rate. Extreme overvaluation finally led to a series of sharp devaluations and the introduction of an auction-determined exchange rate.

A third group of countries has had a long experience of stable nominal exchange rates and a separate commitment to low inflation. In most of these cases the relatively good counter-inflationary record is a result of conservative monetary and fiscal policy being a primary objective. It does not simply follow from a nominally anchored exchange rate. These countries have also increasingly moved towards more flexible arrangements.

CHANGES IN EXCHANGE-RATE ARRANGEMENTS

From the 1960s onwards there have been significant shifts in the types of exchange-rate arrangements utilised by low- and middle-income developing countries, but the most marked changes towards increasing flexibility and real targets approaches have been in the 1980s. In general, the increasing flexibility of exchange-rate policy has been associated with a lowered reliance upon credit policy and increased emphasis upon market-determined interest rates.

During the 1950s and 1960s changes in developed country exchange rates were rare. Inflation rates were low and substantial restrictions applied to capital movements. The method of dealing with international payments imbalances was not to alter exchange rates, but by occasional transfers of international liquidity (e.g. gold) and adjustment of fiscal and monetary policies.

Many developing countries had not attained independence, and their currencies were fixed in value against the metropolitan currency and backed 100 per cent by foreign currency deposits. This is the most extreme case of the nominal anchor, as the volume of domestic money is determined entirely by the outcome on the balance of payments and therefore endogenously determined. Ghana, for example, was pegged to sterling whilst a member of the West African Currency Board, and maintained the peg for another eight years after independence with virtually no inflation. Wages and prices could be set with high certainty against a fixed exchange rate and a low or zero rate of inflation.

By 1970, as the par value exchange system began to loosen among developed countries, several South American countries, and also the Philippines and Syria, had exchange rates which moved within narrow margins of the US dollar. All major currencies (except the Canadian dollar) remained with fixed exchange rates against each other and a par value against gold. During 1970 the Deutsche Mark and the guilder were floated and in August 1971 the dollar was untied from its gold parity rate and the United States abandoned its reserve currency role and guarantee of gold convertibility.

After 1972–3, the fixed exchange rates of other industrial countries broke down under the pressure of large international movements of capital and varying rates of inflation. More flexible exchange rates for developed countries provided a potential long-run benefit of increased monetary independence, which allowed inflation rates to diverge from those in other trading countries. However, this benefit came to be questioned, as it became clear that exchange rates adjusted slowly and imperfectly to differences in external competitiveness.

The exchange rates of developing countries, however, retained exchange-rate pegs fixed to a particular currency or to a basket of currencies, sometimes with discrete infrequent adjustments to the peg. In 1975, thirty-three of sixty-nine low- and lower-middle-income countries had exchange-rate arrangements based on an exchange rate peg to the US dollar, twelve on a fixed peg to the French franc and another fourteen on other single currency pegs (sterling and rand) or currency basket pegs (SDR). Only seven had a more substantial degree of exchange-rate flexibility: five South American countries had frequently adjusted rates against the dollar, and two others (Nigeria and the Philippines) quoted daily changes in rates.

During the late 1970s the peg which many developing countries had to the US dollar became more flexible. Some countries (including Kenya) moved to pegging to a basket of currencies such as the SDR, or a trade-weighted basket, to smooth the impact of fluctuations between major currencies' exchange rates. Predetermined crawling pegs were introduced to deal with rapid inflation, notably in a few Latin American countries where exchange rates were adjusted regularly on the basis of movements in a basket of economic and financial indicators. These were equivalent to nominal anchors, but recognised the persistence of higher inflation than in trading partners.

Those countries which moved to a managed float (e.g. South Korea, 1980; Sri Lanka, 1977) also removed credit ceilings and interest-rate control, and switched to monetary management through reserve requirements, open-market operations and the rediscount mechanism. Indonesia is a clear example of the shift from a nominal anchor towards a real target occurring at the same time as money-market instruments were developed. One result was that intervention to sterilise foreign exchange became possible. The real target adopted from about 1982 was to maintain or increase the competitiveness of the non-oil export sector in line with domestic and foreign price developments. Although speculative attacks upon the exchange rate led to deviations from this policy, real targets were clearly the long-run determinant of Indonesian exchange rates.

In the 1980s a significant number of countries moved further towards market-determined exchange rates by introducing currency auctions or inter-bank trading in foreign currencies, and the role of the central bank, and therefore policy-makers, in exchange-rate determination declined. Between 1980 and 1988, six countries moved to a form of a managed exchange-rate float and a further six had independently floating exchange rates, predominantly moving from a peg to the US dollar. In general the floaters had high inflation records and rapidly expanding money and credit aggregates. There could be little credibility to the announcement of a 'fixed' nominal rate, and severe exchange-rate misalignment made it difficult to assess how the adjustment of the exchange rate ought to be made to follow a real target. The remaining type of exchange-rate policy was to have no (or very little) intervention.

Both internal and external factors explain the reluctance of most developing countries to follow the developed countries towards increased nominal exchange-rate flexibility in the 1970s or to use increased flexibility of the exchange rate to follow real targets. A change in exchange rates was not expected to alter external demand for their exports, since (as small countries) they are price takers in the international market. The supply response of primary commodity exports was likely to be inelastic with respect to price, owing to production bottlenecks (from shortage of capital, poor infrastructure), and the lead time required for planting tree crops such as cocoa implied that the response would be long-term at the best. These arguments suggested to policy-makers that devaluation was unlikely to improve the balance-of-payments position.

Abandoning a fixed exchange rate which was acting as a strong nominal anchor was also thought to reduce the credibility of an anti-inflationary policy, because it would be inflationary in itself. Increased prices for imports would boost money demand and create excess demand for domestically produced goods. Despite pessimism about the effectiveness of exchange-rate policy, there were considerable variations in the actual experiences of developing country exchange-rate arrangements during the 1970s.

THE 'NOMINAL ANCHOR' IN THE FRANC ZONE

The monetary union of Franc Zone countries with France has ensured a monetary policy consistent with a fixed exchange rate over substantial periods of time by passing a degree of economic sovereignty to the developed country.[2] The thirteen sub-Saharan African countries of the Franc Zone have maintained a fixed rate of 50 CFA (Communauté Financière Africaine) francs to the French franc since 1948. The structure of the two monetary unions[3] which collectively set union-wide monetary policy and manage pooled foreign-exchange reserves is described in Chapter 7 on Côte d'Ivoire. The institutional set-up of the monetary unions has allowed a degree of monetary independence at a country level, with low rates of money growth and inflation relative to other sub-Saharan African countries. There have, however, been several problems with the exchange rate as a nominal anchor for monetary policy in the Franc Zone. These include persistent and substantial changes in real effective exchange rates because of price divergence and the inappropriateness of the French franc as the choice of nominal anchor.

Real exchange-rate movements are shown in Figures 12.1a and 12.1b for four Franc Zone economies. Côte d'Ivoire and Gabon are representative of Franc Zone members with expansionary monetary policies and more overvalued exchange rates. Togo and Burkina Faso are more typical of the smaller and usually poorer Franc Zone economies which tend to have a less expansionary monetary policy and lower real exchange rates. It is always difficult to be precise about the extent of overvaluation at a particular moment. During the 1970s some real exchange-rate appreciation is likely to have been appropriate for countries with buoyant commodity export prices (oil, tropical beverages).

From 1986, with the steep fall in commodity prices, some real exchange-rate depreciation would have been more appropriate. The period 1973–80 was one of overall real exchange-rate appreciation resulting from high domestic inflation and rapid economic growth supported by buoyant commodity prices. Between 1976 and 1979 the CFA franc depreciated against the dollar and real exchange-rate rises therefore moderated somewhat. In the 1970s, the real exchange rate appreciated most significantly in Franc Zone countries which experienced a commodity price boom, for example in Côte d'Ivoire (cocoa) and in Gabon (oil). Domestic inflation, the resultant real exchange-rate overvaluation and poor trade performances led

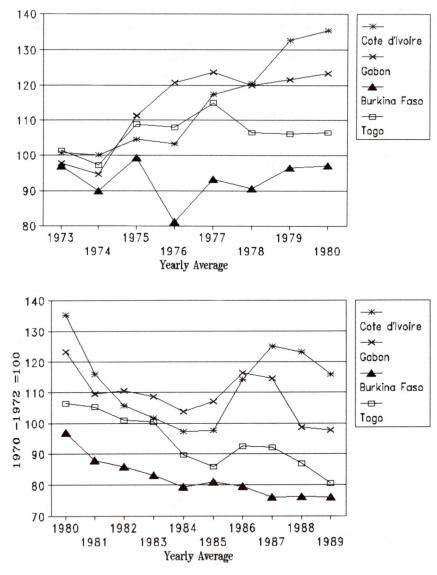

Figure 12.1 Franc Zone real effective exchange rates

to a renewed application of a more restrictive monetary policy in the 1980s and rates of monetary growth slowed. The predominant factor in real exchange-rate movements was the rise (1980–5) and fall (1986 onwards) of the dollar, but some Franc Zone countries (e.g. Togo, Burkina Faso) imposed a more restrictive monetary policy from 1986 onwards and avoided renewed real currency appreciation.

Several factors have limited the effectiveness of the fixed exchange rate as a nominal anchor in the Franc Zone, and sustained the overvaluation and a poor trade performance. First, the weakness of monetary and credit control has encouraged price divergence, and hence real exchange-rate variation. Credit policy has not been rigorously applied, particularly in the larger booming commodity exporters. As Honohan remarks:

> Somehow, at least in the UMOA (West African Monetary Union) the larger and more prosperous countries have gained a disproportionate share in the regional distribution of credit. The major shifts in the distribution of credit over the years in favour of these countries have shown no tendency to be reversed.

(1990b: 11)

Table 12.2 indicates the extent of credit target overshooting for central bank refinancing. Those countries with credit expansion over target also tended to have negative net foreign assets and the highest price divergence from the core country, France. Over the long term these less disciplined countries had more overvalued exchange rates. Although the monetary union as a whole was programmed to have a restrictive monetary policy between 1986 and 1988, the outcome was increasing divergence from the specified targets. The extent of price divergence in Côte d'Ivoire, the largest economy in the UMAO, is shown in Figure 12.2. Price divergence was most significant during the 1970s, particularly in 1977, a year of especially buoyant cocoa and coffee revenues. In the 1980s some of the accumulated price divergence was reclaimed, but during 1986 and 1988 lower French inflation again produced positive price divergence for Côte d'Ivoire.

Table 12.2 Effectiveness of monetary policy in the Franc Zone: central bank refinancing targets (WAMU)

	Ceiling (CFA bn)			Actual over ceiling (%)			Net foreign assets (CFA bn)
	1986	*1987*	*1988*	*1986*	*1987*	*1988*	*1988*
Benin	55	56	56	5.6	11.7	41.3	−47
Burkina Faso	20	25	27	−2.6	0.8	−15.2	76
Côte d'Ivoire	524	507	486	3.6	24.9	31.5	−416
Mali	30	34	34	73.8	58.7	73.0	−19
Niger	38	40	45	1.9	7.6	−8.8	34
Senegal	188	181	168	8.0	10.8	44.7	−222
Togo	25	27	28	−11.2	−10.0	−15.9	−40
Total	880	869	845	6.5	19.9	31.3	−554

Source: Franc Zone Secretariat, *La Zone Franc 1988* (1989), pp. 77, 79 and 185

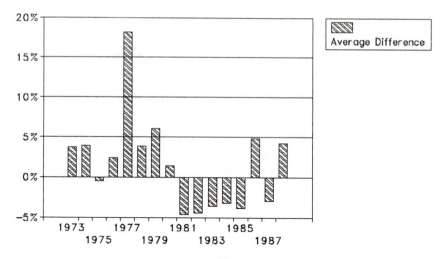

Figure 12.2 Inflation differential Côte d'Ivoire and France
Source: IMF, *International Financial Statistics*

Second, the process of price convergence with the core country, France (a major factor in determining real exchange movements), has been slow and partial. This lack of convergence encourages price-setters to assume that the fixed exchange rate is not a guarantee of relative price stability and to adjust wage demands accordingly. Over the longer term price convergence in Côte d'Ivoire was estimated by Honohan (1990a: 10) on quarterly data to have the following form:

$$dP_t = 0.002 + 1.14 \, dP_{core} - 0.075 \, GAP^{(-1)} + 0.147 DUM$$
$$\quad (0.2) \quad (3.6) \quad\quad (2.4) \quad\quad\quad (6.1)$$

$$RSQ = 0.517 \quad SEE = 0.0237 \quad DW = 2.00 \quad for \ 73.2{-}88.4$$

Where: $P = \log$ CPI Côte d'Ivoire, $P_{core} = \log$ CPI France, GAP = log ratio of the two price indices and DUM = intercept dummy variable.

The coefficient on $GAP^{(-1)}$ illustrates a significant rate of convergence of 7.5 per cent of the price level differential per quarter. The coefficient on dP_{core} is not significantly different from unity.

Slow price convergence within a monetary union is in part the result of current account restrictions. Figure 12.3 shows the ratio of prices in France to Côte d'Ivoire (consumer price indices). Weak price convergence accounts for a large proportion of real exchange-rate variation. Between 1973 and 1980 the weakness of the nominal anchor and slow price convergence allowed Côte d'Ivoire prices to rise 60 per cent faster than French prices.

The third weakness of the franc as a 'nominal anchor' is that the relevance of French prices to Franc Zone inflation has decreased as Franc Zone countries' trade has diversified geographically, in particular to other

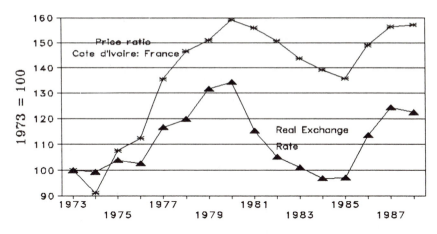

Figure 12.3 Côte d'Ivoire relative prices – real exchange rate
Source: IMF, *International Financial Statistics*

European Community countries and Japan, as discussed in the Côte d'Ivoire study. However, the volatility of the dollar alone is sufficient to ensure that pegging to the French franc is not a stable, and therefore not an effective, nominal anchor. In Figure 12.3, the effect of dollar/franc movements is shown (approximately) by divergences between the real exchange rate and the relative price index ratio. The franc link transmits exchange-rate movements influenced by French and other developed country monetary policies to Franc Zone members.

Even if monetary policy could have counteracted the impact of nominal rate changes through a reduction of the price level, these policies might not have been appropriate. This point is pursued further in the Côte d'Ivoire study, but no strong evidence was found of an adverse output response to credit contraction.

Despite rules designed to ensure monetary control consistent with a nominally anchored exchange rate, the 1980s have been a period of overvalued exchange rates in most Franc Zone countries, and in the larger economies in particular. Arrears in foreign payments have built up and many Franc Zone countries have had recourse to the exceptional financing facilities provided by the French Treasury. The three factors which weakened the linkage between the fixed exchange rate and a long-run monetary policy consistent with that rate were weak control of monetary aggregates and hence substantial price divergence, slow price convergence, and variation in effective exchange rates owing to divergent trade patterns.

For other developing country monetary unions the considerations are somewhat different. Lesotho and Swaziland have a common monetary area with South Africa. Far higher shares of trade with the core country have tended to limit the magnitude of price divergence and increased the speed of price convergence. Long-run monetary policy has been constrained. In the Eastern Caribbean, small island states have very effectively remained at a fixed peg with the US dollar as a result of their small size, high trade integration and monetary control. In contrast, Liberia has issued local currency coins convertible at par with the US dollar without effective restraint. Excessive monetary expansion has lowered confidence in the local currency, which effectively trades at a discount to the US dollar.

RAISING THE ANCHOR: CURRENCY FLOATS IN THE 1980s

Fifteen developing countries[4] in one form or another independently floated their exchange rates during the 1980s (see Quirk *et al.* 1987; Roberts 1989), and seven still had floating rates at the beginning of the 1990s (Ghana, Nigeria, the Philippines, Uruguay, Zaire, Paraguay and Bolivia). Floating is an explicit rejection of both interventionist approaches to exchange-rate setting, the nominal anchor and real targets. For the sake of brevity we use five illustrative examples to display the diversity of success (Ghana, Nigeria, Uruguay, Bolivia and the Philippines).

Before the floating of exchange rates, these financial systems and monetary policy were highly stressed and in crisis:

1　Black market premiums for foreign exchange were high and rising. For example, the premium before floating was 2,120 per cent in Ghana, 250 per cent in Bolivia and 28 per cent in the Philippines.
2　Monetary authorities had practically exhausted gross foreign reserves, had negative net foreign assets and were in payments arrears with overseas creditors (apart from Uruguay). The Philippines, for example, declared a debt moratorium in October 1983; soon after, it was disclosed that the central bank accounts had substantially overstated its foreign assets, which destroyed the credibility of exchange-rate management.
3　Table 12.3 shows for each of the five countries much higher rates of monetary expansion than rates of nominal depreciation in the long-term period before floating. As inflationary expectations adjusted to higher rates of monetary growth and domestic prices rose, the local currency became increasingly overvalued.

The Philippines was something of an exception, as devaluation against the US dollar during 1982 and 1983 had introduced some real depreciation, but monetary policy and inflation took a sharply expansionary turn in 1983, leading to widespread expectations of increasing overvaluation. In the case of Ghana, substantial real exchange-rate depreciation had taken place in the three years prior to devaluation, due to several earlier large devaluations, but floating introduced further incremental real depreciation.

A need for devaluation can also apply to regimes which have a pre-

Table 12.3 1980s floating regimes: exchange rates and monetary growth (%)

Country	Exchange rate appreciation Annual real	Annual nominal	Annual narrow money growth
Nigeria			
Managed float 1976–85	8.05	−3.84	14.65
Independent float 1986–8	−42.85	−41.62	17.48
Ghana			
US dollar peg 1973–82	22.25	−21.88	38.87
Devaluing peg then float (1983–8)	−49.71	−34.57	48.89
Uruguay			
Managed float 1973–82	3.65	−27.75	49.24
Independent float 1983–7	−11.39	−42.78	58.06
Bolivia			
US dollar peg 1973–84	8.71	−36.60	85.73
Independent float 1985–8	−17.49	−80.89	274.23
Philippines			
US dollar peg, managed float 1973–83	0.39	−1.27	15.80
Independent float 1984–8	−5.36	−18.30	12.88

Source: IMF, *International Financial Statistics.*

determined rate of depreciation. With expansionary domestic monetary policy creating an overvalued currency and expectations of devaluation, an outward flight of capital is encouraged, further increasing pressure for a re-alignment. In Argentina in 1979–81 the abolition of exchange controls together with a rapid expansion of government domestic borrowing encouraged capital flight in anticipation of devaluation. Previously, with exchange controls, the black market premium soared prior to anticipated devaluations as a result of illegal capital flight.

Prior to the introduction of floating exchange rates Ghana, Nigeria and Bolivia had fixed-peg nominal anchors and official multiple exchange rates for different types of transactions as a method of rationing and prioritising scarce foreign-exchange resources. In the case of Ghana the exchange rate had remained fixed for years at a time (see Ghana study). As increasing overvaluation shifted transactions into the black market, the relevance of the nominal rate increasingly declined.

In Bolivia increasing rates of monetary growth fuelled inflation, and exchange-rate adjustment against the dollar peg lagged far behind. Uruguay had a unified rate with pre-announced rates of depreciation which were intended to maintain the real value of the currency in line with an inflation rate of over 30 per cent in the year before floating. In the event, depreciation

Table 12.4 Floating exchange-rate regimes: economic background

GHANA (t = 1986) (at float = September)

	Annual data			Quarterly data			Annual data			
	t−3	t−2	t−1	F−1	at float	F+1	t	t+1	t+2	t+3
Domestic credit growth (%)	72.2	50.2	59.7		−26.7		53.1	72.4	−4.8	
Inflation (%)	197.39	39.65	10.31		4.62		24.56	39.81		
GDP nominal growth (%)	112.9	47.0	26.8		49.1		45.9			
GDP real growth (%)	0.7	2.6	5.1		5.2		4.8			
Nominal money growth (%)	40.2	53.7	46.2		14.17		47.9	53.3	46.3	
Discount rate	14.5	18.0	18.5		20.5		20.5	23.5	26.0	
Fiscal pressure	0.86	0.77	0.62		0.77		0.64	0.76	0.76	
B of P pressure	0.00	−0.01	−0.02				−0.01	−0.02		
REER (t = 100)	7	52	66				100	127	134	
Income velocity	8.8	8.5	7.3				7.4	7.0		
Black market premium (%)	2,120						117			

Note: money does not include restricted deposits

NIGERIA (t = 1986) (at float = September)

	Annual data			Quarterly data			Annual data			
	t−3	t−2	t−1	F−1	at float	F+1	t	t+1	t+2	t+3
Domestic credit growth (%)	28.9	10.3	4.9	−5.6	42.6	20.0	14.1	10.4	26.0	
Inflation (%)	23.21	39.61	5.50	18.32	38.24	1.45	5.38	10.52	38.24	
GDP nominal growth (%)	4.6	10.5	12.6				1.2	38.7	23.9	
GDP real growth (%)	−4.2	−6.7	7.9				3.2	1.8	4.0	
Nominal money growth (%)	14.0	11.6	9.0	−11.8	8.9	6.8	2.0	22.4	32.9	
Discount rate	8.0	10.0	10.0		10.0		10.0	15.0		
Fiscal pressure	0.56	0.59	0.57		0.54		0.52	0.53	0.54	
B of P pressure	−0.05	0.00	0.03				0.01	0.06		
REER (t = 100)	67.5	49.0	54.7		30.2		100.0	313.3	292.8	
Income velocity	3.4	3.4	3.5				3.5	3.9		

Quarterly data

URUGUAY (t = 1982)
(at float = Nov)

	t−3	t−2	t−1	F−1	at float	F+1	t	t+1	t+2	t+3
Domestic credit growth (%)	102.8	72.0	44.8	32.7	1,533.8	−7.5	139.3	27.8	59.6	65.2
Inflation (%)	66.8	63.4	34.0	22.6	18.9	139.6	19.0	49.2	55.4	72.2
GDP nominal growth (%)	86.3	60.0	32.8				5.1	43.8	59.1	79.4
GDP real growth (%)	9.8	6.0	1.9				−9.4	−5.8	−1.5	0.3
Nominal money growth (%)	85.4	72.8	49.7	18.95	482.82	−36.97	77.1	13.0	62.3	95.5
Lending rate	68.1	66.6	60.4				58.5	93.6	83.2	94.6
Fiscal pressure	0.03	−0.01	0.02				0.13	0.18	0.25	0.17
B of P pressure	−0.05	−0.07	−0.04				−0.03	−0.01	−0.02	−0.02
REER (t = 100)	148	118	105				100	163	170	176
Black market premium (%)	0.6	0.5	0.2						6.3	0.5

Quarterly data

BOLIVIA (t = 1985)
(at float = QIII)

	t−3	t−2	t−1	F−1	at float	F+1	t	t+1	t+2	t+3
Domestic credit growth (%)	343	171	997	409,500	129,500	705	2,686	140	132	20
Inflation (%)	133	259	1284	4,202	38,822	508	11,749	276	15	16
GDP nominal growth (%)	180	257	1334				12,782	281	17	
Nominal money growth (%)	223	174	1424	15,701	16,036	1,929	6,979	183	46	
GDP real growth (1985) (%)	0.8	−6.6	−0.3				−0.2	−2.9	2.2	2.8
Lending rate	37.0	61.0	149.0							
Fiscal pressure	0.00	0.00	0.00				−1.51	−1.65	−0.73	−0.92
B of P pressure	−0.03	−0.02	−0.03				−0.04	−0.07	−0.08	
REER (t = 100)	204.6	223.0	172.0	103.2	51.7	356.9	100.0	340.0	353.7	372.9
Black market premium (%)	167.3	249.3								

Table 12.4 (continued)

PHILIPPINES (t = 1984) (at float = QIV)	Annual data			Quarterly data			t	Annual data		
	t−3	t−2	t−1	F−1	at float	F+1	t	t+1	t+2	t+3
Domestic credit growth (%)	24.0	23.2	29.8		0.8		5.6	−6.9	−16.4	−7.8
Inflation (%)	13.1	10.6	10.0		32.2		50.4	23.1	0.7	3.8
GDP nominal growth (%)	15.3	11.6	12.8				40.7	13.4	3.2	12.6
GDP real growth (%)	0.03	0.02	0.01				−0.07	−0.04	0.02	0.06
Nominal money growth (%)	18.4	19.9	21.8		64.9		14.8	12.9	9.9	14.4
Lending rate	6.7	6.3	8.1		12.1		12.1	11.5	9.6	9.1
Fiscal pressure	0.16	0.22	0.21		0.22		0.22	0.28	0.41	0.23
B of P pressure	−0.05	−0.08	−0.08				−0.04	−0.00	0.03	−0.02
REER (t = 100)	86.4	83.3	99.0				100.0	91.4	117.1	127.2
Black market premium (%)	2.9	6.3	28.4							

Sources: IMF, *International Financial Statistics*. Black market premiums from Wood, 1988.

Notes: Credit to government includes official entities

GDP real growth at 1980 prices

At float inflation, nominal money and GDP are annualised rates of quarter of float was insufficient and created incentives to falsify current and capital account transactions.

Although the swings in the real Philippine exchange rate were not as dramatic as in the other four countries, Dohner and Intal (1989) argue that exchange-rate adjustment was usually delayed for two reasons: first, Philippine policy-makers looked at the nominal rate's role in domestic inflation, not relative prices or the development of new industries. Second, there was a strong domestic constituency opposed to devaluation, which increased the income of the already powerful (and much resented) sugar exporters. The real impact of devaluation undertaken in early 1983 was then wiped out by a substantial monetary expansion at the end of the year created by government borrowing and losses on forward contracts by the central bank resulting from devaluation and the accumulation of external payments arrears.

We have suggested above a number of reasons for delayed exchange-rate devaluation. In addition, administrative allocation of foreign exchange at grossly overvalued rates created vested interests in maintaining the fixed rate.

In two of the five cases, Nigeria and Ghana, floating rates were introduced as part of an IMF programme in parallel to an official foreign-exchange window for priority imports, e.g. petroleum, and debt-servicing. Introduction of a currency auction in Ghana and the mixed inter-bank trading-cum-currency auction in Nigeria were both performance criteria in adjustment programmes upon which disbursement of official balance-of-payments financing depended. The IMF insistence on the introduction of floating-rate regimes arose from the perceived importance of the exchange rate in economies relatively open to trade and the need to increase the volume of foreign exchange flowing through official channels by narrowing or eliminating the differential between the official and black market rates. But, although external pressure was an important factor in the abandonment of nominal targets, in both countries the case was also strongly argued, by a technocratic faction of economic policy-makers and advisors.

In Ghana the logic of unifying exchange markets was pursued further by legalising street trading in foreign-exchange bureaux. In Nigeria the size of the black market had led to the allocation system breaking down and had discredited the authorities' competence in exchange-rate management.

In the Philippines floating was undertaken just before the agreement of a stand-by arrangement with the IMF and, along with a sharp contraction of reserve money, was thought to be a prior action required for agreement of a stabilisation programme (Dohner and Intal 1989: 544). Uruguay, alone in not having problems of external arrears, and therefore under less external pressure, introduced floating rates independently to stabilise balance-of-payments flows which occurred with the combination of rapid inflation and its crawling peg policy.

In Ghana, Nigeria and Bolivia the magnitude of exchange-rate changes required was substantial and the introduction of a floating rate followed immediately after substantial devaluation of the official (administered) rate. The floats, however, were also a method for deflecting political criticism of devaluation in administered exchange-rate arrangement.

Floating reversed the trend of real exchange-rate appreciation unambiguously in each case, apart from the Philippines. A common factor in monetary policy was a dramatic slowing in the rates of growth of reserve money, credit and broad money. In the Philippines reserve money was contracted in the months before floating by the sale of non-reserve eligible short-term paper at high interest rates, designed to contract banks' domestic lending. In Bolivia, nominal money growth declined from an annualised rate of 16,000 per cent in the quarter of floating to 46 per cent three quarters later, mainly by a sharp reduction in government borrowing and increases in government deposits.

A supportive fiscal policy has been an important element in maintaining monetary control in the post-floating phase, as money creation is unlikely to be responsive to purely monetary instruments such as raised interest rates. This conclusion also appears valid for countries using less flexible pegs: the associated Kenyan study shows that government crowding-out in the credit market occurred, despite increasing market determination of interest (and exchange) rates.

In Nigeria, the fiscal problems were tackled before floating. The federal government deficit fell from 11.6 per cent of GDP in 1983 to 3.8 per cent in 1985. The government cut nominal expenditure by 28 per cent and increased revenue. In 1985 public sector wages were frozen and transfers to parastatals and other government agencies cut or restricted. The second-tier foreign-exchange market opened in September 1986 and the nominal exchange rate depreciated by over 50 per cent in the subsequent quarter. Monetary policy saw tough credit ceilings imposed and a reduction of money supply by a call-in of cash awaiting foreign-exchange cover held with commercial banks. As a result, monetary growth slowed in the two quarters following devaluation, domestic credit growth slowed and, most remarkably, government borrowing declined in the immediate period after floating. The 1987 budget deficit fell substantially. Inflation also dropped from an annualised rate of 38 per cent in the quarter preceding devaluation to less than 2 per cent in the following quarter.

In Ghana, credit ceilings agreed with the IMF were strictly enforced by the Bank of Ghana, and on occasion substantially under-achieved owing to the penalties for commercial banks associated with breaking credit ceilings. The effect was to reduce access to the currency auction for firms without a strong cash-flow position, and thus to reduce the rate of depreciation of the Ghanaian cedi. Over the medium term the reduced access to credit improved firms' stock control but discriminated against those firms importing intermediate or capital goods, because of the financing cost of auction bids.

A further example of the importance of supportive monetary and fiscal policy is given by Bolivia in the mid-1980s. By the end of 1984 Bolivia was facing economic collapse. Inflation was over 1,000 per cent per annum and accelerating, and the fiscal deficit was 28 per cent of GDP, with tax revenues as a proportion of GDP falling sharply, failing to keep pace with inflation. During 1985 events worsened, domestic credit growth accelerated to an annualised 5,000-fold increase and black market exchange premiums widened to several hundred per cent. The institution of a daily auction rapidly depreciated the exchange rate, but inflation, money growth and credit growth also declined rapidly as a result of tight monetary policy and a rapidly reducing government deficit.

Summary

Exchange-rate floating is generally undertaken when the rate has been seriously undermined and official exchange-rate management has little credibility. Widespread black markets make the official exchange rate irrelevant and rapid inflation encourages holding foreign currency or goods. Countries with controlled monetary policies in the immediately preceding and post-float period have achieved a sustained real exchange-rate depreciation by reducing domestic inflation and depreciating the nominal rate. Although the foreign-exchange regime has changed markedly for these countries, there is no marked parallel change in the instruments of monetary policy towards market-based monetary control. This is, first, because IMF programmes have imposed conditionality in terms of nominal money and credit aggregates which are more easily met by administrative control. Credit control is equally effective under fixed or flexible exchange rates and more easily monitored under fixed. Money demand is likely to behave in unpredictable ways during the type of rapid price changes associated with devaluation and floating. Money's income velocity increases as incentives to hedge in goods or foreign currency increase. All this weakens the arguments for targeting monetary aggregates.

Perhaps the most important elements of a successful exchange-rate float are low intervention in the operation of foreign-exchange auctions or interbank markets, apart from developing confidence in the floating system, with, simultaneously, firm control on domestic money and credit, particularly to the government. Limiting the domestic liquidity of importers appears to be the most effective method of arresting exchange-rate depreciation, and directs foreign exchange to those willing to pay most.

REAL TARGETS – A FEASIBLE POLICY OBJECTIVE IN DEVELOPING COUNTRIES?

Some countries have liberalised foreign-exchange markets as part of a sequenced programme closely linked to the development of market-based methods of monetary control and the abandonment of credit and interest-rate targets. The reasons for this reform are the constraints which controlled interest rates place upon development of the financial system (such as weak incentives to mobilise deposits) and the importance now placed on having an exchange rate which offers international competitiveness. By relaxing control on the exchange rate as an instrument and increasing the role of market forces in setting it, even if reinforced by administrative intervention, the incentive to hold foreign financial assets is reduced and the demand for domestic assets increased. In this section we consider two examples of increased exchange-rate flexibility following real targets.

Indonesia

Indonesia, from 1983, is a good example of what may be achieved and the difficulties of implementation. Two factors were important in shifting Indonesia from a fixed dollar peg prior to 1978 to the current managed float, via a series of incremental changes. Firstly, Indonesia has an open capital account, and *de facto* recognition of its financial integration with neighbouring Singapore. Secondly, it is an oil and gas exporter, although the importance of these commodities in trade and government revenue has declined substantially over recent years. Both factors have caused sizeable and uncontrollable shifts in the demand for rupiah-denominated assets over short periods of time, and have placed pressure upon a nominal fixed exchange rate. In 1978, substantial devaluations marked the authorities' intention to adjust the real exchange rate to a new more competitive level; subsequent exchange-rate management, with devaluations in 1983 and 1986, sustained the real depreciation.

The oil price rise in 1973 rapidly increased money supply (endogenously determined, given the fixed exchange rate) and inflation rose from under 7 to over 30 per cent. To control this, comprehensive controls were placed upon credit, and interest rates were kept well below inflation. Credit controls were not effective, however, as the open capital account allowed offshore financial intermediation, and moderate inflation persisted. With a fixed exchange rate the non-oil sector within Indonesia became increasingly uncompetitive, a situation partly remedied by the 34 per cent devaluation in 1978, the first indication that shortcomings in monetary control and competitiveness were to be corrected by exchange-rate realignment. The exchange rate was slowly depreciated thereafter in line with the inflation differential with Indonesia's trading partners. However, the decline in oil prices which began in 1982 highlighted the vulnerability of the economy to fuel-export revenues. If fiscal control was to be maintained, government expenditure had to fall and the exchange rate be adjusted to increase the competitiveness of non-oil exports and raise rupiah oil tax revenues.

The devaluation in March 1983 was a response to oil price weakness and declining foreign reserves. Up to 1986, the exchange rate was depreciated in line with the oil price decline, and import volumes were cut substantially: the public sector reduced capital spending and its import content. The exchange rate was devalued sharply in advance of the oil price collapse of 1986. This coincidence reduced the need for a further realignment when the oil price fell.

The objective of this policy was to maintain a fairly constant terms-of-trade-adjusted real exchange rate. The mechanism was fairly straight-forward: a fall in the oil price reduced export revenues, and led holders of rupiah-denominated assets to expect a devaluation and convert into foreign currency. As a result, considerable pressure came to bear upon the level of foreign-exchange reserves. To stem reserve outflow, the exchange rate was adjusted downwards.

Exchange-rate policy after 1986 was more active and was centred upon maintaining approximately six months' reserves. Adjusting to observed trends in reserves meant that it followed a policy of real targets. The gradual depreciation was intended to discourage expectations of devaluation, but this has not been wholly successful. There have been occasions when the more flexible rate has driven expectations of devaluation, with dramatic monetary effects. This clearly occurred in September 1984 when commercial banks, fearing a devaluation, became reluctant to commit excess funds in the rupiah inter-bank market. This drove the inter-bank rate to a peak of 90 per cent before Bank Indonesia intervened with emergency liquidity and squashed expectations of a rupiah devaluation. Exchange-rate expectations help to explain real interest rates of over 7 per cent in 1985–90, higher than the rate of depreciation. This indicates that devaluation expectations persisted. These real interest rates have proved difficult to lower.

After 1986, the influence of the oil price on the exchange rate diminished. Although the oil price increased during 1987 and 1988, exchange-rate depreciation continued to protect the non-oil export sector, which had grown substantially in size since 1983. Over time, Bank Indonesia developed increasingly sophisticated methods of intervention in the foreign-exchange market. In 1990 the official rate was set twice daily, signalling to the markets the desired direction of change of the rate. A limited amount of sterilised intervention has been possible through sales (purchases) of central bank securities.

In summary, the essence of Indonesia's real targets approach was a staged real devaluation to increase the competitiveness of the non-oil export sector and to increase direct foreign investment. Insofar as the non-oil export sector has boomed from the mid-1980s, the strategy of reducing oil as a share of exports and fiscal dependence upon oil revenues has proved successful.

Botswana[5]

Until August 1976 Botswana was a member of the Rand Monetary Area (RMA), as well as being in a customs union with South Africa. The RMA was an effective anchor in terms of controlling inflation in line with the South African rate, because there were no independent powers of money issue and Botswana was highly integrated with the South African economy. The creation of the Botswana pula, initially at par with the South African rand,[6] permitted the introduction of instruments for a domestic monetary policy (e.g. differing interest rates) and for a discretionary exchange-rate policy. The reasons were the political gain from a national currency and greater control over the Botswana economy.

The early experience of the independent currency was good. Botswana's mineral exports (diamonds and copper-nickel) were increasing faster than imports and foreign reserves correspondingly rose from 2.4 months import coverage to 5.7 months by end 1980. Credit extended by commercial banks during this period fell in real terms, mainly because of weak demand between construction booms (Harvey 1985). A policy of cutting interest rates appears not to have influenced credit expansion. A cautious fiscal policy led to an accumulation of government deposits at the central bank. These fortuitous macroeconomic developments provided a reserve cushion for the Botswana authorities to adjust exchange rates when the need arose.

In April 1977 Botswana received a minor external shock from neighbouring South Africa which raised the customs union tariffs as well as taxes and duties, and lowered subsidies on maize meal (the staple imported foodstuff in Botswana). As almost all consumables are imported from South Africa, the price effect was fully reflected in the Botswana price level. At the time South African and Botswana interests were somewhat divergent: the former was damping demand in response to falling terms of trade and reserves, whilst Botswana desired a mild stimulus to its rather sluggish domestic economy. To maintain real incomes in the face of external price increases, the Botswana authorities had few instruments: raising the minimum wage would affect only the small formally employed sector; import tariffs were set on a customs-union-wide basis by South Africa, and altering domestic taxes on goods would create opportunities for smuggling to South Africa.

They revalued the pula by 5 per cent. Following this, the cost of a basket of imported goods representing half the weight of the CPI rose over the next six months by 16.4 per cent, against 22–5 per cent in South Africa. The gainers from revaluation were predominantly those on low incomes, who spent proportionately more on imports and less on local services than higher income-earners. The main losers were exporters of diamonds, copper-nickel and beef, whose local currency revenues fell (this was partly offset by rising international prices and reduced commodity-export taxation). There were few local producers of domestically consumed tradables whose competitiveness was affected. The positive distributional and price effects of revaluation encouraged the authorities to revalue by 5 per cent again in September 1979, and again in November 1980. On these occasions the reduction of inflation relative to South Africa appeared to be less: a boom in diamond exploitation created extremely rapid GDP growth (22.5 per cent real per capita GDP increase in 1979) and domestic inflationary pressures so that traders tended not to pass on the revaluation effects.

During 1977–80 Botswana had a partial success in using the exchange rate to pursue the target of maintaining real incomes and insulating domestic prices from those of its major trading partners. This occurred despite few independent macroeconomic levers and high trade dependence. The factors associated with the first successful revaluation were clearly adequate reserves, low demand for credit and money, and fiscal caution. An additional enabling factor for revaluation was that Botswana had little importing industry and buoyant, largely extractive-based, export industries.

THE CONDITIONS FOR USING EXCHANGE-RATE POLICY

Although it is a simplification to associate fixed exchange rates with credit control and flexible rates with monetary aggregate control, it is a convenient first approximation, supported by both *a priori* reasoning and empirical evidence in the country studies in this book. The six countries have used credit control as the primary control instrument when exchange rates were fixed: Côte d'Ivoire, Ghana, Indonesia (pre-1978), and China occasionally: Bangladesh, Kenya, Indonesia 1978–83. Credit targets were abandoned in 1983 by the Indonesian authorities when exchange-rate adjustment became more active and interest rates were decontrolled.

The effectiveness of monetary control under flexible rates or of credit control with fixed rates also depends on other factors: the structure of the domestic financial market; linkages between domestic and foreign goods markets and financial markets, and the extent of fiscal imbalances. If the monetary and exchange-rate policies are coordinated with these by regulation or institutional relationships, then monetary policy is likely to be more effective in achieving its primary objectives. Table 12.5 summarises the implications for monetary policy.

In the absence of control of the government deficit, both credit targeting and monetary aggregate targeting are likely to be ineffective with either fixed or flexible exchange rates. Credit control is superficially more effective than monetary control, to the extent that unanticipated increases in credit to government can be offset by reductions in credit to the rest of the economy.

Table 12.5 Monetary policy effectiveness and economic structure in developing countries

Feature	Credit targets	Monetary targets	Relevance
Loss of fiscal control	Weaker – possible crowding-out	Weaker in short run. In long run less effect, particularly if fixed exchange rates.	H I G H
Important non-bank credit market	Weaker – owing to NBFI or informal market	Possibly weaker – dependent on money definition	L O W
Integrated domestic and foreign financial markets	Weaker – net credit can be obtained from offshore markets	Weaker – speculative capital inflows expand reserve money unless sterilised intervention or offsetting reserve money reductions	H I G H

However, the redistribution of credit necessary to accommodate a lack of fiscal control can lower real private spending, output and investment. It can lower future output if government use of borrowed funds is less productive than that of the private sector. In Kenya, the loss of fiscal control led to increases in credit to government which, causality tests suggest, explain reductions in private credit and in its share of total credit. In Côte d'Ivoire, the credit control system has also led to a type of crowding-out: credit for the financing of agricultural exports (largely by a state enterprise) takes precedence over credit for other economic activities, hence, when the demand for rural refinancing rose sharply as a result of a stockpiling policy from 1986 onwards, the credit share of other sectors fell sharply.

The loss of fiscal control is reflected in unpredictable and autonomous increases in reserve money which can affect most monetary aggregates. The problem is similar to autonomous changes in foreign reserves with fixed exchange rates. Its effect, however, depends in part on the exchange regime. The expansionary impact on money supply of excess government borrowing is likely to be less if exchange rates are fixed or inflexible, as increases in credit are offset by reserve losses. Killick and Mwega show for Kenya that, with an inflexible exchange rate, an increase in banking system credit is correlated with a weakening balance-of-payments position.

The efficacy of credit control also depends on whether credit can be obtained outside the controlled credits. In Kenya, this gave an incentive for rapid growth in the less regulated non-bank financial institution market. In low-income countries, the informal financial sector may also limit the effectiveness of credit controls, but the evidence for this is mixed, and the quantities involved may be small (see Chapter 11).

Financial markets integrated with international markets are likely to make the process of monetary control more difficult, particularly with a flexible exchange arrangement. This allows an additional source of credit, which weakens the predictability of the credit-output-expenditure relationship and puts the volume of credit outside the control of the domestic monetary authorities. In Indonesia, the neighbouring financial centre of Singapore has permitted substantial offshore borrowing (and deposit-taking). The extent of financial integration between the two countries was accepted with the removal of all capital restrictions in 1971. After the fixed rate was abandoned, speculative capital flows tended to destabilise domestic money markets, in particular raising interest rates at times of speculative outflow.

In the case of Franc Zone countries, financial integration with France has been total. This has permitted substantial movements of short-term capital and created unpredictable monetary aggregates, but permissive financing by the French Treasury reduced the impact on policy.

In Ghana, the formal sector financial market was poorly integrated with the overseas market: neither interest rates nor exchange rates responded to external developments (until 1983). Shifts into foreign currency as a de-valuation hedge arguably reduced the minimal influence of the central bank on monetary developments.

The main conclusion of this chapter is that exchange-rate arrangements cannot affect the real international value of a currency whose domestic value is declining because of weak monetary control. Where a fixed exchange rate is used to limit domestic inflation, whether in monetary unions, by a fixed peg to one currency (or a basket) or through a predetermined crawling peg, experience tends to show that this is an insufficient tool for controlling domestic prices and monetary policy. Where the nominal tie is strongest, in monetary unions, price divergence and slow price convergence can lock economies into an uncompetitive exchange-rate position. The official exchange rate becomes increasingly irrelevant as foreign-exchange trans-actions shift to the black market. The lack of credibility of monetary policy prevents a return to a new, devalued, fixed nominal rate, and attempts to follow real targets are undermined. Relinquishing official intervention by floating the exchange rate appears to be the best method for reintegrating the official and black market rates, and permits monetary authorities to con-centrate on monetary control. In countries with a reasonable counter-inflationary record the exchange rate can be adjusted to determine external competitiveness or alternatively to maintain the purchasing power of the domestic currency. In terms of policy implementation, this has worked remarkably well, but the country examples have both a relatively open capital account and exports of income-elastic goods.

Part IV

MONETARY POLICY AND THE FINANCIAL SECTOR

13

THE USE OF MONETARY POLICY

John Healey and Sheila Page

The purpose of the last four chapters of this book is to identify some common or frequently occurring experiences in our six country studies, to draw out their lessons for specific questions on the use of monetary instruments, institutional arrangements, and what can be expected of monetary policy, and to examine their implications for broader questions of the use of monetary policy, and the relationship of this to development of the financial sector and of the economies in general. The following seven key questions are posed by this study and have been examined in the country studies:

1 Has there been, or has there evolved, an explicit or implicit monetary policy, and what were the monetary objectives of the government, whether short-term or long-term?
2 How effective has monetary policy been in achieving stabilisation objectives – for inflation or the balance of payments?
3 How effective has monetary policy been in coping with external 'shocks' to the economy?
4 What monetary instruments have been used, and have they been effective in achieving money and credit targets?
5 What have been the main constraints on effective implementation of monetary policy?
6 Has there been a policy for the financial sector, and has it been effective in development objectives – the mobilisation or allocation of financial resources?
7 How important has the informal financial sector been as a part of the financial sector or a constraint on monetary policy?

The first three of these questions relate to when and how governments have used monetary policy, and are dealt with in this chapter. The following three questions go to the central concerns of this study: what monetary instruments can be used in developing countries, and whether there are special difficulties that influence which are chosen, or how effective they are, and the financial sectors within which they must operate. These are considered in Chapter 14. Chapter 15 examines the relationship between the formal financial sector and the informal, and the implications for monetary policy. Chapter 16 discusses the significance of the monetary policies and financial problems discussed here to the broader objectives of developing countries, and views of development.

MONETARY POLICY?

The first question is whether these countries intended to use monetary policy as a 'tool' in their economic objectives. Some tests of this are as follows:

1 Whether there were stabilisation objectives and whether monetary policy was given a part in them: for example, whether there was an intention not to monetise any fiscal deficits.
2 Whether there were prior targets or rules set for money supply or its counterparts for stabilisation purposes.
3 Whether there was an intention to give the central monetary authority some independent status to enable a monetary discipline to be more effectively imposed.
4 Whether the authorities had longer-term development objectives for the monetisation of their economies and the mobilisation of savings by the banking system.

These are questions of strategic intention rather than effective operation.

The broad answer is that none of the countries passed all or most of these tests. Indonesia evolved and pursued clear monetary objectives which were set in a consistent fiscal and external payments policy framework over more than a decade. Côte d'Ivoire, as a member of the CFA system, implicitly subscribed to the system's rules though it did not always keep them. None of the others can be said to have had explicit monetary objectives and consistent strategies for pursuing them. Intermittently, and especially in the 1980s, Kenya and Ghana have had money and credit targets, after periods when fiscal policy was dominant and sometimes irresponsible. Bangladesh could only be said to have had a weak monetary policy. China – a rather special case – is only slowly evolving a monetary policy to fit its economic reforms which decentralise decisions. The evolution of this policy is lagging behind the demands posed by the reforms, though the government seems to have consistently taken an anti-inflationary stance in the sense of avoiding persistent excess demand in the consumer goods markets. It is also a rare case where monetary policy has sought to develop the banking habit and encourage savings.

Let us now look briefly and comparatively at this account of the experiences of the six countries.

A fundamental test of commitment to a monetary policy is whether countries have sought to avoid a fiscal policy which resulted in excessive monetisation of government deficits and have pursued explicit 'rules' or 'targets' in relation to money and credit.

One generalisation is that virtually all of our six countries have since the 1970s evolved a firmer approach to these objectives. Côte d'Ivoire remained a member of the Franc Zone, which has a built-in monetary discipline, although it must also be judged on how far it kept to the CFA rules. The key feature of the Indonesian case has been its willingness to learn from the bad inflationary experience of the Sukarno years (1960s) and to evolve, over two distinct periods, a monetary policy which has deployed both monetary targets and indirect monetary instruments to keep control over the money supply and inflation. The framework for this had two parts: the conservatism of expenditure policy, which achieved the commitment to a balanced budget, and the open capital account, which supported this fiscal stance by providing access to foreign capital inflow while at the same time depending on conservative fiscal and monetary policy to be effective.

In Kenya, and especially in Ghana, commitment has been much weaker. Kenya has had an ambiguous and variable commitment to monetary policy and the objectives of economic stability. Fiscal policy has not been consistent with effective monetary control. Because of the reluctance to increase taxes or control public expenditure, the Central Bank of Kenya has been allowed little influence over major determinants of the monetary situation, namely, the budget deficit and government borrowing from the banking system and overseas. Stabilisation objectives have been abandoned in commodity booms. As Killick and Mwega say 'It is perhaps not stretching things too far to ask whether there has ever been a national monetary policy in the sense of one principally defined by the government'. A monetary policy in the sense of official money credit targets has only been invoked when balance of payments problems have required the intervention of IMF programmes – quite frequently during the 1980s.

There was no serious monetary policy in Ghana from 1973 to 1983, with unchecked monetary growth and high and persistent inflation. During this period the government deficit was the dominant cause of monetary expansion. The resultant collapse in the value of the cedi completely undermined confidence in domestic money as a store of value, and there was a strong shift to transactions in foreign currency. It was not until after 1983 and the initiation of the ERP that overall ceilings were set under IMF programmes, and serious (successful) attempts were made to bring the government budget into balance after deficits in the 1970s rose to 11 per cent of GNP under the Acheampong regime.

The Bangladesh story (1973–87) is less easy to read. There was no monetary policy during the 1973–5 period of high inflation. Under the Zia (1977–81) and Ershad (post-1981) regimes, policies were aimed at bringing inflation under control. Although there were expansionary monetary episodes, policy was effective in bringing average inflation down because of a significant expansion in agricultural output, the inflow of aid, and favourable world markets. Unlike in Ghana and Kenya, fiscal policy has not been allowed to dominate monetary policy. Annual monetary targets have been set, often in consultation with the IMF. The impression, however, is one of a largely accommodating monetary policy. Targets for the money supply (and domestic credit) have been set by reference to expected inflation and planned output for each base period. There has been little fine-tuning for annual variations in food output and availability.

In China there has been a concern with ensuring balance between expenditure and availability of consumer goods and hence an effective anti-inflationary objective. The weakness of the design of Chinese monetary procedures stems from the failure to keep pace with the basic economic reforms taking place; hence some control was lost over the extent of excess demand in the economy. China has been in transition since 1978 from a fully centralised, planned economy towards more decentralised decisions by public enterprises and the introduction of private markets. Although the need for an effective monetary policy has become more urgent, in practice, the basic inconsistency has been in not matching decentralised production and reinvestment decisions in the economy with effective powers for the banking system and the People's Bank to determine the scale and allocation of credit. The People's Bank remains weak because there has been no banking law to regulate lending by the banking system, deposits, interest rates, etc., while private investments have been determined politically and not by the banks using financial criteria like profitability or creditworthiness to ration a limited supply of capital.

A further test of the commitment to monetary policy, at least for stabilisation purposes, is the status and degree of independence given *de jure* and *de facto* to the central monetary authority.

In Côte d'Ivoire the central bank – the BCEAO acting for the countries in the UMOA (the monetary union) – is more independent than that of any other of the six countries. It has the supranational authority of the UMOA, the legal right and obligation to refuse credit to governments, and an exchange rate fixed to the French franc. Lane notes:

> The rule followed is that money supply should be expanded with reference to the level of foreign-reserve coverage. There are two reasons why this is a broadly credible non-inflationary policy ... (i) the BCEAO agency has no particular incentive or statutory authority ... to deviate intentionally from its policy. (ii) Government cannot resort to rolling the printing presses to monetise fiscal deficits automatically.

As the recent history of Côte d'Ivoire shows, however, this has not been allowed to constrain credit creation effectively. There is no other system in our set of six which is designed explicitly for achieving monetary control, though Indonesia under Soeharto comes the closest to it.

When Soeharto came to power in Indonesia after a period of lax monetary control and hyperinflation, the Bank Indonesia was cast in a powerful and fairly autonomous role in money management. This role was exercised by a group of neo-classical economic technocrats who were Western-trained and had the support of the new President. The Bank's position was strengthened by the constitutional provision that the budget be 'balanced', in the sense that expenditure should not exceed revenues plus counterpart funds generated by external assistance.

In other countries, despite the fact that in some cases the central bank began life at independence with formal powers to pursue an independent monetary policy, these powers often lapsed or were legally changed. In Kenya, the central bank had been statutorily obliged to limit the amount of credit it could provide to government, but this provision was repealed in 1972. In Ghana, the West African Currency Board determined the supply of money on similar rules to those of the UMOA till 1957, when responsibility fell to the Bank of Ghana. Created formally independent, the Bank of Ghana continued to control the increase in money supply for the first fifteen years of its existence. Its loss of control occurred in 1972 with the military coup. In recent years the Governor has lacked job security, and control has been exercised by the Ministry of Finance and Planning. In Bangladesh, the subordination of the central bank is less clear, but most decisions have been made by the Governor in close consultation with the Minister of Finance, and also with the IMF.

With the exception of the special case of Côte d'Ivoire, the role of the central bank is not interesting in policy terms in these countries. It is an administrative arm of the government, creating or constraining credit in accordance with its policies. The Governors have not been persons of high prestige, political clout or job security, who would or could take a powerful stand against excessive credit creation. This subordination is normal in centralised countries, where there is only one accepted source of economic policy. It is only in federal countries that size and local power centres can give a central bank a stronger, more independent role.

China is the only potential example among our six countries (unless the role of the BCEAO in the Franc Zone area is interpreted in this way), and there both the central government, politically, and the regional authorities, economically, are too strong for an intermediary to be effective. Experience in the 1970s and 1980s indicates that the People's Bank (central bank) has had no autonomous power to determine monetary targets. The Economic Plan is determined politically by the State Council. Hence, the public sector borrowing requirement (central government and state enterprises) is given for the People's Bank. This largely determines M0 (or currency in the hands of the public) but the People's Bank does have some residual power to influence the other main determinant of M0, the net borrowing of the non-state sector.

The degree of political instability rather than the nature of the political regime seems to be a systematic influence on fiscal deficits and monetising them. The more uncertain are rulers' expectations of the duration of their power, the higher the degree of fiscal and monetary irresponsibility. Why do most countries not see a need to curb the power of the public sector to borrow from the banks as it wishes? Rulers clearly do not like to constrain themselves, but few societies or systems have sought to curb them. Little political research has been done on this subject.

Our case studies do not suggest any obvious mechanisms or solutions to the problem. A constitutional and simple rule like a statutory limit on the size of the budget deficit was used effectively by Indonesia. It was also inflexible under shocks, although it may have prevented worse mistakes. But a constitutional rule only worked there because there was a political consensus which apparently arose from the earlier traumatic experience. Indonesia may suggest two other political or policy features which have a bearing on effective monetary control. First, the system was open so that the public could react and easily 'exit' by taking their capital out of the country if they were not happy with the way money was being managed. Second, the strength of central monetary control did not derive from an independent central bank, but rather from a coalition between the Bank and the Ministry of Finance to resist the pressures of other powerful spending departments. Perceived independence could have weakened it by isolating it.

Finally, how far were the monetary authorities or monetary policies given a clear development role in the long-term monetisation of the economy, mobilisation of savings or efficient credit allocation? In quite a number of cases sectoral policies were specified setting credit targets or constraints, offering low or differential interest rates. The intentions were therefore present but the effectiveness was limited, as the next chapter shows, and the failure of governments to improve the effectiveness suggests that this was not seen as an important role for monetary policy.

On the first two issues, there has been no strong commitment over two decades to government policies for such objectives, whether through the financial sector or other means. In all, the principal retail banks are foreign or state-owned. Foreign-owned banks predominate in Africa. In Indonesia and of course China, the state-owned banks are most important, although a domestic private sector is growing in Indonesia. The establishment of state-owned banks has sometimes reflected a wish to use the banking system to promote monetisation, for example in Ghana after independence, but only in China does there appear to have been a continuing commitment to set up and maintain an extensive network of local banks. This followed the general reforms of the 1970s, which by giving greater responsibility to local enterprises and governments, increased the need for some flexible local credit, but it also served to mobilise household savings. Santorum notes that they were on balance unprofitable, at least until recently, which suggests that they were seen as providing an infrastructure-type service. Indonesia also promoted rural banking up to 1983. Bangladesh does not report any such initiatives.

In Côte d'Ivoire, Lane suggests that monetisation was relatively high from an early date because of the importance of a cash crop, but the other countries do not report this. The formal banks also seem to be more important in the agricultural sector there. Within the period under study, however, there was little change. In contrast, Sowa argues that there is still a major role for barter in Ghana, especially within the subsistence sector.

There was an intention to increase access in rural areas in Ghana, but the series of initiatives reported, all with the same ostensible objective, suggests that it has never been carried through consistently. Although the number of branches has grown, they remain insufficient. There has, indeed, been active discouragement from using the formal sector in the form of confiscation or freezing of bank accounts, demonetisation of high denomination notes, etc., which Sowa plausibly argues will make it difficult to encourage future use of bonds.

Again with the exception of China, the financial sectors in the study countries apparently discourage small or low-income savers or borrowers, seeing them as costly (and perhaps risky) – a normal banking perspective, rather than a developmental one. This supports the evidence from the lack of government initiatives to spread banks that developing this sector has not been seen as an important element in either social or industrial policy.

An alternative approach, treated more fully in Chapter 15 on the relationship between the formal and informal sectors, would be to develop a separate system of informal institutions alongside the formal sector. Where this has been done, however, for example the Grameen Bank in Bangladesh, it has been at the initiative of non-governmental agencies, not of governments.

We can now sum up the results from these six countries. The two cases which show the strongest commitment to monetary objectives are Côte d'Ivoire and Indonesia. They are both economies which have integrated themselves into international capital markets, although complementary liberalising reforms in Indonesia have made this financial integration more effective. Both have had 'rules' for operating their fiscal and monetary policies, although only Indonesia has followed them. Lack of fiscal control and independence for the monetary authority has been a feature of Ghana and to a lesser extent Kenya. Both countries have accepted monetary discipline from the IMF in response to balance-of-payments problems, but have not persisted with them in the Fund's absence. Bangladesh has followed an accommodating monetary policy, again under IMF intervention.

China has been more concerned to create a banking system adapted to the structural changes in the economy, as the government has pursued major reforms which decentralise production decisions and expand the private sector. Monetary policy there would have a more challenging task than in the other countries, since transition between systems makes behavioural responses more unpredictable, and because both policymakers and those who respond to them are learning to do different things in different ways. This has been compounded, in Santorum's view, by a lack of consistency. The decentralisation of decision-making for production enterprises has not been adequately matched by decentralisation of decisions on credit and currency through a banking system which could operate indirectly on the level and allocation of credit through reserve regulation, interest rates and financial criteria. The continuation of central plans, directly administered and politically dominated credit decisions, and weak monitoring has not worked well and has fitted uneasily into the new reforms.

HOW EFFECTIVE HAS MONETARY POLICY BEEN IN ACHIEVING STABILISATION OBJECTIVES?

This is a difficult judgement to make, not only because monetary policy has to be coordinated with other economic policies to be effective, but also because standards of judgement have to be arbitrary. Nevertheless, the authors of the country studies have ventured some views on the effectiveness of monetary policy, at least during certain periods in the countries under review. The following points emerge.

Although other factors have been at work, monetary expansion has been an important influence on inflation in all six countries, and therefore monetary policy had the potential to be effective. It was not always a one-way causal relationship. There is evidence from several studies (Kenya, Bangladesh, Ghana) of feedback of prices on money supply, and in a number of countries real output variations and import prices were clearly a powerful influence and presented difficulties for the effective operation of monetary policy.

Indonesia probably reveals the most successful story of monetary policy at work. It is a story about the evolution of a more effective policy through learning lessons, especially from the 1960s when lax fiscal and monetary policies led to hyperinflation. Hyperinflation was stabilised (1969–73) by moving to balanced budgets and eliminating the monetisation of central government deficits (and later the deficits of state enterprises). Thereafter the use of monetary policy, together with decontrolled external capital movements, to maximise the scope for foreign borrowing and aid was eventually the key to reasonable price stability. Although two oil price shocks in the 1970s and some speculative outflow pressures in the 1980s tested the operation of the policy, it evolved well and inflation was on average very moderate by developing country standards in the 1980s, while growth of output and financial intermediation was not discouraged.

Ghana also experienced hyperinflation and complete loss of confidence in the currency and the banking system. Again inflation was reduced sharply (from about 70 per cent per annum in 1979–83 to about 30 per cent per annum in 1984–8) by tight monetary policy and a shift towards balanced budgets. Nevertheless, it has remained relatively high.

In Kenya, movements in the money supply have been statistically associated with inflation and balance-of-payments problems. Domestic credit to government has been the most powerful influence. Fiscal policy has not been coordinated with monetary policy and monetary policy was not used to help stabilise external price shocks. Nevertheless – although never tightly counter-inflationary – money creation was neither loose nor excessive by African standards. There was no prolonged period of grossly excessive credit creation and inflation has never risen above 25 per cent per annum and fell in the late 1980s.

The other African economy, Côte d'Ivoire, is an interesting test of a policy where the monetary authority has statutory independence, the country is part of a monetary union and the exchange rate has been fixed to a major world currency. Broadly, its experience suggests that monetary policy was effective in keeping inflation lower than the average for sub-Saharan Africa in the 1970s and 1980s. Indeed, its average rate for the 1980s (4.2 per cent) was low by any standards. Lane's conclusion is that the policy worked effectively during the expansionary period of the 1960s and 1970s but not so well during the economic stagnation of the 1980s, and was unhelpful in the adjustment of the economy to changed terms of trade.

An alternative conclusion might be that the policy did not work well (to limit inflation) in the expansionary period and boom of the late 1970s and the cumulative inflation was not fully reversible in the 1980s with a fixed exchange rate. Inflation was reduced to very low levels, but monetary policy would have needed to achieve negative inflation rates to ensure competitiveness with the rest of the world. This demanding legacy stemmed from lack of control earlier. The inability to adjust the fixed exchange rate and reverse the earlier damage then imposed a severe challenge on fiscal and monetary policy. Other policies like unrealistic price support systems for coffee and cocoa increased the pressure. Monetary policy was thus faced with the triple problem of conflicting government policies, instruments limited by fixed exchange rates, and the financial underdevelopment which is discussed in the next chapter.

In Bangladesh and China, with large agricultural sectors and little trade with the rest of the world, monetary policy has been accommodating, partly no doubt because of the priority given to planned growth of output. In neither economy does inflation seem to have been brought under control, though the problems faced have differed greatly. Bangladesh has been confronted with the acute problem of low and fluctuating growth of output, especially food which is desperately needed to match its growing population. A monetary policy cautious enough to prevent runaway inflation but which never brought it down to low and stable levels, could be considered consistent with this. In China, the credibility of the monetary authorities' attempts at stabilisation has been undermined by 'stop-go' policies, with an accommodating monetary policy predominant. Santorum concludes that monetary policy has become less and less effective as a measure for controlling inflation.

Overall, the six studies show governments evolving towards more committed and effective stabilisation policies in the 1980s. The success of monetary policy has clearly varied with the ability of governments to control the demands placed on it from the scale and financing of their budget deficits. Few governments have brought inflation well under control by monetary and fiscal policies, but only in China did monetary control of inflation seem to be slipping further away in the 1980s. Since the study was written, China also appears to have re-established monetary control.

MONETARY POLICY WITH EXTERNAL SHOCKS

One objective of these studies was to assess how able countries with primary product exports were to manage their monetary policy in the face of 'external shocks'. It was expected that unanticipated deterioration or improvement in their terms of trade with the rest of the world or changes in their trade volume because of natural disasters would impose unusual strains, and that poor countries with less developed financial systems would be particularly vulnerable.

Before reviewing the experience in five of the six countries which faced this type of problem in the last twenty years, it might be useful to set out what an 'effective' intervention might look like in fiscal and monetary terms, together with its economic rationale, against which actual actions can be assessed and constraints evaluated.

The interventionist approach characteristic of stabilisation policy argues for state intervention. The first problem is to judge whether the terms-of-trade change is transient or persistent. In the case of a windfall export gain: 'sterilise' the gains to exporters, add to the foreign-exchange reserves, and prevent any addition to the domestic monetary base beyond the permanent income gain or annuity value from investing the gain.

There are two ways to do this. To skim off the 'windfall' to the exporters by holding prices to the producers (if the government is the exporter, as in a marketing board) or by taxing them, which leaves income distribution unchanged. The government or its agency increases its net deposits at the central bank (or reduces its net borrowing). The windfall is saved, not spent on new investment projects or extra current expenditures. The extra public sector deposits at the central bank will be matched by increased foreign-exchange reserves. The second method allows the exporters to retain their windfall gains but the central bank sells equivalent securities to the public to sterilise the aggregate impact on the domestic money base. Either process can be reversed in the case of a terms-of-trade shortfall. Pre-existing foreign reserves are drawn down. Government maintains prices/incomes either for the exporters or for the economy as a whole by altering government expenditure or taxation, or allowing the central bank to buy securities from the public.

Intervention of this kind after a boom might give the following advantages:

1 It ensures that the terms-of-trade/price change gives no false signals to exporters about future prospects. This is true only if the government is more likely to be able to judge permanence than the exporters (or the producers, in the case of a marketing board). In developed economies, and in conventional economic analysis, the reverse would be assumed because it is the exporters who have greater expertise in their own product and the greater financial interest in making the correct appraisal. The judgement on whether a price shock is transient or lasting may not be easy. Past experience may give some evidence on the persistence of price changes. However, there must be a case for a prudent reaction, at least initially. The first oil price shock in 1972–4 in Indonesia was relatively durable and of a novel type. However, in Kenya and Côte d'Ivoire the coffee price bonanza of 1976–7 was clearly transient (it was due principally to frost in Brazil), and not novel.

2 It stabilises the price (and income if the shock is in the terms of trade rather than the volume) for the exporters. This effectively transfers the risk of primary production to the government. Unless there is permanent intervention to hold the price below the international price, it would tend to induce long-term overproduction.

3 It avoids the risk of high inflation because of a sharp increase in domestic demand faced with inelastic domestic output in the short term. The economically efficient alternative would be to permit imports to meet the demand.

4 It should prevent real exchange-rate appreciation which would have to be reversed later. Like point 3, this is an advantage only if it is assumed that the economies of developing countries are more inflexible than those of developed, and that the normal means of increasing flexibility are not available.

5 It should give no stimulus to government expenditure, which may be wasteful and/or difficult to reverse when the boom ends. This embodies an assumption contrary to that of point 1, namely, that the government is not capable of taking correct decisions about the treatment of a windfall gain (or loss), and thus depends on an assumption that the government is either so inefficient or so subject to rules about division of responsibilities (for example, between a central bank and spending ministries) that it can have directly opposed policies, and that the voice

of the former will prevail in a gain and of the latter in a loss.

6   It ensures that any gain gives an addition to the foreign-exchange reserves which can be a buffer against a future 'shortfall' from an adverse 'shock'. In the case of a loss, it assumes that the reserves are already sufficient to act as such a buffer.

It might be added that a process like this requires (i) some prior established policy rather than *ad hoc* intervention, (ii) the identification of 'triggers' for intervention which can be measured or predicted, and perhaps (iii) some institutional arrangements for stabilisation of prices or incomes.

The alternative strategy, of course, is to do nothing, and assume that the monetary and real systems of the economy are mature and robust enough to sustain the shock without intervention. An examination of the strong assumptions required in either case suggests that if a country does have an underdeveloped financial sector, a vulnerable economy, and perhaps a government with conflicting economic objectives, neither strategy is likely to be effective in avoiding a damaging shock to the economy, and indeed that even a developed country will have great difficulties. ('Dutch disease' was first identified in Australia, and has been diagnosed in more than one European country.)

With this in mind, what was the experience of those of the study countries which faced quite sharp terms-of-trade gains and losses, mainly through their export trade? Three countries provide relevant experience; Côte d'Ivoire (coffee boom 1976–9), Kenya (coffee and tea boom 1976–8 and coffee in 1986–7), Indonesia (oil price rises 1973–4 and 1979–80). Bangladesh and China do not provide much evidence on this issue. They are both large and not very open economies where volatility arises more from domestic shocks to supply and demand (e.g. fluctuations in agricultural output) than from external shocks. For Ghana, the challenge of reversing long-term economic and export decline has taken precedence over coping with external price shocks.

Côte d'Ivoire   It faced an export boom (in the late 1970s) and a subsequent collapse of export prices (in the early 1980s). The first point to note is that the country possessed autonomous and efficient institutions for 'stabilisation' and 'sterilisation' in the form of the CSSPA, the CAA and the BCEAO. The established mechanisms fixed the domestic prices received by producers of exported primary products. The CSSPA was a stabilisation fund to insulate farmers from coffee and cocoa price changes above or below a 'set' producer price. Windfall surpluses were syphoned into the CAA, outside the budgetary framework of government. Shortfalls were met by compensatory payments to farmers, financed by net borrowing from banks and the central bank. This device for 'creaming-off' world export prices above certain levels relieved the central bank in principle from having to sell securities to a thin capital market in order to reduce excessive liquidity flowing into the economy. During the coffee and cocoa booms 1977–9, the BCEAO and the CAA operated a voluntary reserve deposit arrangement but this only partially sterilised the rapidly rising liquidity.

Despite these institutional mechanisms, Côte d'Ivoire did not, in practice, operate an effective sterilisation policy. In the 1977–80 boom, domestic credit to both government and private sector increased rapidly; imports rose and no accumulation of foreign assets occurred. With relatively low elasticity of domestic output, inflation accelerated and competitiveness deteriorated. Thus, although the windfall gain was transferred to the state, it was not sterilised, but used for investment expenditure and to redeem domestically held debt, hence giving a fiscal and monetary stimulus to the economy. The money base rose as the 'bonanza' revenues affected the domestic economy and facilitated increased credit to the public and private sectors, despite the damping effect of a money multiplier which fortunately contracts at periods of increased liquidity in Côte d'Ivoire. Net foreign assets did not rise; they fell.

With the collapse of export prices and the erosion of temporary terms-of-trade gains by the early 1980s, the established mechanisms were used to the opposite effect, and an attempt was made to 'sterilise' the loss. The main policy features were:

1   To maintain price support for cocoa and coffee producers, but the level proved unsustainable.
2   To give priority to rural financing from the central bank, but this was used excessively for credit to stockpile surplus export commodities and for price support in 1981–4 and 1987–8.
3   To induce breaches of the statutory money base and ratios and total credit limits. The effect may have been to 'crowd-out' other types of lending or borrower.

It may well have been difficult to forecast early on the length and depth of the terms-of-trade decline for the 1980s. Although the real exchange rate did reverse its appreciation after the 1976–8 boom, the combination of these policies must have inhibited the adjustment of the economy, by providing the wrong signals and incentives. It seems clear, however, that intervening in a fall and not intervening in a rise is likely to produce worse effects than following either policy consistently. The price-smoothing mechanism in Côte d'Ivoire was itself not entirely appropriate, since greater price flexibility would probably have smoothed the incomes of farmers from export proceeds more effectively. Prices in the end gave the wrong signals in the collapse.

Kenya   Here, experience suggests that stabilisation objectives have been abandoned in booms. The study reports that a political decision was made not to tax windfall proceeds, in the face of a boom (1976–8) which was obviously only temporary. A further similar but milder boom in 1986 was left similarly unmanaged. There was no attempt to accumulate net foreign assets or to sterilise the domestic monetary effects of the windfall gains to export farmers by extra taxation, whether by government saving or by selling Treasury bills to the public. On the contrary, a major expansion of public consumption expenditure was accompanied by an expansion in credit to the private sector via reduced reserve ratios. An import boom, a sharp rise in the relative price of non-tradables and a balance-of-payments crisis ensued. There were ratchet effects since it became difficult for the Treasury to control public spending after the boom. Overall credit limits imposed in the aftermath tended to squeeze domestic credit, primarily to the private sector. In the 1986 boom and its aftermath, the increased government expenditure in the boom was mainly 'one-off' in character.

Athough the central bank advised the government to sterilise the extra reserves on both occasions, its warnings do not appear to have been heeded. The main difference from Côte d'Ivoire was in the allocation of the gains. Kenya allowed most of the windfall gain to pass to the export farmers in the boom, and in the slump the credit restraints fell on all private borrowers including the farmers. In Côte d'Ivoire there was a fiscal mechanism which particularly skimmed-off the windfall to the exporters in the boom but supported them in the slump. Only non-rural private sector borrowers were crowded-out of credit in the slump.

Killick and Mwega question whether manipulation of domestic high-powered money to neutralise instability in foreign assets is (i) feasible or (ii) desirable in Kenya. The feasibility doubts centre on the large size of the movement in net foreign assets and the limited possibility for the central bank to sell securities to mop up the excess domestic liquidity or on the limited scope for raising the reserve ratios of banks for the same purpose. Ultimately therefore they see the 'constraint' as the impact on private sector credit: the private sector would be crowded-out directly or via higher interest rates from such a policy.

Indonesia Faced with the first oil price shock in 1974, Indonesia did not behave very differently from Côte d'Ivoire and Kenya. It had no prior strategy; it acted after the major inflationary shock by direct credit controls, and it was not prepared to freeze the increased liquidity in the banking system during the boom. The budget remained balanced, and therefore did not offset the increased private sector liquidity. In fact, foreign assets fell. It was helped, unlike Kenya and Côte d'Ivoire, by greater elasticity of domestic output, but inflation accelerated greatly, suggesting that other corrective responses, from output or imports, were not sufficient. However, in contrast to the coffee cycles, the duration and severity of the oil price hike in 1974 were misjudged by many oil producers.

By the second oil shock in 1979, the government of Indonesia had decided that the costs of inaction were unacceptable, and it managed the boom by sterilising the windfall gains. Net foreign assets rose fourfold (1978–81) matched by increased government deposits at the central bank. Credit rose overall by only 5–7 per cent (1978–80) and inflation was lower than in 1974. But the government had overcome the statutory requirement to balance the budget by 'stealth'. It ran what was effectively a significant surplus because the funds committed for extra development expenditure (as revenues rose in the boom) were not spent, apparently owing to implementation constraints in the construction sector. In spite of the balanced budget requirements, therefore, negative net domestic credit to government largely offset the positive increase in net credit to the private sector. Policy was flexible despite the legal constraints, and was less than 'transparent'.

What general impressions can be drawn from these cases about the management of external terms-of-trade shocks?

None conformed completely to the sterilisation pattern. Only Indonesia in the second oil shock came near to this. Windfalls have normally been passed through into the domestic economy, with little or no sterilisation or accumulation of foreign assets. A severe adjustment in the subsequent slump was therefore required. Both Kenya and Indonesia had two booms of a similar kind within the period studied. The government of Kenya did not change its behaviour, while Indonesia reversed its response.

In only one country, Côte d'Ivoire, was there a prior stabilisation strategy and institutional mechanisms to implement it, but this did not prove effective. Indonesia had no strategy or mechanisms, and its balanced budget strategy was too rigid for this problem. Only unofficial means proved effective. The Kenyan government had a purely *ad hoc* and perverse response to the shocks.

The governments' responses do not suggest great skill at judging the permanence of the price changes. Alternatively, some may have seen the booms as an opportunity to increase government spending, to start programmes which would be difficult to stop, or merely, as in the case of the more one-off expenditures of the second Kenyan boom, to achieve projects difficult to justify in 'normal' circumstances.

There do not appear to be generally applicable monetary or fiscal mechanisms to manage such shocks or to ensure the will to do so. The lack of a developed capital market probably inhibited the sale of securities to institutions and the public to limit excessive liquidity in a boom (as well as the scope for securities purchase in a slump). However, an alternative option, of manipulating the reserve liquidity ratio of the banking system to the same effect, was not used by either Kenya or Côte d'Ivoire, nor was it used by the Indonesians in the first oil shock.

Apart from the 'technical' difficulty of predicting boom behaviour, however, the inhibition appears to be 'political'. There was a general un-willingness to prevent the economy from enjoying the temporary gains by controlling credit when an external windfall gain added to the money base. Any constraints on monetary management could have been avoided by fiscal measures to increase national saving. The governments would have needed to cut their budget deficits and reduce their net borrowing from the central bank or achieve a budget surplus and accumulate deposits at the central bank as a counterpart to increased net foreign assets. There was no apparent economic obstacle to the former in Côte d'Ivoire and Kenya. In Indonesia the balanced budget strategy was a handicap because in a boom it did not allow a surplus to accumulate and in a slump it inhibited a compensatory deficit, although it prevented inflationary financing when incomes fell after the first oil shock.

Finally, what of the politics? The agricultural export business interests of those with political and bureaucratic power in both Kenya and Côte d'Ivoire and the use of the stabilisation mechanism for patronage in the latter country may have influenced the responses to fluctuating export revenues. The government of Kenya also used the bonanzas in 1976–7 and 1986 to escape temporarily from IMF agreements and the constraints which they imposed.

A prudent approach to development suggests a sterilisation policy. The practical obstacles are clearly formidable but there are also serious risks that a policy of non-intervention is not practical in the inflexible and small economies of some developing countries, particularly those which are dependent on a single commodity. There may be a national-interest argument for government intervention in this case, where the potential market responses, of imports, balance-of-payments shocks, etc., pose nationally unacceptable risks of exposure to external constraints on borrowing. Fry (1988: 228) found that 'an accommodative monetary policy regime [is] negatively related to the rate of growth in real GDP'. On the other hand, a 'prudent approach to development' may be a contradiction in terms. Taking risks, and seizing on an increase in available capital to make exceptional increases in spending, may, if the price rise is permanent or the investment highly productive, be seen in retrospect as prescient and intelligent behaviour.[1]

The interests of private economic agents in how a shock is managed are, as always in cases of a choice between the market and commodity stabilisation policy, conflicting and impossible to appraise purely economically. Certainly coffee farmer 'politicians' stand to gain from receiving the full 'windfall' benefits, but they hardly stand to gain from a subsequent inflation, balance-of-payments crisis and crowding-out by the state from bank credit (as in Kenya). Myopia is a common complaint against politicians everywhere, and farmers are not immune. However, politicians in Kenya and Côte d'Ivoire were likely to have longer tenure in office than those in many more democratic societies, and the discussion of inflation earlier in this chapter suggested that these countries performed relatively well because of this. The response to external shocks is a difficult choice, in political, theoretical, and practical terms.

This chapter has shown that monetary policy has been used only inter-mittently, and for a limited range of objectives in the countries studied here. The very different experiences with its use, both among countries and within the same country at different periods, suggest that some of the reasons may lie in choice, of economic or other objectives. But there also appear to be problems in the nature of the financial sectors in these countries. In the next chapter we turn to these.

14

THE FINANCIAL SECTOR

Sheila Page and John Healey

MONETARY INSTRUMENTS AND THEIR EFFECTIVENESS

Almost all the six countries examined have chosen (or been forced by the IMF) to intervene in the financial sector by setting overall credit ceilings for certain periods at least. Either as intermediate targets for these, or, more often, for different, nominally developmental, purposes, targets or constraints for sectoral or public/private components have also been set. Development targets are discussed in the third section of this chapter. Here we consider what mechanisms or instruments have been used to achieve these targets, how effective they have been and what options may have been neglected.

The range of instruments has included:

1 direct intervention to define the credit available to the government and private sector;
2 measures to control lending by the banking system via regulated reserve ratios;
3 measures to influence liquidity by sale or purchase of securities;
4 measures to control the monetary base usually with some liberalisation of interest rates.

Over most of the period 1970–90, Côte d'Ivoire, Indonesia and Bangladesh have had money supply targets from which domestic credit targets have been derived. Kenya has set domestic targets when balance-of-payment problems forced recourse to the IMF. Ghana had no effective targets until as late as 1983, while in China, target credit levels have been implicitly set by the Economic Plan, but designed to offer an accommodating monetary policy.

Direct intervention to achieve credit targets has confronted major challenges. The credit demands of the public sector in certain countries at certain times have required a major part of the total available credit. Credit constraints have affected the private sector particularly strongly because the latter has lacked non-bank finance in a situation of generally thin capital markets. The demands of the government, and frequently those of public corporations in deficit, have taken precedence over those of the private sector. Even when limits on public sector borrowing have been set by government, 'evasion' has occurred by effectively widening the scope of the public sector, and allowing state enterprises to borrow outside the limits. Not only the level, but also the predictability, of public borrowing has been a challenge for credit management.

In some cases, therefore, the application of an overall credit ceiling, combined with a public sector which has been reluctant to raise taxes or cut expenditure sufficiently, has meant an effective squeeze on private sector credit (the extent of crowding-out from credit controls is discussed more fully in the next section).

A concern to set sectoral priorities (agriculture, industry, etc.) has also challenged overall direct credit control. In some cases direct intervention to achieve priorities for the allocation of credit was seen as more important than adhering to overall limits on credit creation, at least until the later 1980s. There were thus at least two policy objectives: financing the public sector and allocating credit to particular economic sectors, which were potentially in conflict with any policy of overall credit limits. Under these conditions, it is difficult to judge whether any failures to meet the overall limits were because the government lacked effective instruments or because it had no mechanism for resolving the conflict of interests.

The problems of credit control and the role of the public sector are well illustrated by two of our three African case studies, and by Indonesia during the period 1974–82. In Ghana, loss of control of money supply through excessive credit to the government and public institutions, particularly the Ghana Cocoa Marketing Board, occurred from 1972, following the military coup. During the 1970s very large budget deficits were substantially financed by credit from the Bank of Ghana, and control of the money supply became very loose. According to Sowa, this was because the military regimes felt less bound to account for their monetary actions before parliament than civil regimes, and were therefore more expansionist.

A radical shift in policy occurred after 1983 (the ERP) with large reductions in both budget deficits and government borrowing from the central bank, admittedly helped by substantial IMF and donor support for the government budget (from a budget deficit of 6 per cent of GDP in 1982, Ghana had a budget surplus of 1 per cent of GDP in 1988). Even then, the credit restraints tended to bite on the private sector more than on the government. In the late 1980s, credit ceilings were an effective tool, and banks which exceeded their limits were penalised by the Bank of Ghana.

Kenya has never experienced a prolonged period of inflationary credit creation, according to Killick and Mwega, although the government and the Central Bank of Kenya have only laid down credit ceilings when there have been IMF programmes. Ceilings have not been exceeded; they do not seem, however, to have been very stringent (annual average increase 12 per cent in 1982). It is therefore difficult to know whether the success indicates effective control and instruments, or lack of serious excess demand and conflicting targets, or an easily achieved target. The Kenya study argues that (i) fiscal policy has taken precedence and the monetary authority has had little option but to take the government domestic financing requirement as given; (ii) forecasts of the government's deficit financing requirement have been over-optimistic and highly unpredictable for planning control of overall credit and money limits; (iii) the result has been that credit restraints fell disproportionately on the private sector, which was crowded-out.

In Kenya, not unlike Ghana, the setting of credit targets with a 'dominant' state borrower leaves the central bank with very limited degrees of freedom, principally to allocate credit among sectors in the private sector. This was the price of quantitative credit controls in Ghana and Kenya, and, in Kenya at least, they had a discouraging effect on the output and expansion of small-scale private enterprises, and those seeking to become established for the first time, as banks favoured established borrowers.

A further effect of credit control when exercised through allocation by banks has been to limit inter-bank competition and interfere with their intermediation functions.

In Indonesia, direct credit controls were used by the Soeharto regime between 1974 and 1982, as indirect controls were neither technically feasible nor politically acceptable. With the government not authorised to issue bonds, open-market operations were ruled out, and rises in interest rates risked antagonising the important support of small entrepreneurs. The targets were set as a residual, taking the government budget deficit and the balance of payments as exogenous. These credit targets applied to commercial banks only and were met remarkably accurately after 1976, in part because the method of setting them and adjustments of targets made them a 'soft' constraint.

A rather different picture emerges in Bangladesh, Côte d'Ivoire and indeed in Indonesia after 1983. In Bangladesh the public sector has not been 'dominant' during the Zia and Ershad regimes. Direct and selective credit controls have been used to achieve 'social' rather than financial priorities, and the private sector has not lost out in credit allocation. It is not clear how restrictive, and therefore how effective, overall credit ceilings have been.

In Côte d'Ivoire and in Indonesia in the later years, there have been credit targets, but in both cases the operative instrument has been the monetary base rather than credit ceilings directly. This has been possible in these very open economies because in both cases fiscal policy has been largely coordinated with monetary policy. Public sector balanced budgets or constrained deficits have given the central bank more freedom to influence the size of the money base and the use of indirect means to influence credit levels, if not always sector allocation.

All these economies have been unable to use open-market operations as a major instrument. The immediately apparent explanation is that they have all had very undeveloped and thin capital markets and it is clear from the country studies that, despite some rhetoric and minor institutional assistance, most governments have not actually encouraged and developed such markets. The private sector evidently sees no immediate reason to create such a market; existing firms have access to external or bank finance and new ones would be even less likely to receive finance from such markets than from banks. It is only the government which wishes to use them for finance, but providing another source of finance for the private sector might make private finance more difficult to control. But the obvious reason that such markets have not developed is that there are serious practical obstacles to a bond market. Low income means too few individual participants to make a market, and many of the insurance, savings, or other institutions which would be major participants in developed countries are themselves state organisations. Government securities are usually sold to a captive market such as state-owned banks, and as a result there is rarely a secondary market in government paper. These limitations and the reasons for them are discussed in more detail later in this chapter.

Even when the central bank has been able to buy or sell securities, the thinness of the market has risked a very strong interest-rate effect which was seen as undesirable in discouraging investment (e.g. Ghana). Only Indonesia as it entered the 1990s was moving towards manipulating short-term interest rates through the sale and purchase of its own securities. Even here, as Lane, Cole and Slade document, speculative surges pushed interest rates on securities to giddy heights, underlining the difficulties in unharnessing the developing capital markets.

The option of controlling the level of domestic credit via the money multiplier by regulating bank reserve ratios seems not to have been pursued by most of the monetary authorities in our six countries. The central banks in Côte d'Ivoire, Ghana, Kenya and Indonesia have used their powers to change cash and liquid reserve ratios of banks, but not as a control. Minimum ratios have been set below levels which the banks have kept for prudential reasons or because of lack of demand for credit. This regulator has not bitten formally, and there is conflicting evidence on whether it has had an influence.

In our group, only Côte d'Ivoire has had a form of monetary base control, although Indonesia has moved toward this type of instrument in the 1980s. To operate on high-powered money (cash and banks' deposits at the central bank) the central bank needs to have considerable control over its short-term assets, credit to government and banks, and over the movement of the net foreign asset position. In the end this instrument failed in Côte d'Ivoire because it did not meet these stringent conditions. Since 1975, although comprehensive targets have been set for money aggregates and sectoral credit priorities have been pursued, the operative policy has been confined to the monetary base. The implicit target for this has been set by statutory limits on refinancing facilities to the government and commercial banks. The implementation of this policy has been based on a set of key 'rules' which, even though they were not all kept, were retained. These have been in essence that (i) there are limits on the amount that the government can borrow from BCEAO to finance its deficit (no more than 20 per cent of the government's previous year's fiscal receipts); (ii) the base money is linked to the net foreign asset position; and (iii) the value of the domestic currency is fixed in terms of the French franc and convertible.

The fixed exchange rate made it important to constrain the monetary base to prevent excessive money creation, inflation and an appreciating real exchange rate. As the central bank could control its refinancing operations for government, a fairly stable money-to-money-base relationship meant that money supply growth and foreign asset coverage could be maintained. Although refinancing ceilings were consistently breached in the 1970s they were adhered to in the 1980s; however, the foreign assets coverage rule (gross foreign assets at least 20 per cent of sight liabilities of the central bank) was consistently breached in the 1980s and net foreign assets (NFAs) fell steadily over this period. The strain on foreign assets in the 1980s was a legacy of rapid credit expansion during commodity booms in the 1970s. There was an 'asymmetry' in that once a fixed exchange rate had made the economy uncompetitive, this could not be reversed by 'negative' inflation in the 1980s or negative refinancing limits. There were simply too few policies open to the government. There were also rather special features of the Franc Zone monetary union which made regulation of commercial bank liquidity more difficult. Some commercial banks in Côte d'Ivoire could borrow directly from parent banks in France; so reduced liquidity which drove up domestic interest rates could have the perverse effect of attracting greater capital inflows, which partially thwarted any sterilisation.

An unstable short-term liquidity preference on the part of the public limited the effectiveness of money base control. At times of rapid liquidity growth people shifted from cash into deposits at the commercial banks. This damped the money multiplier at times of liquidity expansion and in that sense helped monetary control, but conversely the effect of monetary restraint was to reverse shifts into more liquid assets. In the long run, there appeared to be a fairly stable relationship between broad money and the monetary base, but the dangers of an expansionary monetary position were not immediately apparent.

Indonesia is the other country which has shifted to a monetary base control or indirect management and it has also had an open capital market. Between 1983 and 1990 credit ceilings on banks were removed. The central bank leaves the ordinary banks to allocate credit themselves. It operates on the supply of base money and has developed monetary instruments to influence

(i) the reserves of the private and state-owned banks, and hence (ii), via interest rates, domestic demand for money, particularly in relation to foreign currency. There are no statutory monetary rules as in Côte d'Ivoire under the CFA, but there is the constitutional requirement that there should be a balanced budget. Although fiscal policy has therefore not been a problem for monetary management (except under shocks), the bank has had to manage the external account in a way consistent with free capital flows and a flexible exchange rate.

The governments of all the countries have normally used direct controls rather than indirect. Indirect instruments would seem preferable on economic efficiency grounds to direct credit rationing: there must therefore be reasons for their non-use. These have come in part from practical obstacles making it difficult to use indirect methods; these are discussed further in the next section. They also derive from the failure of the countries to take significant measures to develop the financial sector and therefore to make some of these methods more available, which is discussed in the following section. But countries have also in some cases chosen the direct methods. One explanation is that governments wanted the opportunity to set or influence development priorities through intervening in the total supply of credit, or its allocation.[1] To use base money control instead would have made profitability and creditworthiness (or banks' choices) the criteria for rationing credit via interest rates and banks' financial discretion.

It is noticeable that interest rates have been low and often negative in real terms for long periods in a number of the six countries, and have not been used as an instrument for controlling the demand for credit in any of them until very recently. There has been political and indeed ideological opposition to such a regulator in China and Bangladesh and no doubt in the other countries as well. Towards the end of the 1980s, however, views seemed to be changing in countries as different as China and Indonesia. The view that extending new credit is not synonymous with development, and that allocating credit to the most productive types of investment and denying credit to those unable to pay is likely to lead to sustained economic growth, is spreading.

The economic arguments for interest rates as an aggregate means of control are, however, weakened when the productive sector is as dependent on bank finance, and therefore as highly geared, as it is in the other four non-centrally planned economies. It is not therefore surprising that there remains a reluctance to accept the high and sometimes rapidly changing interest rates which may emerge from narrow markets, as noted above in the comments on open market operations. Similarly, the fragmented financial systems do not offer strong grounds for accepting their choice among borrowers as the most efficient allocation. At the high levels of inflation found in cases like Ghana, the effect on the short-term liquidity and cash-flow position of all companies of any non-negative real interest rate would be unsustainable, and calls into question the feasibility of using interest rates as an instrument in high-inflation countries.

There is also the normal advantage of any direct control, provided that it is actually achievable, that it is more certain than an indirect one, if the objective is a fixed outcome, like a ceiling. (This would not apply if a process or a system, such as the creation of an efficient financial sector, were the objective.) Even under the fixed rules of the franc system and with the apparently stable long-term behavioural relationships of Côte d'Ivoire, some of the links required for an indirect control to be effective may eventually be strained too far and break. For a government with policies which it considers more important than developing the financial system, predictability may be more convenient, even at some cost in efficiency (this is one of the most common arguments used for fixed exchange rates). For governments with severe constraints on credit expansion (for example, a fixed exchange rate to defend), predictability may be essential.

For some countries, the choice of a control which offers certainty has not been in their own hands. IMF 'targets' for credit creation have not been targets in the conventional, mid-point, sense, but absolute constraints, and conditions for the continuing availability of IMF credit. In some cases, notably Bangladesh, perhaps also Kenya, they may have been sufficiently accommodating for any form of controlling credit to be unnecessary, but where they were binding, as in Indonesia before 1983 and Ghana after 1982, there was probably no practical alternative to direct controls.

The recent history of Indonesia has been different, and its indirect monetary management offers some interesting experience for other developing countries considering a more liberalised policy. It has abandoned credit controls and developed indirect monetary control, eventually allowing interest rates to be market-determined in a way which reflects the tightness of the money base supply. An inter-bank market has developed as a result. Real interest rates varied between 6 and 13 per cent during 1983–9, which is high relative to those of most of the other countries, and have clearly been used to influence the domestic demand for credit as well as helping to stem the 'speculative' outflows of capital which have been the main short-term challenge for Bank Indonesia.

Despite weak domestic capital markets and lack of government securities, Indonesia has innovated by introducing new instruments, SBPUs and subsidised forward 'swaps' to absorb the excess reserves of the private and state-owned banks, or to relieve shortages of liquidity. Some problems have arisen in the transition to a more liberalised system. Controlling expectations of devaluation with an 'open' external capital account has led to high interest rates. These have met with political resistance. Since some obligations to provide subsidised credit to certain sectors have remained, offsetting action has been required to tighten credit. When there has been a 'crisis' the central bank has tended to step in directly, for example to stop companies borrowing from the banks and to force institutions to buy government securities. Global ceilings on credit were used as a 'back-up' instrument of control. The move to effective reserve management requires existing excess reserves in the banking system to be reduced in order to tighten up and make reserve control bite. These measures have costs. Central bank moves to buy and sell Treasury bills for liquidity control can weaken, and have weakened, infant secondary markets. Thus there may be some trade-off between this type of monetary control and the objective of helping the growth in capital markets. M1 and M2 and inflation have all increased during the later liberalisation period.

CONSTRAINTS ON THE EFFECTIVE IMPLEMENTATION OF MONETARY POLICY IN DEVELOPING COUNTRIES

One of the main purposes of this study has been to examine the constraints or special problems facing developing countries in the execution of monetary policy. Experience suggests two categories of constraints: first those exogenous constraints which arise from the behavioural or institutional character of poor and underdeveloped societies; and second, those which arise from shocks due to uncontrollable events, whether domestic influences (e.g. droughts, floods, good and bad harvests) or external factors such as terms-of-trade changes usually via the prices of major imports or exports, which we assume are more likely to affect developing countries. In addition, there are those constraints which are largely if not entirely 'self-imposed', such as inconsistent or inappropriate policies which create future problems for the pursuit of desirable objectives (for example, loss of confidence in the currency and banks due to excessive credit creation to finance large government deficits).

We are mainly concerned with the first and second categories of constraints, since fiscal or exchange-rate policies which are inconsistent with an effective monetary policy are a matter not of constraint but of policy choice, and in many cases the problems are similar to those already familiar to developed countries. However, it is not always easy to separate these different influences. Uncontrollable external influences like boom or collapse in the price of exports may produce particularly difficult policy choices, and economically damaging policy choices may lead to greater challenges to policy effectiveness.

This section concentrates on domestic behavioural and institutional characteristics and the problems they have posed for monetary control measures. The difficulties and the difficult choices in managing external shocks were discussed in the previous chapter. It is appropriate, however, to emphasise the point made in the first section of this chapter, that constraints like a fixed exchange rate, access to foreign credit, or openness to foreign capital may impose limits on the types of instrument which are used, as well as on how they are used. In principle these may all be 'choices', but they are more serious in their implications for the economy in the case of developing countries (particularly relatively open ones of the type studied here) than for many developed countries.

Changing the exchange-rate policy, as discussed in Chapter 12, is not an easy decision for a developing country without the resources or instruments to operate a more flexible rate, and therefore the need to use credit policy to avoid a real overvaluation may become imperative. Some of our study countries moved to more flexible (or at least more frequently adjusted) exchange rates in the 1980s, and this may have contributed to their greater willingness to consider alternatives to direct controls. As Chapter 12 shows, the conflict between ineffective monetary control and a fixed exchange rate is frequently resolved by a parallel exchange rate, creating efficiency and legal problems of its own, and frequently feeding back through evasion of capital controls on to control of the money supply.

Countries with severe balance-of-payments pressure cannot treat lightly the prospect of losing access to IMF finance. Even the development of a more effective financial sector may itself depend on access to foreign finance. Foreign banks, as in Côte d'Ivoire, can offer access to their own sources of capital, but this also removes part of the domestic financial sector from local reserve or money base controls. The history of both the present industrial countries and the NICs which are beginning to develop financial markets is that the finance for these is initially likely to include a large foreign element. In most of the study countries, foreign lack of confidence in their economic prospects or stability, justified on the macro experiences reported here, is likely to prevent this for the foreseeable future, and therefore weaken this option.

Indonesia is an exception, but this is not entirely because of its own efforts. It is the nearest of the countries examined here not only geographically but in economic approach to the NICs and the new NICs of Asia where such markets have begun to function, and its decision to promote these markets was probably influenced by example as well as by textbook economics. This nearness may also give it more access to foreign finance because of greater awareness on the part of investors and banks of the potential of that area. The corresponding loss of monetary control has already been identified as a problem for the Indonesian government. Securities markets have existed for decades in the major Latin American countries, their importance fluctuating with the success of their economies, and that area also is therefore not unfamiliar to potential investors. African markets would not start with this advantage.[2]

In exploring the behavioural constraints on the monetary authorities, it has been useful to distinguish those which limit their power to influence the money supply from those affecting the demand for money. Demand for money needs to be predictable and the supply of money is predictably influenced by the central bank. The six study countries over most of the period covered (and especially in the 1970s) operated on the supply of money, but by the later 1980s a number had experimented with a more liberalised policy and techniques which require influence over the demand for money.

Constraints on policies to control the supply of money

Africa Our three African countries provide some interesting similarities and contrasts in the behavioural influences on monetary control. In all three the monetary base was the major factor in variations in money supply. Credit to the public sector was the major source of high-powered money. This was a constraint on the central bank in the sense that, for at least two countries, Ghana and Kenya, the government financing requirement was exogenous and dominant. With respect to Kenya the authors are 'deeply pessimistic about its ability to manipulate the monetary base', whether via the domestic or the foreign component. Not only was credit to government out of the independent control of the central bank; the predictability of its level was also poor because of the optimistic and inaccurate forecasts of the public sector deficits. In Ghana this situation was worse until 1984 when the government began to control the scale of its fiscal deficit.

The relationship between total money supply and the monetary base, the money multiplier, has been unstable in all three countries, though in each case the behavioural factors have been different and thus the implications for monetary control. What is perhaps the most 'uncontrollable' parameter for the central bank − the volume of cash willingly held by the public − presented a problem in both Ghana and Côte d'Ivoire. In Ghana between 1976 and 1983 there was a massive fall in the ratio of cash to GDP as people lost confidence in the currency under hyperinflation, and switched domestic financial assets into physical goods and foreign assets. There was also a loss of confidence in the banking system, which resulted in a decline in bank deposits relative to cash. This behavioural trend operated as a 'moderator' of credit creation since it damped the marginal power of banks to create credit from deposits and limited the growth of money supply from its main primary source, expansion of the monetary base.

By 1984 these declines had been stemmed and some confidence restored, but the recovery of deposit/cash ratios was slow and by the end of the 1980s nearly half of the money supply was cash in the hands of the public. By no stretch of imagination can this flight from bank money be seen as an exogenous constraint on the monetary authorities. It was a rational response to irresponsible government policies. Fully restoring confidence remains a challenge for the current reforms in Ghana. The dominance of cash in the total money supply creates an in-built constraint on credit creation, as the money multiplier is kept low. Although the poverty and underdevelopment of the country may be an underlying factor in the strains which helped provoke the lack of confidence in credit, the past failures of policy and lack of confidence in the capability of state institutions seem to be the overwhelming influence.

In Côte d'Ivoire, people's preference for cash as opposed to deposits has been unstable. At times of high liquidity the public has shifted out of cash into less liquid assets and time deposits. This has imposed a constraint on monetary control in the short term because, when the need for a constraining monetary policy was most required, the shift of liquidity into bank deposits allowed the banks freedom to lend more, despite the efforts of the central bank to control primary liquidity. Effective control was also frustrated by the ability of the banks with French links to obtain liquidity from their parent banks when restraint was needed. These constraints operated most powerfully in the expansionary period of the 1960s and late 1970s. During the 1980s these processes have worked in reverse to assist monetary contraction. Lane takes the view that while the existence of informal credit markets maintained the public cash ratio higher than it would otherwise have been, so reducing the size of the money multiplier, it did not generate instability.

In Kenya, unlike the other African economies, the public cash deposit preference seems to have been stable. But the relationship between commercial banks' credit and deposit levels on the one hand and their liquidity on the other appears unstable. This was the main factor in a volatile money multiplier which operated to damp variations in money supply since banks were slow to adjust their lending to changes in the liquidity ratios. This potentially limited the central bank's control over the money supply, but Killick and Mwega suggest that it may arise from an inappropriate specification of liquidity and choice of policy instrument, or that there has been inadequate use of reserve ratios to control credit creation. Either would imply that effective central bank control was available, even if not achieved. They also do not see the informal sector as an obstacle to monetary control.

Asia   In Indonesia, the two major elements of their strategy – avoidance of domestic budget deficits and unrestricted capital movements – gave the monetary authorities both freedom and constraints in controlling money supply. The balanced budget allowed Bank Indonesia greater freedom to influence the monetary base than existed in any of the other five economies. It did, however, contribute to initial difficulties in introducing market-based methods of monetary control, since there was a lack of government paper for open market operations. But while this restricted access to foreign private capital, it attracted foreign aid and public credit, and the government's power to conceal its surplus made shock management easier. Capital mobility engendered instability in the reserves of the banks, owing to speculation on exchange-rate movements and responses to interest-rate differentials. These problems were largely tackled by development of the new financial instruments and by more skilful management of interest rates and the exchange rate in the late 1980s. The experience of Indonesia suggests that given fiscal control there are no inherent behavioural constraints on money-supply control which cannot be overcome by a consistent and credible strategy, combined with innovation, skilled management, and willingness to bend rules. The fiscal control, however, was achieved partly by reaction to the earlier total loss of control, an avenue which, despite its respectable German precedent, may be too costly to offer an acceptable example for other countries. (Latin American experience also suggests that such immunisation may not always be successful.)

In Bangladesh, the main constraint on short-term management of the money supply was imposed by the volatility of domestic food output and prices, due to natural shocks of floods and droughts. The econometric modelling suggests that harvest failures and food price rises were the main explanations of monetary expansion. These monetary expansions seemed to arise because of an accommodating policy of providing credit to meet increased demands from the private sector and also for extra net credit to government for widened fiscal deficits at times of food-supply shocks. Hence there is apparently a strong influence from supply-induced price changes to money supply. However, it is unclear why, in this case, there was not an offsetting damping effect on money growth from good harvests.

The effect of increased money supply on output or prices emerges less clearly, even though over the long term inflation has remained moderately high in Bangladesh. The constraints imposed on a very poor country by periods of domestic food shortages are very real, posing a clear dilemma for a government which did not want to aggravate the situation at such times by a tighter control on private credit. What is less clear from the study is how far such constraints were overriding. To assess this more information would be required on (i) the purposes for which extra private credit was used in flood and drought situations, whether to maintain consumption by farmers who had lost their crops, or for working capital, and (ii) the position on food stocks, private and public, and on availability of food aid or foreign exchange for food imports. Without such micro studies, it is difficult to judge the real constraints on short-term money management in Bangladesh.

Constraints on estimating and influencing the demand for money

In all the studies, the income demand for money has been positive, significant and usually, but not always, stable (see Table 14.1). Income-demand instability does not make monetary policy impossible: variations in the money/GDP relationship can be approached by a series of adjustments and corrections. It may, however, make reasonable current or predicted estimates of income effects problematical, and for a country like Bangladesh, predicting short-term real output has not proved easy. In Indonesia there has been some instability imparted by speculative movements into and out of foreign assets. In Kenya, there has been a stable income demand for money, although money velocity may have been unstable in the short term.

In China, behavioural instability seems to emerge more strongly than in any of the other countries and has clearly impeded the setting and achieving of monetary targets. The estimated income demand for money parameters changed over time, especially after 1978–9 and 1984, and there were lags in the adjustment of desired money balances. The velocity of circulation of M0 has thus been volatile. This instability has not been taken into account by the economic authorities and this hampered their target setting and achievement. Such behavioural instability is not surprising in a society which has been subject to two major waves of policy reform, and indeed the timing of the changes in the parameters seems to reflect the changes in policy of the government and the responses of state enterprises under the new rules, and of households and enterprises finding themselves outside the public sector and with greater discretion.

A related constraint on effective monetary control has stemmed from the lack of 'credibility' of the authorities' stance on monetary restraint. Periods of monetary restraint (one to two years) were followed by periods of 'expansion' with an accommodating monetary policy. This seems to have induced an adjustment of enterprise behaviour, with some able to 'ride' the expected 'cycle'. Hence monetary policy in the later 1980s has become less and less effective in controlling inflation. Interest rates have been used effectively in China to influence the demand for cash by households, but so far they have not been used effectively to control the demand for credit by enterprises. A policy of indirect credit control, varying reserve ratios for banks and allowing banks to influence the demand for allocation of credit through interest rates, is recommended by Santorum. There is evidence that reserve ratios were at least partially used to tie credit creation to the monetary base in China, though no econometric evidence is found that interest rates are related to the demand for credit. Allocation and control of credit have been determined throughout by direct administered methods, with evasion, corruption, political interference and weak monitoring.

The scope for influencing the demand for money via interest rates in low-income countries is an important one. Interest rates would be expected to influence the distribution of people's holdings between narrow money (cash and sight deposits) and time and savings deposits and other forms of financial assets. They would also be expected to affect the demand for credit. The six country studies do not test all possible behavioural responses. The evidence for Indonesia and China, where policies have favoured higher interest rates in the 1980s, is that the expected negative relationship with narrow money aggregates and the positive relationship with term deposits hold. Elsewhere, the evidence is more ambiguous. There is no significant econometric relationship between interest rates and money demand in

Table 14.1 Demand for money: summary results

	Income elasticity	Interest elasticity	Comments
Indonesia	Positive Stable High	Negative and small effect of time deposit rates of state owned banks on narrow money (M1); positive and low on quasi-money (time savings deposits). Negative relationship to risk (swap) adjusted foreign interest rates.	Some instability in demand during periods of devaluation or market crises but instability not systematically tested. Speed of adjustment of demand to variables increased in 1980s.
Kenya	Positive Stable (especially M1) Low Declined over time	Negative but not very significant effect on private demand for credit. Negative effect on savings rates. Insignificant effect on time deposit and quasi-money.	V is unstable and unpredictable presumably because of non-income variables. There is highly significant relationship to previous period money supply which may catch lagged adjustment to past differences between the demand and supply of money.
Côte d'Ivoire	Positive Significant Stable for M1 and M2 Money holdings adjust rapidly to changes in economy.	Negative and significant (M2) for domestic real and nominal interest rate. (No significant link with French/Côte d'Ivoire interest differentials.)	Overall there was no evidence to suggest that money demand was very unstable and income was most important determinant.
Ghana	Positive in short run and long run Significant.	No significant relationships.	Stability of coefficients not tested.
Bangladesh	Positive Significant High (M1 and time deposits).	No significant relationship with time deposits.	

310

China	Positive and greater than unity (M2). Lagged adjustment of money balances (6 months). Long-term parameters not stable.	Negative effect of savings deposit interest on cash holdings.	Parameters and continuous changes in structure of economy have affected agents' behaviour especially 1978–9 and 1984. Instability in V.

Ghana nor with time deposits in Bangladesh. In Kenya there was an insignificant effect on time deposits and a negative but not very significant effect on the demand for credit.

Shifts in the demand for domestic money can occur if it becomes more or less attractive to hold foreign currency. This can happen as a result of a number of influences, but interest rates are likely to be influential in economies which have open capital accounts like Indonesia and Côte d'Ivoire. The studies suggest that the level of the domestic interest rate and the differential with outside interest rates were influential in these two economies.

The econometric work on behaviour in the face of interest-rate variation is not conclusive, but it does not suggest that this behaviour would be perverse. In some cases the expected responses were found, in others there must be agnosticism. Over most of the periods studied, most of these countries had limited interest-rate variation, with low nominal rates and in some negative real interest rates for long periods, so that it is not surprising that the statistical results are weak in a number of cases. In Indonesia and China, where interest rates were varied and raised to significant levels, there was evidence of the expected economic response.

DEVELOPING THE FINANCIAL SECTOR

One of the most surprising conclusions to emerge from the country studies presented here is that, with the exception of Indonesia, they show few examples of countries deliberately trying to develop their financial sector, whether to be able to conduct a monetary policy or for more orthodox development objectives. On the contrary, this sector is usually highly regulated and clearly not regarded as important in its own right. With officially set or regulated interest rates, global, and often sectoral, credit controls, and in many cases, credit for the rest of the economy a residual after supplying state-owned or regulated borrowers, it is difficult to regard the financial sector as a functioning economic actor. This feeds back directly on the scope for increasing its effectiveness for implementing monetary policy, because it implies, as far as the governments are concerned, that developing the sector to make it more effective as a monetary instrument must be justified purely by the benefits that are expected to accrue from monetary policy.

This is at first sight in sharp conflict with both the well-known arguments of administrative and allocative efficiency for increasing the role of monetary and credit institutions (cf. texts like Fry 1988 or Germidis *et al.* 1991) and with the experience of the NICs. Fry considers the financial sector's role in 'providing efficient means for transferring claims over resources from savers (lenders) to investors (borrowers)' to be 'critical' (p. 257), and like other observers regards a financial system capable of implementing governments' credit policies (including sectoral allocation of credit, as well as less controversial ones like transmission of funds and mobilisation of savings) as an important element of the NICs' success. From the studies presented here, it is not clear whether the governments have even considered, and measured, these potential benefits. The existence of selective credit concessions or controls in all six countries may suggest that allocating resources among sectors would not be considered an important function of a financial sector, although within-sector allocation could be improved, but the other functions remain desirable.

It is possible that the informal sector is seen as providing them sufficiently well (this is discussed in the following chapter) or that governments do not see a case for subsidisation of this economic activity. Initiatives by non-government sources to provide financial services, like the Grameen Bank in Bangladesh, have required subsidy, at least of the administration costs and normally of the cost of funds as well (see Chapter 11). Very local small-scale banking does not seem to be commercially viable for a national-size institution, whether governmental or non-governmental, and is therefore very unlikely to be so for a commercial bank. It is not simply 'prejudice', as has been argued in some of the country studies, on the part of banks that deters them, but a reasonable appraisal of the costs and returns. The fact that policies to promote more banks in unprofitable areas have not increased in recent years (and have even been run down) strongly suggests that a renewed interest in mobilisation of domestic savings was not one of the objectives which have led governments to greater interest in financial sectors.

This section discusses first the evidence of financial deepening. If this were strong, it could be an indicator either that there had been a successful government policy or that such a policy was unnecessary because the deepening was occurring without intervention. Neither appears to be the case. The remainder of the chapter considers what governments have done to develop a financial sector capable of the conventional tasks of serving the rest of the economy through transmission and mobilisation of funds, of taking responsibility for such policies as allocation of credit, or of providing an efficient means of implementing the monetary policies discussed in this book.

One possible indicator of increasing monetisation which was discussed in Part I was an income elasticity of the demand for money greater than one.

This was found for Indonesia and Côte d'Ivoire but not for China and Ghana, with an insignificant result for Kenya.

Other indicators of financial deepening are increased ratios of M2 and M3 to GNP, reduced ratios of cash to narrow or broad money, increased time deposits to total deposits, increased financial to total assets and increased density and diversity of financial institutions. The evidence from our country studies shows Ghana to be the worst case. There was some branch development of banking, but directed mainly towards the big urban areas, and of some development banks, but mainly for large enterprises. Most of the above indicators moved in the reverse direction to that required between the mid-1970s and mid-1980s. This was an extreme case, where the loss of confidence in the currency and the banking system was combined with lack of rural development of the banking system.

Côte d'Ivoire, Indonesia and Kenya all have poor records on this score at least until the late 1980s. In Côte d'Ivoire up to 1977 there had been financial deepening and an increase in the banking habit associated with periods of real growth. Subsequently, the process reversed and stagnated. In the 1980s there was no (upward) trend in M1 and M2 ratios to GDP, while domestic and national savings rates fell and there is evidence of a continued outflow of private savings from the banks. In Kenya there was evidence of deepening after the late 1960s, but little progress in the 1980s. In Indonesia the record was poor until the policy changes after 1983. Then, reforms allowed new private banks, and more branches.

In Bangladesh there has been considerable growth of intermediation since 1983 with the liberalisation of the banking system and the spread of private banks. In China, evidence on household savings rates and time deposits confirms increased mobilisation of rural savings. This has been associated with increased numbers and accessibility of savings deposits institutions in rural areas and with increased interest rates on savings deposits. (This was partly to prevent excess liquidity from causing excess demand for consumer goods, as well as to divert income into investment.)

What have been the main policy reasons for this poor or belated progress in increasing the provision for mobilising financial savings? From the six studies the following points emerge.

In all the countries studied interest rates have been low and negative in real terms for long periods; they have therefore had no potential for encouraging investment of savings in financial assets. Only in the 1980s have some of these countries moved towards liberalisation and allowed higher interest rates to encourage portfolio shifts. Indonesia liberalised interest rates after 1983 and had quite high (6–13 per cent) real rates after a long period of negative rates. These encouraged banks to raise deposits for the rest of the decade. China also used interest rates flexibly between 1976 and 1986. Kenya, Côte d'Ivoire and Ghana, however, had controlled low nominal, and negative real, rates until the late 1980s. There is little evidence from these studies that earlier liberalisation of interest rates and higher rates would have increased savings in institutions, but the inflexibility and low level of interest rates and the lack of financial asset alternatives for savers make econometric results unlikely to be helpful, and not all the studies fully test for this.

In the case of Indonesia, China and Côte d'Ivoire, there is evidence that interest rates influence the assets savers hold, but not that saving rates themselves are influenced. In Côte d'Ivoire in 1985 the removal of interest payments on sight deposits appeared to induce a significant shift of deposits to interest-bearing accounts. This emergence of a positive differential of domestic over French rates was associated with expanded demand for money, inflow of foreign capital and reduced outgoing capital flows. In Indonesia portfolio selection has been strongly influenced by relative rates of return on real and financial assets. High domestic interest rates have encouraged time and savings deposits, but these include shifts out of demand deposits. Econometric evidence records a positive relationship between quasi-money and domestic interest-rate variations and a negative relationship with foreign rates. There was also a small negative relationship between narrow money demand and interest rates. Finally, in China, which had flexible interest rates after 1976, there was a positive association with savings deposits and a negative one with currency in circulation on the evidence of household behaviour.

In Ghana, Kenya and Bangladesh the evidence was more ambiguous, perhaps because there was little historical evidence of interest-rate variations. In Ghana, for example, the econometric work suggests that interest rates had no positive effect on the supply of, or the demand for, money, but there was no disaggregation of time deposits or quasi-money and interest rates had been positive in real terms only once since 1972 and had been very low nominally and controlled until 1987. Specific government measures such as the demonetisation of the cedi in 1978, the decision to vet bank accounts in 1982, etc., cannot have helped the confidence of investors in Ghana banks. Interest rates have been decontrolled since 1988.

The operation of monetary policy did not offer any incentives to the commercial banks to mobilise savings deposits. In most of these economies the banks had excess liquidity. Margins between deposit and lending rates have often not been enough to encourage the banks. The exception is Indonesia which in the later 1980s engineered an expansion in private banking to compete with a system which had previously been dominated by an oligopoly. Deregulation has increased freedom of entry and induced a more competitive and aggressive approach to deposit mobilisation. The results have been dramatic: forty-seven new private banks and fifteen joint ventures with foreign banks, 600 new branches opened by private banks.

The evidence does indicate that the countries that have had policies of increasing the numbers of banks or their accessibility to small borrowers have found a response of savings to the number of banks, in contrast to its apparent inelasticity with respect to other instruments like the rate of interest. But in the African countries, although there has been an expansion of branch banking and some innovations (for example, the issue of payment vouchers to cocoa farmers in Ghana to encourage, *inter alia*, the banking habit), the impression is that this was not a priority objective of the central authorities.

The undeveloped nature of capital markets, the lack of financial instruments and the lack of a secondary market for government and commercial securities are important constraints on the use of indirect monetary control. Evidence on whether it is possible to change this situation is limited because the monetary authorities have not usually attempted to do so – except in Indonesia, whose special advantages and problems were discussed earlier. Only that country has made a deliberate attempt to use securities markets to attract foreign capital and reduce the dependence of industry on the equity market. As with its attempt to develop rural networks of banks and ease entry for new banks, this distinguishes Indonesia as having a deliberate policy of developing a functioning financial sector.

The lack of depth and diversity of capital markets in the other countries is, of course, partly a function of their poverty and stage of development. However, government policies have also been unhelpful. In the three African states restrictions on dealings, fixed margins and the governments' desire to preserve low-cost sources of finance for government fiscal deficits discouraged trading and militated against the development of securities markets.

By the end of the 1980s, uniquely among our countries, Indonesia had a secondary market for Bank Indonesia securities, even though the balanced budget strategy of the government was not favourable to the creation of government securities. It also had an active stock market through regulatory reforms. The development of capital markets requires liquidity for holders of paper, and the introduction of a security (the SBI) in Indonesia of uniform and high quality to serve as a risk-free reference interest rate in the domestic market was clearly a valuable contribution by the monetary authority. What is of concern, and illustrated from recent Indonesian experience, is the potential conflict between the pursuit of an effective indirect monetary policy in the short run and the long-run development of indigenous securities markets. In attempting to control liquidity by the purchase or auction of Treasury bills, the central bank may well undermine the functioning of secondary security markets. In narrow markets, any government intervention has a large effect on interest rates. Very high short-term interest rates clearly have an adverse effect on the values of securities in secondary markets.

The development of Treasury bills as a way of mobilising savings in Kenya was hampered by the lack of a secondary market, with few other securities. Côte d'Ivoire has had a stock exchange since 1976 but liquidity has been limited, in this case by government restrictions on bond price movements and on non-national purchase of shares.

Most of the six study countries had for most of the 1970s and early 1980s a system of central credit controls with sectoral priorities set by the government or the central bank. Given the limited success of such controls in their aim to allocate credit, and the damaging effects on efficiency (and in some cases corruption), it is surprising that the system has been pursued for so long. Indonesia is, however, the only clear case among our countries to have turned its back on these.

What effect all this has had on the quality of, or rates of return on, investment in the economy as a whole has not been systematically assessed in these studies. There must be some doubt that this period of credit controls (only now just beginning to be relaxed) has had beneficial effects on efficiency and growth. Other studies (cf. Fry 1988; World Bank 1989) have found a negative association between low real interest rates and economic growth. Although there are clearly causal factors in both directions, the association found in these studies between credit allocation and low interest rates would be consistent with a conclusion that this has damaged the economies. On the other hand, countries like South Korea and Japan have developed successfully with policies of ensuring that favoured industries have received low-cost credit.

It is not therefore clear whether the failures, in the countries examined here and elsewhere, are because the system failed to implement the sectoral policy effectively (the country studies offer clear evidence that this was the case), or because the choices of borrowers were political rather than based on financial or development criteria (several authors suggest this was a problem), or because the policy itself was mistaken.

The failure of selective controls to achieve direction to priority sectors, which usually meant agriculture, was partly because they were not supported by incentives or sanctions on banks sufficient to offset the costs of high risks and controls on interest rates and because they did not constrain credit to low priority sectors (e.g. services, including local commerce) which were more attractive to lenders. The priorities of individual loans were often, in practice, determined on non-financial and non-economic grounds, including those of political support. Credit was also used to finance the survival of heavily indebted enterprises rather than new borrowers, even if they were more promising. Such effects can lead to greater concentration of industry (Fry 1988: 163), with further damage to efficiency, while the effective constraints on competition among banks hurt their efficiency.

Indonesia has introduced competition among banks and borrowers and liberalised interest rates. Ghana and Côte d'Ivoire have begun the process of liberalisation, and there are some signs that Kenya may also move in this direction.

Overall, the authorities in all the countries, with the possible exception of China, do not seem to have had development objectives for their banking systems or the financial sector generally. There has been fairly limited effort to monetise these economies, to mobilise savings, and to ensure the optimum use of scarce savings. There may have been an actual 'urban bias' or a bias towards 'formal organisations' until the mid- or late-1980s, or simply a neglect of other areas. With the exception of China, such a bias among politicians and professionals has not faced any conflict with a strong ideology to encourage efforts to reach out to rural peoples and informal businesses, both in attracting deposits and offering credit.

Clearly in countries where savings are scarce and the number of potential borrowers so small that individual decisions have macroeconomic effects, it is likely that a government taking an active approach to development will want to influence the finance available to different sectors. But if this is done through the financial system rather than through direct subsidies and taxes, it is likely to make it difficult for the financial system to meet 'normal' demands on it, either to implement a macroeconomic monetary policy or to perform its traditional allocative functions.

15

THE RELATIONSHIP BETWEEN FORMAL AND INFORMAL FINANCE

Sheila Page

The individual country studies mention the informal financial sector, if at all, only to consider whether it is an obstacle to government monetary policy. However, it is a major provider of financial services, in these and in all developing countries, at least to some sectors. The Asian Development Bank (1990) in a path-breaking comprehensive survey of its role gathered estimates of the share of informal credit (some are quoted in Table 11.1). The fact that informal sectors exist, and are believed to be of major quantitative importance, suggests that there is a broad demand for financial services and an effective one, in the sense that it can offer an acceptable return to entrepreneurs, even if not to the formal banking and financial sectors. In considering the impact on monetary policy, we must add to this the major role in some countries (Kenya, for example) of the non-bank, but still 'formal', financial institutions.

It is important to recognise that, except in relation to legal monetary policy constraints, the distinction between informal and formal is more conventional than real. They perform the same type of functions, although to different clients or on a different scale. Large national (in some cases, international) financial organisations deal with their counterparts in other industries, and are able to take well-informed decisions about the appropriate risks and returns. Smaller or local or more specialised organisations do the same for their natural clients, and there is no economic distinction between their roles. As other observers have found (cf. Fry 1988: 293), the informal sector is used for investment and working capital as well as consumption expenditures. It may also be used by 'formal'-type borrowers for special purposes, for example for small loans which are 'transaction-cost-intensive' (Asian Development Bank 1990: 190), rather than interest-sensitive or of long duration. Even in China, in spite of regulation of the economy, an informal sector is now emerging for much the same purposes as in other countries, to meet relatively small demands for credit from households, using the surpluses of other households (ibid.).

There appear to be three important aspects of the relationship between the informal sector (or at least some elements of it) and the formal. The informal is complementary to the formal: some elements of it survive in the most advanced countries, and some parts of a formal sector exist in the least developed. The informal is an early stage of the formal sector. And it is an offset (an obstacle or safety valve, depending on the point of view) to monetary regulation and policy. There is no evidence in our study countries of the possible fourth role which can arise (Peru offers examples, see Chapter 11) when informal operators are of major importance in all sectors or when 'informal' means 'illegal', of a parallel economy with the complete separation of an informal financial sector serving only informal producers.

All the indications from these studies and others (Callier 1991) are that the informal sector is frequently a substitute; it can operate in some cases, or for some groups, or even (for example, in agricultural working capital) at some times of year, for the formal sector, with considerable overlap and complementarity.[1] It is not necessarily more or less inefficient, in its own context, than the formal. *A priori* one might expect it to be more efficient because, in the countries considered here, and in most small developing countries, there are very few formal banks, and the consequent oligopoly is frequently not sufficiently well regulated to guarantee competitive behaviour; the informal sector, as Chapter 11 indicates, can be more competitive and more open to entry. In very small communities, however, neither formal nor informal lenders are likely to face competition.

Lack of competition is one reason why the financial sector tends to be highly regulated in all countries. Another, however, is the high risk of fraud. Therefore, an informal financial sector may be a less good substitute for banks than other informal services are for their formal counterparts. This suggests that it may have a preponderance of less eligible borrowers, as the better risks move to the formal sectors, and also that it is more likely to be a precursor than a complement of the formal system.

Certain distinctions do not appear to be valid. One is the suggestion that 'informal' institutions are more likely to have a less bureaucratic relationship with their clients. The greater caution and apparent bureaucracy observed in the larger institutions' relations with small or poor clients are not inherent to banks' way of doing business, but to any organisation's treatment of a new or minor customer. They may treat their own normal clients in the same informal way that the 'informal' sector treats its own.[2] At the extreme, the largest companies (within a country or internationally) may have closely associated banks to manage their financial affairs. The studies here offer examples of NBFIs filling this role in both public and private sectors.

Subsidised, NGO or aid-donor-sponsored, organisations, on the Grameen model, are rather outside the purely financial sector, informal or formal. With both permanent subsidisation (through their aid-financed capital base and volunteer or low paid staffing) and emphasis on certain types of borrower, they are better analysed in the context of (and, in spending terms, in competition with) other social services. Their reliance on group pressure as a guarantee of repayment, on the other hand, is not out of line with more formal banking practice in other close communities where reputation is important: it has been as characteristic of the City of London as of Bangladeshi villages.

In considering how elements of the informal financial sector can develop into part of the formal, two approaches are helpful: examining the criteria for lending and recalling the experience of the developed countries. Three types of lending criteria may be distinguished: against collateral, by assessing the particular project requiring credit, or by assessing the borrower.

Although their requiring of collateral is cited as a criticism of the operations of formal banks among poor or rural clients in the countries studied here, this is common practice when borrowers, and the purposes for which they are borrowing, are unfamiliar to the lender, and therefore difficult to assess. It is also frequently used as an appropriate form of finance for purposes which do not offer a marketable return. Pawnshops and mortgages are not confined to consumers and farmers in developing countries. For new businesses and for working capital, this type of lending may be inappropriate for the borrower, but it may be the only low-risk method for the lender. This is a problem which even modern financial systems in developed countries have not fully resolved, except when the borrower is already known to the lender in the context of other business. In the nature of the process of development, new businesses tend to diminish and cases of prior contact to increase as a proportion of total loans and clients, and therefore the role of collateral lending tends to diminish. This is, however, an area where non-bank systems and lending facilities seem to retain a permanent role.[3]

Assessing an individual lending project, on the other hand, appears to be less related to normal formal banking.[4] The difficulties of administering and enforcing sectoral priorities were discussed in the previous chapter. Lending based on projects, with or without sectoral guidelines, is therefore unlikely to contribute to developing the financial systems. It is not the most efficient way of providing money for a project (subsidies are), and it may not contribute to developing the sector towards which it is targeted, because it places the emphasis on achieving a single object, not developing the activity and the skills of the borrower or the sector as a whole: in the long run, these skills will include having normal credit and banking dealings. For assessing both whether the return on an investment is likely to be sufficient to make a loan repayable and whether it is likely to be repaid, appraising it in the context of the lender's more general knowledge of the borrower, whether individual or firm, is more appropriate, and it is here that local informal lenders and large banks with continuing relationships with their clients are on common ground, and where, as scales change, the former can develop into the latter.

In any active effort to develop the financial sector, in order to ensure or accelerate the evolution of the informal towards the formal, it would be necessary to judge how to encourage appropriate criteria for lending and means of appraisal, including a reasonable regard to risk on the part of borrowers and lenders. Any special treatment should be directed to the special risks posed by and for poor or undeveloped lenders and borrowers. New businesses where each new loan will be a much higher-than-average proportion of total lending and where loans may be a high proportion of total capital, new borrowers, in new industries, and also new lenders are all inevitably involved in a much higher proportion of total financial transactions than would be the case in developed countries. Transaction costs are also larger, because of smaller loans and fewer linkages in the financial sector. If ways of focusing assistance on these can be devised, there is a case for developing the financial sector as part of the infrastructure of a developing country.

This view of the informal sector as an early stage of the formal sector is supported by the experience of the present industrial countries. The informal sector in finance continues to exist, on a very minor scale, in many of the same forms identified in our study countries, including revolving credit from shops, pawning, and intra-family or ethnic group credit. Widespread use of the formal sector is relatively recent. Use of formal bank accounts lagged particularly in the United Kingdom compared with other European countries, perhaps offering one explanation for the greater advances in the study countries which were not British colonies.[5] Existing banks have developed either out of money-lenders or from mutual groups.

The importance of the formal/informal distinction comes principally when there are significant policy measures, whether of subsidy, control, or regulation, that govern the formal but not the informal. A subsidised interest rate or an unlimited supply of credit from state banks distorts the market in favour of those who deal with the formal. In a country where the poor have less access to the formal than those with higher incomes, or rural than urban, or new industry than existing industry, using such mechanisms may be an inefficient or counter-productive means of reaching the groups which are frequently their official targets. (They are, however, efficient means of targeting favoured individuals.) Direct allocation of subsidies will, as always, be more appropriate in efficiency terms. Credit ceilings, discriminatory interest rates, or other controls may have the reverse effect, of damaging formal clients more, if the controls are not applied also to the informal. The effect in this direction is not inevitable, however, as 'formal' borrowers can usually find an 'informal' alternative, and many of our study countries report that the formal banks themselves have set up non-bank subsidiaries. Some of the studies suggest that the offset is not total, because the greater cost of using the informal sector partially constrains credit to the non-priority sectors. Achieving less than the desired result, with an additional inefficiency of allocation, remains an unsatisfactory outcome.

From the point of view of monetary policy, trying to control 'informal' or 'non-bank' sectors has been in many of the study countries a constant effort to keep up with new institutions or new forms of informal finance. This is true also in developed countries, and the evidence suggests that it may be less important to developing countries, first, because small size, low income, and low demand for financial services (along with weak policy implementation) reduce the incentive for an informal sector to grow to avoid the controls, and second, because in many countries, the most used tool of intervention, credit ceilings, does affect the informal because the formal is a major source of credit for the informal. The studies here have little data on how important the linkages are.

The point of view of development or economic efficiency emphasises the opposite risks. The Asian Development Bank argues:

> this 'safety valve' function may be its greatest advantage along with its beneficial equity impact ... in reaching precisely those categories of borrowers who are sought to be benefitted by credit quotas – small and marginal farmers, artisans, small enterprises and exporters.
>
> (1990: 207)

16

MONETARY POLICY AND DEVELOPMENT

Sheila Page

The purpose of the set of studies presented in this book has been to look at monetary policy and the development of the financial sector in developing countries from the point of view of the general development of economies. We may start from analysis of individual questions of effective policy implementation, or correct choice of policy, but we cannot accept the conclusions of what are effectively partial approaches as sufficient. The development of the financial sector into a modern financial system which will serve effectively the economic functions of transmission of funds, mobilisation and transfer of savings, and allocation of credit is clearly an appropriate long-term goal. But it is subject to two basic questions: is it an aim which requires, or which would benefit from, special government policy assistance, or will it happen as part of general development? And the question which must always be most important to an economist, of the choice of priorities: are the financial sectors in the type of country which we are studying in some sense more under-developed than other sectors? Is the need for a more developed financial sector greater or more pressing than a more developed agriculture, or industry, or commerce or education, or any other sector to the extent that whatever resources are available for development should be channelled preferentially to it?

Another set of demands on the financial sector comes from those who look for the most effective means of stabilisation or control of inflation. Again, we must ask: first, whether these objectives are the priority problem for an economy, then, whether they are amenable to government intervention and whether intervention is preferable to other solutions, and, finally, whether it is appropriate to devote resources to developing the existing financial sector to permit certain instruments to be used if other instruments are available.

The financial sector may also face demands from governments which wish to achieve certain distributional or sectoral aims. An economic appraisal here must consider whether using non-financial-sector means is feasible, and might be more efficient.

It is necessary, however difficult, for a government to take account of all these potentially valid, but also potentially conflicting, demands on a financial

MONETARY POLICY AND THE FINANCIAL SECTOR

sector. Then it must choose (if, of course, it is sufficiently interventionist to consider such questions appropriate at all) whether it should attempt to develop the sector; for what purposes and by what methods; and at what level of priority relative to the other demands which it faces.

The governments examined in this book clearly have not (with the possible exceptions of Indonesia and China) actively pursued a policy of developing their financial sectors as an objective in itself. They do not, therefore, share the view of some more advanced developing countries that the financial sector is a leading sector or form of infrastructure which needs to be promoted. It could be that they believe that the informal sectors are so successful that they can turn their attention to more important or more backward sectors. But the previous chapter suggested reasons for regarding an informal financial sector as an imperfect substitute, and the country studies and Chapter 11 offer evidence for this. An examination of their policies as indicated by their monetary and financial interventions suggests that it is more likely that they do not take an approach to development which emphasises any sectoral choice. Their policy (or lack of one) *vis-à-vis* the financial sector is simply one example of this.

One reason for what can appear to be a repression of the financial sector (not of financial relationships and transactions) is that most of our study countries have for most of the period had fixed exchange rates, and, as Lane notes in Chapter 12, fixed exchange rates and credit controls tend to be associated. This could be because of a preference for operating the financial side, domestic and foreign, of the economy in a completely fixed and therefore predictable way, or because of an assumption that the behavioural responses in both the financial and exchange-rate markets are too unpredictable to rely on indirect means of control. Chapter 14 has presented the evidence on this. Alternatively, it may merely reflect a view that both are too unimportant relative to the policies of the government with respect to the real sector for potentially unpredictable or unregulated responses to be allowed the opportunity for disruption. Indonesia, the only counter-example, moved to more indirect methods of intervention in both at the same time, the late 1980s. Related to this is the possibility that it is technically easier to operate a direct than an indirect system, and therefore more suitable for a developing country with limited expertise. This may be true, in absolute comparison terms; but it is not self-evident that the financial sector in developing countries is more deficient or difficult than any other, and therefore that there is a special case for not using or developing it.

The policies which these governments have used with vigour, and, in some cases at least, with effectiveness, have taken a more aggregate, macro approach: total credit controls; exchange-rate policies with capital controls or, later, liberalisation. That they have set sectoral priorities for their banks may seem to contradict this view, but these have not been effective, and, on the evidence here, largely because governments have not made them effective. Our study countries are thus very different in approach from the NICs, which have taken a more sectoral and micro approach, and which have included the finance sector among the sectors to encourage.

Their poverty, vulnerability to external shocks, and narrow domestic markets are sufficient explanations for the fact that, when they implement macroeconomic policies of stabilisation or more generally of exchange-rate or price stability, they have found direct rather than indirect methods of control more suitable. But these limitations do not explain why they have chosen to emphasise macro policies. The difficulties which we expected monetary policy to face from underdevelopment or primary export concentration have been important, but they are not obstacles specifically to the development of a sectorally differentiated policy, whether for the financial sector itself or for others.

One reason for these governments' choice of total credit controls has been their vulnerability to a very specific external pressure: that from the IMF, with a bias towards interventionist macro policy, but non-interventionist sectoral policy. Their dependence on the IMF has also been a reason for using direct controls. To rely on indirect means, e.g. reserve management or other money supply or demand management, to implement a policy of aggregate credit limits, with severe sanctions for overrunning but effectively none for undershooting, is a high-risk choice. It requires fixed and predictable behavioural relationships within the financial sector and between it and the real economy. Accepting a credit-limit policy may require direct intervention in any country, and certainly does in a developing one. To the extent that it actually inhibits the development of a financial sector, it is itself a policy with sectoral effects.

The experience of the NICs has been that primarily sectoral, even firm-specific, policies have been at least strongly associated with successful development. The country studies in this book have not explained why the governments studied have made the opposite choice. It is clearly not because of an ideological choice against government intervention *per se*, since they do intervene in other ways.

Two differences which can influence the potential development of a national financial sector have been identified between the countries studied here and the successful NICs (and many of the now industrial countries which preceded them). The first is the presence in Africa of large foreign banks. This meant that the governments did not themselves need to take an initial view of what the financial sector should be or do (or even, as their presence predates the countries' sovereignty, whether foreign banks should be permitted). The financial sector, therefore, did not force itself on their attention, and its well-being is not of direct concern in the way national firms would be. The second is the absence of an immigrant population equivalent to the Chinese in many Asian countries, with limited economic outlets, and therefore with an incentive to provide financial services, whether informal or formal (the point is stressed by Thomas in Chapter 11). This removed one possible source of a strong indigenous financial sector. Against this, the special characteristics of developing countries which have been the primary focus of this book – poverty and vulnerability to shocks – should have put special pressure on them to develop a flexible financial sector to mitigate the transmission of domestic and external shocks to the rest of the economy. They appear to have failed to do so.

It must be borne in mind that some of these governments faced more immediate problems than those of economic development, including political instability and natural disasters, and all are countries which lack the infrastructure for decision-making and policy-formation to at least the same degree as they lack financial and physical infrastructure. Indonesia, the country which has developed its financial sector and its monetary policy furthest, may have benefited from correct choice and effective implement-ation of economic policies. It is also, however, the country which is best placed geographically to benefit directly from the prosperity of the NICs; best placed in terms of similarity of background and closeness of contacts to imitate them, and attract the attention of foreign capital; and an oil exporter, fortunate because its principal external shocks were positive.

Many of the special conditions in the countries discussed here have made any development or development strategy difficult. The risks attached to any strategy are high. Their financial and non-financial sectors are more exposed to external and domestic shocks, and more vulnerable to them, than those in more mature (and larger) economies. It is not possible to make an absolute distinction between the results of these special conditions and those of the choices which are made in the face of them. Nevertheless, with the possible exception of the external emphasis on aggregate credit limits, the conditions discussed here have not had effects which were more damaging to financial sector development than to other development policies. Some of those which appear to have been particularly inhibiting have themselves been matters of choice (exchange-rate policies in general; membership of the Franc Zone in particular). It is difficult to avoid the conclusion that it is by choice that most of our study countries, most of the time, have failed to intervene in their economies, including the financial sector, in ways that have proved effective in the more successful developing countries.

NOTES

1 THE NEW DEMAND FOR MONETARY DEVELOPMENT

1 Goodhart's law, however, suggests that even here such an approach quickly ceases to be productive.

2 It is arguable that the constraints on finance and needs for adjustment which focused attention on efficiency and cost reduction in general could have led to the identification of financial sectors as a particular source of high costs through underdevelopment, or even to a belief that the financial sector was relatively undeveloped even in the context of the least developed countries (cf. Germidis *et al.* 1991: 23; also Fry 1988: 238). There is little research evidence to support either position.

2 THE INSTITUTIONAL FRAMEWORK

1 This phenomenon features in structuralist macroeconomic models; see for instance Buffie (1984) and Taylor (1983).

2 Bank of Thailand estimates, as reported in the *Far Eastern Economic Review*, 9 March 1987, p. 131.

3 Economic theory shows that thin financial markets are prone to greater volatility than 'thick' markets (Diamond 1987).

4 The IMF distinguishes between 'money' and 'quasi-money' in its *International Financial Statistics*. The IMF defines 'money' as currency plus demand deposits, while 'quasi-money' includes time deposits as well. Quasi-money includes the same types of item as are incorporated in national definitions of broad money (M2/M3), and can therefore be thought of as an internationally standardised M2/M3 measure.

3 AN ANALYTICAL FRAMEWORK

1 Note that the monetary base is not equivalent to the reserve base, for all definitions of the latter exclude currency held by the public (Cp).

2 The fact that these estimations are not simply academic exercises, but are important policy tools, is borne out by cases where inaccurate estimates of money demand have led to unintended policy outcomes. In the case of Chile in the 1960s, for instance, Corbo (1982) shows that because of a misspecification of the demand for money function, the central bank underestimated money demand; this resulted in a restrictive monetary stance and loss of output, contrary to the authorities' intention to pursue an accommodative monetary policy.

4 A FRAMEWORK FOR POLICY ANALYSIS

1 Evidence from developed countries indicates that the demand for credit is less stable and less interest-rate elastic than the demand for money, and Moore and Threadgold (1980) conclude that this control technique has a limited impact in the UK.

2 Policy-makers may find this desirable since it is predominantly a non-tradable sector, and the objective of monetary restraint may be to encourage the switching of output from non-tradables to tradables. However, some construction activity supports the expansion of tradable goods, e.g. silos for storing export commodities, and the long-term use of the method on the sector will be unrelated to the amount of shift desired.

3 A practical problem is that penalties on banks for non-compliance with credit guidelines may be less than profits from breaking them. Okogu (1986) shows how the shifting balance between penalties and profitability has governed the compliance rate of Nigeria's banking system to guidelines on lending to agriculture.

4 This was done in Botswana in 1981, when the authorities took the position that small borrowers would be better-off if at least some credit was available at higher interest rates, rather than having larger firms take most of the rationed loans (Harvey 1985: 33).

5 To deal with the monetary consequences of the sharp rise in foreign-exchange earnings associated with the boom in commodity prices at the time of the Korean war.

5 KENYA, 1967–88

1 Readers wishing to study Kenya's macroeconomic performance in greater depth are particularly referred to Bevan *et al.* (forthcoming). Useful coverage of the 1960s and 1970s is provided in Killick (1981); somewhat fuller discussion of monetary and balance-of-payments aspects is provided in Killick (1984, 1985).

2 Kenya's external debt statistics are a morass of widely varying figures. The government's annual *Economic Survey* provides data showing total debt stock figures which are far below those contained in the World Bank's standard *World Debt Tables*. On the grounds that it follows definitions that are standard across countries and is a more readily available source outside Kenya, we have preferred to use the latter. However, the World Bank's own 1989 *Adjustment Lending: An Evaluation of Ten Years of Experience* contains debt statistics for Kenya which are very much larger than those contained in its *Debt Tables* (World Bank 1991), which makes it all the harder to know which is the best series to use. *World Debt Tables* data have been extended to 1988 by assuming that debt grew in 1987–8 at the same rate as that given in the government's *Economic Survey* 1989.

3 In 1985 the official export volume index stood at 99, with 1982 = 100, continuing a much longer record of stagnation. By 1988, however, the index had risen to 116. See Killick (1985) for a discussion of the longer-term record.

4 However, the entry for 1969–73 should be discounted, as the statistical result of a small absolute increase from a tiny initial base.

5 A curve fitted for the commodity terms of trade for 1964–88 yielded a trend deterioration of 3.4 points *p.a.* (with 1980 = 100). The adjusted R^2 obtained was 0.82 and the t-value of the trend term was highly significant at -10.404.

6 For a valuable account of the functions and workings of the CBK see Kenya Central Bank (1986).

7 Source: IMF, *International Financial Statistics*; Kenya, *Economic Survey*, 1989.

NOTES

8   This can be judged from the following figures:

	1984	1985	1986	1987	1988
Kshs per SDR	15.19	17.74	19.14	23.43	25.03
Real effective exchange rate (1983 = 100)	107	106	92	83	77

The SDR rate is taken from IMF, *International Financial Statistics* and the real rate from Lynn and McCarthy (1989, Table 6) based on IMF sources.

9   Barclays, the Kenya Commercial Bank, the National Bank of Kenya, and Standard Chartered.

10   The Banking Bill, 1989 implicitly defines NBFIs as institutions which accept deposits from the public and on-lend them but which do not offer chequing facilities. However, statistics on the NBFIs exclude building societies, insurance companies, the POSB, development finance institutions, private pension plans and a large number of savings and credit societies.

11   Investigations of the 1986 crisis had revealed both that some NBFIs carried sizeable loans to parastatal bodies on their balance sheets, some of which were of dubious value, and that they were, in turn, heavily reliant for their continued solvency upon large deposits from parastatal agencies, notably the NSSF. Some of these situations were said to be based upon personal relationships between the heads of the NBFIs and parastatals, and a number were believed to be associated with off-the-record transactions between them.

12   See CBK (1989: 47–51) for an account of the changes in banking legislation prior to 1989.

13   An excellent discussion of this topic is contained in an unpublished 1984 'Report and Recommendations on the Money and Capital Markets in Kenya', prepared jointly by the Central Bank of Kenya and the International Finance Corporation.

14   The general nature of our results was also similar to those recently obtained by Tegene (1989) for six other African countries.

15   This is reviewed more fully in Killick (1984: 170–82).

16   See Mwega and Ngola (1988) for an earlier version of these tests.

17   It should be noted, however, that national accounting data on aggregate savings are not very reliable, being derived as a residual and thus reflecting errors on other items.

18   See Blejer and Khan (1984), who find for a sample of twenty-four developing countries that private sector investment is positively correlated with the availability of credit.

19   See Arrieta (1988) for a recent survey of this literature, and the other country studies in this book.

20   See Gelb (1989), who particularly emphasises the potential importance of this productivity-raising effect and who finds substantial econometric evidence of it.

21   This test involved adding constant and slope shift dummies for the second half of the period (1981:2–1988:4) to short-run money demand functions for the whole period, 1973:3–1988:4. The Gujarati test then examines whether these shift dummies are jointly significantly different from zero using the F-test. In our tests they were not significant even at the 10 per cent level for any of the measures of money.

22   Some instability in k could be predicted for our later period, when quantitative credit ceilings were in force. However, the similarity of our results with those obtained by Bolnick for a period when ceilings were rarely used suggests that the instability of k cannot simply be explained in terms of the 'shocks' imposed by observance of credit ceilings.

23   For example, as at the end of 1988 the commercial banks collectively held liquid

assets equivalent to 23.5 per cent of their deposit liabilities, while the prescribed minimum was only 20 per cent (*Economic Survey,* 1989, Table 5.10). This was a typical situation. Table 1.6.3 of the CBK (1989) shows that in every year since 1971 actual bank liquidity has been in excess of statutory requirements, although by fluctuating margins. Taking end-of-year statistics, the mean excess of liquidity in 1971–89 was 37 per cent of the statutory requirement. The mean for 1980–8 alone was 31 per cent.

24 One of our correspondents, for example, refered to a practice by government 'which causes most acute and direct damage to the private sector, i.e. the habit of not paying its bills on time … [I]t is believed that directives have gone out from the Treasury to delay payments for up to 3 months at the end of the financial year, and … preference has been given to contractors etc. prepared to submit invoices dated 1st July.' We were also told of jugglings in the portfolio holdings of parastatals and other agencies around the benchmark dates of IMF programmes in order to maintain the appearance that the government was keeping within credit ceilings.

25 Killick (1984: 206–8) observed for the previous generation of IMF programmes in Kenya that the ceilings did not seem excessively restrictive.

26 See CBK (1989: 10–11) for an interesting and candid account of the difficulties with this experiment.

27 It should be noted that, although taken from official *Economic Surveys*, the data employed do not seem very reliable, with a number of unexplained discrepancies.

28 Indeed, the government's insistence that the NSSF buy government paper, particularly Treasury bills, at sub-market interest rates, creates a strong conflict of interest with the Fund's obligations to maximise the returns on contributions received in order to be able to pay improved pensions and other benefits in the future. In the case of the POSB, the chief result is to limit its ability to offer attractive interest rates to its customers.

29 0.932, 1.145, 0.936 and 0.851 respectively.

30 CBK data admittedly show a high proportion of NBFI credit as going to the private sector. We understand, however, that a good deal of lending to parastatals is, in fact, included in these statistics.

31 On this, see the major study by Bevan *et al.* (forthcoming); and Bevan *et al.* (1989). For a brief earlier analysis see Killick (1984: 179–80).

32 In fact, a modest export tax was imposed late in the boom, but it absorbed only a negligible proportion of the windfall proceeds – and the revenue was, in any case, spent by government.

33 Bevan *et al.* (1989) particularly emphasise the longer-term effects of the boom through its weakening of Treasury control. However, it was not until the early 1980s that budget deficits really threatened to get out of control, and it seems implausible to attribute this to a delayed reaction to the coffee boom. Perhaps a stronger clue is provided by the fact that the holder of the office of Minister of Finance in 1980–3 did not reveal as strong a commitment to fiscal discipline as his immediate predecessor or his successor.

34 It is, as noted earlier, government policy to encourage the development of the capital market. There has been at least one major report on that subject and the government currently has a financial sector adjustment loan agreement with the World Bank for this purpose.

35 See also Ndele (1990), who reaches the same general conclusion.

36 Action may well also be necessary to strengthen the finances of parastatal agencies and thus reduce their credit requirements. We have been unable to get much information about this important aspect of the monetary situation.

6 GHANA, 1957–88

1   Republic of Ghana, *Economic Recovery Programme, 1984–6,* Vol. 1, pp. 15–16.
2   Moreover, in 1967 Ghana registered a negative inflation rate; and that poses a problem for our functional form.
3   A *Ghanaian Times* editorial of 29 June 1989 made reference to a directive from the Ministry of Finance and Economic Planning to the banks, instructing them to suspend the granting of loans temporarily from 1 March 1989.

7 CÔTE D'IVOIRE, 1973–88

1   There is likely to be some double-counting from commercial banks on-lending central bank loans.
2   Carried out by the author on an informal basis 7–8 May 1989 with village chiefs, PDCI leaders and farmers' councils of three villages in the Gagnoa region of Côte d'Ivoire.
3   The new interest-rate policy coincided with, and is generally attributed to, the appointment of a new BCEAO Governor, Alassane Ouattara, in 1988.
4   The broad money measure was found to be preferable to a narrower definition. In 1985 the removal of banks' requirement to pay interest on sight deposits led to shifts towards savings and time deposits. This created instability in the narrow money multiplier but not the broad multiplier.

8 INDONESIA, 1974–90

1   There is no authorisation to issue government debt in Indonesia.
2   Estimates provided by Richard Patten.
3   There was an upper limit to the level of reserve requirements which could be feasibly implemented because the Indonesian Government wished to reduce the real cost of borrowing, particularly for small borrowers.
4   Liquidity credits were not used as a method of monetary control, in contrast to the system used for example in the CFA Franc Zone.
5   An additional factor was that the state-owned banks were encouraged by Bank Indonesia to hold additional foreign-exchange reserves with the funds freed by the reduction of reserve requirements in 1977.
6   See Cole and Slade (1990a and 1990b) for a detailed account of money market development during this period.
7   Some of the larger private banks began to act as informal brokers, intermediating between the state-owned banks and smaller private banks.
8   A swap transaction is a simultaneous purchase and sale of foreign currency for two different value dates. The transaction is usually between a commercial bank and a customer who wishes to borrow offshore and convert into domestic currency. The swap transaction covers exchange rate risk for the customer.
9   Bank Indonesia claimed that it was adjusting the rupiah to a basket of foreign currencies, but never specified what currencies were in the basket, nor how they might be weighted. Actual movements of the rupiah exchange rate were usually measured relative to the US dollar, and expectations were couched in terms of changes against the dollar.
10 The 2 per cent limit was not a floor. Banks have been unable to reduce their cash and working balances with Bank Indonesia much lower than 5 per cent because they cannot have a negative (overdraft) position with Bank Indonesia and most banks are reluctant to make use of the central bank's discount window. However,

an incentive has been created to make banks' cash management operations more efficient.

11 Some government officials describe this sterilisation as 'hiding the oil money'.

12 This group might be contrasted with a more nationalist protectionist approach based in the Ministries of Industry, Technology and Communications.

13 At the time Pertamina was the largest non-Japanese company in Asia (Woo and Nasution 1989: 120).

9 BANGLADESH, 1973–85

1 The use of simple indicators such as the food price index is preferred because the cost of acquiring information to generate rational expectations could be very high in developing countries. However, if agents' expectations are based on the actual and past year's food price rises, then the model is consistent with the rational expectations framework.

2 This formulation was attempted in the estimated model but, since the partial adjustment coefficient was insignificant, it was not used in the model simulation.

10 CHINA, 1949–88

1 The monetary system and monetary policy in China are discussed by Byrd (1983), Bortolani and Santorum (1984), Yang (1984), de Wulf and Goldsborough (1986), and Brotman (1985).

2 An extensive literature exists on the PRS: see in particular, Sinha (1982), Wiens (1983 and 1987), and Lin (1987).

3 Feltenstein, Lebow and van Wijnbergen (1986) found a negative and significant correlation between households' consumption and the real rate of interest on savings deposits, notwithstanding the fact that real interest rates were negative. Their result is particularly interesting, since it is based on an approach, the virtual price index, which takes into account distortions deriving from excess demand in the consumer goods market.

11 THE INFORMAL FINANCIAL SECTOR: HOW DOES IT OPERATE AND WHO ARE THE CUSTOMERS?

1 It is difficult to draw a sharp line between formal and informal financial institutions and provide a definition that will hold for particular institutions in all countries, but in the FFS one would include institutions that are registered, licensed and recorded, i.e. the central bank, the commercial banks and other banks, such as agricultural or industrial banks, that are subject to financial controls and operate to make profits on their activities. In the IFS one would include institutions that are unregulated, unlicensed and/or unrecorded, such as money-lenders, pawnshops, savings cooperatives, credit programmes organised by governments or non-governmental organisations, etc. This is a convenient classification, since in general money-lenders, pawnshops and savings cooperatives are not licensed (and hence are informal), while many of the credit programmes are not directly concerned with profitability and hence differ from the commercial banks and other institutions in the FFS. While informality may involve illegality, this is not a necessary characteristic of informal financial institutions.

2   In discussing problems with slow repayments in Ghana, Levitsky and Prasad (1987) note that 'Participating banks claimed that the Credit Guarantee Scheme was reluctant to settle claims. They believe that the managers of CGS were under the misconception that the measure of success of a guarantee scheme was a low pay-out rate' (p. 69). The fact that the CGS had paid out only 0.5 per cent of the total amount of guarantees over a ten-year period of great economic difficulty suggested that there might have been some truth in the complaints of the participating banks.

3   Levitsky and Prasad quote the problems that arose in a credit guarantee scheme in Cameroon, which had a permitted total guarantee to capital fund ratio of 7:1, but after five years had reached a ratio of only 1.6:1. The agency was severely criticised by the commercial banks for being excessively risk-averse and many of them left the scheme complaining of long delays in processing applications and even longer delays in obtaining settlements to claims.

4   In evaluating the success of credit guarantee schemes, it is important to examine default rates. The choice of measures of default rates raises some interesting technical problems that are discussed in Adams (1988), Bolnick (1988) and Padmanabhan (1988: ch. 10).

5   Levitsky concludes that 'Despite efforts to encourage lending to small scale enterprises, it must be admitted that World Bank lending has hardly benefitted the very small, informal, microenterprises'. He also points out that these credit programmes may have distorting effects on the growth of enterprises: 'The provision of too many special benefits for the small enterprise sector can lead to the creation of "mini-conglomerates" of small businesses in place of the development of larger enterprises' (p. 26).

6   There may be a general tendency for lending agencies to overestimate the size of the 'small' enterprises they are aiming for. For example, in examining the constraints on women's participation in a credit programme in Peru, Buvinić and Berger (1990) report that while the programme aimed to distribute loans with a mean value of US$5,300 per loan, during the first four years of the programme more loans were made but less money was lent in total than was targeted. The average loan size was US$2,362 and they conclude that 'The average mean loan size was lower than projected, in part because of the program's overestimate of the resources available to the average micro entrepreneur in the *pueblos jóvenes*' (p. 697).

7   In his study of pawnshops in China, Whelan (1979) traces the institution back to the last quarter of the fifth century AD, when it was a commercial enterprise restricted to Buddhist monasteries.

8   Schemes based on reciprocity which do not involve money have been developed in some rural communities. In these schemes a group of farmers agree to work together on each other's land in rotation. No payments are made between the members of the group, except that each farmer is responsible for feeding the others while they are working on his land. Johnny (1985) gives examples for Sierra Leone.

9   Seibel and Shrestha (1988) report that their existence has been documented for the Yoruba in Southern Nigeria from as early as 1600. While ROSCAs are not found as widely in Latin America, Vélez-Ibañez (1983) presents evidence of the popularity of ROSCAs among Mexicans in the Southern United States. The importance and popularity of ROSCAs in Korea is discussed in Cole and Park (1983).

10 While it is easy to see why ROSCAs are popular among those who have little or no access to the FFS, they are also popular among wealthier members of many

societies who do have access to that sector (see Cole and Park (1983) on Korea). Part of the attraction may be the absence of project appraisal and flexibility as compared with borrowing from the FFS.

11 Kamara, 1988, reports problems of favouritism and poor repayment rates among those benefiting from favours in Sierra Leone.

12 This contrast between the distance of formal financial institutions from their customers and the proximity of lenders and borrowers in the IFS is made vividly by Timberg and Aiyar:

> The borrowers in the informal market are 'known' parties – under continuous surveillance in the closely packed lanes of the urban wholesale markets. Each bale of cloth that goes in and out is observed by neighbours, the finance brokers and bankers among them; an expensive night on the town is reported and judged the next morning in market gossip. In contrast to the relatively anonymous world of Western businessmen, even in the larger metropolitan centres Indian businessmen live their lives in a narrow social ambit. Most of the intermediaries interviewed seemed incredulous at the suggestion that they would have to ask formal questions of borrowers whose shops they visited every day and with whose business confrères they were in continuous contact.
>
> (1984: 45)

13 Singh (1989) contains an interesting account of how loans from village temples supplement loans from money-lenders in some remote parts of India. See also Nevaskar (1971) and Jones (1990, 1991) on the role of the Jains as money-lenders in India.

14 If obtaining a small loan for a short period of time from a commercial bank would involve three trips (one to collect the forms, a second to return the forms and a third to collect the loan) and if each trip involves a half-day in travelling and transacting the business, the opportunity cost of the time lost in terms of income forgone may be much larger than the saving in interest-rate charges (Christen 1989).

15 While the range of items accepted by pawnbrokers is wide, Bouman (1989: 79) reports that in India interest charges may be up to 10 per cent per month on durables such as watches or radios, as compared to 2.5 to 3 per cent per month on items of gold.

16 The importance of peer-group pressure is confirmed by a number of examples in the experience of Oxfam (Devereux and Pares 1987: 301). For a theoretical analysis of imperfect information in rural credit markets and the operation of peer monitoring, see Hoff and Stiglitz (1990) and Stiglitz (1990) respectively.

17 The Grameen Bank is analysed in some detail because it presents a model that has been exported successfully to a number of countries. However, the group solidarity approach is not the only model to work. Patten and Rosengard (1990) present evidence on the success of the Baden Kredit Kecamatan (BKK) in Indonesia in providing rural credit and mobilising savings. The BKK utilises reciprocity and borrowers are encouraged to repay promptly by the knowledge that such action will allow them to move on in the programme to further loans. However, instead of the group-solidarity approach of the Grameen Bank, the BKK relies on character references from local officials. While this system seems to have worked successfully in Indonesia, it does not appear to have developed in any major way in other countries.

18 In Peru there are fewer restrictions on group formation. For example, there is no requirement for single-sex groups, a fact that may reflect the different position of

urban women in Catholic Latin America. The restriction of only one household member per group operates, but there is no exact equivalence in the urban setting for the requirement that group members should come from the same village; in practice the members of a group come from a small area of the city, usually from a few adjacent streets. Members of a particular group do not have to follow the same occupation. Saving with the lending institutions is not required of the participants. As with the Grameen Bank, the policy of the credit programmes in Peru has been to target women in particular. It is possible that this common feature of different applications of the Grameen Bank system may have contributed to the high repayment rates obtained in these credit programmes, but data showing repayment rates by sex seem to be unavailable, so that a direct comparison cannot be made. Yunus (1988) reports (without providing financial details) on a number of initiatives in the United States, such as the work of the South Shore Bank in Chicago, the Winrock Foundation in Arkansas that was establishing a bank to lend without collateral to welfare recipients, and the Cherokee Nation in Oklahoma.

19 In discussing women's microbusinesses at low income levels, Berger (1989) suggests that 'Because they exist at the margin of minimum subsistence levels, women in this group tend to be risk-averse.... Their desperate living situations may make them eager to take loans if they can obtain them, but their loan investment is unlikely to lead to significant income expansion, and they may be forced to "divert" the loan to consumption' (p. 1022).

20 Sometimes information concerning the IFS may be revealed by regulations affecting the customers of that sector. For example, Cole and Park (1983) provide data for South Korea on the size of the IFS for the early 1970s, when a government decree required all enterprises with a business licence to report informal debts. The total reported was equivalent to 80 per cent of the supply of money at the time and 34 per cent of the then outstanding domestic credit of the banking sector.

21 It is likely that for such clients the impact of monetary policy may be similar through the FFS and the IFS. For example, if interest rates are raised to squeeze credit in the FFS, some borrowers may shift their demand for loans to the IFS by obtaining credit from ROSCAs. One would expect this increased demand to lead to larger discounts in ROSCAs that allocate funds through bidding and hence implicit interest rates will rise in at least some institutions in the IFS.

22 There may be differences in the impact of the inflation tax on the rural and urban poor, depending on the degree of monetisation. To the extent that the rural poor rely on non-market subsistence production and consumption within the household, these activities are not directly affected by inflation. Possibilities for such non-market household activities, particularly in food production, are greatly reduced for those working in cities, who are therefore particularly vulnerable to the inflation tax. The effect of the inflation tax on the poor in Peru is analysed in World Bank (1989).

23 This role has been noted in a number of studies, especially of Africa, including ILO (1988) and Green (1989).

12 EXCHANGE RATES AND THE EFFECTIVENESS OF MONETARY POLICY

1 A classic example of a real targets policy is Australia during the 1980s (Glyn 1989).

2 Until it ended in 1974, the Sterling area, of which many British colonies and ex-

colonies were members, was the principal example of a developed country-led monetary union.

3 West African Monetary Union: Benin, Burkina Faso, Côte d'Ivoire, Mali, Niger, Senegal, Togo. Central African Monetary Union: Cameroon, Central African Republic, Congo, Gabon, Equatorial Guinea and Chad.

4 Bolivia, Dominican Republic, Gambia, Ghana, Guatemala, Guinea, Nigeria, Paraguay, the Philippines, Sierra Leone, South Africa, Uganda, Uruguay, Zaire, Zambia.

5 This section is derived from a survey of monetary policy implementation in Botswana by Harvey (1985).

6 Formally, both currencies were pegged to the US dollar.

13 THE USE OF MONETARY POLICY

1 Keeping the gold under the mattress or returning the talent without increment after burying it in the ground is normally seen as over-cautious, or even 'wicked and slothful'.

14 THE FINANCIAL SECTOR

1 Some may also have wanted to help political supporters or other favoured recipients.

2 The finding by Duesenberry and McPherson (1990) that artificially promoting securities markets may impede their eventual success is also a warning to countries where the initial conditions do not seem to be present.

15 THE RELATIONSHIP BETWEEN FORMAL AND INFORMAL FINANCE

1 World Bank (1990a: 114) suggests that 'loans from moneylenders are used to make a transaction at short notice and funds from formal lenders are used to repay the moneylenders'. This makes the informal sector analogous at intra-national level with the use of bank credit by countries faced with international shocks and slow and inflexible international institutions.

2 Fry (1988: 294) quotes a finding that 'indigenous bankers know their clients better than commercial banks. This reduces information costs.' This seems unlikely as phrased, and is contrary to experience in more developed countries. It is more likely to mean only that informal bankers know their own clients better than commercial bankers know informal banks' clients.

3 In the UK, the use of family finance by recent immigrants is an obvious illustration of the persistence of informal institutions in the context of borrowers who are unfamiliar to formal institutions; such borrowers' use of the Bank for Credit and Commerce International, an insufficiently regulated bank, illustrates the extra risks which stem from their need to use institutions not wholly within the formal system.

4 This suggests possible weaknesses in both NGO and World Bank attachment to projects.

5 Thomas notes also (in Chapter 11) the different experiences of countries with Indian or Chinese immigrants.

REFERENCES

GENERAL REFERENCES

Adams, D.W. (1988) 'The Conundrum of Successful Credit Projects in Floundering Rural Financial Markets', *Economic Development and Cultural Change* 36: 355–67.

Adams, D.W., Graham, D.H. and Von Prischke, J.D. (1984) *Undermining Rural Development with Cheap Credit*, Boulder, CO: Westview Press.

Adekunle, J.O. (1968) 'The Demand for Money: Evidence from Developed and Less Developed Economies', *IMF Staff Papers* 15, 2: 220–66.

Adewunmi, W. (1984) *Loan Management in Nigerian Banks*, Bangor: University of Wales Press.

Aghevli, B. (1980) 'Effects of Banking Development on the Demand for Money', in Coats and Khatkhate.

Aghevli, B. and Khan, M.S. (1977) 'Inflationary Finance and the Dynamics of Inflation: Indonesia 1951–72', *American Economic Review* 67: 390–403.

Aghevli, B. and Khan, M.S. (1978), 'Government Deficits and the Inflationary Process in Developing Countries', *IMF Staff Papers* 25, 3.

Aghevli, B. and Khan, M.S. (1980) 'Credit Policy and the Balance of Payments in Developing Countries', in Coats and Khatkhate.

Ahmed, R. (1981) *Agricultural Price Policies Under Complex Socioeconomic and Natural Constraints: The Case of Bangladesh*, International Food Policy Research Institute, Research Report No 27, October, Washington DC.

Akaike, H. (1960) 'Statistical Predictor Identification', *Annals of the Institute of Statistical Mathematics* 21: 302–17.

Alogoskoufis, G. and Pissarides, C. (1983) 'A Test of Price Sluggishness in the Simple Rational Expectations Mode: U.K. 1950–80', *Economic Journal* 93: 616–28.

Arndt, H.W. (1983a) 'Financial Development in Asia', *Asian Development Review* 1, 1: 86–100.

—— (1983b) 'Two Kinds of Credit Rationing', *Banca Nazionale del Lavoro Quarterly Review*.

Arrieta, G.M. Gonzales (1988), 'Interest Rates, Savings and Growth in LDCs: an assessment of recent empirical research', *World Development* 16, 5.

Artis, M.J. and Lewis, M.K. (1981) *Monetary Control in the United Kingdom*, Oxford: Philip Allan.

Asian Development Bank (1990) *Asian Development Outlook 1990*, Manila: Asian Development Bank.

Aspe, P., Dornbusch, R., and Obstfeld, M. (eds), *Financial Policies and the World Capital Markets: The Problem of Latin American Countries*, Chicago, IL: University of Chicago Press.

Attfield, C., Demery, D. and Duck, N. (1985) *Rational Expectations in Macroeconomics*, Oxford: Basil Blackwell.

Austin, G. (forthcoming) 'Towards a History of Indigenous Credit Institutions in West Africa, 1800–1960', in Sugihara.

Balino, T. (1980) 'The Demand for Money and Its Components in Argentina: Annual Estimations 1935–69', in Coats and Khatkhate.

Barro, R.J. (1978) 'Unanticipated Money, Output, and the Price Level in the United States', *Journal of Political Economy* 86: 549–80.

—— (1979) 'Money and Output in Mexico, Colombia, and Brazil', in J. Behrman and J.A. Hanson (eds), *Short-Term Macroeconomic Policy in Latin America*, Cambridge, MA: Ballinger.

—— (1981) 'Unanticipated Money Growth and Economic Activity in the U.S.', in *Money, Expectations and Business Cycles*, New York: Academic Press.

Barro, R.J. and Grossman, H.I. (1971) 'A General Equilibrium Model of Income and Employment', *American Economic Review* 61: 503–24.

Barro, R.J. and Gordon, D.B. (1983) 'Rules, Discretion and Reputation in a Model of Monetary Policy', *Journal of Monetary Economics* 12, 1: 101–22.

Bera, A.L. and Jarque, C.M. (1982) 'Model Specification Tests: a Simultaneous Approach', *Journal of Econometrics* 20: 59–82.

Berger, M. (1989) 'Giving Women Credit: the Strengths and Limitations of Credit as a Tool for Alleviating Poverty', *World Development* 17: 1017–32.

Bhaduri, A. (1989) 'Moneylenders', in Eatwell *et al.*

Bhatia, R.J. (1985) *The West African Monetary Union: An Analytical Review*, IMF Occasional Paper No. 35, May, Washington DC.

Bhattacharya, S.N. (1984) *Role of Indian Rural Institutions in Economic Growth: a Critical Study*, New Delhi: Metropolitan Book Company.

Blejer, M.I. (1978) 'Black-Market Exchange-Rate Expectations and the Domestic Demand for Money: Some Empirical Results', *Journal of Monetary Economics* 4: 767–74.

Blejer, M.I. and Fernandez, R.B. (1980) 'The Effects of Unanticipated Money Growth on Prices and on Output and its Composition in a Fixed-Exchange Rate Open Economy', *Canadian Journal of Economics* 13: 82–95.

Blejer, M.I. and Khan, M.S. (1984) 'Government Policy and Private Investment in Developing Countries', *IMF Staff Papers* 31, 2.

Bolnick, B.R. (1975) 'Behaviour of the Determinants of Money Supply in Kenya', *Eastern Africa Economic Review* 7, 1.

—— (1988) 'Evaluating Loan Collection Performance: an Indonesian Example', *World Development* 16: 501–10.

Bortolani, S. (1975) 'Central Banking in Africa', Milan: Cassa di Risparmio Delle Provincie Lombarde.

Bouman, F.J.A. (1989) *Small, Short and Unsecured: Informal Rural Finance in India*, Delhi: Oxford University Press.

Bouman, F.J.A. and Houtman, R. (1988) 'Pawnbroking as an Instrument of Rural Banking in the Third World', *Economic Development and Cultural Change* 37: 69–89.

Bruno, M. (1979) 'Stabilization and Stagflation in a Semi–Industrialized Economy', in R. Dornbusch and J.A. Frenkel (eds), *International Economic Policy: Theory and Evidence*, Baltimore, MD: Johns Hopkins University Press: 270–89.

Buffie, E.F. (1984) 'Financial Repression, The New Structuralists and Stabilization Policy in Semi-industrialized Economies', *Journal of Development Economics* 14, 13: 305–22.

Burkett, J. (1988) 'Slack, Shortage and Discouraged Consumers in Eastern Europe: Estimates based on smoothing by aggregation', *Review of Economic Studies*.

Buvinić, M. and Berger, M. (1990) 'Sex Differences in Access to a Small Enterprise Development Fund in Peru', *World Development* 18: 695–705.

Cagan, P. (1957) 'The Monetary Dynamics of Hyperinflation', in M. Friedman (ed.), *Studies in the Quantity Theory of Money*, Chicago, IL: University of Chicago Press: 25–117.

—— (1965) *Determinants and Effects of Changes in the Stock of Money, 1975–60*, New York: Columbia University Press for the National Bureau of Economic Research.

Caiden, N. and Wildavsky, A. (1974) *Planning and Budgeting in Poor Countries*, New York: John Wiley.

Callier, P. (1991) (ed.) *Financial Systems and Development in Africa*, Washington DC: World Bank.

Carbonetto, D. and Carazo, M.I. (1986) *Heterogeneidad Tecnológica y Desarrollo Económico: El Sector Informal*, Lima: Fundación Friedrich Ebert.

Carbonetto, D., Hoyle, J. and Tueros, M. (1987) *El Sector Informal Urbano en Lima Metropolitana*, Lima: CEDEP.

Cardoso, E.A. (1983) 'A Monetary Demand Equation for Brazil', *Journal of Development Economics* 12, 1–2: 183–94.

Carrithers, M. and Humphrey, C. (eds) (1991) *The Assembly of Listeners: Jains in Society*, Cambridge: Cambridge University Press.

Chandavarkar, A.G. (1977) 'Monetization of Developing Countries', *IMF Staff Papers* 24, 3.

—— (1989) 'Informal Credit Markets in Support of Microbusiness', in Levitsky.

Charmes, J. (1990) 'A Critical Review of Concepts, Definitions and Studies in the Informal Sector', in Turnham *et al.*

Chick, V. (1973) *The Theory of Monetary Policy*, London: Gray-Mills Publishing Ltd.

Chopra, A. and Montiel, P.J. (1986) 'Output and Unanticipated Money with Imported Intermediate Goods and Foreign Exchange Rationing', *IMF Staff Papers* 33: 697–721.

Chow, G.C. (1960) 'Tests of Equality between Sets of Coefficients in Two Linear Regressions', *Econometrica* 25: 591–605.

Christen, R.P. (1989) 'What Microenterprise Credit Programmes Can Learn From the Moneylenders', *Accion International Discussion Paper No. 4*, October, Cambridge, MA.

Clower, R.W. (1965) 'The Keynesian Counterrevolution: A Theoretical Appraisal', in F. Brechling and F.H. Han (eds), *The Theory of Interest Rates*, London: Macmillan.

Coats, W.L. (1980) 'The Efficacy of Monetary Rules for LDCs', in Coats and Khatkhate.

Coats, W.L. and D.P. (1984) 'Monetary Policy in Less Developed Countries: Main Issues', *The Developing Economies*, December: 329–48.

Coats, W.L. and Khatkhate, D.R. (1978) 'Money Supply Implications of Commercial Banks' Financing of Government Debt in Developing Countries', *Oxford Bulletin of Economics and Statistics* 40, 2.

Coats, W.L. and Khatkhate, D.R. (1980) 'Money and Monetary Policy in Less Developed Countries: Survey of Issues and Evidence', in Coats and Khatkhate.

Coats, W.R. (1980) 'The Use of Reserve Requirements in Developing Countries', in Coats and Khatkhate.

Coats, W.R. and Khatkhate, D.R. (eds) (1980) *Money and Monetary Policy in Less Developed Countries*, Oxford: Pergamon Press.

Cole, D.C. and Park, Y.C. (1983) *Financial Development in Korea 1945–78*, Cambridge, MA: Harvard University Press.

Collyns, C. (1983) *Alternatives to the Central Bank in the Developing World*, IMF Occasional Paper No. 20, July, Washington DC.

REFERENCES

Conlisk, J. (1970) 'Cross Country Inflation Evidence of the Moneyness of Time Deposits', *Economic Record* 46.

Corbo, V. (1982) 'Monetary Policy with an Overrestricted Demand for Money Equation: Chile in the 1960s', *Journal of Development Economics* 10: 119–26.

Corden, W.M. (1990) 'Exchange Rate Policy in Developing Countries', *World Bank PRE Working Paper No. 412*, April, Washington DC.

Corden, W.M. and Neary, J P. (1982) 'Booming Sector and De-Industrialisation in a Small Open Economy', *Economic Journal* 92, December: 825–48.

Courakis, A.S. (1984) 'Constraints on Bank Choices and Financial Repression in Less Developed Countries', *Oxford Bulletin of Economics and Statistics* 46, 4.

Cuddington, J.T., Johansson, P. and Löfgren, K. (1984) *Disequilibrium Macroeconomics in Open Economies*, Oxford: Basil Blackwell.

Cumby, R.E. and Obstfeld, M. (1983) 'Capital Mobility and the Scope for Sterilization: Mexico in the 1970s', in Aspe, Dornbusch, and Obstfeld.

Cuthbertson, K. (1985) *The Supply and Demand for Money*, Oxford: Basil Blackwell.

Darrat, A.F. (1985) 'The Demand for Money in a Developing Economy: the case of Kenya', *World Development* 13, 10–11: 1163–70.

—— (1986) 'Monetarization and Stability of Money Demand in Developing Countries: The Latin American Case', *Savings and Development* 1: 59–72.

Darrat, A.F. and Webb, M.A. (1986) 'Financial Changes and Interest Elasticity of Money Demand: Further Tests of the Gurley and Shaw Thesis', *Journal of Development Studies* 22, 4: 724–30.

Davis, J.M. (1983) 'The Economic Effects of Windfall Gains in Export Earnings, 1975–8', *World Development* 11, 2: 119–40.

Day, W. (1979) 'Domestic Credit and Money Ceilings Under Alternative Exchange Rate Regimes', *IMF Staff Papers* 26, 3.

Devarajan, S. and de Melo, J. (1987) 'Evaluating Participation in African Monetary Unions: A Statistical Analysis of The CFA Zones', *World Development* 15, 4: 483–96.

Devereux, S. and Pares, H. (1987) 'A Manual of Credit and Savings for the Poor of Developing Countries', *OXFAM Development Guidelines No. 1*, Oxford.

Diamond, P. (1987) 'Multiple Equilibria Models of Credit', *American Economic Review* 77, 2, May (Papers and Proceedings): 82–6.

Diaz-Alejandro, C. (1985) 'Good-bye Financial Repression, Hello Financial Crash', *Journal of Development Economics* 19.

Dick, E., Gupta, S., Mayer, T. and Vincent, D. (1983) 'The Short Run Impact of Fluctuating Primary Commodity Prices on Three Developing Economies: Colombia, Ivory Coast and Kenya', *World Development* 11, 5: 405–16.

Dixit, A.K. (1978) 'The Balance of Trade in a Model of Temporary Equilibrium with Rationing', *Review of Economic Studies* 45: 393–404.

Djanin, A. and Snyder, W. (1986) 'Monetary Control in a Developing Economy, The Case of Indonesia: 1968–82', in D. Cole (ed.), *The Indonesian Financial System*, Cambridge, MA: Harvard University Press.

Dohner, Robert S. and Intal, P. (1989) 'The Marcos Legacy: Economic Policy and Foreign Debt In The Philippines', in J.D. Sachs and S.M. Collins (eds) *Developing Debt and Economic Performance*, Chicago, IL: Chicago University Press for the National Bureau of Economic Research.

Dornbusch, R. and Fischer, S. (1984) *Macroeconomics*, London: McGraw-Hill.

Dornbusch, R.D. and Helmers, F.L.C.H. (1988) *The Open Economy: Tools For Policymakers in Developing Countries*, Oxford: Oxford University Press.

Dow, S.C. and Earl, P.E. (1982) *Money Matters: A Keynesian Approach to Monetary Economics*, Oxford: Martin Robertson.

Drake, P.J. (1980) *Money, Finance and Development*, Oxford: Martin Robertson.

REFERENCES

—— (1985) 'Some Reflections on Problems Affecting Securities Markets in Less Developed Countries', *Savings and Development* 9, 1: 5–15.

Duesenberry, James S. and McPherson, Malcolm F. (1990) 'Monetary Management in Sub-Saharan Africa', Cambridge, MA: Harvard Institute for International Development, mimeo.

Eatwell, J., Milgate, M. and Newman, P. (eds) (1989) *The New Palgrave: Economic Development*, London: Macmillan.

Echavarria, Juan José (1987) *Colombia, 1970–85: Management and Consequences of Two Large External Shocks*, ODI Working Paper No. 20, July, London: Overseas Development Institute.

Edwards, S. (1983) 'The Short-Run Relation Between Inflation and Growth in Latin America: Comment', *American Economic Review* 73: 477–82.

—— (1984) 'Coffee, Money and Inflation in Colombia', *World Development* 12, 11–12: 1107–17.

—— (1988) *Exchange Rate Misalignment in Developing Countries*, Baltimore, MD: Johns Hopkins University Press for World Bank.

Eicher, C.K. and Baker, D.C. (1982) *Research on Agricultural Development in Sub-Saharan Africa: A Critical Survey*, MSU International Development Paper No. 1, East Lansing, MI: Michigan State University, Department of Agricultural Economics.

Fasano-Filho, U. (1986) 'Currency Substitution and the Demand for Money: The Argentine Case 1960–76', *Weltwirtschaftliches Archiv* 122, 2: 327–39.

Fields, G.S. (1975) 'Rural-urban Migration, Urban Unemployment and Under-development, and Job-search Activity in LDCs', *Journal of Development Economics* 21: 165–87.

—— (1990) 'Labour Market Modelling and the Urban Informal Sector: Theory and Evidence', in Turnham *et al.*

Fisher, S. (1974) 'Money and the Production Function', *Economic Inquiry*: 528–9.

Foxley, A. (1983) 'Chile', in Aspe, Dornbusch and Obstfeld.

Franc Zone Secretariat (1989) 'La Zone Franc: Rapport 1988', Paris.

Francis, C. (1986) 'Monetary Policy in a Small Open Economy: The Case of the Bahamas', *Social and Economic Studies* 35, 4: 111–28.

Frenkel, J. and Johnson, H.G. (eds) (1976) *The Monetary Approach to the Balance of Payments*, London: George Allen and Unwin.

Friedman, M. and Schwartz, A.J. (1963) *A Monetary History of the United States, 1867–1960*, Princeton, NJ: Princeton University Press for the National Bureau of Economic Research.

Fry, M. (1982) 'Models of Financially Repressed Developing Economies', *World Development* 10, 9: 731–50.

Fry, M.J. (1988) *Money, Interest, and Banking in Economic Development*, Baltimore, MD: Johns Hopkins University Press.

Fuglesang, A. and Chandler, D. (1988) *Participation as Process: What We Can Learn from Grameen Bank, Bangladesh*, Dhaka: Grameen Bank.

Furness, E. (1975) *Money and Credit in Developing Africa*, London: Heinemann.

Galbis, V. (1984) 'Monetary and Related Policies in Ministates', *Savings and Development* 8, 4: 291–348.

Gelb, A.H. (1989) 'Financial Policies, Growth and Efficiency', *PPR Working Paper No. 202*, June, Washington DC: World Bank.

Germidis, D., Kessler, D. and Meghir, R. (1991) *Financial Systems and Development: What Role for the Formal and Informal Financial Sectors?*, Paris: OECD Development Centre.

Geweke J. (1982) 'Measurement of Linear Dependence and Feedback between Multiple Time Series', *Journal of the American Statistical Association* 77: 304–13.

343

REFERENCES

Geweke, J. (1984) 'Inference and Causality in Economic Time Series Model', in Z. Grilliches and M. Intrillisator (eds) *Handbook of Econometrics*, Amsterdam: North Holland.

Ghai, D. (1984) *An Evaluation of the Impact of the Grameen Bank Project*, Dhaka: Grameen Bank.

Ghatak, S. and Ayisa, C.B. (1987) *Stabilisation Policies, Money Supply and the Role of the International Monetary Fund in Less Developed Countries (LDCs)*, Dept. of Economics, Discussion Paper No. 44, Leicester: University of Leicester.

Gil Díaz, F. (1987) 'Some Lessons from Mexico's Tax Reform', in Newbery and Stern.

Glyn, Andrew (1989) *Exchange Controls and Policy Autonomy – The Case of Australia 1983–88*, Stockholm: WIDER Working Papers No. 64 August.

Goodhart, C. (1984) *Monetary Theory and Practice: The UK Experience*, London: Macmillan.

—— (1987) 'Why do Banks Need a Central Bank?', *Oxford Economic Papers* 39, 1: 75–89.

Gowland, D. (1984) *Controlling the Money Supply*, 2nd edn, London: Croom Helm.

Granger, C.W.J. (1969) 'Investigating Causal Relations by Econometric Models and Cross-Spectral Methods', *Econometrica* 37: 429–38.

Green, R.H. (1989) 'The Broken Pot: the Social Fabric, Economic Disaster and Adjustment in Africa', in Onimode.

Guitian, M. (1973) 'Credit Versus Money as an Instrument of Control', *IMF Staff Papers* 20, 3.

Gupta, K.L. (1984) *Finance and Economic Growth in Developing Countries*, London: Croom Helm.

Hanson, J.A. (1980) 'The Short-Run Relation Between Growth and Inflation in Latin America: A Quasi-Rational Expectations or Consistent Expectations Approach', *American Economic Review* 70, 5: 972–89.

Hanson, J.A. and Neal, C.R. (1985) *Interest Rate Policies in Selected Developing Countries, 1970–82*, World Bank Staff Working Paper No. 753, Washington DC.

Harper, M. (1984) *Small Business in the Third World*, London: Intermediate Technology Publications.

Harper, M. and de Jong, M.F. (1986) *Financing Small Enterprises*, London: Intermediate Technology Publications.

Hart, K. (1973) 'Informal Income Opportunities and Urban Employment in Ghana', *Journal of Modern African Studies* 11: 61–89.

Harvey, C. (1977) *Macro Economics for Africa*, London: Heinemann.

—— (1985) 'The Use of Monetary Policy in Botswana, in Good Times and Bad', *IDS Discussion Paper 204*, Brighton, Sussex: Institute of Development Studies.

Hendry, D.F. and Ericsson, N.R. (1983) *Assertion Without Empirical Basis: An Econometric Appraisal of Friedman and Schwartz "Monetary Trends in ... The United Kingdom"*, Bank of England, Panel of Academic Consultants, Paper No. 22, October, London.

Hoff, K. and Stiglitz, J.E. (1990) 'Introduction: Imperfect Information and Rural Credit Markets – Puzzles and Policy Perspectives', *World Bank Economic Review* 4: 235–50.

Holst, J.U. (1985) 'The Role of Informal Financial Institutions in the Mobilisation of Savings', in Kessler and Ullmo.

Honohan, Patrick (1990a) 'Price and Monetary Convergence in Currency Unions: The Franc and Rand Zones', *PRE Working Paper No. 390*, Washington DC: World Bank.

—— (1990b) 'Monetary Cooperation in the CFA Zone', *PRE Working Paper No. 389*, Washington DC: World Bank.

REFERENCES

Hulme, D. (1990) 'Can the Grameen Bank Be Replicated? Recent experiments in Malaysia, Malawi and Sri Lanka', *Development Policy Review* 8,3: 287–300.
IFAD (1985) *The Role of Rural Credit Projects in Reaching the Poor*, Oxford: Tycooly Publishing for the International Fund for Agricultural Development.
ILO (1972) *Employment, Incomes and Equality: A Strategy for Increasing Productive Employment in Kenya*, Geneva: ILO.
—— (1988) *World Employment Review*, Geneva: ILO.
IMF (1981) *Financial Policy Workshops: the Case of Kenya*, Washington DC: International Monetary Fund.
—— (1986) *Fund-Supported Programs, Fiscal Policy, and Income Distribution*, Occasional Paper No. 46, September, Washington DC: International Monetary Fund.
—— (various years) *International Financial Statistics*, Washington DC: International Monetary Fund.
Jallow, B. (1988) 'Women and Cooperatives in the Gambia', in Mayoux.
Jayamaha, R. (1986) 'Changes in Monetary Policy', in W. Rasaputra *et al.* (eds) *Facets of Development in Independent Sri Lanka*, Colombo: Ministry of Finance and Planning.
Johnny, M. (1985) *Informal Credit for Integrated Rural Development in Sierra Leone*, Hamburg: Verlag Weltarchiv.
Johnson, O.E.G. (1974) 'Credit Controls as Instruments of Development Policy in the Light of Economic Theory', *Journal of Money, Credit and Banking* 6, 1: 85–99.
—— (1975) 'Direct Credit Controls in a Development Context: The Case of African Countries', in K. Brunner *et al.* (eds) *Government Credit Allocation Where Do We Go From Here?*, San Francisco: Institute for Contemporary Studies.
Jones, J.H.M. (1990) 'Rajasthan, India: RPOs in Development Finance', *University of Reading Bulletin 30*: 28–33.
—— (1991) 'Jain Shopkeepers and Moneylenders: Rural Informal Credit Networks in South Rajasthan', in Carrithers and Humphrey.
Kamara, J.M. (1988) 'Women and Cooperatives in Sierra Leone', in Mayoux.
Kamas, L. (1986) 'Dutch Disease Economics and the Colombian Export Boom', *World Development* 14, 9: 1177–98.
Kamath, S.J. (1985a) 'An Investigation of the Demand for and Supply of Money in India, 1951–76', *Weltwirtschaftliches Archiv* 121, 3.
—— (1985b) 'Monetary Aggregates, Income and Causality in a Developing Economy', *Journal of Economic Studies* 12, 2: 36–53.
Kapur, V. (1976) 'Alternative Stabilisation Policies for Less Developed Economies', *Journal of Political Economy* 84: 777–95.
Karunaratne, N.D. (1988) 'Monetarist Perspectives of Papua New Guinea's Hard Currency Strategy', *World Development* 16, 7: 807–20.
Keller, P.M. (1977) 'Controlling Fluctuations in Credit', *IMF Staff Papers* 24, 1.
—— (1980) 'Implications of Credit Policies for Output and the Balance of Payments', *IMF Staff Papers* 27, 3: 464.
Kenen, P.B. (1961) 'The Theory of Optimum Currency Areas: An Eclectic View', in R.A. Mundell and A.K. Swoboda (eds) *Monetary Problems of The International Economy*, Chicago, IL: Chicago University Press.
Kenya, Republic of (1985) *Economic Survey, 1985*, Nairobi: Central Bureau of Statistics, Ministry of Finance and Planning.
Kessler, D. and Ullmo, P.-A. (eds) (1985) *Savings and Development*, Paris: Economica.
Khan, A.H. (1982) 'Adjustment Mechanism and the Money Demand Function in Pakistan', *Pakistan Economic and Social Review* 20, 1: 1–19.
Khan, M.S. (1986) 'Islamic Interest–Free Banking', *IMF Staff Papers* 33, 1.
Khan, M.S. and Knight, M.D. (1980) 'Some Theoretical and Empirical Issues

Relating to Economic Stabilization in Developing Countries', *World Development* 10, 9.

—— (1981) 'Stabilization Programs in Developing Countries: a Formal Framework', *IMF Staff Papers* 28: 1–53.

—— (1983) 'Determinants of Current Account Balance of Non–Oil Developing Countries in the 1970s: An Empirical Analysis', *IMF Staff Papers* 30, 4: 819–42.

—— (1985) *Fund-supported Adjustment Programs and Economic Growth*, IMF Occasional Paper No. 41, November, Washington DC.

Khan, M.S. and Malcolm, D.K. (1981) 'Stabilisation Programs in Developing Countries: A Formal Framework', *IMF Staff Papers* 28: 1–53.

Khatkhate, D.R. (1988) 'Assessing The Impact of Interest Rates in Less Developed Countries', *World Development* 16, 5: 577–88.

Khatkhate, D.R. and Short, B.K. (1980) 'Monetary and Banking Problems of Mini States', *World Development* 8: 1017–25.

Khatkhate, D.R., Galbis, V.G. and Villanueva, D.P. (1974) 'A Money Multiplier Model for a Developing Economy: The Venezuelan Case', *IMF Staff Papers* 21, 3: 740–47.

Killick, T. (1984) 'The Impact of Fund Stabilisation Programmes', in T. Killick (ed.) *The Quest for Economic Stabilisation: the IMF and the Third World*, Aldershot: Gower.

Kmenta, J. (1986) *Elements of Econometrics*, 2nd edn, New York: Macmillan Publishing Company.

Kydland, F. and Prescott, E.C. (1977) 'Rules Rather Than Discretion: The Inconsistency of Optimal Plans', *Journal of Political Economics* 85, 3: 473–91.

Laidler, D. (1977) *The Demand for Money: Theories and Evidence*, New York: Dun-Donnelley.

Laidler, D. (1989) 'The Quantity Theory is Always and Everywhere Controversial – Why?', July, unpublished.

Lal, D. (1984) *The Real Effects of Stabilisation and Structural Adjustment Policies: An Extension of the Australian Adjustment Model*, World Bank Staff Working Paper No. 636, Washington DC.

Lane, C.E. and Page, S. (1991) *Differences in Economic Performance between Franc Zone and other Sub-Saharan African Countries*, ODI Working Paper No. 43, London: Overseas Development Institute.

Laumas, P.S. and Williams, M. (1983) 'An Analysis of the Demand for Cash Balances by the Manufacturing Firms in a Developing Economy', *Journal of Development Economics* 12, 1–2: 169–82.

Lee, S.Y. and Jao, Y.C. (1982) *Financial Structures and Monetary Policies in Southeast Asia*, London: Macmillan.

Leite, S.P. (1982) 'Interest Rate Policies in West Africa', *IMF Staff Papers* 29, 1: 48–76.

Levitsky, J. (1986a) *World Bank Lending to Small Enterprises: A Review*, Washington DC: The World Bank.

—— (1986b) 'World Bank Lending for Small Enterprises', in Harper and de Jong.

—— (ed.) (1989) *Microenterprises in Developing Countries*, London: Intermediate Technology Publications.

Levitsky, J. and Prasad, R.N. (1987) *Credit Guarantee Schemes for Small and Medium Enterprises*, Washington DC: World Bank.

Liederman, L. (1984) 'On the Monetary–Macro Dynamics of Colombia and Mexico', *Journal of Development Economics* 14, 1–2: 183–202.

Lipschitz, L. (1984) 'Domestic Credit and Exchange Rates in Developing Countries: Some Policy Experiments with Korean Data', *IMF Staff Papers* 31: 595–635.

Loxley, J. (1971) 'The Behaviour of the Tanzanian Money Supply 1966–70 and the

Use of Monetary Indicators', in K.S. Lim *et al.* (eds) *Papers on the Political Economy of Tanzania*, London: Heinemann.

Lucas, R.E. (1973) 'Some International Evidence on Output–Inflation Tradeoffs', *American Economic Review* 63: 326–34.

Lynn, R. and McCarthy, F.D. (1989) 'Recent Economic Performance of Developing Countries', *PPR Working Paper No. 228*, July, Washington DC: World Bank.

McKinnon, R.I. (1973) *Money and Capital in Economic Development*, Washington DC: The Brookings Institution.

McLenaghan, J.B., Nsouli, S.M. and Riechel, K.-W. (1982) *Currency Convertibility in the Economic Community of West African States*, IMF Occasional Paper No. 13, Washington DC.

Malinvaud, E. (1977) *The Theory of Unemployment Reconsidered*, Oxford: Basil Blackwell.

Marglin, S. (1963) 'The Social Rate of Discount and the Optimal Rate of Investment', *Quarterly Journal of Economics* 77.

Marquez, S.J. (1963) 'Financial Institutions and Economic Development', in H. Ellis and H.C. Wallich (eds) *Economic Development for Latin America*, London: Macmillan.

Mathieson, D.J. (1980) 'Financial Reform and Stabilization Policy in a Developing Country', *Journal of Development Economics* 7: 359–95.

—— (1982) 'Inflation, Interest Rates and the Balance of Payments During a Financial Reform: The Case of Argentina', *World Development* 10: 813–28.

—— (1983) 'Estimating Models of Financial Market Behaviour During Periods of Extensive Structural Reform: The Experience of Chile', *IMF Staff Papers* 30, 2: 350–93.

—— (1988) *Exchange Rate Arrangements and Monetary Policy*, IMF Working Paper No. 14, Washington DC.

Maynard, G. (1970) 'The Economic Irrelevance of Monetary Independence: The Case of Liberia', *Journal of Development Studies* 6: 111–32.

Mayoux, L. (ed.) (1988) *All Are Not Equal: African Women in Cooperatives*, London: Institute for African Alternatives.

Mayoux, L. *et al.* (1989) *African Women in Cooperatives: Towards a Realistic Agenda*, London: Institute for African Alternatives.

Mazumdar, D. (1983) 'Segmented Labour Markets in LDCs', *American Economic Review* 73: 254–9.

Miller, M. and Orr, D. (1966) 'A Model of the Demand for Money by Firms', *Quarterly Journal of Economics* 80: 414–35.

Minford, P. (1986) 'Monetary Policy in the Light of Rational Expectations', Centre for Economic Policy Research *Bulletin* 14, London.

Mitchell, I.S. and Still, R. (1980) 'Correlates of Consumer Banking Behaviour in the Socialist Cooperative Republic of Guyana', *Social and Economic Studies* 29, 2–3.

Moepi, E. (1988) 'Women in Cooperatives: the case of Botswana', in Mayoux.

Montiel, P.J. (1986) *Domestic Credit and Output Determination in a "New Classical" Model of a Small Open Economy with Perfect Capital Mobility*, Development Research Division Discussion Paper No. 181, Washington DC: World Bank, September.

—— (1987) 'Output and Unanticipated Money in the Dependent Economy Model', *IMF Staff Papers* 34, 3: 228–60.

Moore, B.J. and Threadgold, A.R. (1980) *Bank Lending and the Money Supply*, Bank of England Discussion Paper No. 10, London.

Morris, F. (1985) *India's Financial System: An Overview of its Principal Structural Features*, World Bank Staff Working Paper No. 739, Washington DC.

Moser, C.O.N. (1978) 'Informal Sector or Petty Commodity Production: Dualism or Dependence in Urban Development', *World Development* 6: 1041–64.

—— (1984) 'The Informal Sector Reworked: Viability and Vulnerability in Urban

Development', *Regional Development Dialogue* 5: 135–78.

Mukherjee, N. (1984) 'Annotated Bibliography on Banking and Finance', *International Journal of Development Banking* 2, 1: 33–8.

Mundell, R.A. (1961) 'A Theory of Optimum Currency Areas', *American Economic Review* 51: 657–65.

Myrdal G. (1968) *Asian Drama: An Enquiry into the Poverty of Nations*, Harmondsworth: Penguin.

Neary, P.J. (1980) 'Non-Traded Goods and the Balance of Trade in a Neo-Keynesian Temporary Equilibrium', *Quarterly Journal of Economics* XCV.

Nevaskar, B. (1971) *Capitalists Without Capital: The Jains of India and the Quakers of the West*, Westport, CT: Greenwood Publishing Co.

Newbery, D. and Stern, N.H. (eds) (1987) *Modern Tax Theory for Developing Countries*, New York: Oxford University Press for the World Bank.

Newlyn, W.T. and Rowan, D.C. (1954) *Money and Banking in British Colonial Africa: A Study of the Monetary and Banking Systems of Eight British African Territories*, Oxford: Clarendon Press.

Ng, B.K. (1985) *Some Aspects of the Informal Financial Sector in the SEACEN Countries*, South-East Asian Central Banks (SEACEN), *Staff Paper No. 10*, Kuala Lumpar.

Nsouli, S.M. (1981) 'Monetary Integration in Developing Countries', *Finance and Development* 18: 41–4.

Nugent, B. and Glezakos, C. (1982) 'Phillips Curves in Developing Countries: The Latin American Case', *Economic Development and Cultural Change* 30, 2: 321–34.

Nwankwo, G.O. (1981) 'Techniques of Monetary Control: The Nigerian Experience', *Savings and Development* 2–3: 115–22.

Nwinia, C.S. (1986) 'The Statutory Liquidity Requirements and the Nigerian Merchant Banking System', *Savings and Development* 10, 2: 197–206.

Okogu, B.E. (1986) 'Central Bank of Nigeria Credit Guidelines: a Response Model of Commercial Banks', *Oxford Agrarian Studies* 15: 28–50.

Onimode, B. (ed.) (1989) *The IMF, the World Bank and African Debt*, Vol. 2, *The Social and Political Impact*, London: The Institute for African Alternatives and Zed Books.

Padmanabhan, K.P. (1988) *Rural Credit: Lessons for Rural Bankers and Policy Makers*, London: Intermediate Technology Publications.

Parikh, A., Booth, A. and Sundrum, R.M. (1985) 'An Econometric Model of the Monetary Sector in Indonesia', *Journal of Development Studies* 21, 3.

Patel, I.G. (1954) 'Selective Credit Controls in Underdeveloped Economies', *IMF Staff Papers* 4, 1.

Patinkin, D. (1981) 'Some Observations on the Inflationary Process', in J. Flanders and A. Razin (eds) *Development in an Inflationary World*, New York: Academic Press.

Patten, R.S. and Rosengard, J.K. (1990) *Progress with Profits: the Development of Rural Banking in Indonesia*, Cambridge, MA: Harvard Institute for International Development, April.

Pindyck, R.S. and Rubinfeld, D.L. (1976) *Econometric Models and Economic Forecasts*, New York: McGraw Hill.

Polak, J.J. (1957) 'Monetary Analysis of Income Formation and Payments Problems', *IMF Staff Papers* 16: 1–50.

Poole, W. (1976) 'A Proposal for Reforming Bank Reserve Requirements in the United States', *Journal of Money, Credit and Banking* 8, 2.

Porter, R.C. (1965) 'Narrow Security Markets and Monetary Policy: Lessons from Pakistan', *Economic Development and Cultural Change* 14: 48–60.

Portes, R.D. (1983) 'Central Planning and Monetarism: Fellow Travellers?', in P. Desai (ed.) *Marxism, Central Planning and the Soviet Economy*, Cambridge, MA: MIT Press.

Portes, R.D. and Winter, D. (1980) 'Disequilibrium Estimates for Consumption Goods Markets in CPEs', *Review of Economic Studies* 47: 137–59.

Quirk, P.J., Christensen, B.V., Huh, K. and Sasaki, T. (1987) *Floating Exchange Rates in Developing Countries: Experience With Auction and Interbank Markets*, IMF Occasional Paper No. 53, Washington DC.

Ramirez-Rojas, C.L. (1986) 'Monetary Substitution in Developing Countries', *Finance and Development*, June: 35–8.

Ray, J.K. (1987) *To Chase a Miracle: A Study of the Grameen Bank of Bangladesh*, Dhaka: University Press.

Remenyi, J. (1991) *Credit Where Credit is Due: Income-generating Programmes for the Poor in Developing Countries*, London: Intermediate Technology Publications.

Rhomberg, R.R. and Heller, H.R. (eds) (1977) *The Monetary Approach to the Balance of Payments*, Washington DC: International Monetary Fund.

Roberts, John (1989) 'Liberalising Foreign-Exchange Rates in Sub-Saharan Africa', *Development Policy Review* 7, 2: 115–43.

Rogers, B. (1989) *The Domestication of Women: Discrimination in Developing Countries*, London: Routledge.

de Rosa, D.A. (1986) 'Islamic Financial Policies and Domestic Resource Mobilization', *Savings and Development* 2: 143–54.

Rudcenko, St. (1979) 'Household Money Income, Expenditure and Monetary Assets in Czechoslovakia, GDR, Hungary and Poland, 1956–75', in *Jahrbuch der Wirtschaft Osteuropas*, Vol. 8, Munich: Gunter Olzog Verlag.

Salter, W.E.G. (1959) 'Internal and External Balance: the Role of Price and Expenditure Effects', *Economic Record* August.

Sargent, T.J. (1981) *The Ends of Four Big Inflations, NBER Working Paper*, Cambridge, MA.

Sargent, T.J. and Wallace, N. (1975) 'Rational Expectations, the Optimal Monetary Instrument, and the Optimal Money Supply Rule', *Journal of Political Economy* 83: 241–54.

Sayers, R.S. (1957) *Central Banking After Bagehot*, Oxford: Clarendon Press.

Seibel, H.D. (1989) 'Linking Informal and Formal Financial Institutions in Africa and Asia', in Levitsky.

Seibel, H.D. and Parhusip, U. (1990) 'Financial Innovations for Microenterprises – Linking Formal and Informal Financial Institutions', *Small Enterprise Development* 1: 14–26.

Seibel, H.D. and Shrestha, B.P. (1988) 'Dhikuti: the Small Businessman's Informal Self-help Bank in Nepal', *Savings and Development* 12, 2: 183–98.

Sethuraman, S.V. (1981) *The Urban Informal Sector in Developing Countries, Employment, Poverty and Environment*, Geneva: ILO.

—— (1988) 'The Informal Sector: a Review of Evidence from Selected Asian Countries', unpublished ms, September.

Shaw, E. (1973) *Financial Deepening in Economic Development*, Oxford: Oxford University Press.

Sheehey, E.J. (1980) 'Money, Income and Prices in Latin America: An Empirical Note', *Journal of Development Economics* 7: 345–57.

—— (1984) 'Money and Output in Latin America: Some Tests of a Rational Expectations Approach', *Journal of Development Economics* 14, 1–2: 203–18.

Siddiqui, K. (1984) *An Evaluation of the Grameen Bank Operation*, Dhaka: Grameen Bank.

Sims, C.A. (1972) 'Money, Income and Causality', *American Economic Review* 62: 540–52.

Singh, J. (1989) *Banks, Gods and Government: Institutional and Informal Credit Structure in a*

Remote and Tribal Indian District, Wiesbaden: Steiner Verlag.

Singh, R. (1982) 'An Appraisal of the Impact of Recent Changes in Interest Rates in Guyana', *Social and Economic Studies* 31, 4.

Skully, M.T. (ed.) (1984) *Financial Institutions and Markets in South East Asia*, London: Macmillan.

Spanos, A. (1986) *Statistical Foundations of Econometric Modelling*, Cambridge: Cambridge University Press.

Stiglitz, J.E. (1990) 'Peer Monitoring and Credit Markets', *World Bank Economic Review* 4; 351–66.

Sugihara, K. (ed.) (forthcoming) *Local Supplies of Credit in the Third World, 1750–1945*.

Sundararajan, V. (1985) 'Debt-Equity Ratios of Firms and Interest Rate Policy: Macroeconomics Effects of High Leverage in Developing Countries', *IMF Staff Papers* 32, 3: 430–74.

Sunkel, O. (1960) 'Inflation in Chile: An Unorthodox Approach', *International Economic Papers*, No. 10.

Swoboda, A.K. (1973) 'Monetary Policy Under Fixed Exchange Rates: Effectiveness, The Speed of Adjustment and Proper Use', *Economica* 40: 136–54.

Taslim, M.A. (1984) 'On Rate of Interest and the Demand for Money in LDCs: The Case of Bangladesh' *Bangladesh Development Studies*, 12, 3.

Taylor, L. (1983) *Structuralist Macroeconomics*, New York: Basic Books.

Tegene, A. (1989), 'The Monetarist Explanation of Inflation: the experience of six African countries', *Journal of Economic Studies* 16, 1.

Thirlwall, A.P. (1974) *Inflation, Saving and Growth in Developing Economies*, London: Macmillan.

Thomas, J.J. (1990a) 'Credit programmes for the informal sector', *Appropriate Technology* 16: 20–24.

—— (1990b) 'Exporting the Grameen Bank to the Urban Informal Sector in Latin America', unpublished manuscript.

—— (1991) 'The Regressive Effect of "Double Dualism" on the Financial Analysis of Developing Countries: Whatever Happened to the Urban Informal Sector?', unpublished manuscript.

Timberg, T.A. and Aiyar, C.V. (1984) 'Informal credit markets in India', *Economic Development and Cultural Change* 33, 1: 43–59.

Tshibaka, T.B. (1986) *The Effects of Trade and Exchange Rate Policies on Agriculture in Zaire*, International Food Policy Research Institute, Research Report No. 56, November, Washington DC.

Turnham, D., Salome, B. and Schwarz, A. (eds) (1990) *The Informal Sector Revisited*, Paris: OECD Development Centre.

Vaez-Zadeh, R. and Leite, S.P. (1986) 'Effectiveness of Selective Credit Controls: An Empirical Test Applied to India', *Journal of Development Studies* 22, 3: 558–72.

Vélez-Ibañez, C.G. (1983) *Bonds of Mutual Trust: the Cultural Systems of Rotating Credit Associations among Urban Mexicans and Chicanos*, New Brunswick, NJ: Rutgers University Press.

Villanueva, D.P. and Arya, N.S. (1972) 'Time Deposits in the Definition of Money: Further Cross Country Inflation Evidence', *Economic Record*, September.

Virmani, A. (1985) *Government Policy and the Development of Financial Markets: The Case of Korea*, World Bank Staff Working Paper No. 747, Washington DC.

Vogel, R.C. and Burkett, P. (1986a) 'Deposit Mobilization in Developing Countries: the Importance of Reciprocity in Lending', *Journal of Developing Areas* 20: 425–37.

—— (1986b) *Mobilizing Small-Scale Savings: Approaches, Costs, and Benefits*, Washington DC: World Bank.

Von Pischke, J.D., Adams, D.W. and Donald, G. (eds) (1983) *Rural Financial Markets in Developing Countries: Their Uses and Abuses*, Baltimore, MD: Johns Hopkins University Press.

Wahid, A.N. (1986) 'Expansion and Organization of Monetary Sector: The Case of Bangladesh', *Scandinavian Journal of Development Alternatives* 5, 4: 126–44.

Wai, U.T. (1957) 'Interest Rates Outside the Organized Money Markets in Under-developed Countries', *IMF Staff Papers* 6, 1.

—— (1977) 'A Revisit to Interest Rates Outside the Organised Money Markets of Underdeveloped Countries', *Banca Nazionale Del Lavoro Quarterly Review*, No. 122, September.

Wai, U.T. and Patrick, H.T. (1973) 'Stock and Bond Issues and Capital Markets in Less Developed Countries', *IMF Staff Papers* 20, 2: 253–317.

Whelan, T.S. (1979) *The Pawnshop in China*, Ann Arbor, MI: University of Michigan Center for Chinese Studies.

van Wijnbergen, S. (1982) 'Stagflationary Effects of Monetary Stabilization Policies: Quantitative Analysis of South Korea', *Journal of Development Economics* 10: 133–69.

—— (1983a) 'Credit Policy, Inflation and Growth in A Financially Repressed Economy', *Journal of Development Economics* 13, 1–2: 45–66.

—— (1983b) 'Interest Rate Management in LDCs', *Journal of Monetary Economics* 12: 433–52.

Wilford, D.S. (1977) *Monetary Policy in an Open Economy: Mexico's Experience*, New York: Praeger.

Wong, C. (1977) 'Demand for Money in Developing Countries: Some Theoretical and Empirical Results', *Journal of Monetary Economics* 3: 59–86.

Wood, Adrian (1988) *Global Trends in Real Exchange Rates 1960–84*, World Bank Discussion Papers No. 35, Washington DC.

World Bank (1987) *World Development Report*, Washington DC: World Bank.

—— (1989a) *Peru: Policies to Stop Hyperinflation and Initiate Economic Recovery*, Washington DC: World Bank.

—— (1989b) *World Development Report, Financial Systems and Development*, Washington DC: World Bank.

—— (1989c) *Sub-Saharan Africa: from Crisis to Sustainable Growth*, Washington DC: World Bank.

—— (1989d) *Adjustment Lending: An Evaluation of Ten Years of Experience*, Washington DC: World Bank.

—— (1990a) *World Development Report, Poverty*, Washington DC: World Bank.

—— (1990b) *World Tables 1989/90*, Washington DC: World Bank.

—— (1991) *World Debt Tables 1990–91*, Washington DC: World Bank.

Worrell, D. (1985) 'Preliminary Estimates of the Demand for Money Function: Jamaica 1962–79', *Social and Economic Studies* 34, 3: 265–82.

Zimbabwe Reserve Bank (1986) *Quarterly Economic and Statistical Review: December 1986*, Harare: 7, 4.

Yunus, M. (1988) *Credit for Self Employment of the Poor*, Dhaka: Dhaka Grameen Bank.

—— (1989) 'Grameen Bank: Organisation and Operation', in Levitsky.

—— (ed.) (1987) *Jorimon and Others: Faces of Poverty*, Dhaka: Dhaka University Press.

COUNTRY STUDY REFERENCES

The results of the country studies for Kenya, Ghana, Côte d'Ivoire, Indonesia, and China, and the study of the informal sector were originally published as ODI working papers.

Killick, T. and Mwega, F.M. (1990) *Monetary Policy in Kenya, 1967–88*, ODI Working

Paper No. 39, London: Overseas Development Institute.

Sowa, N.K. (1991) *Monetary Control in Ghana: 1957–88*, ODI Working Paper No. 45, London: Overseas Development Institute.

Lane, C.E. (1989) *Monetary Policy Effectiveness in Côte d'Ivoire*, ODI Working Paper No. 30, London: Overseas Development Institute.

Lane, C.E., Cole, D.C., Slade, B.F. (1991) *Monetary Policy Effectiveness in Indonesia, 1974–90*, ODI Working Paper No. 44, London: Overseas Development Institute.

Santorum, A. (1989) *The Control of Money Supply in Developing Countries: China, 1949–88*, ODI Working Paper No. 29, London: Overseas Development Institute.

Thomas, J.J. (1992) *The Informal Financial Sector: How does it operate and who are the customers?*, ODI Working Paper No. 61, London: Overseas Development Institute.

Kenya

Bevan, D.L., Collier, P. and Gunning, J.W. (1989) 'Fiscal Response to a Temporary Trade Shock: the aftermath of the Kenyan coffee boom', Oxford: Institute of Economics and Statistics, July, mimeo.

—— (forthcoming), *Trade Shocks in Controlled Economies: Theory and an Application to the East Africa Coffee Boom*, Oxford: Oxford University Press.

Brough, T. and Curtin, T.R.C. (1981), 'Growth and Stability: an account of fiscal and monetary policy', in T. Killick (ed.) *Papers on the Kenyan Economy: Performance, Problems and Policies*, Nairobi and London: Heinemann Educational Books.

Grubel, H.G. and Ryan, T.C.I. (1979) 'A Monetary Model of Kenya's Balance of Payments', University of Nairobi, mimeo.

Kanga, M.J.P. (1985) 'Reserve Ratios as Monetary Policy Instruments in Kenya', MA Research Paper, University of Nairobi, June.

Kenya Central Bank (CBK) (1981) *Sources and Uses of Foreign Exchange in Kenya, 1974–79*, Nairobi: CBK.

—— (1986), *Central Bank of Kenya: Its Evolution, Responsibilities and Organization*, Nairobi: CBK, September.

—— (1989) *Economic Report for FY 1987/88*, Nairobi: CBK.

Kenya, Republic of (1986) *Sessional Paper No. 1 of 1986: Economic Management for Renewed Growth*, Nairobi.

Killick, T. (ed.) (1981) *Papers on the Kenyan Economy: Performance, Problems and Policies*, Nairobi and London: Heinemann Educational Books.

—— (1984) 'Kenya, 1975–81', in T. Killick (ed.) *The IMF and Stabilisation: Developing Country Experiences*, Aldershot: Gower.

—— (1985) 'The Influence of Balance of Payments Management on Employment and Basic Needs in Kenya', *Eastern Africa Economic Review* 1, 1.

King, J.R. (1979) *Stabilization Policy in an African Setting: Kenya, 1963–73*, London: Heinemann Educational Books.

Kiptui, M.C. (1989) 'Fiscal Lags, Deficit Financing and Inflation in Kenya, 1967–86', MA Research Paper, University of Nairobi.

Koori, C.G. (1984) 'The Existence and Nature of the Crowding-out Effect in Kenya', MA Research Paper, University of Nairobi.

Maitha, J.K., Killick, T. and Ikiara, G.K. (1978) *The Balance of Payments Adjustment Process in Developing Countries: Kenya*, Nairobi: University of Nairobi.

Mwega, F.M. (1990) *An Econometric Study of Selected Monetary Policy Issues in Kenya*, ODI Working Paper No. 42, London: Overseas Development Institute.

Mwega, F.M. and Ngola, S.M. (1988) 'Causal Directions in the Relationship Between Domestic Credit and Changes in Net Foreign Reserves in Kenya', *Savings and Development* 12, 3.

Mwega, F.M., Ngola, S.M. and Mwangi, N. (1989) 'Real Interest Rates and the Mobilisation of Private Savings in Africa: a case study of Kenya', Nairobi: University of Nairobi, mimeo.
Ndele, S.M. (1990) 'Effects of Non-bank Financial Intermediaries on the Conduct of Monetary Policy in Kenya', Nairobi: University of Nairobi, mimeo.
Nganda, B.M. (1985) 'An Economic Analysis of Monetary Relationships in Kenya, 1968–83', MA Research Paper, Nairobi: University of Nairobi.

Ghana

Atiemo, J.B. (1989) 'Cocobod's Operations: Operational Issues Relating to Purchasing, Haulage and Processing of Cocoa', Paper read at National Seminar on the Cocoa Industry, Accra.
Bank of Ghana, *Annual Report of the Board for the Financial Year ended 30th June 1972*, Accra.
Frimpong-Ansah, J.H. (1971) 'The Ghanaian Banking System and The Challenges of our Time', *Bank of Ghana Quarterly Economic Bulletin* 11, 1.
—— (1989) 'An Economic Analysis of the Cocoa Industry', Paper presented at University of Warwick Workshop, 5 February.
Gockel, F.A. (1983) 'Monetary Control: Theory and Evidence, The Case in Ghana', unpublished M.Sc. Thesis. Legon: University of Ghana.
de Graft-Johnson, J.C. (1967) 'Some Historical Observations on Money and the West African Currency Board', *The Economic Bulletin of Ghana* XI, 2.
Steel, W.F. (1973) 'Social and Economic Statistics of Ghana', Legon: University of Ghana (unpublished).

Côte d'Ivoire

Allechi, M'Bet (1987) 'Estimation d'une fonction de demande de monnaie dans un pays de l'union monétaire ouest-africaine: Le cas de la Côte d'Ivoire', Abidjan: CIRES, mimeo.
—— (1988) 'Savings Determinants and Savings Mobilisation in Sub-Saharan Africa: The Case of Côte d'Ivoire', Abidjan: CIRES, mimeo.
Allechi, M'Bet and Koulibaly, M. (1989) 'European Economic Integration and the Franc Zone: What is the future of the CFA Franc beyond 1992?', Research proposal, mimeo.
BCEAO (1973a) 'Traité Constituant l'Union Monétaire Ouest Africaine', Abidjan.
—— (1973b) 'Accord de Coopération entre la République Française et les Républiques Membres de l'Union Monétaire Ouest Africaine'.
—— (1973c) 'Convention de Compte d'Opérations'.
—— (1973d) 'Statuts de la Banque Ouest Africaine de Développement'.
—— (1973e) 'Statuts de la Banque Centrale des Etats de l'Afrique de l'Ouest'.
—— (1976a) 'La Nouvelle Politique de la Monnaie et du Credit de la Banque Centrale des Etats de l'Afrique de l'Ouest', *Banques et Monnaies* No. 236.
—— (1976b) 'La Distribution Qualitative du Credit et les Nouvelles Règles d'Intervention de la Banque Centrale', *Banques et Monnaies* No. 237.
—— (1987) 'Politique Monétaire de la BCEAO et Incidences sur les Agents Economiques depuis la Crise de 1974', *Banques et Monnaies* No. 366.
—— (1988) 'Activity Report 1986/87', Lomé: West African Development Bank.
Bhatia, R.J. (1985) *The West African Monetary Union: An Analytical Review*, IMF Occasional Paper No. 35, Washington DC.
Bourse des Valeurs (1988) 'Rapport d'Activité 1986', Abidjan.

REFERENCES

Bulletin de l'Afrique Noire (1988) 'Résultats des 50 Premières Entreprises Ivoiriennes', No. 1420, 8 September, Paris.

Duruflé, G. (1989) 'Structural Disequilibria and Adjustment Policies in The Ivory Coast', in B. Campbell and J. Loxley (eds) *Structural Adjustment in Africa*, London: Macmillan.

Fichier des Banques et des Etablissements Financiers, Côte d'Ivoire (1988) Ediafrica, Paris: IC Publications.

Franc Zone, (various issues) 'La Zone Franc, Rapport', Paris.

Guillaumont, P. *et al.* (1988) 'Participating in African Monetary Unions: An Alternative Evaluation', *World Development* 16, 5: 569–76.

Kouamé, P. (1988) *Intégration Monétaire en Afrique de l'Ouest*, Abidjan: Nouvelles Editions Africaines.

Krumm, K.L. (1987) *Adjustment in the Franc Zone: Focus on the Real Exchange Rate*, Washington DC: World Bank Trade and Adjustment Division.

Medora, R. (1987a) 'The Gains From Pooling Reserves in the West African Monetary Union', Toronto: University of Toronto, mimeo.

—— (1987b) 'Real Exchange Rates and Monetary Policy in WAMU', Toronto: University of Toronto, mimeo.

Ministère de l'Economie et des Finances (1988a) *Projet de Loi de Finances pour la Gestion 1989: Rapport Economique et Financier*, Abidjan.

—— (1988b) *Etudes et Conjuncture*, various issues.

de Mowbray, P. (1989) 'Structural Adjustment and the Franc Zone', London: School of Oriental and African Studies, University of London, mimeo.

Ouattara, A.D. (1987) 'Union Monétaire et Intégration Economique: Experiences et Leçons à Tirer', BCEAO symposium, Dakar, Senegal, 20 October.

Riddell, R.C. (1990) 'Côte d'Ivoire', in R.C. Riddell (ed.) *Manufacturing Africa*, London: James Currey for the Overseas Development Institute.

Schiller, C. (1988) *The Fiscal Role of Price Stabilization Funds: The Case of Côte d'Ivoire*, IMF Working Paper WP/88/26, Washington DC.

Thill, J., and Pelletier, M. (1989) *Développement du Secteur Privé en Afrique*, Paris: Ministry of Cooperation and Development.

Touré, A. (1985) *Les Petits Métiers à Abidjan: L'Imagination au Secours de la Conjuncture*, Paris: Karthala.

den Tuinder, B.A. (1978) *Ivory Coast, The Challenge of Success*, Washington DC: World Bank.

World Bank (1988) *Côte d'Ivoire: Mobilising Domestic Resources For Stable Growth*, Washington DC: World Bank.

Indonesia

Ahmed, S. and Kapur, B. (1990) *How Indonesia's Monetary Policy Affects Key Variables*, World Bank Working Paper Series No. 349, February, Washington DC: World Bank.

Asian Development Bank (1987) 'Improving Domestic Resource Mobilisation Through Financial Development – Indonesia', *Asian Development Bank Staff Paper No. 40*, Manila: Asian Development Bank.

Boediono (1985) 'Demand For Money In Indonesia 1975–84', *Bulletin of Indonesian Economic Studies* XXI.

Binhadi, and Meek, P. (1988) 'Implementing Monetary Policy In Indonesia', Chapter 4 of *Visiting Specialist Papers*, 17th Seanza Central Banking Course, Sydney, Australia, October/November.

Cole, D.C. and Slade, B.F. (1990a) *Financial Development in Indonesia*, Harvard Institute

for International Development, Development Discussion Paper 336.
——— (1990b) 'Development of Money Markets in Indonesia', Cambridge, MA: Harvard Institute for International Development, Program on International Financial Systems.
Indonesia Bank (1989) 'Controlling the Money Stock through the money market', Monetary Division Discussion Paper, mimeo, unpublished.
——— *Annual Report*, various issues.
——— *Monthly Report*, various issues.
——— *Weekly Report*, various issues.
Indonesia Central Bureau of Statistics, *Indonesian Statistics*, various issues.
——— *Economic Indicators*, various issues.
Odano, S. and Soekarno, (1988) 'Demand for Monetary Assets in Indonesia, 1976–86', Paper submitted to EAEA conference, Tokyo.
Patten, R.S. and Snodgrass, D.R. (1987) *Monitoring and Evaluating KUPEDES (General Rural Credit) In Indonesia*, Harvard Institute for International Development, Discussion Paper 249.
Sundararjan, V. and Lazaros, M. (1987) 'Financial Reform and Monetary Control in Indonesia' Paper presented at a conference sponsored by the Federal Reserve Bank of San Francisco, September.
Woo, W.T. and Nasution, A. (1989) 'Indonesian Economic Policies and Their Relation to External Debt Management', in J.D. Sachs and S. Collins *Developing Country Debt and Economic Performance* 3, Cambridge, MA: National Bureau of Economic Research.

Bangladesh

Ahmed, S. (1984) 'Inflation in Bangladesh: Causes and Consequences', Ph.D. Dissertation, Boston University, USA.
Hoque, A. (1986) 'Plan Objectives and Economic Policies in Bangladesh: 1972–84', *Economic Bulletin for Asia and the Pacific* 37, 1: 67–77.
Hossain, M.A. (1988) 'Macroeconomic Problems and Policies in Bangladesh 1972–85', *Economics Discussion Paper, 18/88*, La Trobe University, Victoria, Australia.
Huda, M.N. (1986) 'Objectives and Instruments of Monetary Policy in Bangladesh', *Journal of the Institute of Bankers, Bangladesh* 24: 1–10.
Islam, N. (1977) *Development Planning in Bangladesh: A Study in Political Economy*, London: Hurst and Company.
Islam, R. (1980), 'Foodgrain Procurement, Input Subsidy and the Public Food Distribution System in Bangladesh: An Analysis of the Policy Package', *Bangladesh Development Studies* 8, 1 and 2: 89–120.
Kirkpatrick, C.H. and Nixson, F. (1976) 'The Origins of Inflation in Ten Developing Countries: A Selective Review', in M. Parkin and C. Zis (eds) *Inflation in Open Economies*, Manchester: Manchester University Press.
Mahmud W. and Osmani, S.R. (1980) 'Impact of Emigrant Workers' Remittances on the Bangladesh Economy', *Bangladesh Development Studies* 8, 3: 1–28.
Osmani, S.R., Bakht, Z. and Chowdhury, A. (1986) 'The Impact of Fiscal Policy on the Monetary Sector of Bangladesh', *Research Report No. 50*, Dhaka: Bangladesh Institute of Development Studies.
Parikh, A. and Starmer, C. (1988) 'The Relationship between Money Supply and Prices in Bangladesh', *Bangladesh Development Studies* 16: 59–70.
Sohrabuddin, M. 'Monetary Policy in the Third Five Year Plan', *Bangladesh Journal of Political Economy* 7, 1: 198–209.
Taheruddin, M. (1977) 'The Demand for and Supply of Bank Credit in Bangladesh:

An Empirical Analysis', *Bangladesh Development Studies* 5: 443–9.

Taslim, A. (1980) 'Inflation in Bangladesh: A Re-examination of the Structuralist – Monetarist Controversy', *Bangladesh Development Studies* 8: 23–51.

Wahid, A.N.M. (1986) 'Expansion and Organisation of Monetary Sector: The Case of Bangladesh', *Scandinavian Journal of Development Alternatives* 5, 4: 126–43.

China

Balassa, B. (1982) 'Economic Reform in China', *Banca Nazionale del Lavoro Quarterly Review* 142: 307–33.

Beijing Review (1984) 'Decision of the Central Committee of the Communist Party of China on reform of the economic structure', 27: I–XVI.

Bortolani, S. and Santorum, A. (1984) *Moneta e banca in Cina*, Milan: Giuffre.

Brotman, D. (1985) 'Reforming the Banking System', *The China Business Review* March, 17–23.

Byrd, W.A. (1983) *China's Financial Systems*, Boulder, CO: Westview Press.

Chen, C.H. (1988) 'Determinants of the Money Supply in Mainland China', Taipei: Chung Hua Institution for Economic Research, mimeo.

Cheng, H.S. (1981) 'Money and Credit in China', *Federal Reserve Bank of San Francisco Economic Review* Fall: 19–36.

Chow, G. (1987) 'Money and Price Level Determination in China', *Journal of Comparative Economics* 11: 319–33.

Ellman, M. (1988) 'China's OTC Markets', *Comparative Economic Studies* 30: 59–64.

Feltensein, A. and Farhidian, Z. (1987) 'Fiscal Policy, Monetary Targets and the Price Level in a Centrally Planned Economy: an application to the case of China', *Journal of Money, Credit and Banking* 19: 137–56.

Feltenstein, A., Lebow, D. and van Wijnbergen, S. (1986) 'Savings, Commodity Market Rationing and the Real Rate of Interest in China', *World Bank CPD Discussion Paper No. 27*, Washington, DC.

Gong, Z. (1985) 'Household Saving in China', London: Birkbeck College, mimeo.

Goodstadt, L. (1979) 'Why Bankers Have Become Heroes in China', *Euromoney* January: 78–85.

Grub, Phillipson and Sudweeks, B.L. (1988) 'Securities Markets and the PRC', *China Newsletters* 74: 11–16.

Hsiao, K.H. (1971) *Money and Monetary Policy in Communist China*, New York: Columbia University Press.

Huang, D., Gong, C., Mengcan, H., Shengye, Z. and Yingjie, H. (1981) *Shehuizhuyi Caizheng Jinrong Wenti* (Fiscal and monetary problems under socialism), Beijing: Chinese People's University Publishing House.

Lin, J.Y. (1987) *The Household Responsibility System Reform in China: a peasant's institutional choice*, Economic Growth Center, Discussion Paper No. 526, New Haven, CT: Yale University Press.

Macroeconomic Research Office (1987) 'The Macroeconomy in the Process of Reform: distribution and use of national income', *Jingji Yanjiu* 8: 16–28.

Naughton, B.J. (1986) 'Saving and Investment in China: a macroeconomic analysis', Ph.D. dissertation, Yale University.

—— (1988) 'Macroeconomic Management and System Reform in China', Paper presented at the conference 'The Chinese Developmental State: Change and Continuum', at the Institute of Development Studies, University of Susssex, April 7–9.

People's Bank of China (1983) *Jinrong Goikuang* (Survey of Banking), Beijing: Banking Publishing House.

REFERENCES

Portes, R.D. and Santorum, A. (1987) 'Money and the Consumption Goods Market in China', *Journal of Comparative Economics* 11: 354–71.

Reynolds, B.L. (1987) 'Agricultural Reform, Rural Savings and Growth in China', Paper presented at the 'Conference on China in a New Era: continuity and change', Manila, August.

Santorum, A. (1987) 'Expenditures and Portfolio Behaviour in China', Associazione Borsisti Luciano Jona Working Paper 17.

Sherer, J.L. (1988) *China. Facts and Figures, annual, Vol. 10, 1987,* Gulf Breeze, FLA: Academic International Press.

Shi, L. (1982) 'Jiandingde Zhixing Wending Huobide Frangzhen' (Resolutely carry out a policy of currency stability), *Zhongguo Jinrong* (Banking in China) 2: 204.

Sicular, T. (1988) 'Plan and Market in China's Agricultural Commerce', *Journal of Political Economy* 96: 283–307.

Sinha, R. (1982) 'Production Responsibility System: the Pandora's Box', *Land Reform* 1/2.

State Statistical Bureau, PRC (1987) *Statistical Yearbook of China 1986,* Hong Kong: Economic Information Agency.

—— (1988) *Statistical Yearbook of China 1987,* Hong Kong: Economic Information Agency.

Wiens, T.B. (1980) 'Price Adjustment, the Responsibility System and Agricultural Productivity', *American Economic Review* 73: 319–24.

—— (1987) 'Issues in the Structural Reform of Chinese Agriculture', *Journal of Comparative Economics* 11: 372–84.

de Wulf, L. and Goldsborough, D. (1986) 'The Evolving Role of Monetary Policy in China', *IMF Staff Papers* 33: 209–42.

Xu, J. (1987) 'The Stock-share System. A New Avenue for China's Economic Reform', *Journal of Comparative Economics* 11.

Yang, P. (1984) 'Banking', in G. Yu (ed.) *China's Socialist Modernization,* Beijing: Foreign Language Press.

Yue, H. (1988) 'China Opens Securities Market', *Beijing Review* 31: 20–1.

Zhang, E. (1981) 'On Banking Reform', *Beijing Review* 20 July: 24–7.

Zhongguo Jinrong (1984) 'People's Bank of China Promulgates Provisional Regulations on Several Questions Concerning the PBC Functioning Exclusively as a Central Bank', 12: 29–30.

Zhou, Z. and Zhu, Li (1987) 'China's Banking System: current status, perspective on reform', *Journal of Comparative Economics* 11: 339–409.

INDEX